Cultural Shaping of Violence

Cultural Shaping of Violence

♦ victimization, escalation, response ♦

Edited by Myrdene Anderson

Purdue University Press ♦ West Lafayette, Indiana

Library of Congress Cataloging-in-Publication Data

Cultural shaping of violence / edited by Myrdene Anderson.
    p. cm.
Includes bibliographical references and index.
  ISBN 1-55753-345-8 (cloth) -- ISBN 1-55753-373-3 (pbk.)
  1. Violence--Cross-cultural studies. I. Anderson, Myrdene, 1934-

  HM886.C847 2004
  303.6--dc22
                            2003026950

Contents

Acknowledgments

The editor appreciates all the peaceful encounters where the cultural shaping of violence received proper attention—in symposia, courses, and ordinary conversations. In the final flourish before publication, the following colleagues and students, near at hand and far away, provided provocative insight, especially for the "bookend" chapters: Scott Baxter, Devika Chawla, Jeff Gill, Gene Jackson, Michael S. Koskey, Kalevi Kull, Floyd Merrell, Robert Paine, James Pavisian, B. Frédérique Samuel, Chrys Taylor, and O. Michael Watson.

Likewise appreciated is the untitled painting by former colleague, artist, and biologist Ben Olson, which graces the paperback cover of this book.

Cultural Shaping of Violence

Chapter I

Introduction: The Careless Feeding of Violence in Culture

Myrdene Anderson and Cara Richards

Acknowledging and Recognizing Violence

Violence has emerged as a major concern, globally and locally, as history has turned the leaf to another decade, a new century, a fresh, still single-digit millennium. How have we survived, individually and collectively, when in fact the numbers of terminal victims, or "megadeaths," due to various obvious kinds of violence in the last century, number 10 percent of those living at the beginning of it (Hobsbawm 1994: 12; Eagleton 2003: x)? Certainly, violence is the tragic marker of this historical moment, self-consciously poised as it is between the embarrassments of past progress and the tenuous promise of a future encumbered with overpopulation, (other kinds of) pollution, a disembodied cybersociety, and a threadbare institution: the nation-state (Anderson 1996, Gastil 1993, Keane 2002, Tuan 2002).

All of this was palpably the case before September 11, 2001; since then, all assessments of past and future pale as we are rendered speechless, at least in the West, and especially in North America. We experience a collective astonishment at the ratcheting up of global terrorism and at all the responses to it, including fear, leading to as well as magnified by "homeland security" in the United States, and the dreaded war, or wars.

Meanwhile, mundane cultural expressions of violence thrive in the usual sites of individual pain and societal inequities. Insofar as most persons become consciously aware of violence nearby as well as in exotic locations mainly through the media, rather than as witness or through gossip, they may not perceive much of violence as all that immediate or threatening—unless and until they recognize themselves as victims. The media, the Janus-faced tricksters, manage to distance us even as they make their content intimate; perhaps this is summed up in connotations of the "virtual." Yet, in every society, some violence is palpable close to home—particularly *in* the home—and in every society still other sites and styles of violence impact every individual, directly or indirectly. The more shaped and nurtured by culture, the more violence can be rendered to appear innocuous or inevitable, or not to appear at all: invisible—at once both opaque and transparent.

Contemporary media themselves constitute another source of disturbance, as they graphically report, in real time and then in iterated segments ad infinitum, the hitherto unspeakable and even unthinkable—yet nonetheless imitable. This mediated information assaults our every sense and sensibility. As though adult terrorism, ethnic cleansing, child soldiers, and children killing other children were not enough, the media are also saturated with what one might call recreational violence. The news (though never new or true), the documentaries, soap operas, reality series, and—dare it be said—sports and the stock exchange altogether epitomize the recreational violence attracting persons of all ages, genders, and walks of life into a post-modern addiction with a novel sort of dull, mediated "reality" craving ever more of our attention. Indeed, beyond the print, the radio, and the TV, many seek further saturation via the Internet, computer games, and video arcades. While the youth in affluent societies may be more afflicted and addicted than others, the situation is both general and increasingly global.

Thanks to the relatively immaterial media and the ideas/ideals they promulgate, and to the material traffic in people and goods around the planet, humans living today over the brink of the millennium participate in a synchronicity described as "global monoculture." Each individual culture—working through its historical patterns, societal habits, and psychobiological constraints, and subjected to sheer unmitigated serendipity—integrates macro- and micro-level dynamics to generate a somewhat unique worldview with its own set of habits, preferences, avoidances, and expectations. The Rorschach of phenomena labeled "violence" in each culture—so labeled by insiders or by outsiders—will likewise be culture-specific at each of their conjunctions in space and time.

There has been considerable debate during recent decades about the possible human propensity for violence against other humans, and also against other animals, plants, other living things, and the ecosystem as a whole; when it comes to material culture and the built environment, humans have amplified their capacity for violence as it can occur both in the construction and in the destruction of artifacts. One ongoing discussion about influences on or determinants of human behavior, labeled "nature or nurture," long predates the current debate between sociobiologists and culture-determinists. Fortunately, most scholars now eschew "either-or" questions, especially those purporting to pinpoint antecedent "causes" in a simplified linear or predictive model. Reducing phenomena as nuanced as those encountered in culture, society, and behavior to algorithms of cause and effect actually insults the complexity we seek to understand. In its precipitation and in its consequences, violence qualifies as a complex, but not inevitable, attribute of human culture and behavior.

Apropos the discussion of nature/genetics versus nurture/culture, the transcendent response to "either-or" is now embodied in the contemporary litany of "both-and" and in the emerging mantra of "neither-nor"; yet any mechanical antidote also sidesteps the real issues about what the meaningful units of and processes for analysis might be, and how, even perhaps why, they function, or misfire, as they do. The wisdom in understanding both the culture-bound and the culture-free or universal aspects of violence may lead to less folly in prevention, intervention, and denial. This collection of articles inspects some of the ways that the cultural shaping of violence occurs, foregrounding the variety of situated meanings in the experience of violence—whether confronted directly or indirectly. There will be no magic pill or silver bullet, there can be no quarantine, when the subject is violence. Violence is neither sickness nor accident, neither malady nor enemy; *it is us.*

Anthropologists, and others who gaze critically at the patterns and puzzles of human behavior, have useful observations to bring to these debates about "human nature." Violence occurs in many guises and in many settings and with many consequences. It is also sometimes noticeable by its very absence or by the shock following our blindness to it. To define "violence" operationally may not open up discussion as fruitfully as we can accomplish by unpacking specific, if intuitively delimited, instances of "violence." That is the agenda here. Violence usually ensues from intent and agency in the case of individual actors. At the cultural or structural level, violence generally appears as an entropic element, one that erodes both constituent selves and extruded society (and ecosystem, as will be argued). Violence at any level may be negatively sanctioned and/or rewarded, at least intermittently. Intermittent reinforcement has powerful consequences (Bateson 1977), as violence comes to be stylized, enabled, managed, curtailed, and rationalized— and most importantly suspensefully anticipated and indelible—within the fabric of culture itself, by perpetrators and victims alike. Violence is less a virus than an old-fashioned parasite, collaborating in some mutuality with its host-matrix. *Again, it is us.*

Whether there are commonalities across cultures in the conditioning of each genre of violence may be a moot issue. Yet, given the physical and social dependence of children within families, and sometimes females within society, it seems useful to start with conditions close to home and family. The family itself serves as the initial crucible for enculturation and socialization, whose processes, "adaptive" or otherwise, simultaneously mimic and foreshadow processes of the larger system.

The editor, Myrdene Anderson, is indebted to Cara Richards for jumpstarting this project on the cultural shaping of violence, which was set into motion by Richards's extensive research on infanticide. Because that research on the killing of children culminated in a book-length study, *The Loss of Innocents: Child Killers and Their Victims* (Richards 2000), we recommend that volume. There, Richards selects and probes for patterns in more than 800 infanticide cases from 1971–1993 in the United States, involving more than 1,000 victims and 990 perpetrators. Infanticide is just one topic neglected but not entirely overlooked in the present volume; others will be mentioned in the epilogue. In any event, with or without analysis, it would hardly be feasible to catalogue and chronicle all types of violence, everywhere, throughout history. There is no typology or taxonomy for violence that could address the perverse persistence of the process that, were violence even more pernicious, might wipe itself out altogether along with its culture-bearers.

Even though the documentation in this volume does not exhaust all the ways humans have found to be inhuman and inhumane, the chapters do range from domestic affairs to war and torture, and touch on every continent. It would be presumptuous to subject all of this data to ethnological comparisons and contrasts; what we have is apples, orange-sections, and banana-peels. So, instead, the authors focus on close readings of particular conditions conducive to, amplifying, mediating, dampening, or preventing violence, and to its inadvertent nurturance within the social (including anti-social) tensions that configure personal and historical experience.

Pretext

The organization of this volume around the first four major sections—parts one, two, three, and four—moves from what some have called direct violence toward the more clear instantiations of structural violence, or from the (inter)personal to the social, and from the domestic to the cultural (including the political). Johan Galtung (1969, 1990) re-inspects these rather over-determined paired distinctions and suggests adding a third category, cultural violence. His original contrast was between direct and indirect (called there structural) violence. For him, cultural violence can legitimize either direct or indirect violence, all of which can thereby reverberate throughout a society. Most social scientists would probably consider the structural already to implicate institutions and the cultural. Regardless of legitimization, all patterned violence will be cultural, so the utility of Galtung's third distinction seems only to exclude truly "random" acts of violence, and the violence that might slip out of our analytic powers by not resolving to the social. This volume will be more inclusive.

Following this introduction (chapter one), the four main sections contain twenty-five chapters (chapters two through twenty-six), and the editor has appended a fifth section, part five, containing two chapters in her voice.

The altogether twenty-eight chapters, involving twenty-eight authors of seven nationalities, document violence in twenty-two distinct cultural settings in seventeen nation-states on five continents. Most of the authors are anthropologists, but also represented are persons trained in psychology, sociology, criminology, pedagogy, literary studies, consumer sciences, and business management; secondarily some authors have experience as teachers and therapists, and in policing, soldiering, consulting, and activism, besides living in the world. Three of the chapters take a cross-cultural ethnological approach to investigate some feature relating to violence, such as kinship, politeness, and armed conflict.

The first of the four sections, part one, "Children and Women First? Violence Close to Home," deals with relations between generations and genders. Three authors consider the quality of life for children in inner cities and areas of civil strife. The geographic settings for these studies are the United States (Linda McDonald and Anna Richman Beresin, in chapters two and three, respectively), and Ireland, with a reference to Australia (Linda J. Rogers, chapter four). Children take up much of the slack in a society while waiting in the wings, absorbing the behavior of others, and they often bear silent witness to the violence around them. Sadly, learning well, they are also capable of being more, or less, than "just" victims. Happily, sometimes their behavior turns out to be more sensible than that of their elders.

As with children, sometimes women too seem to be regarded as resilient and durable, or perhaps expendable, or even peripheral to the scenes of the crimes of violence. These very assumptions can also render women as handy victims. Too frequently women find themselves stretched to the limit as they try to secure family life in an inhospitable environment, or when physically violated by assailants. The geographical contexts of three more studies in part one are the United States and Mexico (Cathy Winkler, chapter five), Brazil (Sarah Hautzinger, chapter six), and African immigrants in the United States (Jon D. Holtzman, chapter seven). In fact, geographic and cultural dislocation may exacerbate interpersonal violence close to home. Domestic violence victimizes the entire intimate social fabric of the family, not just the most typical recipients of abuse, namely the women and children—and pets, the scapegoats that too often slip under the radar. Domestic abuse *and neglect* as well as sexual predation have repercussions beyond the family, violating the social fabric of the entire community, leaving everyone ripped up emotionally and ill at ease, permanently, with other vulnerable individuals becoming fearful as well.

Part two looks into the "Social Regulation of Anti-Social Behavior." Here the issues pivot on the nature of kinship (Wade C. Mackey and Nicole Sault, chapters eight and nine, respectively), to the role of women in a gendered arena (Claudia Fonseca and Myriam Jimeno, chapters ten and eleven, respectively), and to the culturally nuanced practices of politeness (Dov Cohen and Joe Vandello, chapter twelve). The first of these, chapter eight, provides a state-by-state and international ethnological comparison of the positive consequences of the presence of fathers in the household, showing impressive negative correlations with indices of crime. The other studies in this part focus on Mexico, Brazil, Colombia, and the United States. Besides other family members, godmothers, friends, and neighbors, the ethological dimensions of politeness in a society can frame potential for anti-social behavior as well as for civility. The last chapter in part two, like the first, is comparative, looking at cross-cultural patterns in politeness and their ramifications.

Part three, "Institutional Architectures Mediating and Memorializing Violence," brings together studies of police culture (Steven V. Lutes and Michael J. Sullivan, chapter thirteen), with a focus on the United States in general and San Francisco in particular; pre-modern and modern warfare (Barton C. Hacker, chapter fourteen); the sculpting of civilians into soldiers by the military in Israel (Eyal Ben-Ari, chapter fifteen) and by the U.S. Marine Corps (Rhonda J. Moore, chapter sixteen); and the enduring and subliminal violence of colonialism, referencing Palestinians (Nada Elia, chapter seventeen), Pacific Islanders (Katerina Teaiwa, chapter eighteen), and Arab-Africans (a second essay by Nada Elia, chapter nineteen). Among the case studies in part three, there is one, Hacker's chapter fourteen, which also surveys broader ethnological data concerning a single institution, warfare. The ethological and ecological repercussions of intra-cultural institutional confrontations and inter-cultural violence show no signs of subsiding with this millennium. Indeed, the dislocations of persons, the extraction of raw materials, and the importing *and* exporting of labor *and* services accompanying neocolonialism all contribute to the major systemic pathologies on the planet, which come up for discussion in the next section.

The fourth section, part four, "Escalating Ecologies of Perturbation," addresses the dynamics between people and their environments in space and through time. This theme obligates close attention to the complex and interlocking constraints of natural resources, cultural resources, sociopsychological conditions, and the long arm of history itself. The violence documented in this section weighs particularly heavily: it is less personal but more personally devastating, bigger than the family and still larger than the socio-ecosystem, deeper than one's experience in the world and still deeper than history or even prehistory. The media, with various motivations, attempt to communicate such large-scale insults to the human condition, but our language cannot suitably classify them, and our cognitive faculties short out. Each case implodes on itself.

While any single individual portrayed in earlier sections may be violated more than once, even daily—in the family, in the streets, by insidious discriminations, and in the cultural invention and intervention called war—an outsider may posit that the victim could walk away, turn the other cheek, or just focus on the positive. In part four we are confronted by situations so severe, with possibilities for regulation so bleak, and with escalating outcomes so over-determinedly tragic, that there is no way to "blame the victim." Instead, the reader joins the victim in grief and despair.

Perturbations within the social and ecological system often engage longer calendars, and hence have kinky, nonlinear histories that do not readily unravel. The first three authors in part four deal with resource imbalances infecting the social fabric, in Indonesia (Glenn Smith, chapter twenty), in Peru (Bartholomew Dean, chapter twenty-one), and in Taiwan (Charles Trappey, chapter twenty-two). Three more authors document instances of politically inspired abuse-unto-torture-unto-murder in Guatemala (Frank M. Afflitto, chapter twenty-three), in Haiti (Glen Perice, chapter twenty-four), and in Romania (Gila Safran Naveh, chapter twenty-five). Finally, an in-depth longitudinal survey of Colombian violence (Mario Fandino, chapter twenty-six) reveals not just trends, but cycles whose trajectories puncture the future. Ethnographic and historic depth may not be available for each society, and when they are, the evidence may not always point to cycles. Nonetheless, the cycles of bloodshed in Colombia suggest that some violence in the world today may seethe while latent, and may orbit into cultural patterns yet to be so much as suspected.

Following part four are two chapters by the editor under the umbrella of part five. Chapter twenty-seven, about the seemingly non-violent Saami reindeer breeders of Norwegian Lapland, would be an anomaly in this volume were it not an opportunity to braid together historical trajectories of both subtle and incontrovertible violence in a setting of colonialization, together with deconstructions of patterned infelicities relating to material culture and the ecosystem, all tying in with violence when painted with a more inclusive brush. Here colonialism, technology, and alcohol play pivotal roles.

Thereafter, the final chapter twenty-eight serves as an epilogue for the volume as a whole, picking up on the issues and genres of violence barely sampled in the introduction and other chapters, to close the volume with some more positive approaches in the prevention of, curbing of, and coping with violence. There can be no meaningful synthesis of the patterns and particularities from the chapters of case studies that precede the epilogue, and a straightforward recapitulation would be redundant—but more must be said. If one dare refer to the subject of violence as vast, this collection is poor, incomplete, inconsistent, and indefinite, although hardly inconclusive. So much remains on the table, and even more under it. We have mentioned infanticide, for example, but then there is also animal abuse, correlated with both infanticide and the abuse of children and others. On the subject of abuse, it's often reported as intransitive, A hits B. The literature underreports, if not disregards, the inverse of the equation, B hitting A. Traditional or typical victims are seldom portrayed as perpetrators, so children rarely abuse adults, women rarely abuse men, and is it even possible to say that a pet can abuse its caretaker? Well, actually, that can probably be taken as an index of previous intransitive abuse becoming transitive. The literature also disregards the tangled nonlinear heterarchies so prevalent in natural systems (McCulloch 1945), where A can peck B, and B do the same to C, but C has a leg up on A. Families afford ample examples of heterarchies, and these are no less evident throughout culture and the ecosystem.

The epilogue deals further with Galtung's cultural violence in the contemporary world, incuding terrorism. No single other contribution in this volume addresses global terrorism per se, yet each author presciently prefigures it, unpacking the unfortunate patterns found at different scales in various cultures. Local, state-level, and global terrorism have had long histories that insulated publics have chosen to ignore. No longer. Lamentably, "nine-one-one" personified as tragedian and trickster will be writing its own history for a long time to come, eventually to become less surprising, more suspenseful, and forever incomprehensible. That is our fear.

Fear itself figures into all genres of violence, as does sacrifice, and even healing. An extremely valuable collection of seminal writings on violence, *Violence and Its Alternatives*, was assembled by Manfred B. Steger and Nancy S. Lind in 1999. In fact, any number of works on violence came out during the late 1990s and even more since then. Can one wonder why! Here and in the epilogue, however, we will take gentle issue with the implications of suggesting "alternatives" to violence. Would "alternatives" trivialize violence? It might then seem that cultural violence will be obvious and perversely logical, that it comes about through rational or irrational choice, and that it can be addressed and mended within the system through a combination of recognition plus enlightened agency. In addressing the cultural shaping of violence, any alternatives at all will be uniquely embedded, visible or not, in the fabric of the culture. Today more and more scholars recognize this, and also that violence is neither universal nor indelible in culture, nor is it in biology either. For once and for all, aggression is not "genetic," nor is it a necessary precursor to violence. All the same, to be maintained, both violence and any endemic "alternatives" also need care, feeding, and selection, and these processes integrate both long-term phenomena such as biology, and cultural habits of substantial vintage, along with agency drawing on unique individual experience. This merits expansion in the epilogue.

For the ordinary practitioner in society, the quotidian exists on the surface plane of the obvious but un-inspected, not at deeper cultural levels. Christopher M. Hann (2002: 259) has related these by referring to the realm of the cultural as "congealed sociality." What practitioners do, mindfully or not, will feed back into the culture, but in trickles and lumps. To find and nurture "alternatives" to violence will not be an option for everyone or for every society, nor will these be typologically comparable alternatives, let alone solutions. But we do have instances and labels for some practices, and if uttering them can do magic, if also "alternatives" can be self-fulfilling prophecies, then we might try them on for size: non-aggression, dispute-resolution, conflict-avoidance, passive-resistance, optimism, reconciliation, performance therapy, trust, love—but not denial. These issues, too, will be served up in the epilogue.

References

Anderson, Myrdene. (1996). On the menu, upon our plates, and then its taste in our mouths. In *The Story of Progress*, edited by Gosta Arvastson and Mats Lindqvist (Acta Universitatis Upsaliensis; *Studia Etnologica Upsaliensis*, 17), pp. 11–12. Uppsala: Uppsala University, Almqvist and Wiksell International.

Bateson, Gregory. (1977). Some thoughts about intermittent reinforcement. Unpublished article manuscript; Bateson Archive, University of California, Santa Cruz.

Eagleton, Terry. (2003). *Sweet Violence: The Idea of the Tragic*. Oxford: Blackwell Publishing.

Galtung, Johan. (1969). Violence, peace, and peace research. *Journal of Peace Research* 6.3: 167–191.

———. (1990). Cultural violence. *Journal of Peace Research* 27.3: 291–305.

Gastil, Raymond Duncan. (1993). *Progress: Critical Thinking about Historical Change*. Westport, Connecticut: Praeger.

Hann, Christopher M. (2002). All *Kulturvölker* now? Social anthropological reflections on the German-American tradition. In *Anthropology Beyond Culture*, edited by Richard G. Fox and Barbara J. King, pp. 259–276. Oxford and New York: Berg.

Hobsbawm, Eric. (1994). *Age of Extremes: The Short Twentieth Century*. London: Penguin.

Keane, John. (2002). The triangle of violence. www.wmin.ac.uk/csd/staff/keane/JKTriangle.htm.

McCulloch, Warren S. (1945). A heterarchy of values determined by the topology of nervous nets. *Bulletin of Mathematical Biophysics* 7.2: 89–93.

Richards, Cara E. (2000). *The Loss of Innocents: Child Killers and Their Victims*. Wilmington, Delaware: Scholarly Resources, Inc.

Steger, Manfred B., and Nancy S. Lind. (1999). Introduction. In *Violence and Its Alternatives: An Interdisciplinary Reader*, edited by Manfred B. Steger and Nancy S. Lind, pp. viii–xxvi. New York: St. Martin's Press.

Tuan, Yi-Fu. (2002). Progress and anxiety. In *Progress: Geographical Essays*, edited by Robert David Sack, pp. 78–96. Baltimore: Johns Hopkins University Press.

◆ Part One

Children and Women First?
Violence Close to Home

Violence converges from the bottom-up, top-down, and side-ways. Individuals most apt to find themselves in this convergence will do so at home and/or as children. After children, women run a close second in victimhood. But this is not to say that either children or women are either passive or chained by convention, or that men have a corner on perpetrating these never-faceless crimes.

It is important to view violence as an attribute, first of culture, acculturation, and socialization, rather than of individuals or from a deterministic biology. Women and children share all those systems with men. Quite aside from any social actor asserting agency in the prevention of, commission of, and resistance to violence, traditions continually change, from within and without. These chapters inspect some of the manifestations of and antidotes for violence close to home.

Chapter II

Violence Absorbed:
Lives of Children in an American City

Linda McDonald

Children live primarily in the context of home and school. As learners and participants in both arenas, they knowingly and unknowingly take in an array of values, mores, standards, and specific information from those settings, and develop skills to operate within them, cultivating what Vico referred to as the capacity to "read between the lines" (Burke 1985). Achieving this astuteness becomes a survival strategy for the urban children whose stories are told in this paper. Their narratives chronicle the effect that progressive and cumulative acts of violence absorbed from daily life have on their development.

Discussion pertaining to the effects of violence centers primarily on violent adolescent or adult behaviors that might be attributed to previous conditions (Maxfield and Widom 1996; McCloskey, Figueredo, and Koss 1995; Schwab-Stone, Ayers, Kasprow, Voyce, Barone, Shriver, and Weissberg 1995). While valuable, these studies cannot detail the cultural context of the child and subsequent shaping in the child's lived experience. Violent acts of shooting and stabbing are obvious and effect the child's psychological development; however, mundane violence emanating from home and school, and understood by children in this study, amplifies insidious daily occurrences of violence to create a developmental map evident through their language (Bruner 1990; Vygotsky 1962).

The children in this study are students (K-5) at Hoover School, a neighborhood public school located in the inner city of a large Midwestern metropolitan area. Neighborhoods surrounding the school reveal boarded up storefronts with signs on others announcing that merchants sell money orders and lottery tickets, cash welfare checks, and accept food stamps. Multiple family dwellings display peeling paint, torn screens, bottles, paper, and a number of vehicles in yards. Any new structure is a contrast, and often displays a temporary sign, "Built by Habitat for Humanity."

The one hundred-year-old school mirrors the neighborhood, situated next to a forty-eight-acre blighted area of deserted factories recently identified as a former toxic waste dump, now earmarked as a "priority development site" for the city (*The Plain Dealer*, January 14, 1996). Entrance is through the "yellow door" once the buzzer is pressed and the visitor identified. A walk through the school reveals ceilings where water leaks caused plaster to become so saturated that it crumbled and fell, exposing structural boards between the floors. Paint on the walls is chipped and peeling, and two large windows on stairway landings are broken and boarded up. Several classroom doors display "value" words such as sharing, courtesy, friendship, and honesty. Bells mark the end of academic periods; students walk single file, by gender, through the halls when changing classes. Talkers receive detentions.

Approximately 90 percent of the 540 Hoover children are poor, based on the percentage of those who receive free or reduced-price lunches. All but four students are African-American. Basement lunchrooms have seven-foot ceilings and stone walls, each supervised by one parent volunteer. Lunch in Styrofoam boxes and containers of milk are served on a tray with plastic ware. Children's voices reverberate amid shouts of "Don't talk!" from the frustrated lunch volunteer who dispenses detentions and/or loss of playground time. The school slogan is posted on the lunchroom wall: "Do our best, obey each rule, and make Hoover a model school." Absent is any evidence of support, concern or strategies for the children meeting these goals.

Safety and behavior are intricately related for children. "My mother said if I act up she going to whoop me. She say if my name be up on the board and I'm bad, that mean I'm getting a whoopen." Children not in required uniform get their names on the board. A "whoopen" is administered with a belt, a "spanken" with a hand. One girl explains she got in trouble "only once when I was talking. I had to stand on the carpet with my hands on my head when I first went to school; now I don't talk anymore." Gone are her curiosity and the inquiry necessary for critical thinking and intellectual growth. It is impossible to "do good in school" when no strategies to implement "goodness" exist. Normal child behaviors of walking or talking to friends are restricted and rewards are external; little or no opportunity exists to internalize controls or to make choices.

By fifth grade, children possess a sophisticated understanding of classroom and interpersonal dynamics, and unfortunately the barrier created by this teacher prevents Regina from sharing her insights. "Sometimes one person do something. The teacher blames the whole class if someone misbehaves. Like we have to write 600 times." She explains that she can't tell the teacher this punishment is unfair because more punishment would be meted out; school and home reality are in direct conflict as parental instructions are to "tell the teacher" if she has a problem. Regina reflects that writing doesn't keep the bad kids from being bad. By not being accessible to the "good" kids, the teacher drives them to join forces with the "bad" ones, and reinforces the "Why bother?" attitude ever present among the children, and narrows the range of school behaviors available to children.

The state of family is fluid and site specific. Joan understands family as, "It's like some people don't have a mother, or some people don't have a daddy. Some people don't have neither one of the parents. A family is a mother, a father, or just a mother or just a father, and you put all your relatives together." Other children respond, "people that live in your house with you and you have a nice relationship," or "when somebody has a baby, and then you're a family," to "blood and love." Although extended and inclusive, support relationships are fragile and often transient.

Little if any distinction exists between girls' and boys' narratives from kindergarten through second grade. All examine what they know about their world and the mediators used to move through the various institutions in their lives. The typical child for these grades is Ken, a kindergartener, who informs me, "Rotweillers save you from bad people. Get one right now. Y'all feel better, y'all got some dogs" [to gain protection from people with guns]. He lives with his mother, who is separated from his stepfather, who is in jail for beating Ken and his mother, and he discusses living in a number of homes with mom before the current arrangement with his grandmother and his brother. Ken explains his mom's instruction "not to be bad, and don't fight in school; get good grades and do homework more neatly to get in first grade." He adds he got in trouble for walking fast and having the teacher classify the behavior as running. The teacher wouldn't believe him and put him in the corner. Ken takes care of his brother and says if he had lots of money he would buy clothes and shoes for himself, his brother, and mom. He often plays "exterminator" at home to pick up the bugs in the house. The stage is set as Ken tries to retain taught values, "My uncles be smoking not cigarettes, the other stuff, and they be drinking beer and wine, and so do my daddy, and one of my grandma's drink too, but two don't. Bad people do drugs, and when they have a friend that's involved in guns and uh...that other stuff, if he tell you to come on, just say no." By age five, Ken already knows adults cannot be relied on and feels the impact of violence and dissonance of values in his world.

Friends are to share, and this includes endorsing fights. "Best friends take each other back if we fight, we stay together." If somebody fights a friend, "We all go fight the person who did it, because my grandfather say if somebody fight somebody, you try to stop it, and if they hit you, you hit them back. He said I could fight anytime I want to if somebody get in my face, I just fight them." A moral dilemma exists between church values and world reality, "God don't like evil, if a person be mean, you should still be nice." According to this logic, if she follows God, she will be beaten up. In a conflict between God and Grandpa, the reality of Grandpa is dominant. Conflict resolution occurs through fights although the result may be physical injury or school detentions. One girl explains, "I try not to fight because I think that's wrong, and because some kids you fight they take out a knife and stuff, and try to stab you and stuff; she'll push me into the wall and I'll walk off and she'll punch me in my back. Then I'll tell the teacher, and then she'll [the girl] be like 'I'll get you after school.'" The girl cannot tell the teacher who should keep her safe, and the dance of danger escalates reaching a point where no safe ending seems possible.

Early understandings of gender differences emanate from observed adult relationships, "My step-dad don't whoop me no more because, I don't want his hands on me. He only whip his kids now. Sometimes he tap her [his daughter] with the belt. If I get in trouble like after school, my mom she is hitting me. Sometimes when I be screaming, she be punching me, then she get back the belt and then hit me." Third graders know, "In the old days, boys did nice things to girls, now it's just boys hurt girls, like they bend their wrists and stuff." "James, he want to hit girls, and he always want to have a girlfriend. She shouldn't have no boyfriend like I don't have one because you too young. You don't know what he might do, he might smack you and all that, but he treat her right; he give her money, but that's still wrong."

Third-graders' experiences and worries sound more adult than child-like. Death is not an abstract concept confined to bad dreams from scary movies, but rather an omnipresent reality. A boy tells about his mom's undefined illness, "Sometimes my mother she...she starts getting a little weird and stuff and gets sick. Mom gets sick 'cause last time almost, she couldn't breathe that day when we got home. The ambulance came, and she had fell down and then my brother's dad had turned on the fan so she could get a little air, and then the ambulance had to come pick her up." He matter-of-factly tells that his sister nearly died when her heart stopped. Another boy recounts in an understated way that his mother died when he was six, "and so a lot of things changed." Illness and death are accepted daily occurrences, but create yet another form of isolation for the child. The question persists, who is a constant and consistent caregiver and advocate for the child?

Evidence of a concern for personal safety begins to generalize to an upset condition, sometimes approaching outrage, as third-graders tell personal experiences about danger related to drugs, guns, shootings, and police. "Here we have a lot of violence and people selling drugs." The boy hears gunshots four times a week, and has constant fear, "I think I'm going to die, gettin' shot on my way to school." "At night times when people be walking around in gangs, I be seeing police; I hearing policemen, and I be hearing firecrackers. Sometimes I think that they be guns; I be scared." Children know how gangs evade the police. Once a gang was "shooting dice and stuff, and then he [Mr. Y] called the police, and they all ran. And Little Wayne [age thirteen], he was on his go-cart and went in this backyard and parked it, and then hid in the backyard, and the police couldn't find them. Once, the police was called and someone ran in my backyard and got on my garage and hid and ducked down, and then the police tried to look up there, but they couldn't climb the gate cause they were two old guys." He describes another incident, "The police pulled out a gun because they thought it was a grown-up running from them, but it was a little kid, and they shot up in the air, and he still kept running." The message is clear; police cannot be depended on to provide safety.

Traditional values of goodness, loyalty, and responsibility exist simultaneously in the interviews, but their significance to Hoover children is very different from suburban children (Tillman and McDonald 1994). The standard admonition to "do good [in school], don't fight, and don't get your name on the board," contradicts "grandma told me never fight in classroom, but if they want to fight me outside, fight them outside. Don't be scared, fight them back or pick up a stick or something and knock them out." A boy explains he was taught to recycle and pick up litter, and about the role of a friend. "A friend 'lie up' for you. Sometimes I get in trouble, and the other person lies for the other, like you like one person, like the O.J. Simpson thing...like...but I think it's that like well one person gonna lie up for his friend. But he don't have to suffer the consequences. And my friend didn't lie up for me, cause I didn't start it, and he lied, just lied for his friend, and I felt it was really unfair. Then I was like, I didn't say anything, and then I got back at him. When he got in trouble again, I was like one of his friend's witnesses, when his friend's friend, and I was like yea, he did start it with this other boy, because he start hitting him, and the way I got back on him was when he went outside, he like (facial expressions and sounds), and he had hit me, and then I hit him across his face, and that's what made it even!"

Jamae, a typical fourth grader, says her family "be moving because these drug dealers, they being by the house, they be in the hallway." She explains the drug culture, "They be gambling and stuff, and they be smoking their joints, and they be across the street and writing stuff, it begin with a 'W,' I forget, and then they be giving white stuff. They be like 'hey you want some of these?' Me and my sister be going over there and sometimes, they be walking across the street and me and my sister go over here." Her mother taught her to cross the street to escape the dealers, but she "would like to go to Washington, D.C., to meet the President and ask, 'Could we get the drug dealers off the streets, and get rid of the guns and stuff, and make them use more useful things, make them use cars, tools, useful things.' Collect all the guns, knives and stuff." Jamae reaches to find someone who can establish some safety for her life and chooses the highest, most powerful symbol in the United States, the president. She optimistically believes surely someone must care about children's safety.

Isolation from teachers and parents is sometimes self-imposed as a means of physical and emotional survival. The history of Don, age ten, typifies the frustration of a child who has experienced violence in every area of his life from everyone with whom he has contact. After his suspension, Don watched a citizenship movie and reconstructed the event to redefine himself, "the only people that go is the citizens, and so that's why I think I'm good. If you do good things, you get rewarded." He tells, "My mother keep hittin' me and it feels just like I want to hit her back, but I'm not gonna hit her cause she my mother and I just feel

I want to get out of there. She be hittin' me with, in the face with her rings and stuff." His mother drinks and smokes; her fiancé lies and tells her Don's selling drugs, and his sister hits him with broomsticks and burned him with an iron. Don's personal struggle not to hurt his mother whom he loves is as real as the anger and contempt he feels. Personal safety is a chronic worry, but few avenues of escape or support are available for a ten-year-old.

Will tells about visiting his older sister and seeing police involved in a case of "mistaken identity." A "friend's friend" had reportedly been playing football in the street and ran to use his aunt's bathroom at the same time the police were following another man. "He looked just like him, so they were driving and he looked behind him and he heard the siren, so he just kept on running faster and faster and then he ran into his auntie's house and just stayed there and hid, cause he didn't know why they were running after him. The police found him and they beat him with the night stick and arrested him because after they beat him, they sprayed mace into his eyes, and they arrested him." After the police left with the man, a third policeperson, a woman was beaten by the residents of the housing project as they "started throwing bottles at the car and took a night stick away from her and started beating her." The boy asks the interviewer if she's heard about "the thing about Rodney King." Regardless of the degree of accuracy of the boy's report, the perception of victimization remains and in fact is seen to exist beyond his immediate neighborhood and generalizes to the national level. Police as symbol of protection has changed to one of aggression.

Multiple moves and schools are the norm rather than the exception. Friends, and often parents, become transient too. The tentative nature of childhood becomes even more vulnerable and carries with it a threat to the achievement of success in school, college, or workplace. Michelle has been to five schools; they move when "my mother gets tired of the house, or something broke and the landlord won't come fix it. Then we'll move till she get a better house, but it's hard because she got all them kids [eight children] and people don't want to take kids in an old house."

Contradictions abound and coexist as an embedded element of childhood. A more powerful description of this paradoxical life is evident in the following vignette of a boy and his black Labrador retriever: "I let her jump up on the bed with me when nobody's looking. I feed her when nobody's looking. I'm not supposed to do that, and I close the door and I beat her up." The nature of friendships being "someone who's there for you, and accepts you," takes on a different significance at fifth grade. Someone fun and willing to help you with your problems may or may not include "school goodness," thus raising new issues in the friendship dynamic. When the single available option for conflict resolution and the primary criterion for a friend both consist of fighting, the choice is clear, and rather than seen as a bully (Byrne 1994), the most successful fighter feels empowered in a culture that recognizes the importance of survival. A powerful account of the fragility of association is told by Binjamin Wilkomirski (1996), about his childhood in the concentration camps of Poland where the need to survive created distrust of anyone new.

Descriptions generated by the children and the symbols they recognize as effective in navigating the dynamics of family, school, and friends depicts world knowledge observed and experienced. It is within that world that they define themselves, a process identified by Blumer (1969) as symbolic interaction. The children's narrative texts represent experiences that imply a complex interaction of cognitive, affective, and connotative dimensions (Bruner 1986; Linde 1993; Tappan and Brown 1989). In authoring or telling a story, children claim responsibility for the experience, thus taking cognitive ownership. For Hoover children, that ownership means absorbing violence from every corner of their lives, and the Bakhtinian (1986) dialectic of the "I for myself" and the "I for others" becomes a necessary coping structure.

By fifth grade, attitudes and values from the personal, lived culture are embedded and become the central organizing structure for children. Abandonment by parents and teachers has forced the boys and girls to rely on each other or become totally isolated, a greater threat to safety. There is no choice; survival means becoming like those around you. Missing in the lives of children in this study is any attitude of playfulness or realistic vision of a future different from the present. Imagination is a luxury absent when basic needs are not met; and without the capacity to see into the future, it becomes difficult to have the motivation to self-improve (Dorris 1989), suggesting that the children in this study have a limited range of adult experiences.

The adult family members who share their lives with Hoover children also attempt to survive: they work, care for children, offer their understanding of "do good in school," and strive to provide a physically safe home; however, they too were once children in the same neighborhood. Vygotsky viewed each culture as providing children the necessary tools, technical and psychological, whereby they could become full participants in their culture (Wertsch 1985: 78). When the world is filled with contradictions, determining which tool better serves children becomes critical to survival, and when the measure of daily violence is taken, one can hear the assimilated scripts which allow children to simultaneously care for a friend or dog, while at the same time beating the dog or friend who doesn't "lie up" for you. Childhood is indeed a process of guided participation (Rogoff 1990).

References

Bakhtin, M. M. (1986). *Speech Genres and Other Late Essays*, edited by Caryl Emerson and Michael Holquist. Translated from the Russian by Vem W. McGee. Austin, Texas: University of Texas Press.

Blumer, Herbert. (1969). *Symbolic Interactionism: Perspective and Method*. Englewood Cliffs, New Jersey: Prentice Hall.

Bruner, Jerome. (1986). *Actual Minds, Possible Worlds*. Cambridge, Massachusetts: Harvard University Press.

———. (1990). *Acts of Meaning*. Cambridge, Massachusetts: Harvard University Press.

Burke, Peter (1985). *Vico*. New York: Oxford University Press

Byrne, Brendan. (1994). *Coping with Bullying in Schools*. New York: Cassell.

Dorris, Michael. (1989). *The Broken Cord*. New York: Harper Collins Publishers.

Linde, Charlotte. (1993). *Life Stories: The Creation of Coherence*. New York: Oxford University Press.

Maxfield, Michael, and Cathy Spatz Widom. (1996). The cycle of violence: Revisited six years later. *Archives of Pediatric andAdolescent Medicine*, 150: 390–395.

McCloskey, L., A. Figueredo, and Margo Koss. (1995). The effects of systemic family violence on children's mental health. *Child Development*, 66: 1239–1261.

Rogoff, Barbara. (1990). *Apprenticeship in Thinking: Cognitive Development in Social Context*. New York: Oxford University Press.

Schwab-Stone, M., T. Ayers, W. Kasprow, C. Voyce, C. Barone, T. Shriver, and R. Weissberg. (1995). No safe haven: A study of violence exposure in an urban community. *Journal of American Academy of Child and Adolescent Psychiatry* 34.10: 1343–1352.

Tappan, Mark B., and L.B. Brown. (1989). Stories told and lessons learned: Toward a narrative approach to moral development and moral education. *Harvard Education Review* 59: 182–205.

Tillman, Linda, and Linda McDonald. (1994). Decision making perspectives of young children (K-5): Choices in the world of young boys and girls. 1994 paper later published in *Proceedings: Fifth Congress of the International Association for Semiotic Studies,* 1995. Berkeley, California: University of California Press.

Vygotsky, L.S. (1962). *Thought and Language.* Cambridge, Massachusetts: Massachusetts Institute of Technology Press.

Wertsch, James V. (1985). *Vygotsky and the Social Formation of Mind.* Cambridge, Massachusetts: Harvard University Press.

Wilkomirski, Binjamin. (1996). *Fragments: Memories of a Wartime Childhood.* New York: Schocken Books.

Chapter III

School Power, Children's Play, and the Timing of Recess Violence

Anna Richman Beresin

There is a growing literature that examines the controlling aspects of schooling as a framework for studying children inside the classroom in a Foucauldian sense (Ball 1990; Bourdieu and Passerson 1990; Devine 1996). Yet, little or no attention has been paid to how schools frame the interactions inside the playground, an arena ironically referred to as one for "free play." Recent psychological literature on school yard play has advocated the release that recess provides and the significance of peer-led activity as a social and cognitive learning domain (Blatchford and Sharp 1994; Hart 1993; Pellegrini 1994), while classic game studies in folklore and anthropology have eloquently described children's activities as playful reflections upon the larger cultural and historical frameworks (Opie and Opie 1969, 1988; Sutton-Smith 1981, Sutton-Smith et al. 1995). The present study focuses on the institutional framing of children's games within the arena of an urban, public elementary schoolyard in the 1991–1992 school year, contributing to what Helen Schwartzman (1978) has described as the "ethnographies of childhood."

Violent episodes were indeed visible, and almost predictable, but rarely at the time of play. The playtime was instead filled with peer-led activities such as jump rope, hopscotch, handball, and basketball. Actual violence could be found in the transition back to the classroom when the bell rang indicating the end of recess. This can be contrasted to the mock-violent play, also known in the literature as "rough-and-tumble," exhibiting a very different dynamic than actual violence. If one can demonstrate that the adult-constructed transition back to the classroom brought on actual violent interaction, and not the play period itself, then it raises some important questions about policies that limit or eliminate play.

Daily fieldwork was carried out during the fifteen-minute break known as morning recess, which lasted from 10:30 AM to 10:45 AM. Extensive observation was also done in classrooms, in the lunchroom, in the gymnasium, in the hallways, at school wide events, and in the neighborhood at large. Of the 300 students at play on the playground, 104 third, fourth, and fifth grade boys and girls were the focus. Forty-seven served as native experts, and gave their own commentary as they watched themselves at play on videotape. Video footage allowed for repeatable analysis, and was encoded with a running clock so as to render comparable visually recorded information with audiotaped sound and field notes. In order to examine the interact ional patterns of both play and violence over time, two video cameras were set up, one from the second floor window facing the school yard, and another eventually set up on a roving tripod with the author on the playground itself.

The children knew the author was studying recess and were eager to offer their insights and considerable expertise on the subject. No footage of actual violence was shown directly to either children or staff in order to make clear that the ethnography was not intended to get any person in trouble. Footage of general interaction, play, and games were shown to children in single-gender, small groups, and separately to staff. Recess was described by one fourth-grade boy leader as a time for "playin' and fightin'." The question was, how were they distinguishable, and in what contexts did playing, fighting, and play-fighting emerge.

The timing of actual fighting was clear to the children. The fourth grade girls talked of the difficulty of ending their play, and of the frequency of fights while lining up to go back to class. That was their time to "slap someone upside the head" or to try to run away (a practice officially prohibited by the staff during lining-up time).

Not unlike transitions in rites of passage, the procession back to the building was filled with tension (Turner 1982). A group of fourth-grade boys offered that going in from recess and lining up was an awful experience, one mixed with the ambiguities of ending play in a restrictive school, and the chaos of the transition itself.

> —Some people run, and then most people just hang out and keep doing what they're doing.
> —Yup.
> —No.
> ARB: Is it hard to come in, or are you glad to come in?
> —I don't want to come in (pause).
> —I think going in is the worst part of school.
> —Yes it is.

Mock-violent play has been studied most extensively and most usefully by animal ethologists such as Karl Groos (1976/1901), Robert Fagen (1975) and Owen Aldis (1975) and by scholars of face-to-face communication such as Erving Goffman (1963) and Adam Kendon (1990). The primary distinction in mock-violent play, among both allo-animals and humans is in the presentation of the face and the small metacommunicative messages that tell the players that this action is jest, and not to be taken seriously. The clearest distinction between mock-violent and real violent interaction is said to be that when mammals play mock-violently, they tend to stay together after the bout is over, and that their faces are in part visible to each other. In real violent interactions, the actors separate, if they are permitted to do so (Boulton and Smith 1989; Pellegrini 1994). At the end of recess, this is especially difficult to do, as the adults are directing the students to stop playing and get in line. Conner (1989) has cautioned that the labeling of interactions as violent may be subjective and calls for a less rhetorical and more exacting definition of the phenomenon.

Following the children's cues and the distinctions described by the ethological and human communication literature, the video footage from both the roving camera and the wide angle camera were analyzed for incidents of actual versus mock-violence.

The following is a summary of the roving, up-close camera coding. Attention was paid to whether the actors separated, and to facial cues. (Activities noted but not counted in the tally as fitting the category are in parenthesis. Single pushes, if not escalated, are not included here, as they appeared whenever a game was interrupted—the reason being that the camera was often focusing on a game and the game was interrupted by an outsider wishing to be photographed.) A dash indicates no clearly observable conflict.

The time of the bell is also recorded below, as it is significant in its relation to the timing of the activity and the violence. The actual time of the bell and the clock on the video camera may not have been synchronous; one of the two clocks might have been fast or slow. The important thing here is the timing of the bell in relation to the activity to be described below:

Date	Description	Time of Action	Time of Bell
3/10	a) play fighting sustained between boy and girl, slapping, hair pulling	10:37:64	
	b) real punches/fight in line	10:42:16	10:42:00
3/20	playing turned into brawl stopped by aide	10:43:12	10:41:56
5/6	——		
5/7	girl is knocked down and she cries	10:47:29	10:47:26
5/11	a) two boys wrestle lazily and part	10:45:28	10:44:25
	b) girl approaches camera and announces plan to "beat this boy up right now."	10:47:31	
5/12	——		
5/13	——		
5/14	——		
5/15	——		
6/1	in back of line, fourth-grader kicks third-graders	10:48:39	10:47:37
6/2	a) playfighting borderlines with real pushing	10:43:39	
	b) teacher grabs jump rope, yanks it, children keep playing	10:50:03	
	c) boxing in line, children separate	10:50:28	10:49:00
6/3	a) elaborate mock fight, victim runs away, "Don't kill him," they theatrically cross camera	10:40:20	
	b) observer to mock fight starts to pinch another observer ; "Let up, you're killing me," they exit together)	10:40:42	10:48:00
6/4	——		
6/22	a) "I socked him, I finally socked him" announced to camera	10:45:54	10:43:52
	b) immigrant boy is on floor, in tears, is being pushed by another; building reentry	10:47:11	10:47:58

In more than half of the footage with the roving camera, which was focused on the game interaction, images of real fighting appear. And in all of these, with one exception, the fighting occurs within a minute and a half of the ringing of the bell. Some of these examples occurred within seconds. The violent talk had a wider window, of about two or three minutes, but the violent aftershock of the bell was clearly visible, even with this initial small sample. The last example shows a larger three-minute, 18-second gap, but it was only 47 seconds before the walking back into the building. The transition may indeed be two-fold, given the extended waiting period. There were days when no violence, mock or real, was visible in front of the camera. And most significantly, violence was visible in fewer than half of the days, and when it did occur, it was visible in six out of seven cases, as part of the transition period, and not in the playtime.

The wide-angled footage recorded general traffic patterns, and was coded for blatant violence in the larger play period and the lining-up process as well. Note that some times are recorded with hour, minute, seconds, i.e., 10:44:21, and some are noted with minutes and seconds by a counter, i.e., 25:34, depending upon which wide-angled camera was in use. Again it is the relation of the timing of the action to the bell, and not the absolute time that is significant here.

Date	Description	Time of Action	Time of Bell
11/4	a) real fights, pushing, kicking in back of line, leads to a ripple effect	10:44:21	
	b) more real fighting, escalated, they separate, withdraw face gaze	10:44:35	10:42:38.
11/8	——		
11/15	a) real fight, slugging, they separate	10:41:56	
	b) much wrestling in line		
	c) fight in line, visible anger	10:44:18	10:42:26
11/18	a) three rounds of mock but direct fighting at beginning of recess;	10:30:04	
	third is real fight,	10:30:42	
	broken up by older girl	10:31:02	
	b) brawl with crowd, ended by aide	10:31:50	
	c) fight, student thrown to ground, retaliation	10:42:48	10:42:24
	d) girl hits in line as retaliation	10:44:22	
11/25	a) boy is pushed to ground, actors stay together	10:32:48	
	b) fight begins	10:41:42	10:42:44
	c) fourth grader pushes everyone in line	10:43:22	
	d) girls punch and kick as retaliation	10:43:53	
6/1	a) play fighting is joined by boy who is less playful, and is seriously pushed	25:34	24:37

6/2	a) as line is about to go in, fourth-grader is about to hit third-grader, other third-grader and then teacher intervene	21:49	20:17
6/3	a) fight starts, two on one, victim stalks back later, they separate	21:47	20:59
6/4	a) in line, third grader, second in line grabs person in front, throws to ground, grabber is hurt, leads to ripple of pushing	34:14	33:46
	b) kicking, pushing, banging, two boys test the boundaries away from the line	34:18	
	c) in line tagging becomes hitting, then retaliation by being thrown to ground, chain reaction to four couples, male and female, sparring harshly	36:22	

Here eight out of nine examples showed distinct violence in the lining up procedure, with six out of eight occurring in less than two minutes from the bell. Only two violent episodes in the wide-angle footage occurred away from the transition period. (Some of the non-line-up conflict occurred right at the beginning of recess, and may be connected to lack of stimulation or activity options in the beginnings of the play period.) A ripple effect is also visible in several of the tapes: pushing leads to retaliation, sometimes from bystanders, who then are involved and bump into another student.

Several factors are contributing to the escalation of tension and palpable violence at the end of recess. During the games themselves, the children were in charge of their own peer groups, but the ringing of the bell signaled that the peer period was over, and that the teachers and teachers' aides were now in charge. Yet during the five- to ten-minute transition period at the end of recess, teachers were often not yet outside, leaving, quite literally, no one in charge. Secondly, the lining-up formation itself, in this time of leaderless transition, placed students head-behind-head in close proximity, not permitting the usual reading of facial clues to regulate messages of mock and real violence. It is at this point that the teachers emerged and saw chaos, substantiating their claim that when they "see" recess, they "see" violence. But to confuse the part with the whole is to deny children the opportunity to play, an interference likened to the denial of free speech. The violence is then displaced; the punishment is upon the children, who are blamed for the transitional structure of "the worst part of school." In this light, children's strategies to "keep on playing" and to "keep doing what they're doing" reflect a stance not of defiance, but self-imposed structure.

References

Aldis, Owen. (1975). *Play Fighting*. New York: Academic Press.

Ball, Stephen Jay. (1990). *Foucault and Education: Disciplines and Knowledge*. London: Routledge.

Bourdieu, Pierre, and Jean-Claude Passeson. (1990). *Reproduction in Education, Society and Culture*. Translated from the French (*La reproduction*) by Richard Nice. London: Sage Publications.

Blatchford, Peter, and Sonia Sharp. (1994). *Breaktime and the School*. London: Routledge.

Boulton, Michael, and Peter K. Smith. (1976). Issues in the study of children's rough-and-tumble play. In *The Ecological Context of Children's Play*, edited by Mariane Bloch, and Anthony Pellegrini, pp. 57–83. Norwood, New Jersey: Ablex.

Conner, Kathleen. (1989). Aggression: Is it in the eye of the beholder? *Play and Culture* 2.3: 213–217.

Devine, John. (1996) *Maximum Security: The Culture of Violence in Inner-City Schools*. Chicago: University of Chicago Press.

Fagen, Robert. (1976). Modeling how and why play works. In *Play: Its Role in Development and Evolution*, edited by Jerome S. Bruner, Alison Jolly, and Kathy Sylva, pp. 96–118. New York: Basic Books.

Goffman, Erving. (1963). Face engagements. In *Behavior in Public Places,* pp. 83–111. New York: The Free Press.

Groos, Karl. (1976). The play of animals: Play and instinct. In *Play: Its Role in Development and Evolution*, edited by Jerome S. Bruner, Alison Jolly, and Kathy Sylva, pp. 68–83. New York: Basic Books. Article first published in 1901.

Hart, Craig. (1993). *Children on Playgrounds*. Albany: State University of New York Press.

Kendon, Adam. (1990). Some functions of the gaze in two-person interaction. In *Conducting Interaction: Patterns of Behavior in Focused Encounters,* pp. 51–90. Cambridge: Cambridge University Press.

Opie, Iona, and Peter Opie. (1969). *Children's Games in Street and Playground*. Oxford: Oxford University Press.

———. (1988) *The Singing Game*. Oxford: Oxford University.

Pellegrini, Anthony D. (1994). *School Recess and Playground Behavior*. Albany: State University of New York

Schwartzman, Helen. (1978). *Transformations: The Anthropology of Children's Play*. New York: Plenum.

Sutton-Smith, Brian. (1981). *A History of Children's Play: The New Zealand Playground 1840–1950*. Wellington: New Zealand Council on Educational Research; Philadelphia: University of Pennsylvania.

Sutton-Smith, Brian, Jay Mechling, Thomas W. Johnson, and Felicia R. McMahon. (1995). *Children's Folklore: A Source Book*. New York: Garland.

Turner, Victor. (1982). *From Ritual to Theatre: The Human Seriousness of Play*. New York: Performing Arts Journal.

Chapter IV

Growing Up with Violence in Northern Ireland: Making Meaning of Institutionalized Violence

Linda J. Rogers

This analysis focuses upon two boys, age nine and eleven, who live in two different housing estates in Northern Ireland. They took part in a study I conducted to investigate children's perspectives of their interactions at school, at home, and at play with their peers. During the course of 1997–1998 I interviewed about 140 children. These children were tangential participants and victims of the accepted discourses of violence that they inherited by being born into their various families and communities. The way these children dealt with their individual dilemmas paradoxically placed them into deeper, unintentional, and unavoidable risks in their daily encounters with teachers and peers.

I will use narrative analysis (Linde 1993) and applied semiotics (Danesi and Rogers et al. 1999), and touch upon discussions of "thirdspace" as developed by Edward Soja (1996) in order to make my sense of the children's stories.

I begin with a minimal introduction to the children and the schools that they attended. For the purpose of this discussion, however, I will describe a single school, Ballybaile, in Northern Ireland. The school, the teachers, and the conditions of the social and economic lives of the people living in that community, with a few adjustments for an older or newer building, a different religious orientation, more or less sun, could be easily blurred into many schools, even the schools where I had taught in Western Australia over 10,000 miles and a seemingly different culture away.

Ballybaile is a "controlled" school—that is, a school in a Protestant neighborhood, or housing estate. Catholic schools are termed "maintained," and in the general area I stayed there were three schools that integrated Catholic and Protestant children. The two Protestant schools where I interviewed took the name of the area, therefore, when a student went to Ballybaile Primary, he was "from Ballybaile."

Myles, aged nine, was a Ballybaile boy. His eighteen-year-old school was bright, filled with wonderful art work created by the children, and had a fairly stable teaching staff. The principal had been there many years and knew the children by name. The first day I set foot in the school I was walked about by the Deputy, a young woman, Stephanie O'Neill, who spoke to each child personally. Ms. O'Neill was an experienced teacher and loved her work and the school. The younger children swarmed to her and often received a hug, a pat, or some form of affectionate notice. It seemed to me to be a place of warmth and to be deliberatively supportive. Further, I was impressed by the dedication of the teachers. Each stayed after school until five o'clock almost every evening preparing lessons or working on special projects. In her concern for a researcher she had never met, Ms. O'Neill went to painful efforts to ensure that the conditions of the study were successful. She randomly selected the students, making certain there were an equal number of girls to boys, personally sent out the invitation-to-participate letters of consent to parents, and interviewed me quite carefully, preparing me to be sensitive and respectful of the community life.

Ms. O'Neill was knowledgeable about the demographic information that statistically described the socio-economic conditions of the lives of the parents and their children. There were 265 children in the school, including two special units of children with mild learning disabilities. Most of the parents were unemployed and those who were employed mainly had jobs in local shops. Few belonged to the P.T.A., and only a few parents came to see school plays. Many of the children also had artwork on display in a town approximately five kilometers away—it was an outcome of the school having an artist in residence. The children had been taken to see their work but few parents went.

Ms. O'Neill described the school as a "haven," a place the children were happy to attend. Although people in that community often moved from housing estate to housing estate, many of the parents had attended the school themselves.

The parents of Ballybaile children were represented as being welcome in the school, as being sought after to participate in the life of the school. I was told, and did see, that parents often came in to visit with the Headmaster, Mr. Davis, and freely discussed their problems with him and asked him for personal advice. This was a common feature at the two schools the boys attended.

One of the major events the school had just participated in was the Heartstone Project; the school teamed up with a Catholic School to work on issues of violence and reconciliation. A group of children from the school had visited the Prime Minister of Southern Ireland, the Republic of Ireland, and asked questions of her. Individual pictures of these children were prominently displayed alongside a local newspaper article that had a photo of the children with the Prime Minister. One aspect of the project was to train children as peer mediators—the immediate effect of this program was quite noticeable, as it had eradicated bullying on the school grounds. Although the reconciliation program had been in effect for a number of years, Ms. O'Neill described the school and estate population as "staunchly Protestant—no mixing or mingling with Catholics." Around the housing estate I had noted the curbs were painted red, white, and blue, and on the walls of some of the buildings were drawings and names indicating membership and loyalty to particular Protestant sectarian groups.

This particular aspect, "the troubles" that permeated the lives of some of the children in this school and in others, was unique to Northern Ireland. I cannot explain "the troubles" of Northern Ireland, nor why the situation—so difficult and devastating over a long period of time for so many people—is still unresolved. Many people I met who live there find it beyond their explanation. It is, of course, all about the discourses of power and rage and grief. It keeps fueled through the violence that is acted out among and between adults, but many children's lives are grimly affected. They grow up in it, become accustomed to it, and perhaps, as Burgess (1993) suggests, become immune or anesthetized by the expectation and anticipation of violence. People whom they love are affected by it, and they learn about it through direct and indirect experience. It is compounded by silences, leaving them to make meaning of events that sweep them up. The two boys I interviewed, in different housing estates, were deeply affected. Myles was nine at the time I spoke to him, and Ryan, eleven.

Myles

Myles was the third child I interviewed at Ballybaile. He had a very bright smile and I wrote in my notes that he wore a brightly colored woven wristband—I commented upon it and he nodded. He had chosen it himself—he said he liked nice colors. He listened carefully and responded thoughtfully, choosing his words. I had been told that he had a difficult year. His dad had left his mother and moved in with another woman in the estate, around the corner. Myles was in the same class with a girl who now lived with his father. Myles had found it difficult. His schoolwork had slipped and his attention frequently drifted.

It was not an uncommon situation. Many women in the estate were not married and their families consisted of children fathered by different males. I had been told that one of my questions, one that asked, "Who lives in your house?" was not a sensitive question to ask. Many families would be suspicious that a question such as that was structured in such a way as to give officious social workers access to information. It was a question that was considered intrusive. I did not ask it. I did ask Myles where he lived and if he could tell me about his family. He tells me he lives with his step-dad now and has two brothers, one 17 and one 4, and two sisters, one 12, and the other a baby. He says that their dads are not his dad. But his dad doesn't live with him anymore. The interview changes when I ask if anything has ever scared him. He looks up and quickly says that he is scared of dying. I repeat that, "of dying?"

> L.R. Is there a special reason? Do you know anyone who has died?
>
> M. Yes. My best friend's father, Donald George. My best friend is David George, but I haven't seen him for a long time. I don't know where he is.
>
> L.R. Why is that?
>
> M. I don't know. They just came and took everyone away.
>
> L.R. Did that happen recently?
>
> M. Yes. One night I just went to bed and when I got up the next morning it had happened and they were all gone.
>
> L.R. Can you tell me what happened?
>
> M. Well, I think that his friends killed him—they called him out in a lane and they just shot him. That scares me too—how would you know, I mean he was a good man, he was a real dad. When my dad moved away, he said, "Don't worry Myles, you can come over here and go fishing with us. I need another lad." And I went over there all the time and we did all kinds of things together. David was my best friend and I loved his dad. And his friends came for him and called him out . . . how could I ever trust a friend now, if his friends did that to him?
>
> L.R. I see. Were you able to see your friend and tell him about how you feel and that you are sorry his dad died?
>
> M. No. I just went to bed that night and everything was fine. But, in the morning he was dead and they were all gone.

L.R. Do you know where?

M. No.

L.R. Did you ask your mother?

M. She just said I shouldn't think about it.

L.R. Do you think about it a lot?

M. Yes. I try to imagine what it is like.

L.R. What, what do you try to imagine?

M. What it is like to be dead?

L.R. I see. What do you do or imagine when you do that?

M. Well, I wake myself up very early in the morning, before anyone else is up and I lie very still [he stretches out his legs] and I put my hands over my ears [he cups both hands and places them over his ears] and I shut my eyes tight [he does] and I lie like that for as long as I can. I try to imagine what it must be like for him. And that I can keep him company.

L.R. For him?

M. For Mr. George.

L.R. Do you tell anyone this?

M. No.

L.R. Did you ever ask your teacher, or did you ever tell her you were worried about dying?

M. I asked her about dying but she said I should think about living and getting on with things.

L.R. What about your mom?

M. She's pretty busy with the new baby and she just says I should get on with it.

L.R. Do you go to church?

M. No, not really.

L.R. Do you, do you think that maybe he is in heaven?

M. I don't know. I just am scared because I have to die some day and I wonder what it is like and . . .

L.R. Well, for just now I have an idea, but would you mind if I mentioned to your teacher that you are feeling sad about your friend and his father, and if I mentioned it to Mr. Desmond, maybe he could find where the family went, would you like that?

M. Okay.

L.R. But, for today, I'd like you to try something for me, something that you can imagine. Will you try something?

M. What?

L.R. I want you to do something today, just a little thing that you would think would have made Mr. George proud of you. Just something little that you would be glad that he knew about, something that you might tell him. Like doing well in class or doing well in sport, or taking care of your little sister well . . .

M. And?

L.R. And, in your mind, I want you to concentrate on what you did and why he would be happy and then I want you to imagine that you could put that in a box and wrap it up.

M. With nice wrapping, paper and ribbons?

L.R. Yes, if you like. Then send it to him.

M. Send it to him? Do you think he'd get it?

L.R. I'm sure he would. And, I want you to find me tomorrow and tell me about it. Okay?

M. Okay.

Immediately after the interview I questioned the principal, Mr. Desmond, for corroboration. He confirmed that Mr. George had been shot in a sectarian incident the previous November. The principal followed up on what happened to the George family. Two days later he came to me with amazing information. Mr. George had indeed been shot as reported. The account had been written to appear as if he had died. In fact, one of the bullets was lodged dangerously close to his heart, making an operation terribly risky. The family had been moved out immediately and Mr. George taken to a major hospital in another community. The authorities did not want anyone to "know" that Mr. George was still alive in case another attempt was made on his life. We were not allowed to tell Myles anything about the family.

The day after the interview with Myles, he came up to me beaming; he had done what I suggested, and he knew Mr. George had got "it" and he could send him other things. Also, the principal, Mr. Desmond, and his teacher had talked to him and he said he felt better. I told him to tell his teacher or Mr. Desmond when he starting thinking or felt sad.

Myles had not been given counseling—he had not been considered affected by the incident as he had not been a member of the immediate family. He was peripheral to the violence, someone who lived across the street from it. There was no venue for psychological services for a child who lived across the street, for someone so outside the membership of what a typical family is considered to be. But, Myles considered himself a member of that family. He had reauthored (Bakhtin 1986) an effective self as a son of a "real" father. He told me "a dad" lived with "a mum," a "real dad" married the mum. Mr. George was a real dad, and Mr. George had incorporated Myles into his "family" when Myles' father moved away.

Myles' coping strategies were interesting. He began questioning adults as to what happened. Answers were not forthcoming, perhaps perceived as difficult or beyond the understanding of a nine-year-old. He was admonished to "get on with," to go about the business of his life, but he had recast his life after its first disruption and had re/incorporated it into his new desired family system. The "real" son, David, was not only bio-logically connected to his father but bound by the public, socially prescribed civil and religious ceremony of marriage, not common for that community. David is the child that public gaze would recognize as having "lost" his father to violence, and whose grief, if it was openly demonstrated, would be sanctioned as valid. People, or "the others," could recognize that child as having sorrow and perhaps rage. Myles' grief went without witnesses; in effect, he held no valid claim to the ongoing dilemma. But, in his imagination he created the closeness he longed for—he could even be physically close to Mr. George each morning and "keep him company." He could, in fact, be closer to the believed dead Mr. George than he was to his daily experiential world—the world of homework and chores and stepfathers.

The space that Myles occupied was an imagined or symbolic placement of desire. He could keep company with a man he thought was dead, and be loved and give love—he could demonstrate the loyalty he felt to Mr. George early in the morning lying in his bed with his eyes shut and his hands over his ears. His grief could function in the inner plane of his choosing—a place he could make and powerfully situate himself beyond the admonitions of his mother or his teachers. He did not so much displace his feelings as re-place them, re-situate himself in a world beyond the control of events and other people. It was a space/place that he could envision and structure himself. He was the one who crafted time and propelled himself into a space of caring. He knew the best time in "real world" time to be beyond the comment of family or others who did not recognize his need. He could perhaps tolerate actual time and actual events because of his ability to transcend these and attempt to build himself into knowledge that was otherwise unavailable to him.

Soja (1996: 5) discusses the concept of thirdspace, a place of creative restructuring, of "othering," a place of extraordinary "openness . . . where geographical imagination can be expanded to encompass a multiplicity of perspectives." Myles, through an accident of a question opened his carefully crafted plane of longing, his thirdspace plane of interaction. His daily world could then be reappraised, his daydreaming, his "loss of enthusiasm" be reinterpreted and symbolically relocated to a level of interaction where adults witnessed a child experiencing loss and disengagement on a tragic level. He was not "just another" child whose dad left home, although that could be considered enough; his grief could be an undefinable other...worthy of extra consideration, of exploration, of pondering possible multiple strategies of evolving solutions, and he no longer fit neat categories of known behaviors.

It is interesting how few people in that narrative were considered "a part" of the event. The practice of social recognition and social gaze avoidance is one of the issues in this incident and in many places where violence is seen as an on-going phenomenon. The only people "near to" that episode that Myles' community seemed to grant connected-ness were the immediate family. Counselors did not come into the school to discuss David's disappearance with other children or teachers. The nearness of violence did not enter into the household discussion that Myles heard or related by any means other than as a silencing—a stillness beyond the understanding of Myles—a silence that bewildered him and left further commentary as somehow a comment on the questioner as not being right, not stiff upper lip, not "getting on with it," "not our business." It becomes almost immediately a literal and figurative distance. It can also be seen as a measure of the danger that people anticipated. It certainly positions commentary as dangerous and as extraneous. It creates and sustains a placement of mystery and fear where friends may not be friends and where community is reduced to individual holders of power, obscured and empowered by silence.

Ryan

Before the interview with Ryan at Derrycarrick began, I was told to be sensitive with Ryan, as his father was in jail in Belfast for having taken an active part in a sectarian murder. Ryan was a quiet, slim, shy boy. He was quite polite and soft spoken. He gave me the impression of someone timid. The interview was in two parts; the first part consisted of the interview protocol. I had noted his comments about his father during the interview. Ryan simply said his father was in prison and now his mum drove a taxi. He said that they used to go once a month to see his dad.

> L.R. What did he say to you?
>
> R. To be good, not to give me mum any trouble.
>
> L.R. Do you know why he is there?
>
> R. No.
>
> L.R. So, no one has ever said, why . . .
>
> R. No.
>
> L.R. Do you miss him?
>
> R. Yes, I think he will come home after a long time, maybe when I am 16 or 17.

When I asked him if he ever got in trouble he said, "Sometimes." He tried to be good. He said he sometimes got in trouble with the teacher, or had fights. He was not more forthcoming and I didn't press as him as I was conscious of his background. However, to my surprise, when the interview ended, he asked me if I could help him.

> L.R. Help you, how, what would you like me to help you with?
>
> R: With my sad spot.
>
> L.R. Your sad spot.
>
> R. Yes.
>
> L.R. Where is it? Is it in a particular place?
>
> R. (He nodded.)
>
> L.R. Can you show me?
>
> R. (He pointed to an area just under and to the left of the heart.) There. I have to work very hard keeping it there, keeping it small, or else it grows.
>
> L.R. What happens when it grows?
>
> R. It fills me all over and then I start crying and I can't stop.
>
> L.R. Does that happen very often?

R. Every night.

L.R. Do you tell your mum?

R. Yes.

L.R. What does she say?

R. She says I have to get on with it. I have to stop.

L.R. Do your sisters know?

R. Yes. They just say I have to get on with it.

L.R. What do you do then?

R. I sit in my room in the dark and I cry. I don't come down.

L.R. Does your teacher know?

R. No. I'm afraid to tell her. She yells at someone sometimes in the class and, even though it isn't me she's yelling at it starts to grow, and I have to spend all my time keeping it small so it doesn't grow in class.

L.R. Does she yell at you?

R. No, but sometimes I get in trouble because I haven't done my work or been able to hear what we are supposed to do.

L.R. Then what happens?

R. Then it is worse.

L.R. What else makes it worse?

R. Well, I hate yelling and loud noise . . . and

L.R. Do you fight?

R. Sometimes. I have to.

L.R. How do you feel about that?

R. Well, sometimes I get in trouble and then I get worse and it gets worse, the spot. It's always there.

L.R. What would you like to happen?

R. [He looks up quickly.] Go away. If I could go away, far away from here, where no one knew me. To New York or somewhere in America, or to . . . Australia.

L.R. Do you think you'll do that when you're older?

R. I hope so . . . I want to be far away, far away from here.

L.R. Do you think it would help if I said something to your teacher . . . would you let me say something?

R. (He nods.)

I tell Ryan that he can speak to me anytime he likes . . . he nods. I pause and tell him that his teacher and the principal have my telephone number and that if he wants to talk to me any time I am here, he can. I ask how he feels now. "A little better," he says.

I tell the headmaster at Derrycarrick, as soon as the interview is over, that I am worried about Ryan, and why, as Ryan has given me permission to talk to him. Mr. Poldark is somewhat incredulous. Ryan's sister works near the school and has never mentioned this. He goes to check. He returns to me shortly afterwards, clearly troubled. The sister has just told him that Ryan cries himself to sleep most nights, often rocking back and forth saying that no one loves him. The sister had thought that this was just normal behavior. . . She says that to me as well later that day.

Two weeks later I see Ryan at an overnight camp with the rest of his class. He is happy, scrambling over rocks. He comes rushing up and says he feels a little better. Mr. Poldark needs him to help him fish so he's going to go with Mr. Poldark and help him fish. Soon.

Mr. Poldark nods. He has often taken a personal interest in particular children. Ryan now has someone just for him . . . at least for now. It is hard for me to think of Ryan without grief. One aspect of further worry is that the mother has stopped going to Belfast to visit the father and rumor has it that she has a boyfriend. Mr. Pollock is worried that this also troubles the boy.

Ryan's spot, or site of psychic and corporal pain, moves. He needs to place his hand upon it, "to keep it small." It needs the warmth of his hand, his humanly created warmth to deactivate and firmly situate "the sad spot" into a bodily region. It acts on its own. It overwhelms. He could be overwhelmed, again, in public. This is the site where he recognizes the mass of feeling within him, where it gathers. Just there. When he can control it, he has a measure of safety.

Unlike Myles, Ryan is recognized by the system as connected to trauma. But his connectedness is not a relationship of sanction, one of protection, overall pity, and support. He has a conflicted presence...his father is a political prisoner, or a murderer. To some, the father can be seen as an active part of resistance to oppression, or as a destroyer. The son, as a symbol of the father, is marked by the father's positioning. That marking brings Ryan into public gaze, not as a child, but as a child representing the action of belief and retribution. He is held in that gaze as a consequence and inheritor—"sometimes the boys, they tease me."

> L.R. What do they tease you about?
>
> R. They try to make me fight. And, if I do, then, then I'm just like m'dad and if I don't, then I'm a sissy.

Ryan is placed or symbolically replaced in the community as if in a trial of training to take his father's role—a logic of replacement. Can this human be the other human? Who Ryan is, the child that is Ryan and how he feels—where he is in finding a self that can cope with the extraordinary experience of which he is a tangential part through biological connection—is not the subject of the community discourse. Ryan's experiences offer a false binary—his father's role or that of the sissy. As the one human took on the role of executioner or avenger, here is another of his blood, a creature object like him, "like father, like son."

Nemeroff and Rozin (1994: 158) present the "magical law of contagion" as a natural human response. This theory maintains when people come into contact with people or objects that are stigmatized, or in this case set apart, that through a magical influence there is a transfer of the properties that acts almost as contagion. This is especially important when considering a vital connection. That which is inside, and presents a danger or attraction, can move outside and penetrate an inside without being seen. It can even move from an external outside object to contaminate an inside.

Mary Douglas (1992) points out that deciding what is an object and distinguishing that object from a context cannot be taken for granted. In Ryan's case, the object blurring moves from the act committed by Ryan's father into the body and personality of the son—does the son become the father? Is the son reduced to his biological connectedness, an over-determined sign of the father's act?

Ryan's own body begins its insidious rejection of the false binary opposition—the sad spot is not "of the father," is not part of the "just get on with it" modus operandi that orchestrates the acceptable ranges of responses in the housing estate. Ryan cannot even control the sad spot—it operates as a seemingly automatic rejection of the object blurring, it asserts a dangerous difference and reduces the eleven-year-old to a crying, rocking, wounded child at night. But who can hear him? What self does he have that can participate in opening the debate? Where can he safely explore growth and experiment with role or career? In his case, a stranger, a not-member, accidentally opened the thirdspace placement, the place where Ryan lived out his fears and pain—the possibility that Ryan wanted an "other" life, but one that he did not know how to make in the everyday world of acts and consequences. In his imaginary life, his space of safety, he would escape to a far away world, a place where his inheritance as "the son of..." was not known, a space where his body could be his again—his own self-structuring and where he could be the determiner of his being. While at his school, Derrycarrick, Mr. Poldark offered to open the line of possibilities available for Ryan. The pathways that appeared to lead into either emotional deadening or despair seemingly, for this time, may have been avoided (Terr 1990).

Where do we begin to move away from children? How do we all quickly move into "othering" and distancing ourselves so that we find the ability to resist knowing about trauma that is happening? And, when do we find the time, the place, and the energy to break the social sanctions of "interference" to be able to ask the questions that open the opportunities for resistance, witnessing, and change?

I transcribed the field notes and did much of the background reading for this project while I was in Western Australia collecting data there. One afternoon, driving home after having a lengthy visit with a dedicated school psychologist who had introduced a modified anger management program for the children in that school, I listened to the Prime Minister of Australia being interviewed on the national radio station. He was being questioned about policies he was presenting to Parliament, which would entail cutting current funds for lower income families and educational projects.

The gist of the Prime Minister's commentary was that it was time for low-income families and people in depressed economic areas to take charge of their lives. I wondered how the children would fare with even fewer support systems. It was not that these children, or Ryan or Myles, had an identity to reframe or resituate into larger, welcoming communities. Instead, many children are reduced to holding on, using much of their energy simply to maintain what ideas of self they can grasp, instead of seeking the challenge of developing out into life.

The children need the social flow of active people who have the time and energy to encourage and support a possible emergent self into a being that holds and claims a sense of humor, curiosity, adventure, and that recognizes tenacity. Although, right now, these children need us, in not too many years we will need Myles and Ryan to determine the shape of their adult years for themselves. I have no answers, only the narratives of children who attempt to make meaning of and adjust into a family, located in a particular community. It is difficult enough for children to sort out the confusing messages of the adult world without having to withstand the dangers of situated and established modes of violence. I was struck by the thought that I could provide any number of actual empirical examples that would easily demonstrate the dangers of that current government's policy but that all too often, the theory behind the policy that shapes what happens to children is more important than the people the policy affects.

References

Bakhtin, M.M. (1986). *Speech Genres and Other Late Essays*, edited by Caryl Emerson and Michael Holquist. Translated from the Russian by Vem W. McGee. Austin: University of Texas Press.

Burgess, T.P. (1993). *A Crisis of Conscience*. Aldershot, England: Ashgate Publishing Limited.

Linde, Charlotte. (1993). *Life Stories: The Creation of Coherence*. London: Oxford University Press.

Rogers, Linda, Susan A. Tucker, and Marcel Danesi. (1999) A forum for inter and transdisciplinary discourse. *International Journal of Applied Semiotics* 1.1: 3–6. Ottawa: Legas Press.

Douglas, Mary. (1992). *Objects and Objections*. Toronto Semiotic Circle Monograph Series 9. Toronto: Toronto Semiotic Circle.

Nemeroff, Carol, and Paul Rosin. (1994). The contagion concept in adult thinking in the United States: Transmission of germs and of interpersonal influence. *Ethos* 22.2: 158–186.

Rogers, Linda. (1997). Field Notes from Three Schools, Northern Ireland, May–June, 1997. Unpublished document.

Soja, Edward. W. (1996). *Thirdspace*. Cambridge, England: Blackwell Publishers.

Terr, Lenore. (1990). *Too Scared to Cry*. New York: Basic Books.

Chapter V

Believed and Not Believed: Community Reaction to Rape in Mexico and the United States

Cathy Winkler

After decades if not centuries of silence about the crime of rape (Sanday 1996), the 1970s feminist movement encouraged people who were raped to speak up about such: truth that violence occurs (Brownmiller 1975). Since friends and family of rape victim-survivors are in the process of developing coping strategies, we still don't know what to say or how to act toward or as a victim-survivor (Winkler 1991, 2002).

As I experienced people's ambiguity to the attack against me in the United States, I longed for the support of my friends in the rural town of Olinala in the state of Guerrero, Mexico, where I did my research (1980–1982) (Winkler 1987). There I studied a situation of institutionalized rape. Their practice of mountain marriages was the precursor for rape, and in the 1950s and 1960s as in the United States, the crimes of rapists were hidden and silence was a victim's blight.

Mountain Marriage

Prior to the 1970s, marriage in Olinala occurred in four forms: civil marriages, church marriages, free union, and mountain marriages. Economics orchestrated the choice of marriage. Those who had money, usually landowners, could afford both a church and civil marriage. Those with some funds opted only for the civil marriage. Those couples without assets moved in together in the house of the husband's parents.

In the earlier tradition, mountain marriages were an exciting event in which the kidnapper, and his fellow horsemen, rode up and captured (*robar*, to steal) a young woman. While some women did arrange for their own kidnapping, others were alarmed when they were carried off into a new life. All women yelled for help as their bodies were grabbed and thrown over the horse, but the people in the community believed that every woman had agreed with their capture and that the screams were self-protection against the anger of their parents, cheated of their wishes for a formal wedding. The term *robar la mujer*, to steal a woman, meant to steal her from her parents/family, not from herself.

A joke in the community came from an actual event in which a kidnapper, slow to act, almost thwarted the pre-arranged kidnapping. Maria and Juan had secretly decided to elope and to have a mountain marriage. On the prearranged day, which was a Sunday— market day and a good day for people to linger around in various areas talking and shopping—Maria silently walked to the designated corner, far from her family who might stop the kidnapping. Along came Juan riding up on his horse to "capture" Maria. As Juan leaned over to grab and force Maria over the horse, Maria yelled: "*Ayudeme, ayudeme* [help me, help me]." Juan, though, had trouble getting Maria over the horse. People nearby, who were not family and thus not allowed to interfere in family matters, heard intermingled within Maria's yells for help a quiet voice that whispered: "*Apurete,*

apurete [hurry up, hurry up]." The "hurry up" comment demonstrated that Maria was an accomplice in the kidnapping.

In the mountains, the kidnappers had a code of honor that respected the wishes of the woman kidnapped: No man should touch a woman sexually without her permission or physically force her to have sex. To force a woman physically to have sex could damage her internally and such internal damage could prevent her from having children: Hurting one person could result in hurting others not yet born.

When discussing this code of honor with women unwillingly kidnapped, the code held another meaning. While all women agreed that the kidnapper honored the code, the woman's decision was situationally inevitable. Any kidnapped woman who returned to the town, whether she had had sexual intercourse or not with the kidnapper, would still be sentenced to a life as a wife to the kidnapper. The community would assume that she was part of the prearranged kidnapping and that she had had sexual intercourse with him in the mountains. The truth was irrelevant: From the perspective of the women, they had no option once they had been kidnapped. Eventually they would have to succumb to the kidnapper sexually whether they desired it or not. Their fate was sealed. Sexual intercourse for procreation was their only solution to bring some peace into their lives. Kidnappers, who set up a situation in which they forced women to decide to have sex, committed rape.

Silence and Isolation

In the United States, we can speak up *for* our rights and *against* violence, or can we? While some Olinaltecan women kidnapped were silent about speaking out and were isolated into a marriage of inconvenience, we women victims in the United States can speak up, and yet we receive silence from our listeners who later isolate themselves from us. That is how "Gail" treated me:

> I am ashamed of myself because I did nothing. I didn't call her. I didn't write to her. I couldn't talk to her about it. I didn't want to hear about it. I still can't read her account of what happened that night. I hugged my pain and my anger to my breast and I did nothing. Although I feel deep emotions, I can't express them. And I don't cope with others' emotional problems.

Gail's reaction was avoidance: she silenced and isolated herself from me. Susan on the other hand had regular contact with me as I stayed weekends at her country home, 45 minutes away from work and the crime scene. For three months, I worked with the police and a private investigator to find the rapist and by the fourth month, we had his identity. His blood was sent off to the laboratory for DNA fingerprinting analysis. This new method of scientific identification has freed the victim of stranger rapists from the trauma of identifying the attacker. [DNA analysis became legally available in the course of my long struggle in pursuing the case with the police (Lewis 1988). Although the case took seven years to get to trial and was aired on *48 Hours* (May 11,1994), the rapist finally received five life terms.]

This ongoing investigation was, at that time, part of my life and a part of my life that I discussed as the details unfolded. "Susan" was perceptive of how people reacted to what they felt was an investigation that never ended:

Cathy continued to talk about the rape for months. I began to notice some people avoiding her in order to avoid hearing about it. I began to appreciate the spirit of this woman even more as time went on because, as the intended support of people around her began to wane, and she was experiencing the cruelty imposed by insensitive, ignorant people, she pushed on, trying to work and resume a 'normal life'.

To mention rape is to resurrect our fears for ourselves or others, or memories of past assaults. Many people, even professional feminists as in the case of "Ellen," suggested professional listeners instead of their own time. When asked for help by attending a meeting on an unrelated matter, Ellen responded by writing a letter instead of calling me in person.

> I wish I could be more helpful to you. As you said, this time will be very difficult for you. If you need extra or new support now, I'd like to suggest some folks you might consult. These women, all licensed psychologists, were suggested by my husband, who is a licensed psychologist. After I told him the general nature of your experience, he mentioned Sue [who] has had extensive experience working with battered women [Was I battered or raped? Are these the same?].

Ellen's support as a feminist was to get advice from her husband and then send me to a therapist for weekly sessions at $50 to $75 per hour, not covered by my medical insurance. The silent presence of Ellen sitting next to me during a meeting did not occur. Ellen did not even formally reject my request to be my listener, just to be an extra set of ears, wordless and inactive. She could not even support me that much. I have since written two articles addressing the constraints of counselors against victim-survivors, and how these constraints are rape-like (Winkler 1994a, 1994b).

Isolation in Socialization

While the isolation by some of my friends was imposed on me, the period of isolation by work for young teenage Olinaltecans in the 1960s and earlier was due to patterns of interaction which inhibited socialization among young people. First, work isolated both young men and women in distinct domains of labor. For the young women, housework was a tedious, uncompromising and nondismissal job. One of the most difficult chores was grinding corn for tortillas. Most households averaged four to six hours of grinding corn per day to feed the family. Cleaning the dirt floor was a daily duty. Frijoles or beans demanded three to four cooking hours over a stove whose flame was constantly fed by wood. Of course, clothes washing was by hand and included dirt-filled clothes due to either the children playing on dirt floors, the arduous work of the women around the house, or the men and young boys working in the fields.

The male domain for six months of the year was in the mountain areas growing corn and beans. For many, these fields were several hours' walk from their homes. Even though no crops were grown for the other six months due to the drought conditions, men and young boys still needed to go to the mountains for their daily water supply. The heavy workload along with the geographical distance of the male and female work places isolated young adults from socializing with each other.

Then the miracle of water pipes transformed the patterns of social interaction. In the 1950s, fresh spring water was piped into the community, but only to the corners of each block. Water is continuously needed in a home with the extensive demands of daily cleaning and cooking. Young lovers were ardent suppliers of buckets of water for the home: their good deeds hid their multiple rendezvous. These new faucets were outlets to socializing. Some days, a household needed a lot of buckets of water, and young adults arranged their bucket errands to meet simultaneously at the corner faucet. Many arranged mountain marriages occurred over a bucket of water.

In the late 1950s and 1960s, electrically run corn grinders further increased the number of rendezvous by young people. While the corn grinding stores were few in number, by the late 1970s there were seven located around the town and quite busy throughout the day. A meeting along the way to the mill or back was always a possibility. A common trick was to leave the bucket at the mill and meet at the prearranged place to converse. For those days when two meetings were desired, a person would drop the bucket off and rendezvous with the friend. An hour or two later, s/he would return to the mill, but coincidentally, pass the meeting place. Electricity decreased the time for work and increased the time for amour.

Emphasis on education also had a dramatic impact on patterns of interaction of young people. Most children attended second or at the most fourth grade in the 1950s. In the 1960s, the number of grade schools increased to four with a junior high opening up in the 1970s and by 1982 the first class graduated from high school. The majority of the children graduated from the sixth grade and a great majority completed junior high by the 1970s. Regular daily interaction for nine months each term could have a profound impact on socialization. The isolation of Olinaltecans began to dissipate and an openness settled into the community.

Culture of Denigration

For myself in the United States, I felt a cultural environment of people who not only isolated and silenced me, but who responded in a negative manner to the rape attack and the following investigation—not directed at me so much as at the issue of rape. Speaking at times became impossible. My experience of a wonderful, blissful sleep the first night after the attack, without discussion of it with my friends, remained unexplained.

> Slowly my eyes opened, but I continued to hug the remnants of my dream. This was Wednesday, the first morning after the attack. My dream vision was one of paradise, a paradise filled with multiple colors of flowers that were blooming everywhere. Surrounding me were bright, cheery pallets of vivid and striking arrays and tones of flowers. It was more than a visionary splendor. The luscious and titillating smells of gardenias, a flower that is a special favorite of mine plus roses, lilacs, and other aromas awakened my senses and hugged me with a comfort of peace and contentment, alerting my senses to the gusto of life.

> As I slowly opened my eyes—not wanting to lose that delightful display, the first rays of sunlight peeked into my room, almost blending into the paradise vision of my dream. That dream occurred after the best sleep in my life, and the morning brought the most fantastic dream

imaginable. Both of these I experienced with relish. My place of sleep was a vacation spot of rest and relaxation. My body was soothed by the gentle breeze that eased into the attic haven. If viewers had seen my first facial response, I'm sure they would have seen a smile of contentment. Then I walked downstairs to breakfast.

But no one let me speak while focusing on their own dreams. "Nightmares haunted my dreams," wearily responded Susan as we exchanged greetings that first morning.

> Linda popped out of her bedroom, hugged me, and was ready with a response for me: "Oh, Cathy. I had some horrible nightmares also. Several times I woke up throughout the night. It was rough getting to sleep and then staying asleep. It must have been terrible for you, hon. How are you doing after last night?"

People assumed that their experiences must be the same as mine and they repeated tales of nightmares to me. The truth of my paradise dream did not fit in with their culturally over-determined experiences.

The negative environment continued with people wanting me to mimic their pain as noted by "Alecia":

> I felt that you were academizing your pain. I understood that as I did the same thing myself. You kept intellectualizing it. How long did it take you to cry? Sometimes I felt like screaming at you, "Cry, God damn it; admit that it hurts, really feel the pain," let it all out. You were so stoic, so obsessed with and determined to demonstrate that "no one was being sympathetic to your attack or to your pain."

While Alecia noted that I reacted in the same manner as she had reacted after the rapist had attacked her, she did not want to accept my similar behavior. She felt that she should have cried immediately and she felt that I should cry on command and with her. For me, I was in a state of numbness that lasted months. There is no one set pattern for how a person reacts after an attack: the forms of trauma are multiple and varied.

More unsuspected turmoil from others was awaiting me when I returned to work. I had informed the departmental chair that due to the nervous reactions which the members of the department were feeling—all the women, both faculty and staff and a wife of a male faculty member, had their own memories of past assaults—and because they directed their tension at me, I would not be in the office for a few days and would only attend my classes. She had my home phone number. No call came those days. The next week back at work, I opened the office department door and stared at a dozen dead and faded yellow roses that my sister had sent me the previous Thursday. Those dead roses were not the result of aging: there was no water in that 12" deep vase. How could 12" of water dry up in three days! The secretary had dumped out the water, and the rest of the members of the department watched the roses die.

The people in our culture, perhaps because we do not know how to treat each other after a crisis of rape, do not provide a supportive and comforting environment for victims. In part because many of them, tortured in the past, still live with unresolved trauma, and in some cases, they have anger at current victim-survivors who receive some support. All people need support: past and present victim-survivors.

Olinaltecan Parental Protection and Distrust

Likewise, Olinaltecans' negative environment for victims was part of their past history. Parents distrusted young people to select a mate for life. One of the reasons was due to the history of land redistribution earlier this century, which precipitated much homicide and fear. As a result, parents in the 1950s and 1960s wanted to be sure that their children did not form unions with the children whose parents had participated in those killings.

A second reason that parents had little trust for their children's ability to decide was due to the community's understanding of *el susto* or trauma. Olinaltecans believe that no child should be traumatized. The community members all keep the secrets of the parental crimes from the children. A child should never be told that his or her parents were murderers: that is a cultural crime—with horrendous implications—in Olinala. The deeds of the parents are not the fault of the children. Therefore, to protect the children of criminal parents, all children remain unaware of criminal acts by any parent. Adults do discuss in front of the children favorable and disfavorable deeds, but do not alert children to the specific people. One child could easily tell another child, and the truth would then reach the child of the guilty parents and that child could be traumatized: such an act is culturally almost defined as crime. For children to become socially healthy and responsible adults, the community protects all children until adulthood that begins around the age of fifteen.

The parents' protection of the children—while quite admirable and crucial in a child's development—also resulted sometimes in unfavorable mountain marriages for some women. Parents would show their deference, while unexplained, toward their children marrying children of criminals. Instead, the parents would arrange parties for their children to meet potential partners from acceptable parents. In cases when two young people became interested in each other and knew their union was against one or both sets of parents, they then arranged a kidnapping for a mountain marriage. One woman noted that, after she joyously returned from her mountain honeymoon, she discovered that her husband had murdered people. Unsuspectingly, she agreed to wed a man who would always be a criminal in the eyes of the townspeople.

A third form of indirect protection centered around care for the elderly. Family members took care of each other until death. In order to ensure later nursing care for themselves, the parents would raise the eldest daughter not to marry but instead to serve her aging parents. Therefore, the eldest daughter in a family was either convinced against or prevented from marrying. This position of the parents could encourage either a daughter to participate in a kidnapping or a kidnapper to take action to rescue his loved one.

The fourth reason is for the protection of girls. While Olinala is a community with multiple cultural backgrounds, unlike the indigenous, Nahuatl villages in the surrounding mountains, the use of Spanish and the two hundred fifty year documentation of selling lacquer art work in non-Nahuatl shapes indicate a strong Euro-influence. With evidence of the Euro-influence then, it is not surprising to find social patterns similar to Europe in this supposedly isolated, mountain town. In this regard, the parents raised the young women in a protective manner. The idea that young women cannot be trusted to make a sound judgment was popular in the 1950s and 1960s. While a decision made by a young woman such as her participation in a kidnapping was upheld, the parents disapproved of her method and her decision.

Target Self-Esteem

The distrust, protection, need for elderly care, and lack of education were the basis for how parents in Olinala judged their children, and such patterns of judgment have parallels in the United States in how we make statements which target one's self-esteem. Instead of using a style of negotiation, we tend to use a confrontative style and state how a person should express herself.

The week after the attack, while staying at a friend's house, a previously planned party took place. Since my face was bruised, my attendance at the party was strictly because of their encouragement. With trepidation, I experienced the first greeting: "Oh, I am so sorry for what happened. How could this happen to you?" Her pity response reflected her self-denial and pity is false sympathy. She had emphasized in her statement *to you* and that emphasis pointed out that she was not a victim type. She continued: "Oh, I am so sorry *for you*. I know you didn't intentionally mean for this to happen *to you*." Embedded in her sorrow was her knowledge that she was not the type of person to be raped. Rape could not be part of her good life. She rejected the fact that the act of rape was an attack against all people, and instead braided into her words the idea that rape is selectively wrong. But rape does not selectively occur.

I grabbed the free seat at my friends' table, but unfortunately, another seat was available, and "Judy" found it. While I had freed myself from the pity person, she was not the only insensitive person.

> "Well, you must be the *bruised lady* that Stephanie [my daughter] told me about. She told me there was a black and blue lady here. Ha, ha, ha!"
>
> "Did your daughter tell you why my face is bruised?"
>
> "No, I didn't ask."

How appropriate! We make jokes of others' misfortune and do not even think to ask what caused that misfortune.

Another part of that pattern of misjudging is the blame category. If we blame someone else, then we do not have to take responsibility or feel guilty. "Rob" and "Gerri" were the landowners of the house where the attack had occurred. He noted his reactions:

> I was angry at you, Cathy, just because you were the victim. Again, I expected you to move out but your rape forced me to have to deal with the house when I would have preferred to have life run smoothly. I'd rather worry about things that would never really happen. So I did blame you for your own rape. I always knew that no one deserves rape, but I had to continue to get along with Gerri. It was easier to blame you for our problems. I needed someone to be angry at and you were convenient. I wanted to be angry at the rapist, but he was not available.

Rob demonstrated his blame on me in multiple ways: "your rape," "your own rape," "to blame you for our problems," and "no rapist available." Of course the problem of renting the house had to be someone's fault, according to Rob. If a rapist does not materialize, then we inappropriately seek the next closest person: the victim-survivor. I received the blame and the guilt for the rapist's acts and the repercussions from his attack.

My private life, my home life, and even my work life contained people eager to judge or misjudge me. The first day back to work I saw the chair of my department and asked her whether we could get the locks on the front door of the office changed since the rapist stole my keys and knows where I work. The simple request initially netted me a diagnosis of "paranoia," from another woman!

My professional life also encountered callous judgments and mistreatments. Professionals who had spoken, written, and experienced rape themselves had negative comments for me. To several of these women I sent the first chapter of my book that described the rape attack. In that chapter, I attempted to be honest about my thoughts and details about the movements and words of the rapist for those three and half hours. The chapter was used at Harvard University to explain rape violence, and numerous editors of academic presses pursued me to sign a contract with them.

The assistant editor for a series on violence told me that my book would be accepted dependent on the editor's decision, but she added that she felt that would not be a problem. For months, "Jean" gave me the royal treatment. She was so excited about the book that she told other editors at the press and this information got back to me. How many authors named Winkler are writing a book on rape! Then the assistant editor called and told me the book was rejected by the editor. Her voice betrayed her feeling of sadness. At the next conference, I introduced myself to the editor and asked her why she had rejected my book. Her response was:

> "No one will believe you were raped that way. You could not think or act like that. To the reader, the rape will seem like a fabrication. You have to be true to life."
>
> "Do you mean I was raped the wrong way?"
>
> "No, but you have interjected more material in there than really happened. You could not have thought that way."
>
> "I have had over two hundred of my students read this account and they believe it. Are those two hundred people along with a dozen professionals wrong?"
>
> "That's just a fluke. I'm sorry about this. I know how hard it is, but you are too close to your rape. You need more distance. You know, I was raped too."

This editor has never admitted publicly that a rapist attacked her. Instead she has written about others' tortures—objectively. For her, distance was necessary at that historical time to succeed academically, but should she reject a subjective account from someone who is willing to speak?

"Sharon" was no different. She too had suffered a terrible ordeal of rape and had testified against the rapist. She ran a crime center in a major city and had published first-hand accounts of rape. Thinking that I would get understanding and respectable criticism, I sent her a copy of the first chapter on the attack. Sharon answered with this letter:

> There's no pleasant way to say this, but . . . I'll do it quickly: while I realize this is an early draft, I find this very poorly written and conceptualized and full of factual errors ???—Would like to discuss this with you—try. More soon—Sharon

How does one make factual errors on a rape attack? Did I get the rape wrong? While people have many meanings for the reasons why they respond, I was not able to discover from either of these writing professionals their reasons for protecting their self-esteem and negating mine. On the other hand, I was able to discover the multiple meanings behind the kidnappings in Olinala.

Meanings of Kidnappings

In the 1950s and 1960s, the most prominent perception of mountain marriages celebrated the self-esteem of the kidnappers and his male friends. The action and daring, the ability to outwit the young women's parents, the take-charge action, and the chance for real love to blossom were their foci. The community reverberated the positive feelings of the kidnappers by cheering them on. The community supported two people who wanted to commit themselves for life to each other. Within a year, there might be another member to this community and another reason for joy. The parents of the young woman were disillusioned: The hoped-for wedding was now impossible. More tragically, the child with whom they had spent fourteen to maybe twenty years would not be seen daily in their home.

Women's experiences in mountain marriages vary from being an active participant to interested party to unsuspecting victim. Let me begin with an active participant's experience. Maria Jesus, with a huge smile, recounted the months prior to the kidnapping. Her responsibility was to bring water to the house from the corner water pump. There she met Ricardo. As the days, weeks and months passed, Ricardo spent a few minutes each day wooing Maria Jesus. They timed their visits to the water faucet. Since Maria Jesus' parents would not agree with her marriage to Ricardo who had captured her heart, she and Ricardo arranged one Sunday for the kidnapping. At a prearranged time and place, Maria Jesus stood at a safe distance from all her members of her family and at an easy enough location for Ricardo and his friends to kidnap her. The kidnapping occurred, and that Sunday night in the mountains, Ricardo and Maria Jesus had sexual intercourse to insure their union. With time, perceptions have changed, and her parents and her husband now work together. Even today, she remembers the cheers of the people in the community as she was carried off to the mountains screaming, with a secret glee, for "help."

Women as interested parties told of their kidnappings. Some young women could never leave their homes; yet standing in the doorway and watching people in the street was, for a few minutes of relaxation each day, allowed by the parents. Rosalda told me how this young man had caught her eye. He would pass each day at the same time as she was waiting in the doorway. At first, they only exchanged interested glances. Then, they began to exchange a few words of salutation. To talk more than that would arouse the suspicions of her parents. At this point, she learned his name, Guatelupe: "What a beautiful name!" To get around the handicap of silence, Guatelupe would pay Rosalda's brother a few centavos to deliver a secret written message to Rosalda. While people only attended a few grades, most people either have learned enough to write a few words or could find a confidant to read the messages and write further notes. Education helped lovers' interests. Over a period of time, Guatelupe knew Ricarda's dedication to her because he had said the important words in a note: "I want you to have my children." Symbolically, this phrase for Olinaltecans carries the meaning of commitment. For a man to want a woman to have his children is one of the highest acclamations of love: Children are the center of life. The following Sunday, Rosalda and Guatelupe, using a plan similar to that of Maria Jesus and Ricardo, rode off into the mountains that protect young lovers from discovery.

Shortly after moving in with Guatelupe and his family, Rosalda learned the truth: He was a drunk. He had visited her in his sober moments and hid his bottled times from her view. Her husband now, her husband for life, was an alcoholic. Her own family rejected her for her betrayal of them and would not let her return. As they perceived it, she must take responsibility for her actions. Because of his unreliability in working, Rosalda had to suffer raising her children on only the efforts of herself and her sometime husband. She stated that her difficult life was due to her parents' desire to keep her ignorant of people's reputations in the community. Without birth control, she had eleven children and told me how for decades she only slept three or four hours a night in order to complete the work of the house and produce artisan products for sale. She raised her children so that, when they began to get near the marital age, around thirteen or fourteen years old, they knew the traits and dispositions of the young men in the town. Her error, as her family liked to point out, would not be a mistake made by her children. Her kidnapping was one that turned bad.

For all women who did not expect a kidnapping, their life with their family ended one Sunday when they were transferred, without any previous knowledge of the upcoming event, to the mountains and thereafter permanently to their parents'-in-laws house. All women agreed that the method of marriage was, in all aspects, unpleasant and grueling. During a peaceful stroll around the market, while waiting leisurely in their front doorway, or while walking casually for a bucket of water, a group of men grabbed these women, bound their arms and legs, threw them over a horse with their stomach and body battered by the galloping of the horse on rocky and mountainous terrain, taken to an unknown and hidden area in the mountains, forced to sleep outdoors without the comfort of a home or bed, left to eat tortillas and beans that were a day or so old, and imprisoned to listen to this kidnapper who stole her life.

Every single woman rejected the method of mountain marriages, but the life after the kidnapping impacted their interpretation of the act. For those men who were good husbands, who were dedicated, worked hard, and helped raise their children, the women learned to love the kidnapper and regretted only the marriage method not the marriage partner. For those women who discovered that the kidnapper was a rejected man in the community, the method of marriage and their husband for life were both disasters—unavoidable and unendurable. They acknowledged that their life was without pleasure.

Just as kidnappers with the support of the community tried to control and make life decisions for some women against their will, people in our culture likewise take that action. The historical control in Olinala occurs in terms of current control in United States.

Control Movements and Decisions

Back at work, my departmental chair defined for all the faculty the cultural environment for the year when she yelled at me: "Your rape is causing havoc in the department." Her impatience escalated during the winter season when she told a colleague that "Cathy is using her trauma to avoid department responsibilities." At the department meeting to decide the applicants for the new tenured position, the chair made the announcement, before people had made their list of nominees, that "Cathy is not qualified for this position.

Her rape research is not an urban project and that type of research does not fit into our department's interests." For that year, she explicitly controlled the decisions of the faculty members by her announcements against and mistreatment of me.

In a less explicit manner, "Rose," like many other people, wanted to control my movements.

> I listened more attentively to the things you were saying and the way you expressed yourself. I sort of kept score of how much of our conversations were about the rape and how much about other things. At first everything you said was rape related. Then as time passed, other things crept in. I became anxious for you. I equated it with the death of a loved one, an event that traumatizes, *How could you let this be taken away from you?* (emphasis added).

For Rose, recuperation and the investigation were to last a few weeks, and then everything would be back to normal. If it wasn't back to normal, then it was my fault: "How could you let this [normal life] be taken away from you?" While Rose and others were asking this same question, I kept asking myself: How can we let rapists keep attacking, torturing and destroying people and their friends and families? Isn't it inhumane to allow a rapist to destroy people, and when possible, shouldn't we try to stop these attackers who bludgeon people's lives? This culture that negates rape and yet refuses support or rights to victim-survivors confuses me even to this day. As an anthropologist in Olinala, I experienced a phase of confusion but only initially.

Acculturation and Change in Olinala

When I arrived in Olinala in 1980 to live for two years, the times had changed. People still spoke of mountain marriages, but none occurred. Not understanding their meanings behind their words and not having observed a mountain escapade, the threat by the townspeople—that some horseman might kidnap me—kept me alert. While there were few horses in the streets, I avoided all horses. If I saw one, I quickly knocked on a person's house to spend time with them. When I went around corners, I first spied down the street to ensure visibility of all people and nonvisibility of four legged creatures that weighed 2,000 pounds. One point I was sure about: a kidnapper needed a horse for a kidnapping, and no horse meant no kidnapping. While I frequently asked people about their serious but humorous comment to me—*"Un hombre va a robarte, Catalina; vas a ver"* (a man is going to steal you, Cathy; you will see), the truth from those with whom I trusted is first that the possibility of a kidnapping did exist; that was the explanation for their seriousness. Second, they remembered the exciting and successful kidnappings and that explained their joyousness. Third, they enjoyed, and never lost this aspect of their enjoyment, joking with me. Their conclusion was that there was always a possibility that a mountain marriage could happen.

After a year, I again asked my trusted Olinaltecan friends about the possibility of a mountain marriage. Now, they said, it is not possible because you have established your reputation. Acting as a diplomat around the town endeared me to the people, and for that reason, no kidnapper would dare risk his reputation against mine. Therefore, a kidnapper's control is superseded today by community support as a control. In Olinala, I earned control through my actions, but in United States, my actions resulted in contradictory interpretations.

The incidence of mountain marriages was somewhat common in the 1950s and 1960s and several occurred during each drought season from October until April. By the 1970s, the number of mountain marriages was infrequent: one every two to three years. While these were still called mountain marriages, the meaning and result had changed. The code of honor by kidnappers had decreased, and the term *robarte* was now used with an additional word: *robarte con fuerse,* to steal with force or to rape. The women raped did not have to marry the kidnappers, and respect for these women remains high today.

Kidnappers suffer one of two consequences: if the family of the victim-survivor can not kill them, then they seek exile for life. Their crime is a crime for life: no rehabilitation or sanctions are allowed or accepted. My investigation revealed the names of the rapists from the 1970s who were either buried in the ground or in exile. While the family recognized and openly admitted that their male member was a rapist, they also protected him by keeping the location of that exile strictly secret.

How did Olinala smooth out their history of contradictions to expose hidden rape? In a community where the activities of a select few rapists were covered up in the applauded mountain marriages, later enhancements in economics and education have altered the patterns of interaction and exposed the criminals and their crimes.

The impact and availability of education were important as a route to succeeding economically in such jobs as clerks, secretaries, teachers, nurses, or specialized training: all resulted in salaried positions but demanded an education. The tripling of the number of grade schools and the extended number of years that a child spent in primary and secondary (junior high) augmented people's interactions. Education became a route to succeed monetarily in the community or elsewhere. The years in school broke the isolation. Interaction, once a rarity, was now a daily occurrence. Young adults did not need the excuse of bypassing parental house control because they were now able to talk and laugh with everyone.

The redistribution of land impacted access to wealth. In the 1930s, the town had two economic classes: the wealthy landowners and the landless poor peons. The 1940s redistribution of land resulted in every family owning or accessing land to grow crops. With a guaranteed food supply the family could spend the nonagricultural season working as artisans, while an expanding tourism industry assured outlets for products.

A town that promoted a cultural pattern that protected rapists now had repatterned itself. The result is that kidnappers' praise turned into kidnappers' crime—a crime against the family and the community. During the 1982 kidnapping, the people in Olinala stopped and focused on resolution of the crime. Until the woman was safe, the community was partially paralyzed and after the capture of the rapist, the healing occurred in different degrees but for everyone.

Reverberations of Rape: United States

We in the United States too frequently focus only on the victim-survivor without realizing that those around the victim-survivor are also severely impacted by the attack. Many of the emergency phone calls to rape crisis centers are not from the victim-survivors but from friends and family members of the victim-survivors. "Rose" pointed this out:

I wanted to ease your pain, but I really didn't know how to go about it. I talked to several mutual friends who were little help in showing me what to do. Their reactions varied from "Oh, my, how terrible!" to "I told her she should carry a gun."

The woman at the local rape crisis center was a calming influence. I guess I really didn't realize my own turmoil until then. That talk with a disinterested but trained and sympathetic third party helped me to put things into a better perspective. Rape is no longer distant or isolated. It is a reality.

"Gerri" also stressed that the rape of one person extends beyond the victim-survivor:

Untangling and acknowledging these layers of feeling has helped me realize the need to make others aware that there is more than one victim in rape. Our culture represses healthy sexuality and promotes sexual violence and abuse. This creates ambiguity, anxiety, and fear about what to think or how to heal those involved in sexual assault, including those who, like us, are peripheral victims of sexual crimes. We're all victims.

The damage of the rapist is severe because we are a culture that still covers up the crimes of the rapist. We have not learned to discuss rape or treat each other fairly.

Summarizing Changes in Olinala

While the people in the United States are learning to be more open to the crime of rape, the Olinaltecans have already experienced multiple changes impacting the mountain marriages.

They are now rare. In the 1950s, marital rape that began with the mountain escapade and was later protected by marriage has now turned into murder or exile for the kidnapper. The severity of the penalty matches the severity of the crime. In the 1950s there were a number of kidnappings annually, some of which covered up forced sexual intercourse or rape. In the 1970s, the number had decreased to one every two to three years.

Nowadays, the actions of the kidnappers are not glorified. A rapist today can not hide under the guise of marriage. There is no longer any code of honor for kidnappers. While many men admitted to me they stole their wives against their will, the wives revealed that the sexual intercourse then was not physically but situationally forced. Yet today, even the parents of the kidnappers reveal the truth of the crimes of their sons.

Archival records are suggestive. There are instances in which numerous young men in their twenties and thirties died on the same day. The reasons listed for their deaths range from loss of blood to heart attacks. According to verbal accounts, these deaths were a result of gun battles and executions. People remembered the places, days, and times of those murders. Even today, while some of the murderers are still alive, retribution is sought. These murderers cannot leave their homes: their only safe haven.

Ethnocentrism vs. Self-Denial: Respect vs. Second Assault

How is it that Olinaltecans have succeeded in changing their perceptions and we in the United States, despite our feminist movement, punish victim-survivors? We critique other cultures as traditional while applauding ours as modern. The former is a result of our ethnocentrism and the later is a result of our self-denial. For Olinala, the changes between 1950s and 1980s resulted in a solution to rape while for the United States the damage by the rapist parallels the damage by the people around the victim-survivor.

In the United States, besides a physical rape there ensues a second assault on the survivor of rape. "While these second assault comments do not *individually* match the horror and trauma of the rape, the *accumulative* effect of prejudicial and antagonistic statements toward the survivor does have a compound effect that is *more cruel* than the rape attack itself" (William and Holmes 1981: 2). Its cruelty is in part the fact that lack of understanding and in part that we survivors, depending on these people for support and comfort, experience instead a panorama of ignorant and intrusive treatment.

The second assault is a *cultural process* of rape that is enacted by the accumulation of negative responses by friends and family who individually duplicate the processual traits of the rapist. The second assault entails isolation and silence; cultural denigration; undermined self-esteem; confusions of control, contradictions, and support. Our insensitivity results in our initial feelings of sympathy for the victim-survivor turning into anger against her/him. We have to blame someone without realizing that either we are blaming the wrong person or the situation is to blame, not a person. Who are these people who wrote these statements for this chapter? They're my friends, good friends whom I appreciate for their good intentions and honesty.

One of the most deadening aspects of U.S. life is the assumption that we are better off than we were in the past and better off than other people in the world. This assumption blinds us to the enormous problems we face. This chapter demonstrates that the act of the rapist reverberates throughout our society and that this further traumatizes the survivor. Perhaps, we can learn from Olinaltecans who believe the word of a woman violated and who will never forget nor allow a rapist in their community. Justice for women does exist in some places in this world.

References

Brownmiller, Susan. (1975). *Against Our Will*. New York: Simon and Schuster.

Lewis, Richi. (1988). DNA fingerprints: Witness for the prosecution. *Discover* (June): 42–51.

Sanday, Peggy Reeves. (1996). *A Woman Scored: Acquaintance Rape on Trial*. New York: Doubleday.

Williams, Joyce E., and Karen A. Holmes. (1981). *The Second Assault: Rape and Public Attitudes*. Westport: Greenwood.

Winkler, Cathy. (1987). Changing Power and Authority in Gender Roles. Ph.D. Dissertation in Anthropology, Indiana University. Ann Arbor: University Microfilms.

———. (1991). Rape as social murder. *Anthropology Today* 1.3: 12–4.

———. (1994a) The meaning behind rape trauma. *Many Mirrors; Body Image and Social Relations*, edited by Nicole Sault. New Brunswick: Rutgers University Press.

———. (1994b). Rape trauma: Contexts of meaning. *The Body as Existential Ground*, edited by Thomas J. Csordas. Cambridge: Cambridge University Press.

———. (2002). *One Night: Realities of Rape*. Walnut, California: AltaMira Press.

Chapter VI

"Here the Cock Does Not Crow, for He Is Not the Lord of the Land": Machismo, Insecurity, and Male Violence in Brazil

Sarah Hautzinger

On men's gender and kinship roles in poor, predominantly Afro-Brazilian families in the city of Salvador, Northeast Brazil, anthropologist Klaas Woortmann observed what he called a "subjective marginality." This perceived sense of being peripheral to their families and wider society, together with concrete poverty, "strongly inhibits men from fulfilling roles of masculinity as defined in the dominant culture," Woortmann argued. "Here the cock does not crow, for he is not the lord of the land" (1987: 21).

My study, also based in Salvador, concerned masculinity and domestic violence. Such masculinities, somehow seen as "falling short" of normative expectations, have implications for the practice of domestic male violence against women. Are men who are unable, or disinclined, to fulfill the role of primary breadwinner and authoritative head of household as prescribed in the dominant culture more likely to resort to violence as a compensating "resource" for power and control?

In broaching the connections between economic hardship, poverty, and violence, I do not wish to suggest that the insecurities and instabilities generated are exclusive to the poor. A ubiquitous insecurity exists for Brazilians of all classes and ethnic backgrounds, deriving directly from Brazil's ongoing economic crisis. Many if not most Brazilians feel that their worlds are perpetually spinning out of control. In some sense, the situation of the Brazilian middle class could be understood as even more unstable, or subject to dramatic and unforeseeable change, than that of the Brazilian poor, because the middle class has more to lose. Nonetheless, the crisis of the poor is certainly more existential, immediate, and desperate.

Without negating the usefulness of Woortmann's "rooster" metaphor, my research suggests an alternative reading: that precisely when the "rooster" feels his masculine identity threatened or called into question, does he begin to "crow," strut and puff, and that part of this display may involve physical aggression against a female partner.

Within Brazil, the Northeastern *macho* is particularly renowned. As a result, it is often assumed that the Northeastern woman must in turn be singularly submissive. Instead, and in keeping with a contradictory aspect of Salvador's image, my research portrays indomitable women whose mettle matches that of the most consummate macho. These contrasting images of men and women suggest that Salvador's singularly high (registered) indices of domestic violence may have as much to do with confrontation and contestation of male authority within conjugal relationships as with simple male dominance.

This research was inspired by my learning that Brazil, in response to pressure from its feminists, had created the world's first all-female police stations. The specialized stations are staffed by policewomen and respond exclusively to women with complaints about aggression by men. After a year of fieldwork in Salvador's women's police station and elsewhere, I moved into a *favela*, or slum, with interest in gaining a more intimate perspective on men's subjective experience of conjugal discord, and to understand when and how violence was seen as a tolerable, inevitable, appropriate, or reprehensible result. The final phase of fieldwork, in which focus groups were convened with community men and women who had participated in earlier phases of the research, zeroed in on the question of how institutional criminalization and delegitimation of male violence are affecting the cultural tolerance for such aggression on the ground, with particular attention to male peer groups.

My intention in engaging men in conversations about male violence came as an effort to redress the striking absence of subjective male voices in the discourse on domestic violence, in Brazil and elsewhere. When a study includes a section on men and masculinity, it is inevitably informed by women's voices, and rarely moves beyond a reductive "profile" of the typified, authoritarian, and macho "batterer" on the one hand, complemented by a beleaguered, esteem-drained female "victim" on the other. Unfortunately, this reductive tendency hampers ethnographic endeavors about domestic violence from doing justice to the variability, complexity, and ambiguity of violent relationships. Specifically, the elements of contestation and confrontation seen in clashes where the male-female balance of power is more symmetrical, and where the violence is often mutual, are generally ignored.

The case of Brazil—a country historically infamous for social codes virtually mandating men to "wash their honor with blood" (by killing wife, her partner, or both) when subject to female adultery—calls into question treatments of violence that assume it to be somehow opposed or destructive to cultural meanings. However reprehensible, if in Brazil violence is something that can wash honor, then it is constitutive of meaning and value. Even as the so-called "legitimate defense of honor"—and yes, it is always male honor—is becoming a less and less viable tactic for absolving wife-murdering Brazilian men, and even as male impunity is slowly diminished through increasing criminalization, it is undeniable that male violence still holds positive connotations and values in the popular culture. Not only *can* a man use violence to "prove" that he is, in fact, a man, or to preserve his masculinity; he is often *required* to call upon violence, particularly when his other options are few for succeeding in the high-maintenance, labor-intensive work of continuing to "be a man."

Male Honor as Metaphor for Male Power

While it is clear that the majority of severely violent domestic eruptions don't directly involve issues of betrayal or adultery *per se,* the fact that nearly all of the focus-group discussions revolved around these themes is significant. Female adultery supplies a critical key scenario, revealing the place where violence is most probable and most readily defensible. In such circumstances, men find it most *necessary* to avoid their descending to the category of *corno* (cuckold). To be a *corno* was constantly contrasted with being a man: to be a *corno* is to be a non-man, to have one's masculinity neutralized. What male honor and female adultery tell us about being or failing to be a man helps to reveal the models of power operative in more mundane, everyday expressions of domestic conflict and aggression.

As domestic assault itself becomes criminalized, alternative modes of washing or maintaining male honor are beginning to emerge. Like the man who threw acid into the eyes of the rival he found in bed with his wife, some men still employ explicit violence, but fall short of drawing blood and actual homicide. Another man perceived a visitor under his bed when he arrived home and called neighbors to the door to "see a lovely painting in his house." Then, with witnesses at the door and revolver close at hand, he ordered the intruder to leave and to take the wife with him as his punishment. He was praised by the men in the focus group where the story was recounted as having "more than" preserved his honor: He showed himself to still be in control and calling the shots, while brandishing a threat of violence that was believable enough that he did not need to use it.

In relating these examples, men expanded on the mandate to be in control. Men whose wives' leashes were too long, whose wives could be found constantly chatting in other people's doorways, or whose wives traveled alone without husbandly vigilance, were described as *acomodados* or *conformados*. One man made the either/or options quite clear: "You have the *conformados*, and then you have the *perigosos* (dangerous ones)." By conforming and accommodating to circumstances rather than dictating and directing them, by failing to pose a threat of being dangerous, such men suffered painful jokes and derision from their male peers. They were constantly referred to as "giving a big empty space (*vazão*)," or opportunity for being cuckolded. Being a *corno* also plays into underlying homophobia: The man whose honor is destroyed when his wife is unfaithful is figuratively "getting screwed" by the other man, losing irreparably in the hierarchy game. This transmutation, of course, rides on the premise of the woman being understood as a mere extension of her husband's agency, sphere of influence, or jurisdiction.

One case frequently mentioned in several different focus groups illustrates this point. In this instance, neighbors were certain that a woman had committed adultery with another man; of interest to onlookers was the fact that the husband failed to produce an adequate reaction—violent or otherwise—toward preserving his honor. The case was discussed in a group of older men, including three men in their late forties or fifties, all of whom had self-disclosed histories of violence of various levels (from "destroying the house" to a case my assistants and I knew involved chronic battery). This group, which laughingly dubbed itself "the gang of machos" [*a turma dos machistas*], produced an account representative of prevailing values around violence and masculinity. Jorginho, a man known to be a wife-batterer and the only one who lived in the immediate area where the case occurred, began by telling about how the volatile information reached his ears.

> Jorginho—... one day when my wife was there, a conversation arose about a guy who lives here that was being wronged [*prejudicado*], let's just say, *corno*. ... I went to [the person who was gossiping] and I said, oi, I hope this conversation doesn't happen again here in this place, and especially when my woman is here. ... Talk about it elsewhere, but not here. ... The

situation got more and more heated, when on a certain day, he was coming home, arriving in the door, and he saw the *banana* [mess] there. He saw it, no one told him, because he was the type that for him, everyone else was a *galhudo*. "You're a *galhudo*! You're a *galhudo*!"

Sarah—What's a *galhudo*?

Carlos (research assistant)—Horns [*chifres*].

Sarah—Ah.

Jorginho—[Tells in detail about the man arriving and seeing] ... Because how is it that you are a married guy, you have responsibility with your family, how are you gonna find another guy in your bed ... on top of your woman?

Hélio—Ave Maria!

Jorginho—So, the people here were adding fuel to the fire... [but] God cooled it down, threw water and cooled it down. About fifteen days later, my youngest son calls me: "Jorginho, come quick, Fulano [so-and so] is going to kill Fulana [the wife] and the *otro* [the "other"; the lover]—he's got a gun in his hand!" So I went ... I told him to put the gun away. But in this interval he'd thrown the other guy out [of the neighborhood], the guy almost broke his neck...He tore this [indicates the skin at his neck] all apart.... [Goes on to explain how he wouldn't let the guy inside his house (anymore?), how "friends" shouldn't be allowed inside one's house in general].

Although it seems that Jorginho is saying the man showed himself capable of a "re-action," later he returned to the incident and made clear that whatever action the man had taken was inadequately resolute.

Jorginho—... He didn't have any consideration for himself as an individual. ... So, right away, the person should isolate [himself] ... Because, in a case like this with me—I am a MAN!! With me, I'm not going to do anything to her, but I'm simply going to leave the locale. Not stay there, living, because it's ugly for me if all the guys are looking at me and laughing in my face. He arrives here below and everyone's psst-psst [gossiping]. ...

Hélio—The people here are horrible.

Carlos—And he's still living here?

Sarah—What if he had avenged himself ... ?

Hélio—He had to be a man. He lacked the machismo [here: ability to be a man].

Jorginho—He was not a man! Sarah, it's just like he said, he wasn't a man!

Flávio (research assistant)—What do you think he should have done?

Jorginho—Anything! Anything at all. So that his name...

Sarah—For example ...

Jorginho—Anything! So he wouldn't have doubted his own name! Even a shout, he needed to give, but he didn't do anything: he was paralyzed.

Not all the men in this group agreed that the cuckolded man should have left the neighborhood, just as not everyone thought that he necessarily had to react with violence to preserve his honor. But there was a consensus over his need to do something—anything—to preserve his name, his honor. This consensus was frustrated by the lack of an appropriate option, particularly in the face of violence becoming an increasingly delegitimated response.

Another group comprised of some of the youngest male participants, many of whom have been raised in female-headed households, discussed this same case. Most maintained that they would not need to "react," or actively avenge their honor with violence. The unfaithful woman had already shown her morals to be beneath those of her man in the eyes of all, so he had already won: "My honor stays right where it was."

Chico, the group's most outspoken member, begins by hypothetically placing himself in the betrayed man's place.

Chico—... from the moment I put her in my house, she changes. Her change is going to hurt [*prejudicar*] her, not me, because you know for the man, *não pega nada* [nothing sticks; no harm done]. ... If she takes someone else: I accept it. You know why I accept it? Because this already happened with me, you understand? I'm going to pass by and the guys will say, "Ah, Fulano [so-and-so] is a *corno*." I'm going to say, "Not me," I'm still going to have high morale, you know why? Because *she's* doing something that everyone will always criticize, and I'm not. When [the guys say], "Ah, but your woman made you a *corno*," I'll say, "She did not make me a *corno*, no: Do you think her actions were correct?" The question's going to stay in the air like that. Which is to say, I'm going to continue with my head held high.

If this happened with me ... I'd break up with her. My personality isn't like just any man's: While they're over there thinking about making fun of me, I'm going to go about living my life. ... Because of the *gozações* [jests, mockeries], do you think I'm going to grab her, beat her; am I going to kill her? No: I want God to help her and not to abandon me ... let her live her life and let the guys talk, make *gozações*. If they think that to show them that I'm the *maioral* [the boss, the greatest], that I'm the *machão* [big macho], ... no way!

Pablo—First, you're going to lose your freedom, so what's that going to resolve? You took away her life and also lose your freedom, and you can lose your life as well.

Chico—Of course! Why should I do anything to her...

Pablo—If you think of doing it to someone else, it can also happen to you.

Itamar—It could even hurt you... .

Chico—Understand, Itamar, ... if it got to the point where I killed her and her family afterward, what's going to happen? Maybe not with me, ... but if he doesn't avenge himself with me, he'll get my brother, an aunt of mine, even my own mother, and then what? ... I could stop, and analyze, and avoid all that, understand?... [They can call me *corno*] ... and of course I'm going to be hurt by that, inside, but I'm not going to show this to him, because he's there talking, "Ah, man, aren't you going to do anything? What about your honor?" No. My honor stays where it was!

This important difference, where a man views his female partner's agency and subjectivity as disjoined from his own, seems to result at least in part from the effects of recent criminalization, as the risk of "losing my liberty" was always cited. At the same time, as members of the poorer socioeconomic classes, these men would perhaps never have been party to the same level of impunity before the law that their middle- and upper-class counterparts enjoyed. It is not surprising, then, that a second deterring factor, that of local, vigilante revenge played out between families, is painted in such a vivid picture.

That this assertion of "autonomous male honor" is a relatively new and precarious form of resistance to inculcated norms and scripts is evident in the very insistence with which these scripts still insinuate themselves into Chico's thinking, forcing him to engage in a dialogue with them. He claims his honor is immune to the aspersions of his circle of male friends and neighbors, and yet he has rather exhaustively articulated in his own mind how he will respond to them, and indeed, he identifies the moment in which "the guys" are questioning his honor as precisely the juncture in which he would typically be compelled to use physical violence.

This research focuses on a case study involving an extended family that aptly demonstrates this generational shift. In fact, both Jorginho and Chico—the two focus-group participants whose views are contrasted above—are family members. My familiarity with the family spans four living generations of an extended family, in which four distinct conjugal forms exist: matrifocal (single mothers, peripheral fathers), authoritarian couple (with domestic violence), nuclear couple (more egalitarian), and parallel (married men with more than one stable relationship). The family has lived in the neighborhood—once considered remote jungle but now fairly central as the city of Salvador has expanded—for six generations. A *terreiro* (temple) of Candomblé (Brazil's most prominent Afro-Brazilian religion) has been part of the settlement since anyone can remember.

The backbone of this family is formed by the women: the widowed *mãe-de-santo* (mother-of-saint, or Candomblé priestess) matriarch; her only daughter who runs the household; her granddaughter; and great-granddaughter. Each of the conjugal forms given above are present in the extended family, affording an opportunity to compare corresponding styles of masculinity. As represented here by Chico, the sons of autonomous mothers (of matrifocal or nuclear couples) seemed far more disposed to view female partners as discrete agents than were sons raised by authoritarian fathers and subordinated mothers. Relatedly, younger sons of matrifocal and nuclear families were the most likely to subscribe to alternative models of male honor whose preservation did not mandate the use of violence.

Masculinity, Machismo, and Zero-Sum Power

What hasn't changed, even in emergent alternative models, is the one-up-one-down, zero-sum model of power. Indeed, informants explained the occurrence of domestic violence by saying that either the woman or the man "always needs to be on top," "doesn't want to be the one on the bottom," or "always wants to be in the right." Explicit in these accounts is that if one is right, the other is wrong; if one is on top, the other is on the bottom. These determinations are measured by concrete outcomes (rather than discrepant interpretations or perspectives), deriving directly from differential power, and frequently, brute force.

Weighing in the double standard for female versus male fidelity, where male infidelity is seen as inevitable and expected and female infidelity is calamitous, it is clear that the balancing act enabling men to uphold their masculinity requires that the woman's position be perpetually insecure, off-balance and at risk. The difference, perhaps, lies in the fact that women's power is forcibly relativized by the inevitability of her partner's extra-conjugal sexual activities: Her task of negotiating power cannot be as absolute as "washing honor with blood," and tends to fall more into "weapons of the weak" resistance strategies (Scott 1985).

Woortmann relates his assessment of symbolically castrated "roosters," cited earlier, to the legacy of slavery and racism and resultant "social disorganization," particularly as manifested in the prevailing matrifocal kinship patterns of the poorer socioeconomic classes where families are often dominated by mothers, grandmothers, aunts, sisters. In the under-employed socioeconomic stratum I studied, women may receive lesser remuneration for each labor-hour, but nonetheless often have more *consistent* earning power as domestic servants, washerwomen, and small-scale, informal market merchants. Consequently, women often serve as primary sustainers of their families, which and implicitly underline their male partners' inadequacy as providers.

The forms masculinity takes under such circumstances must further be considered in light of *machismo* as an overriding gender ideology. Lancaster's vision of machismo in Nicaragua is as an ideology, a "political economy of the body," and a system of exchange

> ... between men in which women figure as intermediaries. To maintain one's masculinity, one must successfully come out on top of these exchanges. To lose in this ongoing exchange system entails a loss of face and thus a loss of masculinity. The threat is a total loss of status, whereby one descends to the zero point of the game and either literally or effectively becomes a *cochón* [queer] (1992: 237).

Here Nicaraguan masculinity, under the specific ideological shaping of *machismo*, becomes inherently perishable, high maintenance, and subject to challenge, attack, and siege. This model is applicable for Bahian men of all classes, but raises the question of how the difficult task of upholding masculinity is further aggravated by marginalizing economic, racist, and kinship organization factors.

My argument here differs from stigmatizing "culture of poverty" or "culture of violence" theories. Rather, it focuses on how individual men negotiate gendered identities, power and authority in the face of limited resources, both material and behavioral. The man disallowed from exercising control based on earning power, social prestige or status, or patriarchal authority in the family may rely more heavily on alternate power "resources," of which violence is but one example.

Other ways of thinking might employ Peter Wilson's (1973) "respectability" and "reputation" as contrasting value complexes in the Anglo-Caribbean, or Roberto da Matta's (1991) contrasting *casa* (house) and *rua* (street) spheres for Brazil. These authors relate respectability and *casa*, respectively, to values associated with whiteness, affluence, and women on the one hand, and reputation and *rua* with the lower classes, blackness, and men on the other. Reputation and *rua* valorize play over work, adventuresome virility as opposed to the overly domesticated "auntie man," and roguery and rebellion over conformity and accommodation. (See also Besson (1993) for a critique of Wilson's tendency to ignore Caribbean women's radicalism, and Mintz (1971, 1981) for how Afro-Caribbean gender relations may afford women greater economic autonomy without threatening male partners than in non-Afro-Caribbean counterparts.)

The intention here is emphatically not to suggest that violence actually occurs more frequently, or with greater severity, in poorer classes or in minority ethnic groups: there is no evidence for that. Rather, I want to consider the possibility that men whose disadvantaged social locations cast greater doubts upon their masculinity might rely more on violence as a positive resource in constructing male identity (positive in the Foucauldian sense of creating meaning/value). Clearly, class or ethnic distinctions are not overdetermining in this respect, yet it is reasonable to consider the influences they have for creating stress and insecurity and for how the tenacity of violence as a strategy might result.

This concern is defensible insofar as feminist and other activism against male violence may at times be working at cross-purposes. On the one hand, the feminist movement encourages questioning and rebelling against male domination and authoritarianism. The fruits of this questioning should come as no surprise: questioning it produces conflict and contestation.

The feminist movement is committed to the eradication of male violence against women, but yanking the crutch of violence out from under men without trying to understand what infirmities the crutch was supporting creates the risk of generating more insecurity, more conflict, and potentially, more violence. Moving beyond palliative measures in combating male violence entails distinguishing between conflict and violence: recognizing conflict's dynamic, transformative potential on the one hand, and seeking ways of dissolving an overdetermined, causal relationship between conflict and violence on the other. The more we understand about what enables men to be secure as men, and the more we know about how instabilities create the "need" for men to call upon violence to continue being men, the closer we come to helping men break violent habits.

References

Besson, Jean. (1993). Reputation and respectability reconsidered: A new perspective on Afro-Caribbean peasant women. In *Women and Change in the Caribbean*, edited by J. Momsen. London: J. Curry.

Lancaster, Roger N. (1992). *Life is Hard: Machismo, Danger and the Intimacy of Power in Nicaragua*. Berkeley: University of California Press.

Matta, Roberto da. (1991). *Carnivals, Rogues, and Heroes: An Interpretation of the Brazilian Dilemma*. South Bend, Indiana: University of Notre Dame Press.

Mintz, Sidney W. (1971). Men, women, and trade. *Comparative Studies in Society and History* 13: 247–269.

———. (1981). Economic role and cultural tradition. In *Black Women Cross-Culturally*, edited by Filomina C. Steady. Cambridge: Schenkman.

Scott, James C. (1985). *Weapons of the Weak: Everyday Forms of Peasant Resistance*. New Haven: Yale University Press.

Wilson, Peter. (1973). *Crab Antics: The Social Anthropology of English-Speaking Negro Societies in the Caribbean*. New Haven: Yale University Press.

Woortmann, Klaas. (1987). *A Família das Mulheres*. Rio de Janeiro: Tempo Brasileiro.

Chapter VII

Transformations in Domestic Violence and Conflict Resolution within a Midwestern U.S. Nuer Refugee Community

Jon D. Holtzman

Migration and Family Discord

The relationship between social change and transformations in family violence has become increasingly problematized in recent years. While conventional wisdom has held that Westernization and other types of social change lead to increased family violence, due to a variety of factors related to the disruption of the social fabric (Gelles and Cornell 1983), recent studies have suggested a more complex picture. Morley (1994), for instance, has found that the relationship between "modernization and wife-beating" is complex—while tensions arising from the political context of kinship relations may diminish, other factors such as alcohol consumption frequently exacerbate pre-existing problems. Although social change has been found to increase family violence in some contexts (Savishinsky 1976), in others the opposite effect is the case (Erlich 1966). In his broad cross-cultural survey Levinson (1989) finds that there is not a unidirectional relationship between social change and increases in family violence, calling instead for specifying the types of relationships that may serve to mitigate or vitiate family violence within the particular context of social change.

In this paper I will analyze transformations in domestic violence and conflict resolution through a focus on the changing nature of gender, kinship, and marriage among Nuer refugees from Africa's Sudan who have recently settled around a community I will refer to as Wacohtia—an outer-ring suburb of a large U.S. Midwestern city. Drawing on research undertaken in Wacohtia since December 1995, I compare processes of domestic violence and conflict resolution among Nuer couples living in the United States with the nature of these processes in Sudan, drawn from both informants' accounts and published ethnography (Evans-Pritchard 1940, 1951; Hutchinson 1996).

Since mid-1994 when Nuer refugees began arriving in Wacohtia in significant numbers, domestic violence has emerged as an important issue, both within the refugee community and for the agencies involved in the resettlement process. Within the context of war, flight, and resettlement, a variety of new tensions have entered the Nuer conjugal relationship, already significantly transformed through displacement. Expectations of male employment, changes in male sociability and drinking, transformations in spatial dimensions of gender relations, gendered differences in second-language competence and in the ability to negotiate a new cultural environment, and the need for new forms of cooperation between spouses have all conspired to create a variety of marital tensions not present in Sudan. These new tensions are arising within the context of Nuer marriages which are now extricated from the wider kinship network in which they are traditionally embedded—this network constituting the normal context for conflict resolution afforded to Nuer couples. Factors largely internal to Nuer social relations will be discussed in relationship to cultural, ideological, and legal dimensions related to life in the United States in framing domestic violence and conflict resolution within the Nuer refugee community.

Background to This Study

Beginning in mid-1994, Nuer refugees—mainly from the Eastern Jikany tribe of Nuer—began resettling in Wacohtia in significant numbers. The refugees are from the bloody and protracted civil war in southern Sudan. Most of them had spent five to ten years in refugee camps in Ethiopia and Kenya prior to resettlement in the United States. Despite this prolonged period of displacement, virtually all are substantially enculturated in rural Nuer life, and speak Nuer as their primary or only language. They are divided fairly equally between primary refugees, who were resettled directly in Wacohtia, and secondary migrants, who joined the community from other Midwestern communities, and such areas as upstate New York and San Diego. The population is quite young—with few individuals beyond their early thirties—and lives mainly in nuclear families, with some single individuals. Extended kinship networks are not present. While the size of the population has fluctuated significantly, and is difficult to track because of substantial migration in and out of the state, it has generally been on the order of approximately 300 individuals.

By early 1996, domestic violence had emerged as a visible problem in the community. A number of incidents occurred in which police were involved, including at least one in which a woman was seriously injured. Additionally, several women fled their husbands to women's shelters. While some amount of "wife-beating" is socially sanctioned within Nuer culture, in the United States it clearly was not. Social service agencies involved with the Nuer made great efforts both to make Nuer men understand that wife-beating was not acceptable, as well as to inform women of what they should do if hit or threatened.

Nuer Marriage in the Sudanese Context

Within the Sudanese context, Nuer marriage is embedded within the wider kinship network. Bride-wealth cattle—normally in the range of twenty to twenty-five head—are collected from an array of the groom's kin, and are commensurately distributed within the bride's kinship network. Consequently, not only is the kinship network substantially involved in the marriage itself, but it is invested in the continued well-being of the marriage—in the event of divorce some or all of the bride-wealth cattle needs to be returned. Hutchinson (1996) details Nuer gender relations in Sudan, including discussion of historical changes in the marital relationship, particularly the role of the courts and the ways in which the age of women affects their status vis-à-vis their husbands.

Quarrels that occur between married couples in Sudan frequently revolve around men's perceptions of the failure of women to cook or perform other household duties. Nuer men and women in Wacohtia agree that in Sudan women must do what their husbands tell them to do, and that failure to obey may result in violence inflicted upon the wife. Female adultery—real or imagined—may also be a source of tension.

In instances of domestic violence—particularly if it is severe or if a woman's actions do not render it justifiable in Nuer culture—it is common in Sudan for a woman to flee the home. In doing so she will normally seek refuge with her family, and relatives from both sides will seek to mediate the dispute. Beyond the well-being of the couple, they may have considerable incentive to resolve problems, since divorce would result in the return of bride-wealth cattle. As such, they may try to calm the parties as well as exert pressure on them to stay together.

New Sources of Tension

A variety of factors have led to new sources of stress in Nuer marriages in the United States. This is, of course, to be expected, given the radical changes in daily life brought about in the transition from agro-pastoralist, to displaced person, to resettled refugee in the United States. Concomitant with these lifestyle changes, men's and women's roles and responsibilities to one another are similarly transformed.

One dimension of this is that men and women are in a variety of ways pushed closer together, both literally and figuratively. Among Nuer in Sudan, men and women are spatially divided, with women staying in their homes and men staying together with one another in the men's space, *thokat*. Similarly there is a well-defined gendered division of labor, with women assuming roles such as milking and cooking, and men in herding and the bulk of cultivation. In the United States, husbands and wives live together, usually in small one- or two-bedroom apartments, sleeping in the same room and frequently the same beds.

Accompanying this is significantly more mutual dependency between men and women in daily life. While there is a weak tendency toward men working and women staying home (particularly because of greater English competence among the men), there is significant intermingling of these roles. It may be difficult for women to single-handedly manage the home-care roles for which they would be responsible in Sudan. In addition to aspects of life in the United States that render women's traditional roles more complex, they may have additional activities such as part-time work and/or English as a Second Language (ESL) classes. The absence of older people places the full burden of child care upon the couples themselves.

Consequently, substantial coordination and cooperation between husband and wife may be required for the care of the home and the children. This may push men to assume roles from which they are culturally prohibited, particularly cooking, and may also force changes in male sociability. While going to a friend's house for a day or two in order to drink and socialize may be quite normal in Sudan, in the United States it may place undo strain upon the wife, particularly when an unforeseen event (e.g., a sick child) arises which the wife cannot effectively handle if she lacks linguistic competence.

Among the primary sources of friction is insufficient money, as Nuer couples rely on public assistance and/or low-paying jobs. Disagreements frequently arise concerning how money should be spent, and women may suspect that men are hiding some portion of it in order to use it for things such as alcohol, or in order to remit it to their own relatives in Africa. This tendency toward suspicion over money may be a particular problem when money is placed in bank accounts. Because of low rates of literacy, women cannot verify the amount of money placed in bank accounts, and may have a difficulty accessing it (if only because of an inability to write checks).

Issues of money further play themselves out in ways directly related to transformations in the conjugal bond associated with displacement and resettlement in the United

States. Frequently the marriages of Nuer couples did not occur in ways that render them fully legitimate within Nuer culture. While Nuer marriage traditionally entails the transfer of approximately twenty to twenty-five cows from the family of the groom to the family of the bride, this was generally not possible for couples marrying in refugee camps, in transit, or in the United States. While they generally maintain that these cows will be paid by relatives (if they have not been already), this normally takes the form of the remittance of funds to purchase cows, or as payment in lieu of cows. Without such payments, the very legitimacy of the union, and hence the status of the women, is subject to scrutiny. While Nuer remaining in Africa understand the problems which have caused difficulties in performing the marriage in the prescribed manner, it is considered important to compensate for this in other ways—particularly through cash remittances. Failure to do so may indicate that a couple is, perhaps, not truly married, and that the wife might be regarded as being of dubious character, having simply run off with a man rather than being married properly.

A final new source of significant stress in Nuer marriages is quite simply new forms of gender relations that are brought about by life in the United States. While in Sudan men may wield considerable control over their wives, women find that in the United States they may enjoy much more freedom to do as they please. These messages are to some extent promoted through social service agencies, as well as simply being apparent to Nuer women who see the behavior of American women in the wider culture. While in principle many Nuer men may accept that women could be allowed more freedom—as they understand American women to have—many maintain that their women are "too primitive" and do not have the abilities, the social skills, and the judgment to exercise that freedom in a proper way. Consequently, while women may be more prepared to question the judgment of their husbands, their husbands are not always correspondingly prepared to accept it.

These factors, then, conspire to produce considerable tension in the marriages of many Nuer living in Wacohtia. I will now turn to transformations in processes of domestic violence and conflict resolution itself, examining the ways in which changed kinship structure and political-legal context have changed the way in which these processes take place.

The Changing Context of Conflict Resolution

"When a man and woman argue, the first thing she says is that she is going," states a Nuer husband in his late twenties. But where does she go? While the structure and rhetoric of argumentation may remain similar between the Sudan and the United States, the implications of "leaving" are very different. As previously noted, few individuals in Wacohtia have a local kinship network beyond the domestic group, and women in particular lack kin. The few individuals who have kin present are males, either brothers or groups of male cousins. As such, if a women wishes to leave the home in a dispute, there is no culturally legitimate place in which she may seek refuge from her husband in the absence of relatives who should normally fill that role.

The absence of a wider kinship network means not only that women may have difficulties in obtaining refuge from a difficult home situation, but also that the traditional mechanisms of conflict resolution are not available. While Hutchinson (1996: 229) notes the effects of British-initiated policies in decreasing the influence of the kinship network on Nuer marriage (in the words of one Nuer "the fate of marriage was increasingly put into the hands of two people who couldn't agree about anything"), the parents, siblings, uncles, and aunts continue to have considerable influence over a relationship in which they have a tangible stake. In contrast, in Wacohtia the "two people who couldn't agree on anything" are placed in the position of resolving disputes themselves without the aid of kin in calming individuals and mediating their disputes, without the pressure that kin may exert in order to preserve the marriage for the sake of the wider interests involved.

In short, then, while facing new and unfamiliar sources of tension in the marital relationship, Nuer couples have ostensibly been extricated from those mechanisms that traditionally constitute the medium for conflict resolution, the wider kinship network. An important result of this is a readiness of Nuer women to seek resolution of disputes outside of the Nuer community, through the involvement of police and women's shelters.

Hutchinson (1996: 228–229) notes what appears to be a somewhat similar phenomenon among Western Nuer where "I could not help but be struck by the steady stream of battered and abused women who sought sanctuary there (the chief's home) until their husbands could be summoned and their domestic difficulties aired in court. In that region many women seemed to regard the courts as a sort of marriage counseling service in which they would expect to receive a just hearing." This was, however, wholly absent among the Eastern Nuer, who are present in Wacohtia and among whom Hutchinson also worked. Social service agencies have actively promoted among women the idea that if they are hit or feel threatened, they should call the police and/or seek safety at a women's shelter.

While the rhetoric of "I am going" may remain constant, the meaning changes in each setting. In Sudan the wife would go to relatives, who would seek to resolve the issue within a kinship network, the members of which have to a high degree shared values and goals. In the United States, in contrast, she might go to a women's shelter—an institution associated with the state with its foremost goals the protection of women, rather than the preservation of marriage. Within this context, "dialing 911" has taken on a life of its own within the Nuer community, with the readiness of women to seek the police becoming an additional source of gender-based tension. While Nuer men generally acknowledge that there are times when it is appropriate for women to seek police intervention, they maintain that calls are made when it is not appropriate, when women further their cause within disputes. They feel that the threat of dialing 911 has become part of the rhetoric of conflict, ostensibly a weapon to be used against men regardless of the threat of physical violence. A Nuer husband in his early thirties suggests, for instance, "If you just look at a woman like you are serious she dials 911."

Settling Disputes under Resettlement

Ascertaining exact and concrete facts about the nature of domestic violence—among Nuer refugees and the wider American community—is frequently difficult. Whether the frequency and severity of domestic violence actually differs between Nuer in the United States and Nuer in Sudan is impossible to determine given the frequent reluctance of individuals to speak openly. While refugees maintain that the problems are largely driven by the stresses of life in the United States, domestic violence is certainly prominent in contemporary Nuer life in Sudan (Hutchinson 1996). Conversely it is unclear to what extent women have used "dialing 911," or the ability to flee to women's shelters, as threats against men in instances in which circumstances have not warranted it, particularly given the different perceptions of men and women.

What does invite a greater degree of precision are the ways in which the nature of domestic violence and conflict resolution have been reshaped through the processes of social transformation concomitant with the refugee experience. First, regardless of whether domestic conflict and associated violence exceeds that found in Sudan, the conflict that arises is derived from very different sources, as gender roles and relationships are recast in the context of the resettlement process. Second, the extrication of the conjugal relationship from the wider kinship network has reshaped the meaning of marriage and its significance in the wider community. This has most significantly affected processes of domestic violence and conflict resolution by removing the medium through which issues are most readily resolved.

Finally, the role of the state in reshaping the nature of domestic violence and conflict resolution should be emphasized. This is the case both in rather straightforward ways, through both education and active involvement in domestic conflict, as well as in more subtle ways involving the interplay of Nuer and American social institutions. I have shown, for instance, that while similar modes of argumentation continue to be used within the context of domestic conflict, the meanings become very different when these invoke the state, rather than the kinship network.

The processes described in this paper are ongoing, and the means to address the issue of domestic violence is a point of continued interest within both the Nuer refugee community and agencies involved with resettlement. Men have, for instance, become more sensitive to the legal context of domestic violence in the United States, while both men and women have become more active in discouraging women from going to women's shelters, or staying there if they have gone, and rather encourage them to resolve the problem within the home. Given the early stage of resettlement which the Nuer are still in, it should be expected, further, that gender relations will continue to be transformed, as other normative patterns emerge and as women gain greater linguistic competence in English, allowing them a wider range of interactions with the local community. As such, it will be intriguing to see how these factors affect the continued development of new means of conflict resolution in the American context.

References

Erlich, Vera St. (1966). *Family in Transition: A Study of 300 Yugoslav Villages.* Princeton: Princeton University Press.

Evans-Pritchard, E.E. (1940). *The Nuer.* Oxford: Oxford University Press.

———. (1951). *Kinship and Marriage among the Nuer.* Oxford: Oxford University Press.

Gelles, Richard, and Claire Cornell. (1983). *International Perspectives on Family Violence.* Lexington, Massachusetts: D.C. Heath and Co.

Holtzman, Jon D. (2000). *Nuer Journeys, Nuer Lives: Sudanese Refugees in Minnesota.* Boston: Allyn and Bacon.

———. (2001). Dialing 911 in Nuer: Gender transformations and domestic violence in a Midwestern Sudanese refugee community. In *Immigration Research for the Next Century: Multidisciplinary Perspectives,* edited by Nancy Foner, Ruben Rumbaut, and Stephen Gold. New York: Russell Sage Foundation.

Hutchinson, Sharon. (1996). *Nuer Dilemmas: Coping with War, Money and the State.* Berkeley: University of California Press.

Levinson, David. (1989). *Family Violence in Cross-Cultural Perspective.* Newbury Park, California: Sage Publications.

Morley, Rebecca. (1994). Wife beating and modernization: The case of Papua New Guinea. *Journal of Comparative Family Studies* 25.1: 25–52.

Savishinsky, Joel S. (1976). *Stress and Mobility in an Arctic Community: The Hare Indians of Colville Lake, Northwest Territories.* Ann Arbor: University Microfilms.

◆ **Part Two**

Social Regulation of Anti-social Behavior

Somehow, violence slips back and forth through the interstices between family and society. Each transition occurs within complex networks of feedbacks and feedforwards, with the result that violence may be amplified, maintained, or reduced, even when not directly addressed. The dynamics of personal violence may be regulated through abstract notions of honor and shame, through concrete practices and feelings such as reprimand, humiliation, fear, and politeness, and through the intervention of persons standing in culturally significant role relationships, such as fathers, mothers, and godmothers—all coming up for attention in the following chapters.

Chapter VIII

Violent Crime and the Loss of Fathers: Beyond the Long Arm

Wade C. Mackey

The Social Father: A Universal

One of the founding graybeards of anthropology, Bronislaw Malinowski (1927), believed that "the principle of legitimacy" is one of the pillars upon which the organization of the family was built. Malinowski stated that "the most important moral and legal rule concerning the physiological side of kinship is that no child should be brought into the world without a man—and one man at that—assuming the role of sociological father, that is, guardian and protector, the male link between the child and the rest of the community..." Hartley (1975) echoed Malinowski: "With hundreds of societies in the world having varied beliefs and customs, different environmental problems, and differences in group size and organization, the principle of legitimacy comes as near as any social rule to being truly universal." In turn, "legitimacy" is derived from "marriage," another cross-cultural universal (Brown 1991, Van den Berghe 1979, Stephens 1964, Levinson and Malone 1980, McCary 1975; cf Gough 1968). "Marriage," inter alia, serves to legitimize the wife's children (see Fisher [1983] for a complementary discussion predicated on *The Sex Contract*). Once married, the man is expected to provision and to protect his children: the children who had become his through the ritual of "marriage."[1] Accordingly, the role of "fathers" is to nurture his young to independence. It should be noted that, for the discussion here, it is irrelevant whether fathering is strictly a "social invention" (Mead 1949; cf Harlow 1971, and Smuts and Gubernick 1992), which exists only as part of the thin veneer of civilization, or whether fathering exemplifies an independent affiliative bond "built" into our species (Mackey 1985, 1996. cf Lovejoy 1981). What is relevant is the putative impact that the presence/absence of an on-going social father may have upon the level of violence within his community.

It is argued below that, in addition to the more vegetive function of keeping his children alive, "fathering" may play a more subtle role in enhancing the viability of the father's community. Framed a little differently, the social father may be an invisible prophylactic in minimizing violence within his community.

Fatherlessness and Violent Crime

It is arguable that, if a responsible and continuous adult male role-model is unavailable to young, developing boys, then those boys would become more prone to engage in deviant or anti-social behavior. That is, there is a tendency for children from fatherless homes to be over-represented in categories of unwanted behavior (Mackey 1985, 1996).

The lack-of-appropriate-role-model argument can be made in an anecdotal/idiographic mode. It can also be subject to a nomothetic, empirical corroboration. The empirical route seems like an interesting path to follow. First, let's look at the U.S. mega-tribe, and then a cross-cultural sample will be examined.

The Abraiding of the U.S. Social Father

Since the 1960s there has been a systematic peeling away of the U.S. social father from the mother-child(ren) dyad. Approximately 2,000,000 children per year are separated from an on-going social and biological father due to processes outside of the control of the "father." In 1992, nearly 1,225,000 births or 20.1% of all births were to single parent mothers (U.S. Bureau of the Census 1995) and 1,075,000 minor children were involved in a divorce (U.S. Bureau of the Census 1995). In up to 90% of the divorce cases, it is the mother who receives custody of the minor children (Sitarz 1990, Sack 1987). It should be noted that wives predominate as the petitioner in all divorce situations and further noted that when minor children are involved, the wife's tendency to petition for divorce increases and the husband's tendency to petition decreases (Mackey 1993, National Center for Health Statistics 1989). In a divorce situation with minor children, a social father had been present with the child for some duration. In single-parent births, he was not.

To see if there were a relationship in the U.S. between rates of violent crime and rates of out-of-wedlock births, the two indices were analyzed, by state, across the 50 states.

Out-of-wedlock births, by state, were obtained form the Vital Statistics of the U.S. [U.S. Bureau of the Census (1992: 6)]. Rates of violent crime, by state, were obtained from the FBI (U.S. Bureau of the Census 1992: 181)].

Across the 50 states, violent crime rates were significantly related to the percentage of all births that were born to unwed mothers ($r_P = .655$; $p < .001$; 2-tailed). As the percentage of out-of-wedlock births increased, so did rates of violent crime. Over 40% ($r_p{}^2 = (.655)^2 = .429 = 42.9\%$) of the differences in violent crime rates can be attributed to differences in the levels of out-of-wedlock births. See Appendix I for the data by state. (Note that if the District of Columbia is added to the sample, the correlation increases to .825; $p < .001$; 2-tailed).

Thus, within the framework of this inquiry's parameters, there, indeed, is a linkage between violent crime within a community and the level of single parent births within that community.

Cross-cultural Perspective

Arguably, this connection between unwed mothers and violent crime may be a (epi)phenomenon that is highly specific to the U.S. mega-tribe. To discover whether the linkage between violent crime and births to unwed mothers was more particularistic to the cultural matrix of the United States, or exemplified a more thematic cultural dynamic, a similar analysis was conducted across cultures, specifically, across nation-states.

A/any/all cross-cultural analyses are hampered by the problems of meaningful and comparable units of analysis. [See Ford (1961) for a discussion on cultural "units"]. Analyses on rates of crime are often problematic because of the lack of consonance among countries in the definitions and reporting of various crimes. However, one "crime"—murder—does seem to be universally accepted as a "crime" with reasonably concordant definitions (Archer and Gartner 1984; Daly and Wilson 1988). One may muse on the high validity of the level of death as a dependent variable. Accordingly, rates of murder in the United States [U.S. Bureau of the Census (1992: 181)] were correlated with illegitimacy rates in the United States—across the 50 states—and then were compared to similar figures generated by cross-cultural data (Smith-Morris 1990, United Nations 1992). Note that the United Nations defines "illegitimacy" in the following manner.

"Legitimate refers to persons born of parents who were married at the time of birth in accordance with the laws of the country or area. Illegitimate refers to children of parents, who, according to national law, were not married at the time of birth, regardless of whether these children have been recognized or legitimized after birth" (United Nations, 1992, p. 104).

The United States. The relationship—across the 50 states—between murder rates and illegitimacy rates was significant ($r_P = .749$; $p < .001$; 2-tailed). As illegitimacy rates increased, so did murder rates. Over half ($r_p^2 = (.749)^2 = .561 = 56.1\%$) of the variance in murder rates can be attributed to differences in illegitimacy rates. See Appendix II for the data by state. If the District of Columbia is included, then the correlation coefficient increases to $r_p = .8565$; $p < .001$; 2-tailed.

Cross-cultural data. There were usable data from the U. N. sources for 44 countries in which both murder rates and illegitimacy rates were reported to the satisfaction of the United Nations. See Appendix II for data by country. The relationship was positive and significant ($r_p = .429$; $p < .01$; 2-tailed).[2] Across cultures, as murder rates went up, so did the proportion of single-parent births.

Discussion

Violent crime and illegitimacy

Before the results of the relationship between violent crime and illegitimacy are discussed, two caveats and qualifications should to be presented. To wit: (1) Problems in the reporting of (violent) crime are legion, and (2) If the focus is cross-cultural, then the legionary problems in the reporting of (violent) crime are intensified.

On the other hand, given the very real existence of the two caveats, the above sources of "error variance" would tend to lessen or to lower, if not submerge, any index of association that was being computed. Hence, in spite of large amounts of noise in the system, significance was still reached and, thereby, it suggests that the relationship between violent crime and rates of illegitimacy is more real than merely apparent. With the above qualifications squarely ensconced in the background, some interesting patterns emerged in the foreground.

Violent crime (including murder) is associated with single parent births. The single parent is the mother, not the father. The association is fairly robust. If the father is systematically precluded from or abraded from the mother-child dyad, then violent crime within the community is expected to be under pressures to increase.

Several points become germane here.

(1) Neither the single mothers nor their babies are committing the crimes. Violent crime is predominately committed by men, especially young men (Bartol 1995).

(2) In virtually all cultures, family functioning is almost totally immune from formal penal codes, law enforcement, and the legal institution. Marriages cannot be coerced,

nor, in the main, can be abortion, abstinence, or the use of contraceptives. Men cannot be coerced into the role of social father. All of these items are, to one degree or another, related to illegitimacy, and not one of them can be meaningfully modified by acts of governance. The long arm of the law does not reach so far. Illegitimacy is quite beyond the long arm of the law.

(3) The pattern appears across cultural boundaries: an increase in unmarried mothers is aligned with an increase in violent crime. Thus, a *unique* cultural matrix with an unusual set of ecology and economics and social structure does not seem like a productive explanation for the *patterned* trends.

(4) Although correlation does not demonstrate causality, neither does it preclude causation. In this instance, it seems clear that illegitimacy is not causing violent crime. Nor is violent crime, by men, causing out-of-wedlock births. The divining of the causal links that do serve to mesh single parenthood with violent crime remains beyond the scope of this paper. There is, however, the intuitive specter that, perhaps, Freud (1964) was flirting with a real phenomenon when he constructed the Oedipus complex [see Fox (1980) for a complementary conjecture]. The exact nature of that flirtation or phenomenon may well remain only a specter.

(5) Lastly, the relationship between biological, but not social, fathers and those individuals who commit crimes appears to be unknown and only barely knowable. Accordingly the concatenation between elevated rates of illegitimacy and violent crimes is similarly unknown, but probably more knowable. What does seem clear is that the continuous presence of a social and biological father does reduce the level of violent crime within a community. Those who are charged with the task of reducing violent crime would be well advised (i) to consider ways and means to maximize incentives for men to enter into and to remain in the father-role, (ii) to consider ways and means to minimize the disincentives of the father-role, and (iii) to relay to women the potential costs to them, their children, and the commonweal of precluding a son from his father. The effect of autonomous, on-going father-child relationships seems to immunize, at least partially, the growing boy from violent crime (Mackey 1985, 1996). The exact mechanisms of the putative immunization have yet to be isolated. Accordingly, those specialists interested in child development and those cultural anthropologists interested in marriage and the family and those criminologists interested in crime and criminals seem to have a splendid knot to untangle.

Moslem Swath and Europe, or Fundamentalism vs. Gender Equality

Two sub-groups of countries are of special interest to this inquiry and represent a bifurcation on how cultures incorporate the "social father" and the "status of women" into their overall cultural matrix.

Muslim swath. One tine of the bifurcation is a Moslem swath of countries that begins at Mauritania and sweeps eastward to Pakistan. This collection of cultures has been slow or retrogressive in forging equality between the genders. Ethnographic accounts of the relevant Moslem countries invariably refer to the strongly patriarchal character of their political and economic structures. Rarely is the question addressed: Is the country patriarchal? The emphases invariably revolved around how the patriarchy developed and/or how it is maintained.

For example, Ahmed (1992) writes: "The subordination of women in the ancient Middle East appears to have become institutionalized with the rise of urban societies and with the rise of the archaic state in particular..." and, as Islam crystallized its theology, "Implicit in this new order was the male right to control women and to interdict their interactions with other men. Thus, the ground was prepared for the closures that would follow." See Kadioglu (1994) for a parallel argument for women's role in Turkey. Toubia (1988: 2–3) makes the case quite clearly: "Arab women are dominated by men in every area of life in the patriarchal family system: state, political party, trade union and public and private institutions of all types." She noted that over 97% (97.2%) of the Yemeni women, as late as 1975, were illiterate. Badran (1995: 5) notes that "the woman was perceived as essentially or exclusively, a sexual being, unlike the man who was only partly understood in terms of his sexuality." Gerami (1996: 157) views the current version of Islamic fundamentalism as "nipping a very young feminist movement in the bud and under the banner of nature's mandate, pushed women further into the family. They managed to cast woman's individualist identity as a perversion of her nature plotted by Western imperialists." Obermeyer (1995: 370) observes that the "Islamic emphasis on complementarity rather than equality in gender roles" makes dialogue with a worldview predicated on equality rather than complementarity extremely difficult. The women of Islam have difficulty in obtaining a divorce and also have, in the context of comparatively high birth rates, low proportions of out-of-wedlock births.

Europe. The second tine of the bifurcation, Europe, has experienced the recent tendency for an increased and unfettered access by women into economic and political power structures. Although this tendency has been viewed as an appropriate and positive event, when aligned with enhanced political and economic power, a more problematic consequence to the enhanced power has also arisen—the preclusion of the social father.

For example, a working definition of individual freedom would probably include some reference to money and to political freedom. Women's relative access to economic and political realms can be indexed by their increased participation in tertiary education, i.e., education beyond the "high school"/secondary level and by their success in reaching parity (compared to men) in income. Alternative indices could, of course, be developed by different inquiries.

Women's Equity and Single Parent Births

Data from 49 countries were found which had both the percent of women in tertiary education and the percent of births to unwed mothers (see Appendix III). The relationship between the two indices was significant ($r_p = .367$; $p < .05$; 2-tailed). As the proportion of women in tertiary education increased, so did the proportion of out-of-wedlock births. Approximately 13% ($.367^2 = .134 = 13\%$) of the variability in single parent births can be attributed to changes in the level of female participation in tertiary education. For the data by country, see Appendix III.

There were twenty countries in which both the ratio of women's income (to that of men's) and the percentage of out-of-wedlock births were available. The relationship between the two indices was significant ($r_p = .649$; $p < .01$; 2-tailed); as the ratio approached unity, the proportion of single parent births increased. Nearly 42% ($.649^2 = .421 = 42\%$) of the differences in the level of out-of-wedlock births can be attributed to changes in the income ratio. See Appendix III.

There were 18 countries that reported all three indices. The relationship between the percentage of single parent births and the two indices of women's equity (proportion of women in tertiary institutions and the ratio of women's earnings to that of men's) acting in tandem was significant ($R = .758$; $F(2,15) = 8.61$; $p < .01$). Over half (adjusted $R^2 = .514 = 51.4\%$) of the variance in single parents can be attributed to changes in the other two variables.

Hence, two quite disparate biocultural formulae are in competition with each other. One, the Moslem swath, has (i) a high rate of annual natural increase (mean = 3.0%, s = 1.1%; n = 21)[3] and (ii) restricted options for its women. Two, Europe has a (i) low rate of annual natural increase (mean = 0.4%, s = 0.3%, n = 29). [Note that the Moslem rate of natural increase is more than seven times the Europe rate and is also significantly higher than the European rate {t [48] = 10.3; p < .01, 2-tailed], and (ii) enhanced options for their women. The benefits of the "European" system can be envisioned as increased freedom for women, some consequences are lesser population growth and fatherlessness. The pattern of the "Moslem" system is population expansion and greater father-child interaction, with restricted freedom for women.

Reduced fathering in a community eventuates in pressures for increased violent behavior by that community's men. As culture's structure increased freedom for women, unintended *sequelae* might include enhanced levels of anti-social, or deviant, or violent behaviors within those cultures.

Synopsis

A series of choice points have made themselves available to the world's community of nations or mega-tribes for the 21st century. Will these communities make an attempt (1) to maximize incentives and minimize disincentives (rather than the reverse) for growing boys to enter into the role of social father and for already grown men to stay in that role? And (2) to encourage women to re-evaluate the net benefits/costs to abrading the social father from his child?

Raising an incompetent and dependent child into a competent, independent adult is not a sinecure. Costs abound for the caretakers. Moral indignation that intones the mantra of "be more responsible" is probably not convincing to the target of the moral indignation. Whereas the release from "social fatherhood" may serve the ends for a particular individual, if occurring en masse across a community, the results might well be deleterious overall (see Hardin 1968) for the classic presentation of the dilemma between corporate and individual needs).

Its own violent (young) men are one of the problems with which any organized society must deal [see Harris (1974, 1977) for discussion and examples]. The addition of an on-going social father seems to tamp down violence within a society. The erasing of such "fathers" is associated with increased rates of violent crime. To the extent that a society's fathers are systematically removed from the fathering role, the more that society ought to expect its level of violent crime to increase. Because there are no viable societies with any length of history that have had men, as a class, avoid the role of social father, no one has any idea on the competitive quotient that fatherless societies may have versus those societies which assume/mandate fatherhood. Neither data nor theory exists to constitute a store-house of knowledge on the viability of fatherless societies. To date no such society has existed. A real experiment is currently being conducted within the laboratory of the

U.S. and elsewhere. The hypothesis is being tacitly tested: "Are fathers supernumerary?" As in any other true experiment, the results are unknown until the final datum is tabulated.

Notes

1. The avunculate, of course, more disperses authority and nurturing within a family. However, children within the avunculate also are expected to be born to a married woman.

2. The two rates—for illegitimacy (6.7) and for murder (38.7)—were also available for the Philippines. However, the Philippines' murder rate of 38.7 was over 8.5 standard deviations (sd = 4.09) over the sample mean of 3.62. Accordingly, the Philippines was enough of an outlier to be excluded from the sample. If rankings were used to generate the correlation coefficient (r_s) and if the Philippines is included in the sample, then the relationship between illegitimacy and murder rates is significant ($r_s = .889$, $p < .01$; 2-tailed, n = 45). If the Philippines is not included in the sample, the correlation, based on ranks, is still significant ($r_s = .896$, $p < .01$; 2-tailed, n = 44).

3. The rate of natural increase is found by subtracting (crude) death rates from (crude) birth rates.

References

Ahmed Leila. (1992). *Women and Gender in Islam: Historical Roots of a Modern Debate*. New Haven: Yale University Press.

Archer, D., and R. Gartner. (1981). Homicide in 110 nations. In *Readings in Comparative Criminology*, edited by Louise I. Shelley. Carbondale: Southern Illinois University Press.

Badran, Margot. (1995). *Feminists, Islam, and Nation: Gender and the Making of Modern Egypt*. Princeton, New Jersey: Princeton University Press.

Bartol, C.R. (1995). *Criminal Behavior: A Psychosocial Approach* (4th edition). Englewood Cliffs, New Jersey: Prentice Hall.

Brown, Donald E. (1991). *Human Universals*. New York: McGraw-Hill.

Chagnon, Napoleon. (1977). *Yanomamo*. New York: Holt, Rinehart and Winston.

Daly, Martin, and Margot Wilson. (1988). *Homicide*. New York: Aldine De Gruyter.

Fisher, Helen E. (1983). *The Sex Contract: The Evolution of Human Behavior*. New York: Quill.

Ford, C.S., editor. (1961). *Readings in Cross-cultural Methodology*. New Haven, Connecticut: HRAF Press.

Freud, Sigmund. (1964). *The Standard Edition of the Complete Psychological Work of Sigmund Freud*, translated and edited by J. Strachey. London: Hogarth.

Gerami, Shahin. (1996). *Women and Fundamentalism: Islam and Christianity*. New York: Garland.

Gough, E.K. (1968). The Nayars and the definition of marriage. In *Marriage, Family and Residence*, edited by Paul Bohannan and John Middleton, pp. 49–71. New York: Natural History Press.

Hardin, Garrett. (1968). Tragedy of the Commons. *Science* 162: 1243–1248.

Harlow, Harry. (1971). *Learning to Love*. San Francisco: Albion.

Harris, Marvin. (1974). *Cows, Pigs, Wars, and Witches*. New York: Random House.

————. (1977). *Cannibals and Kings: The Origin of Cultures.* New York: Random House.

Hartley, S.F. (1975). *Illegitimacy.* Berkeley: University of California Press.

Human Relations Area Files (HRAF). (1949). New Haven, Connecticut: HRAF Press.

Kadioglu, A. (1994). Women's subordination in Turkey: Is Islam really the villain? *Middle East Journal* 48: 640–662.

Levinson, David, and M.J. Malone. (1980). *Toward Explaining Human Culture: A Critical Review of the Findings of Worldwide Cross-cultural Research.* New Haven, Connecticut: HRAF.

Lovejoy, C. O. (1981). The origin of man. *Science* 211: 341–350.

Mackey, Wade C. (1985). *Fathering Behaviors: The Dynamics of the Man-Child Bond.* New York: Polonium.

————. (1993). Marital dissolution by sex of the petitioner: A test of the man-child affiliative bond. *Journal of Genetic Psychology* 154: 353–362.

————. (1996). *The American Father: Biocultural and Developmental Aspects.* New York: Plenum.

Malinowski, Bronislaw. (1927). *The Father in Primitive Psychology.* New York: Norton.

McCary, J.L. (1975). *Freedom and Growth in Marriage.* Santa Barbara, California: Hamilton.

Mead, Margaret. (1949). *Male and Female.* New York: Morrow.

National Center of Health Statistics. (1989). Children of Divorce. Vital and Health Statistics Series #21, DHHS Pub. No. (PHS) 8901924. Washington, D.C.: Government Printing Office.

Obermeyer, C.M. (1995). A cross-cultural perspective on reproductive rights. *Human Rights Quarterly* 17: 366–381.

Sack, S.M. (1987). *The Complete Legal Guide to Marriage, Divorce, Custody and Living Together.* New York: McGraw-Hill.

Sitarz, Dan. (1990). *Divorce Yourself: The National No-fault No-lawyer Divorce Handbook.* Carbondale, Illinois: Nova.

Smith-Morris, M., editor. (1990). *The Economist Book of Vital World Statistics.* New York: Times Books.

Smuts, B.B., and D.J. Gubernick. (1992). Male-infant relationships in nonhuman primates: Paternal investment or mating effort? In *Father-Child Relations: Cultural and Biosocial Contexts,* edited by B. S. Hewlett. New York: Aldine De Gruyter. pp. 1–30.

Stephens, W.N. (1964). *The Family in Cross-cultural Perspective.* New York: Holt, Rinehart, and Winston.

Toubia, Nahid. (1988). *Women of the Arab World: The Coming Challenge.* London: Zed Books, Limited.

Van den Berghe, P.L. (1979). *Human Family Systems.* New York: Elsevier.

UN (United Nations). (1992). *Demographic Yearbook.* New York: United Nations.

USBC (U.S. Bureau of the Census). (1992). *Statistical Abstract of the United States: 1993* (113th edition), pp. 69, 181, 384. Washington, D.C.: Government Printing Office, pp. 69, 181, 384.

————. (1994). *Statistical Abstract of the United States: 1995* (115th edition.). Washington, D.C.: Government Printing Office.

Appendix I

Rates of illegitimacy and rates of violent crime across states (U.S. Bureau of the Census 1992).

State	Rate of illegitimacy[1]	Rate of violent crime[2]
Maine	21.8	143
New Hampshire	15.7	132
Vermont	19.8	127
Massachusetts	23.8	736
Rhode Island	24.9	432
Connecticut	26.3	554
New York	31.9	1,181
New Jersey	24.1	648
Pennsylvania	27.9	431
Ohio	28.0	506
Indiana	23.8	474
Illinois	30.9	967
Michigan	24.5	790
Wisconsin	23.4	265
Minnesota	19.5	306
Iowa	19.4	300
Missouri	27.1	715
North Dakota	16.9	74
South Dakota	21.8	163
Nebraska	19.3	330
Kansas	19.6	448
Delaware	29.1	655
Maryland	28.9	919
Virginia	25.2	351
West Virginia	23.5	169
North Carolina	27.7	624
South Carolina	31.6	977
Georgia	31.7	756
Florida	30.2	1,244
Kentucky	22.6	390
Tennessee	29.1	670
Alabama	29.8	709
Mississippi	39.4	340
Arkansas	27.7	532
Louisiana	35.3	898
Oklahoma	23.8	547
Texas	19.6	761
Montana	21.7	159
Idaho	16.1	276
Wyoming	18.5	301
Colorado	20.5	526
New Mexico	34.5	780

1. Births to unmarried women, percent of total births (1989)
2. Offenses known to the police per 100,000 population (1990)

State	Rate of illegitimacy[1]	Rate of violent crime[2]
Arizona	30.8	652
Utah	12.7	284
Nevada	23.5	601
Washington	23.4	502
California	30.0	1,045
Alaska	24.6	525
Hawaii	23.8	281
(District of Columbia)	(64.3)	(2,458)

1. Births to unmarried women, percent of total births (1989)
2. Offenses known to the police per 100,000 population (1990)

Appendix II

Rates of illegitimacy and murder across the United States (n = 50) (U.S. Bureau of the Census 1992) and across nations (n = 44) (Smith-Morris 1990, United Nations 1992).

State	Illegitimacy[1]	Murder[2]
Alabama	29.8	11.6
Alaska	24.6	7.5
Arizona	30.8	7.7
Arkansas	27.7	10.3
California	30.0	11.9
Colorado	20.5	4.2
Connecticut	26.3	5.1
Delaware	29.1	5.0
Florida	30.2	10.7
Georgia	31.7	11.2
Hawaii	23.8	4.0
Idaho	16.1	2.7
Illinois	30.9	10.3
Indiana	23.8	6.2
Iowa	19.4	1.9
Kansas	19.6	4.0
Kentucky	22.6	7.2
Louisiana	35.3	17.2
Maine	21.8	2.4
Maryland	28.9	11.5
Massachusetts	23.8	4.0
Michigan	24.5	10.4
Minnesota	19.5	2.7
Mississippi	39.4	12.2
Missouri	27.1	8.8
Montana	21.7	4.9
Nebraska	19.3	2.7
Nevada	23.5	9.7
New Hampshire	15.7	1.9
New Jersey	24.1	5.6
New Mexico	34.5	9.2
New York	31.9	14.5
North Carolina	27.7	10.7
North Dakota	16.9	0.8
Ohio	28.0	6.1
Oklahoma	23.8	8.0
Pennsylvania	27.9	6.7
Rhode Island	24.9	4.8
South Carolina	31.6	11.2
South Dakota	21.8	2.0
Tennessee	29.1	10.5

1. Births to unmarried women, percent of total births
2. Offenses known to authorities per 100,00 population

Texas	19.6	14.1
Utah	12.7	3.0
Vermont	19.8	2.3
Virginia	25.2	8.8
Washington	23.4	4.9
(Washington, D.C.)	(64.3)	(77.8)
West Virginia	23.5	5.7
Wisconsin	23.4	4.6
Wyoming	18.5	4.9

Country	Illegitimacy[1]	Murder[2]
Argentina	32.5	0.2
Australia	15.5	4.2
Austria	22.4	1.3
Bahamas	62.1	12.2
Barbados	73.1	4.0
Belgium	5.7	3.1
Brunei	0.4	1.9
Canada	16.9	2.2
Chile	31.8	5.6
Costa Rica	37.2	4.0
Cyprus	0.4	1.7
Denmark	43.0	1.25
Fiji	17.3	2.0
Finland	16.4	1.1
France	19.6	4.05
Greece	1.8	0.85
Hong Kong	5.5	1.2
Hungary	9.2	2.3
Ireland	7.8	0.5
Israel	1.0	1.7
Italy	4.4	1.5
Jamaica	84.3	18.0
Japan	1.0	1.2
Luxembourg	8.7	7.0
Malta	1.2	1.8
Mauritius	26.0	2.4
Mexico	27.5	7.4
Netherlands	8.3	1.2
New Zealand	24.9	2.9
Norway	25.8	0.9
Panama	71.9	4.6
Peru	42.6	1.2
Portugal	12.4	3.0
South Korea	0.5	1.3
Spain	3.9	2.3
Sri Lanka	5.4	18.9
Sweden	46.4	1.7

1. Births to unmarried women, percent of total births
2. Offenses known to authorities per 100,00 population

Country	Illegitimacy[1]	Murder[2]
Switzerland	5.6	0.9
Tunisia	0.3	0.7
U. K.	19.2	1.3
U.S.A.	21.0	8.6
Venezuela	53.9	8.4
West Germany	9.4	1.5
Yugoslavia	8.4	5.4

1. Births to unmarried women, percent of total births
2. Offenses known to authorities per 100,00 population

Appendix III

Values for the three social indices: Percentage of all births born to single parent mothers, percentage of tertiary students who are females, and the ratio of female to male earnings (Smith-Morris, 1990; United Nations, 1985–1992).

Country	% of single parent births	% female tertiary students	ratio of female to male earnings
Australia	15.5	49	1.00
Belgium	5.7	47	.62
Denmark	43.0	50	.84
France	19.6	51	.81
West Germany	9.4	41	.73
Iceland	47.1	54	.90
Japan	1.0	37	.52
Luxembourg	8.7	34	.66
Netherlands	8.3	42	.76
New Zealand	24.9	48	.77
Switzerland	5.6	32	.67
United Kingdom	19.2	46	.695
United States	21.0	53	.68
Czechoslovakia	6.8	42	.68
Hong Kong	5.5	35	.77
South Korea	0.5	30	.48
Sri Lanka	5.4	41	.71
Cyprus	0.4	49	.585
Egypt		33	.68
Kenya		26	.85
Costa Rica	37.2		.72
Paraguay	33.3		.88
Austria	22.4	46	
Finland	16.4	50	
Greece	1.8	49	
Ireland	7.8	43	
Italy	4.4	47	
Norway	25.8	51	
Portugal	12.4	54	
Spain	3.9	50	
Sweden	46.4	53	
Bulgaria	11.4	56	
East Germany	33.8	52	
Hungary	9.2	53	
Poland	5.0	56	
Brunei	0.4	51	
Fiji	17.3	35	
Philippines	6.1	54	
Mauritius	26.0	36	
Israel	1.0	46	
Malta	1.2	36	
Tunisia	0.3	37	
Argentina	32.5	53	

Country	% of single parent births	% female tertiary students
Bahamas	62.1	70
Barbados	73.1	49
Bermuda	31.2	51
Chile	31.8	44
El Salvador	67.4	43
Mexico	27.5	36
Panama	71.9	58
Peru	42.6	35
Puerto Rico	26.5	60
Venezuela	53.9	47

Chapter IX

The Godmother as Mediator: Constraining Violence in a Zapotec Village of Oaxaca, Mexico

Nicole Sault

Discussions of the factors contributing to violence usually focus on the role of men, ignoring women participants or portraying them as silent onlookers and victims. Although there have been some ethnographic studies of women's participation in violent behavior, as well as female resistance to it, there has been little attention to the roles that women play in circumventing or quelling violence.

This chapter examines how godmothers act to reduce the seriousness of violent encounters among men in a Zapotec village in the Oaxaca Valley of southeastern Mexico. In this village violent acts do occur, especially when men are drinking at fiestas; but senior women who are godmothers are called upon to calm arguments, stop fights, and restore order. The expectation is that no man would argue with or strike his godmother, for she above all others deserves his respect and gratitude. Nevertheless, the social changes associated with increasing modernization, mass media images, and external political conflict have undermined community ties and the traditional high status of godmothers, leading to increased and more severe violence.

Introduction: Call the Godmother!

At a household fiesta after a baptism in a Zapotec village, people are eating and drinking, talking and laughing into the dark of the evening, when suddenly the merriment is broken by shouts and cries. Quickly a circle of people gathers around two inebriated men rolling in the dirt of the house patio, grappling with each other over a perceived insult and challenge. Neither man is armed so the audience does not seem greatly alarmed, but the reaction is quick, for the people immediately cry out "call for the godmother!" The consensus is that the godmothers of the men should be notified and asked to come and break up the fight. Meanwhile, the observers look on and comment about how the fight began, the motivations, and implications. But of greatest immediate interest is making sure that no one is seriously injured.

This was the first fight that I had witnessed in Oaxaca, and I was interested in the reaction of the audience. Their response was concern. Once the men in the circle verified that there were no weapons involved they did not try to intervene. They just stood in the circle, carefully watching. Meanwhile, everyone called on older women to step in, either the godmother, the mother, or an older sister of either man. Eventually the fight ended and everyone went back to partying. The conversation briefly focused on the fight and the character of each man involved. The attitude was that fighting at someone else's party was in bad taste because it is disrespectful to the hosts and an affront to the village as a whole. Some people seemed to enjoy talking about the behavioral details that preceded the fight, but the general attitude was disapproval toward both men.

The fight began and ended suddenly, but what surprised me most was the reaction of the audience—the women calling on each other to step in and break up the fight, while the men accepted this as the most appropriate response. Knowing how Zapotec girls are raised and the expectations of godmothers, I should have recognized that this mediatory role is routine behavior for women, especially if they are godmothers.

Socialization for Mediation

The expectation that people will step in to mediate and the ability to do so are taught to boys and girls from an early age as they learn about respect, cooperation, and responsibility. These are the values that are traditionally admired by Zapotec men as well as women, despite the common stereotype of the ideal Mexican man as an aggressive macho.[1]

Respectful behavior is demonstrated by showing deference, regard, and consideration for the feelings and needs of others in the group. This same ideal exists in another Zapotec community of the Oaxaca Valley, where Selby remarked on the elegant manners of villagers: "the soft-spoken manner, the ritual greetings, the enormous care not to offend, the specially groomed vocal inflections to indicate every shade of respect, the kissing of hands, and above all, the gravity of manner that marks a man of respect" (1974: 4). In general, all members of the community deserve a basic level of respect, especially those who are older, senior kin, or leaders. Children as well as adults are accorded respect. For example, if a small child is playing it is wrong to snatch the child up and quickly leave. This shows lack of consideration for the child's feelings and the child may become ill as a consequence, for the child's soul may be left behind, since the souls of children are not yet securely attached to their bodies. Proper behavior toward the child means telling the child to get ready to go because it is time to leave. The expectation is that once told, the child will obey and prepare to leave.

From childhood on, both men and women are taught the values associated with extended family structures of dependence training societies: cooperation, obedience, and sharing (Sung 1985, Wolf 1966: 69–70). These values are communicated through extended breastfeeding and co-sleeping patterns, a high degree of physical contact between kin, sharing meals together, participation in family rituals, and parallel work patterns in which children work alongside their parents or other senior kin. At an early age responsibility is encouraged by giving young children small tasks that contribute to the welfare of the family, such as making tortillas, sweeping the patio, drawing water from the well, herding, chopping vegetables, fetching firewood, and running errands. A sense of identity comes from participation in the kin group, rather than focusing on the self or an age-based peer group.

For Zapotec villagers a sense of respect is intertwined with dignity and trust. This sense of dignity can be seen in the way that people walk. Zapotec market women are noted for their erect bearing that conveys pride and confidence. Being raised to believe they are worthy and deserving of respect gives children a sense of dignity. Most small children are treated with a great deal of affection and solicitude, being embraced, held, and kissed by everyone from their parents and siblings to senior kin and other children in the village. Small children are rarely punished. When they cry, fuss, or misbehave they are held and played with, both to distract their attention and to reassure them. Among the Zapotec, children are socialized through "skinship," a high level of bodily contact that is considered "essential to the development of a sense of well-being and interdependence in the child" (Hendry and Lebra, as cited in Pader 1993: 126).

From their embodied experience of being wanted and loved, children develop a sense of trust for close kin, but they are also taught to distrust outsiders. Just as the family represents the womb of security in which everyone should feel safe, the outside world is a place of danger where people and things cannot be trusted. Everything scary, mean, nasty, and bad is portrayed as coming from outside the family, whether it is bad air, a black dog, sprites and witches, envious neighbors, the evil eye, or people from the city and the federal government. Trust is accorded to an outsider only gradually, when that person has earned it through respectful language and reliable behavior.

Yet respect is neither absolute nor unwavering. Respect flows out of one's interactions with others, and it can be earned or lost. To be accorded respect one must embody the values of the society: to conduct oneself with decorum and humility, to honor senior kin, to fulfill one's obligations, to share generously, to cooperate in village activities, and to show consideration toward others. Such people are calm, speak in low tones, and move with grace. High praise is to say a man or woman is respectful, responsible, and fulfills their obligations. By contrast, people who are stingy, divisive, or volatile are looked down on, as are those who act in a noisy, abrupt, or aggressive manner. Some of the worst things that you can call a person are selfish, disruptive, or irresponsible.

The Power of Words

Part of becoming an adult is learning how to use language skillfully. Verbal ability is greatly admired, whether in ritual speeches, jokes and metaphors, quick retorts, or good counsel. Those who embody community values and can also demonstrate agility and creativity with words gain great prestige. They are asked to preside at ritual gatherings by making elegant formal speeches that express key elements of the Zapotec worldview (El Guindi 1986). Those who can entertain with playful banter and teasing are appreciated for their ability to create laughter and ease tensions. Quick and clever retorts are admired as key to demonstrating the ability to defend oneself.

From a young age children are taught to be respectful, but also to defend themselves. The expectation is that rude or aggressive behavior should not be tolerated, and the appropriate response is a vigorous verbal display. As Chiñas observed along the coast of Oaxaca, that Zapotec women regularly move about in public areas as market vendors or messengers, where they are vulnerable to assault, so "it becomes imperative that women behave in ways designed to leave no doubt in anyone's mind as to their virtue. Thus Isthmus Zapotec girls are socialized to rebuff improper and undesirable attention. Members of both sexes greatly admire 'a woman who defends herself' by devastatingly insulting remarks directed toward would-be lotharios" (Chiñas 1973: 110).

Women use language in self-defense, but they can also use strong language to make a peremptory strike and take over a situation. For example, one day in the late afternoon I was traveling by bus between two villages, accompanied by a young Zapotec woman. I was going as far as the last stop, but she was getting off before that. As the bus was quite full, we were standing at the back, among a number of men from other villages. She had previously warned me that men from one of the villages were notorious for being aggressive and violent. Observing that it was growing dark, she became worried about my welfare. I did not know anyone else on the bus and I had a way to walk once I got off. Suddenly she began talking in a very loud voice, decrying the way that men carry on, saying: "men are shameless dogs, for they will stick it anywhere." As she continued her tirade all the men around us turned away and moved off, seeming to shrink down so as to be less visible. When she finished she smiled, convinced that she had established a protective shield around me. Then she said good-bye and left. For the rest of the ride the bus was very quiet. At the last stop I got off and peacefully walked the rest of the way back to the village where I lived. Though public space is often viewed as a male domain, women have ways of taking over that space and making it their own. Verbally shaming men is one powerful way to do this.

In Zapotec communities defending oneself should be done with words first and foremost. Violence does occur, but this is a sign that words have failed. It means that someone has lost control of themselves or others. Sometimes children are punished physically, a handful of men are known to beat their wives, and a few women beat their inebriated husbands. On rare occasions women fight with each other, but what is most frequent is for drunken men to quarrel. But the man who resorts to violence is admitting verbal defeat. A man who uses violence against women or children is viewed as out of control, or a coward who takes out his frustrations on others. All acts of physical aggression, whether by men or women, were criticized by others. They openly criticized people in two other villages as notorious for their violent behavior, places that should be avoided or only entered cautiously when accompanied by others. By contrast, they spoke well of other villages where the people were well mannered. The Zapotec ideal is to use words to resolve disputes. When people resort to violence they lose some of their humanity and sink in the estimation of others.

The Zapotec emphasis on using words to resolve conflict flows out of what Nader calls a "harmony ideology" (Nader 1990). In Talea, the Zapotec town she studied in the Sierra of Oaxaca, people respond to conflict by seeking mediation in the village court. Nader points out that violence per se is not the problem, for Taleans view violence as a sign of disruption in social relationships, and it is the broken relationships that must be addressed. They do not focus on the violence itself (which is a Western category), for violence is only a symptom of a deeper problem (1990: 243). The Taleans are more interested in discovering the motive for violence in order to resolve the situation and maintain community values of balance and unity. The legal model of traditional Mexican society emphasizes communalism, compromise, and conciliation; in contrast, individualism leads to adversarial relations and group fragmentation (1990: 304–305). The Zapotec do not think in terms of individuals as points on a map, they think in terms of relationships between people, and whenever relationships are disrupted this can ripple out to affect many others.

Women Mediators and Defenders

Many scholars have described conflict escalation and resolution in relation to court systems or examined the historical context for violence in Mexico, but Beverly Chiñas is one of the few who discusses women's roles in this area. In the Isthmus of Tehuantepec on the southern coast of Oaxaca, Chiñas found that Zapotec women perform crucial roles in supervising, mediating, and policing their community. There is a high level of aggression and violence related to land disputes and outsiders, but women work together to bound and control aggression so that the violence can be prevented or subdued (Chiñas 1973: 86). Women's roles include monitoring local conditions, maintaining order at fiestas, protecting women from assault, and defending the community against outsiders.

Because men are often away working in their fields, during the day women predominate in the markets and streets as well as other public areas and homes. This means that women can practice surveillance, gather information, and act as messengers or reporters. In their roles as market vendors and shoppers, women can also move more freely than men without arousing suspicion (Chiñas 1973: 102, 111). Velez Ibañez has made similar observations regarding the highly urban community of Netzahualcoyotl in Mexico City, where most men leave daily to work elsewhere and women remain to work and oversee the community. Women control the communication networks in Netzahualcoyotl, selectively relaying news according to what they choose to share with men (Velez Ibañez 1983: 118–119). I found that not only women but also girls have important roles as messengers, couriers, and controllers of information. Rather than sons, mothers trust their daughters with more information to deliver, and if a woman has to leave her house she will instruct her daughter on what to say if someone arrives and asks questions.

Chiñas notes that Zapotec men have formalized policing roles at fiestas that include guarding the entrances to keep out uninvited men and maintain order, but women have informal policing roles as well: "whenever a male guest, encouraged by too much *mezcal* [agave liquor] begins to behave improperly, an elderly kinswoman intervenes" (Chiñas 1973: 104). Either his aunt, grandmother, or godmother will try persuasion or the stronger measure of verbal shaming, but if he resists then she will physically push him toward the male guards and let them take over.

I observed similar behavior among Zapotec men and women at fiestas, the women cajoling or scolding the men to keep them in line. People expect women to be able to drink and maintain their composure, rather than becoming quarrelsome, aggressive, or emotional. Even though the women drank as much mezcal liquor as the men, it was the women who maintained a vigilant eye over all the fiesta proceedings. The women carefully monitored who was present, how much they drank, and their emotional states. When the women deemed it necessary, they would intervene by: serving food to sober men up, finding a place for inebriated men to lie down or walking them home, distracting or ridiculing men who were quarrelsome, and physically intervening to break up fights.

Age ranking differentiated women's roles, for girls and young women would carry information to the older women who then gave the orders on what to do next or stepped in to break up any argument or fight that erupted. People are expected to socialize and may discuss issues at fiestas, but loud arguments are definitely discouraged as inappropriate and offensive. Quarrelsome people are closely watched and forced to leave if they become difficult. In one case Chiñas observed women kin dancing a drunk man into a bedroom, getting him into a hammock, and locking him in to sleep it off until the next morning to avoid potential conflict (1973: 107).

When I asked about women breaking up fights, one man explained that people call in a man's mother or godmother to break up a fight because no man would ever think of hitting such an important woman, no matter how drunk he was. The only reason a man would strike these women, he explained, would be if the man had become *marijuanado* because some outside evildoer put marijuana in his mezcal.

The women themselves get angry, but they are less likely to become violent and threaten community solidarity since they express their anger more privately, within the family, according to Chiñas (1973: 101). What I found is that women are more likely to stick to using words, and less likely to express their anger physically. In the village I studied there was one old couple who fought fiercely, engaging in heated verbal exchanges, during which the husband would take out his old rifle and brandish it about. At that point the wife would get out her old rifle and wave it around as well. But people did not seem worried about this exceptional behavior. In their youth the old couple had both fought in the Mexican Revolution and long ago developed this rancorous interactional style. Neither ever came to serious harm, and eventually they both died at advanced ages. When I met the old woman she was still quite formidable.

The more typical way that conflict between women is expressed is through fear of the evil eye or witchcraft, both of which may be attributed by young women to old women: "evil eye beliefs differentiate women in the community, revealing points of conflict as well as support networks across generational lines" (Sault 1990: 70). In this Zapotec village "older women have the authority to tell others how to behave, to give orders, and to scold. They also have the right to ask for things, including children. . . . When a young mother says she fears the evil eye of an old woman, she is also verbalizing her discomfort about the power asymmetry in that relationship" (1990:80). Here words express women's fear, but they also become a weapon that can be used against others. According to Selby, "symbolic exchange is the major activity that creates community," by reinforcing relationships among villagers, and when people are engaged in these exchanges then neither will label the other a witch, for witchcraft is by nature an anti-social activity (Selby 1974: 128). Whether the accusation is of giving the evil eye or practicing witchcraft, in each situation the victim accuses the suspect of antisocial acts that threaten her family and the community.

From the adult women Zapotec girls learn to protect each other from men. This "esprit de corps . . . which goes beyond kinship and beyond ethnicity, allows women to cooperate in many situations" not open to men (Chiñas 1973: 111–112). In Tehuantepec Chiñas found that "women cooperate in overt nonformalized roles to protect one another from sexual aggression" (1973: 104). A woman alone is much more vulnerable, but if there is any other woman around, she can be appealed to for aid. In fact, it is not even necessary to ask for help. Zapotec women will defend others whenever the need arises.

Zapotec women will also rise to defend male as well as female members of their community against outsiders. Since the men are often away during the day, women may actually be more active in defending the community during daylight. Again, this has been observed by both Chiñas and Velez Ibañez. Chiñas argues that Zapotec "women can act aggressively toward the dominant mestizo power structure with less fear of reprisals than can men" (1973: 111). For a mestizo man to respond with force publicly might be viewed as a sign of powerlessness or cowardice. He is better off simply retreating, rather than risking a crowd of women forming to attack him.

Velez Ibañez describes how women's support networks for defense coalesced in Netzahualcoytl, where he observed several incidents in which women attacked outsiders who threatened the community: "The use of violence and confrontation was not specific to men. . . . Many daytime confrontations . . . involved women" (Velez Ibañez 1983: 119–120). He describes one incident he observed that involved "a local municipal judge, a land developer's representative, and two policemen from the municipality, who came to serve eviction papers on a lot owner" (1983: 120). The women's network notified local residents, and within minutes thirty-two women with their children gathered, accompanied by three men. The women surrounded the house lot and prevented the eviction notice from being served. When the judge, the developer's representative, or the police tried to cross the street they were blocked by about a dozen women who insulted them. Women continued to gather until forty to fifty stood together, calling the outsiders cowards and sissies. When one of the policemen advanced against the women, they picked up rocks and taunted him until "the women eventually chased the males from the street, pelting them with rocks, tearing the coat off the representative, and jabbing a stick into the anus of the judge" (1983: 120–121). Velez Ibañez goes on to describe other incidents in which women burned down the huts of mortgage payment collectors, after first looting the huts, throwing out the workers, or stripping a man and throwing him into a sewage ditch (1983: 121).

Other more recent examples of women defending their communities can be found all over Chiapas, in towns like La Realidad and Bachajón, where Mayan women have driven out soldiers of the Mexican government or armed paramilitary groups. In the 1997 Saul Landau film *The Sixth Sun,* the final scene shows Mayan women shouting at the government soldiers atop enormous tanks, using the traditional tactics of publicly shaming men for their wrongdoing in assaulting the town.

Why the Godmother? Liminality and Mediation

Up until now I have discussed the mediation roles of women in general, but the women who are godmothers to many people have preeminence. The godmother's role as a mediator in situations of conflict and violence grows out of her role as a mediator par excellence in other areas of life. The godmother is the main person who mediates on behalf of her godchild between this world and the next, combining aspects of both physical and spiritual worlds in protecting the child.

During the baptismal ceremony the godmother holds the godchild in her arms and some of her essence is transferred to the child such that: "the godparent's character and destiny become intimately connected with those of the godchild" (Sault 1985: 230). At this moment a mystical link is created between them, which gives the godmother special power to enlist supernatural protection for her godchild. She is also entrusted with the physical well-being of the child, and is expected to be knowledgeable in herbal curing. Whenever the child becomes sick the first person to be called is the godmother (not the godfather). In these ritual and healing roles godmothers share many aspects in common with midwives, shamans, and curers. Most ceremonies also involve godfathers, but their role as spiritual guardians and healers is secondary to that of the godmother. The godfather's role has more political and economic overtones. People chosen to be godparents are generally of somewhat better economic standing, but it is seen as improper to choose godparents only for financial gain, and in fact some of the people most often chosen are of quite ordinary means. They are chosen because of their traditional skills in oratory, healing, religious leadership, and mediation.

As the "second parents" to a child, the godparents have important roles in educating their godchild in village ways and traditions, and may also train the godchild in specific skills. Godparents should see to the spiritual formation of the godchildren, making sure that they receive all the sacraments of the Catholic Church, but the godparents are also asked to assist with the formal education of the godchildren if they need financial support or housing to attend junior or senior high school in another town.

At all the important moments in a child's life, the godparents are invited to be present as witnesses and advisors. When a godchild decides to marry, the godparents are immediately advised, for they are closely involved in the marriage negotiations and serve as go-betweens. At a godchild's wedding the godparents provide special gifts, including a chest, a grinding stone, and icons for the house altar. The godparents also serve as counselors to their godchildren, and will intervene if a married couple is having marital problems. The godparents are called in because their advice is taken most seriously, and they have the right to admonish or punish their godchild. When a godchild dies the godparents (or a member of their family) provide the casket or the grave clothes, depending on whether the godparent is the sponsor of baptism or confirmation (El Guindi 1986).

Being asked to sponsor is an honor for the godmother and the godfather, elevating their prestige within the community. It indicates that they are esteemed for their good character and abilities. In a general way it increases their influence in the community as a whole. People defer to the sponsors of many children, and their opinions carry more weight. They are invited to many fiestas, not only from a sense of obligation, but because their presence gives importance to the occasion. When these influential people attend a fiesta other villagers will view it as more significant and be more eager to attend also (Sault 1985: 230). At the fiestas "godparents are treated as honored guests and perform supervisory roles—giving orders to others and delegating responsibility for different tasks" (1990: 232).

When a person becomes a godmother (or godfather) their power and status in the village is enhanced because the godchild's family becomes indebted to the godparent's family. *Compadrazgo* or godparenthood is structured as an asymmetrical relationship in which the godparent occupies the superior position in relation to not only the godchild, but also the godchild's parents (El Guindi 1977: 14). A request to sponsor involves a formal petitioning ceremony in which the parents and their close kin take a candle and gifts of food, drink, and cigarettes to the prospective godparents, and in elaborate speeches the parents (and their representatives) ask that the child be sponsored as an act of charity, a favor that God will repay. Sponsorship cannot be reciprocated or reversed, so the favor can never be returned or repaid. The child's parents are forever indebted to the godparents and must always show them respect and deference.

Respectful behavior includes ritual kinship terms of address and reference in either Zapotec or Spanish, deferential greeting behavior, and visiting patterns. When the parents and children encounter the godparents on a village path or street they bow their heads, shake hands, and ask a blessing. During the feast days for *Diá de los Muertos*, or Day of the Dead, the godchildren and their parents visit the homes of the godparents to take them gifts of candles, food, drink, flowers, and cigarettes (El Guindi 1977). The parents and godchild are also expected to perform favors for the godparents and provide assistance whenever needed. They are expected to refrain from gossiping about the godparents, to support them if legal problems arise with others, and to assist in their fiestas. Godparenthood brings greater security to both the godchild and the godparents by extending their network of trusted kin who can be relied upon in times of illness, crisis, or old age (Sault 1994: 307–309).

The role of godparent is one of mediator between the forces of life and death on behalf of the godchild, and between the godchild's family and others in ritual contexts within the village. This mediatory role is recognized and honored by not only the godchild's family but others throughout the village, and it is extended to other contexts.[2] The godparents are invoked to address disputes or conflict by calming and advising people, and the godmother is asked to actively intervene and pull a man out of a fight. Note that the godmother is the ideal person to ask, because she is the last person any man can argue with, let alone strike. She has the authority of the godfather combined with the emotional power of a mother figure. The importance of her role is ritually marked in all of the village processions, for a godmother is always chosen to lead the way, bearing an incense-burner filled with smoking copal incense to purify and protect.

Changing Contexts for Harmony versus Adversarial Models

Violence within villages is intimately connected to the violence between villages, which in turn develops in a context of warfare among different political entities. This long history goes back to the Mixtec conquest of the Zapotec and later the Aztec conquest, and followed by the Spanish conquest and centuries of colonial control. The land shortage has continued for centuries, and land disputes have been endemic. But rather than serving as a nuisance to the state, centralized governments have benefited from the ongoing village conflicts and actually perpetuated them, for whenever the state steps in to resolve a conflict the state gains control. Arbitration creates dependence on the central government, which becomes the source of moral superiority that admonishes the villages to cease fighting. It is much easier to control a region that is fragmented by local conflict for then larger political alliances are precluded (Dennis 1987).

Nader's research shows that the Zapotec of Talea are all too well aware of these issues, and this is why they focus on keeping conflict within the village. When conflict spills beyond the village boundaries then Mexican government officials and lawyers take over, to everyone's loss and expense. The Zapotec of Talea use the "harmony model" of conflict resolution as a way to restrict the encroachment of external power in "a political ideology that is counter-hegemonic" (Nader 1990: 307). The local court officials of Talea "are vigilant in disputes that threaten the whole. Their tolerance for contentiousness and litigiousness is generous as long as the bounded community is protected. For this reason the communities are peaceful though not conflict free" (1990: 313).

Nader's analysis of a harmony ideology that emphasizes reconciliation applies to the village that I studied, but I would add that in addition to the village court, respect for godparents is an important instrument for maintaining a harmony ideology of resolving disputes before they spread. The problem for Zapotec villagers is that conflicts are increasing and the boundedness of villages is weakening, which is affecting women's roles as godmothers.

Since I first came to the village in 1977 the rate of change has been accelerating. Earlier there were no locks on doors, few patios had gates that closed, and crime of any sort was unusual. Only barking dogs guarded the houses and livestock. There was no market and the only transportation was a bus that arrived once in the morning and once in the evening. The only outsiders who arrived during the day were the elementary school teachers and occasional street vendors who were familiar to everyone. If a stranger entered the village, such as a visiting health officer, people noticed and commented to others so that eventually everyone found out. I soon learned that there was never any anonymity or privacy. But this also meant that the village was extremely safe at all hours of day or night.

When I visited the community in 1996 I found a dramatic change in the atmosphere of the village. Everyone has locks on their doors, and many have iron gates to secure their house patios. Buses enter the village several times a day, and a few young men have cars used as taxis. This is very convenient for travel to and from the city, but it means that outsiders are more prevalent. Outsiders are renting or buying property and living in the village. Meanwhile, more of the village's youth have left to work in Oaxaca City or Mexico City, and even more have migrated to the United States to work. People complain about the presence of outsiders, and the ways in which living in the United States has influenced those who have returned to the village. Robbery and assault are much more common.

In particular, one incident stands out. Every year for the patron saint's fiesta a modern band, or *conjunto*, plays tropical music in front of the town hall. In the past this dance was open for all the villagers to come and watch. Men, women, and children all attended, standing around on the edges of the basketball court that was transformed into a dance floor. Those who wished to dance paid a small fee to buy a ticket and dance all night. It was an exciting and happy event for dancers and onlookers alike. But now all this has changed. The dance floor is surrounded with cyclone fencing and plastic sheeting to screen it out from public view, so that only those who pay can watch the band or the dancers. The one narrow entrance into the dance area is posted with numerous guards and ticket prices were 35 pesos, quite a large amount when a day's salary in Oaxaca City was 27 pesos. Now the bands blast rock music from a stage high above the dance floor, shimmering with electric light shows. When I complained about the changes a woman explained that the dances became too dangerous and village officials could not control the problems. There were many increasingly violent young men from other villages coming to attend the fiesta. She blamed their violence on the drugs they use after living in the United States. The dance is no longer a community function. It has become an exclusive event screened off for those younger people who can afford the high price of a ticket.

This incident reveals an increasing fragmentation in this small village as out-migration and in-migration increase and the mass media and schools teach that the source of knowledge and meaning lie beyond the village in the city. Back in the early 1970s, Selby heard people in another village complain that "the children have no respect or manners any more and that it is impossible to teach them because they listen too much to the schoolteachers . . . they don't even know how to say 'hello' to their godfathers any more" (Selby 1974: 4). I have heard the same complaints in the past, but imagine what people are saying now!

In other areas of Oaxaca it has been noted that "the separation of religious from civil hierarchies in indigenous communities and the increasing secularization of for-mal political decision making" have meant that "women lost their most formal re-maining link to institutional community politics" (Stephen 1991: 159). While the re-quirement for religious service was dropped, new requirements for fluency in Spanish and experience with state bureaucrats have become the new basis for selec-tion to community political posts, which eliminates most women from consideration. What were formerly the responsibilities of women fiesta sponsors, or *mayordomias*, are now taken over by male officers in the civil hierarchy. Under the old civil-religious ranked system of offices, political authority was "rooted in age, ritual ex-perience, and community service. Under this system, ritual and politics were inte-grated entities. Respect and authority that stemmed from ritual were readily transfer-able to politics" (1991: 160). This gave women a source of ritual authority that flowed into political influence. According to Stephen, now that the fiesta sponsor-ship of *mayordomos* has weakened, the main source of ritual authority for women is sponsorship of life-cycle rituals as godmothers.

This has also been the pattern for the village where I worked, but the more recent trend I see is the weakening even of life-cycle sponsorship for women, and for men as well. The larger political and economic problems of the Mexican nation impinge upon this small village in terms of land scarcity, inflation, tax increases, unemploy-ment, fear of violence, religious conversion to Protestantism, and population move-ments. All this has contributed to the instability of the village, and undermined the traditional authority of both godfathers and godmothers. At a big rock event that is screened off from the public there is no role for godmothers to intervene on behalf of community values, since older women are no longer able to attend as part of the au-dience.

What appears to be occurring is a basic shift in the way people perceive and re-spond to conflict and violence. According to Nader, "changes from harmony to con-frontational or adversarial law models and back have been documented by historians for a number of societies" (1990: 304). She cites Kagan's work on Castilian courts in which he argues "that with geographic mobility and fragmentation of the primary group came an increase in the number and types of disputes, which could not ade-quately be resolved by the informal mechanisms of conciliation and compromise.

The adversary process and style were henceforth used as a political and economic legal strategy" (1990: 304–305).

The evidence suggests that the harmony ideology of Zapotec communites supports a strong role for godmothers as mediators who uphold community values and resolve problems before they reach the courts, but in a changing system where an adversarial model of competing individual interests is promoted, the godmother's role is severely undercut. Godparenthood ties are diminished by the flux in population, as both godchildren and godparents leave the community either temporarily or permanently and create sponsorship ties elsewhere. But even within the village, the godmother's ritual authority no longer carries over into the political sphere with the same strength as in the past.

Conclusion

Much of the literature on violence and conflict resolution has been dominated by psychologists, political scientists, historians, or ethologists. When anthropologists have looked at these issues, the focus is usually on men engaged in intergroup violence such as feuding and warfare. In these descriptions women are usually onlookers or victims, either silent or weeping. Although there is now more research on violence against women, such as rape and battery, the example of the Zapotec shows that women can be more than victims or spectators. Because the Zapotec have social institutions that create a sense of local community and personal responsibility, women can actively intervene in male-to-male conflict to restore order and they can effectively prevent male aggression against women through female solidarity. Yet these roles are currently being undercut by changes in social institutions, community identity, and personal responsibility to redefine gender roles and women's power. As ritual roles are replaced by secular offices, godmothers will find it increasingly difficult to intervene and offer protection or mediation to others in their community.

Notes

1. According to Chiñas, "the phenomenon of machismo, so often cited as a male characteristic in Latin American cultures, seems to be largely absent in intragroup relations in Zapotec culture. Where such behavior is evident, it is negatively sanctioned. A man who acts muy macho is derided as an overbearing bully, and a woman who mistreats or takes advantage of one weaker than she, is similarly criticized (for example, a mother who strikes her child)" (Chiñas 1973: 111).

2. According to Selby, if a conflict continues, the godfather is called in to settle the dispute and prevent it from expanding and disrupting other relationships (1974: 48).

References

Chiñas, Beverly. (1973). *The Isthmus Zapotecs: Women's Roles in Cultural Context.* New York: Holt, Rinehart, and Winston.

Dennis, Phillip. (1987). *Inter-village Conflict in Oaxaca.* New Brunswick, New Jersey: Rutgers University Press.

El Guindi, Fadwa. (1977). Lore and structure: Todos santos in the Zapotec system. *Journal of Latin American Lore* 3: 3–18.

———. (1986). *The Myth of Ritual: A Native's Ethnography of Zapotec Life-Crisis Rituals.* Tucson: University of Arizona Press.

Landau, Saul. (1997). *The Sixth Sun: Mayan Uprising in Chiapas.* Meridian Productions.

Nader, Laura. (1990). *Harmony Ideology: Justice and Control in a Zapotec Mountain Village.* Stanford: Stanford University Press.

Pader, Ellen J. (1993). Spatiality and social change: Domestic space use in Mexico and the United States. *American Ethnologist* 20: 114–137.

Sault, Nicole. (1985). Baptismal sponsorship as a source of power for Zapotec women in Oaxaca, Mexico. *Journal of Latin American Lore* 11: 225–243.

———. (1990). The evil eye, both hot and dry: Gender and generation among the Zapotec of Mexico. *Journal of Latin American Lore* 16: 69–89.

———. (1994). How the body shapes parenthood: Surrogate mothers in the United States and godmothers in Mexico. In *Many Mirrors: Body Image and Social Relations,* edited by Nicole Sault. New Brunswick, New Jersey: Rutgers University Press.

Selby, Henry. (1974). *Zapotec Deviance: The Convergence of Folk and Modern Sociology.* Austin: University of Texas Press.

Stephen, Lynn. (1991). *Zapotec Women.* Austin: University of Texas Press.

Sung, Betty Lee. (1985). Bicultural conflict. *Journal of Comparative Family Studies.*

Velez Ibañez, Carlos. (1983). *Rituals of Marginality: Politics, Process, and Culture Change in urban Central Mexico, 1969–1974.* Berkeley: University of California Press.

Wolf, Eric. (1966). *Peasants.* Englewood Cliffs, New Jersey: Prentice-Hall.

Chapter X

Honor and Violence in a Brazilian Slum: Gendered Checks and Balances in the Politics of Everyday Life

Claudia Fonseca

The Research Setting

Based on two years of ethnography in a sub-proletarian squatters' settlement, I examine how, in the absence of any influence from the formal law system, the code of honor establishes an uneasy balance in social relations. Considering the expected behavior according to sex and generation, we look in particular at the way in which "reputation" provides a certain protection, thereby conferring no little weight to female gossip, pitted against male brute strength.

In the analysis of a group of urban poor, violence, considered in the light of the notion of "honor," appears as a constitutive element of the social order. Violence in this group is not a "spontaneous" reactive impulse. It is undeniably linked to economic and political discrimination to which the poor have been submitted for generations. However, to reduce the phenomenon to such a deterministic dimension, to see it as merely the residual product of dominant society, is to overlook the fundamental creativity—even in the most adverse conditions—of human culture. I propose, therefore, to look into the "internal" mechanisms that attribute a meaning and regulate the use of physical violence in an urban squatter settlement in the south of Brazil.

Our commentaries are based on ethnographic field research carried out in the early 1980s in a settlement of around 750 squatters—Vila do Cachorro Sentado (Sitting Dog Vila)—planted in the middle of a middle class neighborhood about seven kilometers from downtown Porto Alegre (approximately 1,000,000 inhabitants), the southernmost state capital in Brazil. The terrain, belonging to a neighboring state mental hospital, has been alternately occupied by and then cleared of squatters two or three times during the past three decades. While some are rural migrants, most of the vila dwellers have long acquaintance with urban living. Of mixed ethnic origin—including Italians, Portuguese, German, Polish, native Indian, but principally black African—the adult men, mostly illiterate, earn their living as rag pickers, junk dealers, night watchmen, handymen, and occasionally as construction workers. The women, when they are employed, are usually cleaning ladies. Often, the young men complement their earning through theft, and the women of all ages engage in episodic begging.

It is hard, impossible even, to maintain any sort of privacy in this teeming settlement wherein mingle seven to eight hundred people in a lot which measures little more than a football field. The tiny one- and two-room shacks are not designed to shut people in, and, particularly in summer, the front doors close only at nighttime, when dwellers are inside at rest.

Most people have few daily engagements outside the vila and spend their days at the vila's informal gathering places: women wash their clothes at the vila's single public spigot, men squat in front of the general store sipping the traditional *chimarrão* (tea in a gourd). On the main dirt-covered road, just wide enough for a small truck, children play soccer, or putter with homemade go-carts. Here, anonymity is totally out of the question. Knotted paths may change shape—with a new house sprouting up here, an old shack torn down there—witnessing incessant additions and transformations. But the changes stay within the limits of the familiar world. Newcomers are usually brought in by a friend or relative already living in the area. Even people who move away seem to follow a predictable circuit, moving to neighborhoods where other ex-residents of the vila have preceded them, and then back again.

Hand in hand with the intense social activity, comes a functional interdependence between neighbors. Legal access to water is the privilege of a handful of residents who live along the front edge of the vila, near the highway. Other residents manage the money and know-how to tap the main lines, providing pirated services to their own homes and, often at an exorbitant rate, to nearby "clients." The dispute for the internal regulation of these vital commodities is inevitable and unending since only the very few can get along without depending on neighbors.

Despite its poverty, this group, should not be considered "marginal." The neighborhood residents participate fully in an urban economy, acting within the informal sector of the economy as well as occasionally being employed. Vila residents are fully conscious of the fact that, because of their miserable living conditions, their low level of education, and the irregular or even shady character of their economic activities, they are considered by the dominant sectors as repugnant dregs of society. However, this group has grown used to a certain symbolic autonomy—not only because they are "excluded" from the conventional system of prestige, but also because they live in a small, well-delineated enclave, shut in by walls built by cautious middle-class neighbors whose back yards would otherwise give onto the vast "empty" lot. In this relative autonomy, where formal law has very little influence, violence plays a key role in maintaining order.

Honor

I have adopted the concept of honor as defined by Pitt-Rivers, one of the pioneers in this line of investigation: "the nexus between the ideals of a society and their reproduction in the individual through his aspiration to personify them" (1977: 1). The discussion will develop along two analytical axes: one emphasizes the function of the individual psyche, personal pride, and the effort to ennoble one's self-image through socially established norms; the other focuses on a code for social interaction where personal pride is bargained as the fundamental symbolic item of exchange. The notion of honor may seem somewhat out of place in this analysis of urban poor. However, Pitt-Rivers allows for this sort of possibility, affirming that the question of honor tends to stand out among brigands as well as aristocrats—there where "might makes right," where people are *outside* and not necessarily *above* a central law.

The vila residents enjoy close ties with friends and relatives in other urban neighborhoods with more of less the same profile. The upper classes, however, hardly ever penetrate into their space. Brazilian social workers are few and overworked, with little time or disposition to make "home visits." In fact, aside from two Catholic-sister volunteer workers from the local parish and a stray university student doing social sciences research, representatives from the mainstream society simply avoid the vila. Several residents claim that their better-off cousins refuse to set foot in the place, others admit that they are ashamed to give their address to friends. Truck drivers refuse to enter the vila to make deliveries since the local youth find it great sport to jump on the moving vehicle in order to carry off merchandise (beer and soft drinks are a preferred target.) Thus, despite their ties to global society, this group remains relatively isolated.

Here, mechanisms of social control have little to do with those witnessed in the dominant sectors of society. It is inconceivable for a vila resident to go to the police for protection against his neighbor. The avoidance of theft or bodily harm is each man's own affair. According to a young woman who, after leaving the vila, began to date a police-man, the Vila do Cachorro Sentado is referred to by the police as "The Lawless Vila" (*A Vila Sem Lei*). The strong men of the group are those who are able to impose their will on others, either through physical violence, or through financial holds, such that there emerges a political pyramid with shopkeepers, armed men, and young delinquents at the top, and with the old and timid, as well as women in general, at the bottom. This political order does not, however, function mechanically. For, as we will see, to redress the bal-ance of power, the meek may resort to the language of symbolic exchange, using the code of honor, and thereby neutralize the advantage others hold over them.

Personal Pride

Men and their honor

A young bachelor's major strategy for bolstering his public image is to accentuate quali-ties of *bravura*, virility, and generosity. *Bravura* in a form of courage—the courage nec-essary, for example, to kill a formidable adversary, to save a mate in danger, or to resist police torture rather than inform on friends. It is a masculine form of solidarity not far removed from that known to the military ranks. Virility comes into light especially with regard to sexual conquests. A young man's reputation also includes social virtues such as a love for children and generosity. During periodic potlatch-type binges, these young men, each time they fall into some money, manage to spend great sums in very little time. Take, for example, the case of Juarez, eighteen, just after receiving the equivalent of 400 dollars for wooden planks he stole from a construction site. Arriving at the house of Dana, full of wine, Coca-Cola and other delicacies, he ostentatiously offered presents to each new arrival. To Dona Maria, an elderly lady reputed to have curative powers, he offered money to include him in her prayers; to me, he offered money ("to pay your taxi home"), and then he started organizing a barbecue for the following day. Exactly because these young people possess no palpable marks of prestige—children, wife, car, or di-ploma—they appear to be constantly exaggerating their own personal virtues.

A married man affirms his virility by fulfilling his role as husband and father. In the first place, he should be a good provider. How he does this is nobody's business. For ex-ample, the professional thieves—all of them younger than twenty-five—are known but seldom criticized for their livelihood. "I have nothing against the *maconheiro*s" (literally, marijuana-users), claims Rosalina, mother, mother-in-law, and wife of solid job-holders. "They carry on their activity elsewhere. It's none of my business." Solange, a mother of four who just established a relationship with a young thief, praises her new husband's qualities:

My ex-husband, father of my children, was very refined, well-educated, but he never had a job. What good is a cute husband when you're dying of hunger? I was the one who had to work. My new man won't let me work. He says, 'You have everything you need—a house, food and clothes. Why would you want to work?' When we moved into the new house, I complained because we had no table. He went out and a couple of hours later, came back with a table as well as extra cash. He's very smart. My former husband, despite all his education, wasn't nearly as smart.

The woman who has a job humiliates her husband, bringing to public attention the fact that he can't support her. The problem is that most men in the vila, especially the young ones, have access only to irregular and badly paid jobs. To support a family demands aggressiveness. Obviously, it is not by making polite inquiries that one finds a job; nor is it by earning a minimum salary that a man can expect to support his wife and children. (On the average, the wives of *maconheiros* live slightly better than the wives of young unskilled laborers.) Aside from a handful of older men, the salaried workers' families live on the limits of misery, with, literally, a gnawing hole in their stomachs. Living with this sort of "failure" undermines one of the fundamental bases of a man's social identity. The fact that many husbands and fathers are confronted with the same dilemma helps to create a certain solidarity through which men band together, scorning their family obligation, to drink away the little money otherwise earmarked for the family's welfare. Self-disgust (due to the inability to fulfill family obligations) is thus redirected toward the source of humiliation (women and children) and, in part, is counterbalanced by the prestige associated with generosity among friends.

In the second place, a married man should demonstrate sufficient *bravura* to protect the women of his family from aggression. Since it goes without saying that unaccompanied ladies will be accosted by the local youth, potential aggressors are never lacking. By supposing thus, married men flatter their young rivals and at the same time increase their own prestige as protectors of the homes. But, protection slips surreptitiously into control over female sexuality. Since legal marriages are extremely rare, a man's rights over his wife are established by, and last only as long as, their cohabitation. A woman thus "married" owes her spouse strict fidelity. Transgressions occur but the risk of brutal punishment (tolerated if not encouraged by public opinion) is so great that they are held at a minimum.

Whereas a husband concentrates a good part of his energy on the control of his wife's sexuality, a woman's brother or father sees his as a primarily protective role. However, even *this* protection involves no small measure of male rivalry. In every one of the paternally headed families, the adolescent girl had to run away from home to be married since her father never approved of her beau. (The elopement relied in general on the mother's complicity.) It would appear that the father's opposition depends neither on the age nor the choice of mate, but rather on the principle of masculine pride: he could not peaceably cede his daughter to another man. After a girl leaves home, the rivalry between males may act in favor of women since it discourages alliances between a husband and his in-laws. Once a woman "marries," her father and brothers are no longer responsible for her sexual behavior. Their major role becomes that of protection against potential aggressors, including her husband.

Honor among women

There is no particular notion of honor linked to single women. Whereas a man's public image is indexed by several activities (sex, bravery, family, occupation), a woman's revolves around a single area—that of female domestic tasks. She must be a devoted mother and a good housekeeper. The criticisms I usually hear of women go something like this: "My brother was right to leave that girl—she was so negligent, her baby died before it was a month old." And the defense runs along the same lines: "My mother-in-law says I don't deserve my husband because I don't take care of him as I should. But his clothes are always clean, his meals always hot, and the baby is well cared-for. What else does she want?"

A woman who lives with her parents may be praised because of her love of children, the help she gives to her mother, and the like, but she will never be fully recognized until she has her own home—a feat accomplished either by getting married or by having a baby. An unwed mother or divorcee may rely on her motherly virtues to bolster her public image, swearing that she'll never remarry because it wouldn't be good for the children. (Since it is a biological father's role to support his children, a woman's second spouse would be considered a fool to support her children by a previous marriage; consequently he usually pressures his wife to farm her children out to a grandmother, godmother or willing neighbor.) However, in fact, women seldom stay single for long; the overwhelming majority of divorced women remarry, perhaps even several times.

One may easily imagine that this behavior has more to do with material survival than questions of honor or prestige. The sexual division of labor, according to which men go out to work and women stay to care for the home, theoretically permits a rational organization of activities necessary for social and biological reproduction. But, strangely enough, single working women, even those with many children, often seem to have a higher standard of living than many of their married neighbors. Because these women control the family income, they needn't worry about wheedling money from the husband, or chiding him to keep a regular job. Why then remarry? By remarriage, a woman has the hope not only of receiving some affection, but also of raising her status. One always suspects that a single woman has no man because she wasn't able to get one. Furthermore, a husbandless woman is a thorn in the side of the community—a challenge to male virility and an object of constant female jealousy. A husband to neutralize the woman's sexuality nicely settles the affair. Furthermore, if the man has recognized virtues, these will enhance his wife's status still more.

People do not generally criticize women for their sexual past; their virtue concerns others only when it begins to threaten the domestic peace of a neighbor. The few times I heard that a woman had been called a whore or wanton slut by some neighbor, it was gossip carried through someone from outside the vila: the Catholic sister or a student volunteer. Otherwise, the commentaries I heard were much more moderate. For example, Eli, the only professional prostitute who lived in the area, a comely and prosperous mother of four, was well spoken of by her neighbors. She, as did other single women, took great care not to provoke the jealousy of her neighbors: "I never have anything to do with the men here. I don't even go to the dances. They [the other women] can say nothing against me." In another example, we see how sexual flaws are minimized in relation to other female qualities:

My ex-husband's lawyer came after me with a bunch of accusations. And I said, yes, it's true—I've done this, and that. So what? Ask the neighbors: who pays for my children's food? I've sold lettuces on the street corner, I've begged from door to door at the bourgeois houses there on the hill, to put a roof on my house, I carried tiles from downtown to here in the vila— on my back! And I did it all for my kids. So! No one can say anything against me.

Nonetheless, jealous wives demand a minimum modesty from the women in the vila. The only girl I knew who regularly transgressed the norm of female modesty was known as "loony Regina" (*Regina a louca*). She strolled the streets in short shorts "half naked"; she openly expressed her sexual desires to certain of the men; and was once surprised in *flagrant delit* with a married man from the neighborhood. I was present one day when she began to taunt Seu João, a highly respected leader in the zone: "People say your wife is going to leave you because you can't get it up." Her sister-in-law, standing nearby, immediately covered up, declaring: "You know she's half off her rocker." "Not just half," responded Seu João. And then, reestablishing the norm: "Anyhow, you know she's lying. My wife never speaks of our private life to anyone." The young women her age all avoided Regina, calling her "nauseous," but her greatest punishment, the worst imaginable, was to remain single—because no man in the vila wanted to be associated with her.

The Social Dimension of Honor

Up to this point, we have considered the values that constitute personal pride: the individual honor of different social categories. Keeping in mind that honor straddles the two domains—individual psyches (self-image) and social interaction (the system of conduct)—it is now possible to look at the specifically social dimension of honor and the way it functions as a code of conduct regulating the network of social relations and guarantees group coherence.

"Group coherence" by no means implies that the vila's residents live in happy harmony nor that they share all the same values. On the contrary, we found there clear divisions along the lines of morality. For example, while certain people would never engage in theft, the moment a policeman enters the area, looking for one of the local *maconheiros*, a web of complicity springs up among nearly all members of the community. Although different individuals may have different values, the social isolation imposed from without as well as the need for daily exchanges within the vila obliges people to recognize a code of interaction permitting the unraveling of everyday activities.

The importance of physical clout

Women as well as men brag about their physical prowess and take apparent glee in recounting exploits in vivid detail. For example, one woman gloats about having battered another: "I may be little, but you better not mess with me." And some may even brag about winning out over men: for example, to explain why she keeps an iron bar behind the counter, Dora (wife of the local merchant), describes how the last customer to make a pass at her ended up with a badly broken arm. An ex-prostitute, barely twenty, proudly describes how she wielded a razor to slash a client's face when he tried to force her to do more than she had agreed on. Stories on such themes are told and retold in the gossip circles. Those who witnessed a Saturday night fistfight will joke about it: "I had a front-row seat." And one girl, describing the fracas of the previous night, lamented, "There were three fights going on at once. I kept running back and forth to take it all in, and ended up missing them all!" Another woman comments on the dispute simmering between two neighbors: "I'd pay to see that fight when it breaks out!" Although very young children may possibly be frightened, their older brothers and sisters quickly enter into the spirit of the game. Two young informants, eight and nine years old, glitter with emotion as they tell me how Nina, the sister of one, had broken a bottle on the chest of an aged relative, and how Dione, the other's sister-in-law, had landed two good blows on her husband's chin.

In the vila, because of physical proximity as well as patterns of intense sociability, spectators are ever-present, but they hardly ever interfere in a fight. A storekeeper who let the retreating loser of a rather rough fistfight take refuge in his shop was severely criticized by his neighbors: "We won't go there anymore to buy our groceries!" When a group of men, sharing an afternoon beer in front of a tiny corner bar, discover that the screams they heard on the previous night came from a local youth, roughed up by his cronies during a neighborhood dance, they shrug : "Who in his right mind would go out to investigate what was happening? Anyhow, if he didn't want to get beat up, he should have stayed home. Nobody made him go to the dance."

Manifestly, violence is among the socially acceptable manners to resolve conflicts. However, the fact that we underline physical force as an important element in the vila's social organization by no means implies that we are dealing with a "less civilized" or "more natural" form of social life. There exist specific cultural limits to the exercise of violence and those who break these limits suffer severe sanctions. Murder, as far as I could see, is never approved of. There are two big families in the vila, linked by marriage. When a youth in one family killed an adolescent from the other, the conditions were perfect for a sort of Mediterranean vendetta. Nothing of the sort occurred, however. The killer's parents simply closed their store for a couple of months, an act interpreted by the community as penitence, and then things went back to normal. Other people accused of murder (a woman who supposedly poisoned her husband's lover, an adolescent who stabbed his neighbor because of an off-color joke) left the vila because of the pressure. Another storekeeper whose son nearly killed a friend, one of the local boys, sold his store and left the vila the day after "the accident." Assured that the victim had not died, the aggressor's father started a campaign to clear his name: the wounded boy was a *maconheiro* who had tried to hold up his store. Three weeks later, the man was back in the vila with his store now on a different corner.

According to the norm, children and pregnant women are definitely off limits. The respect for this taboo marks the limits between the vila's young bandits and outside aggressors who respect no limits. People are quick to remind you, "The police don't respect anyone—not even babies and pregnant women!" Of course, it happens that parents (particularly the mother) administer a heavy-handed beating to their child. Such episodes represent the rare occasions on which neighbors (particularly those who are family relations) will interfere—particularly if it appears that the father or mother is getting carried away. A wife who wants to leave her husband will receive general encouragement if she can persuade people he's battered her during a pregnancy. On the other hand, if she isn't pregnant, she will probably be considered capable of defending herself.

The importance of physical violence in daily life gives a distinct advantage to the *maconheiros* over other members of the community, and to the men over other members of their household. Let us now look into the tactics that permit the "disadvantaged" to redress the imbalance of power.

The neutralization of physical force

Whereas the *maconheiros* may be useful as protection against *outside* aggressors, they represent a threat that must be controlled within the community. Early on in the project, I discovered that vila dwellers were divided into two sorts: those who lived in fear and continually complained of the "dangerous elements" in the neighborhood, and those who had no complaints. The latter felt "respected." The former did not, and with cause, for they suffered near-daily aggressions: a child sent out to buy bread would be accosted and "lose" his money, a chicken coop would be found empty, a door forced open and the gas bottle stolen. One woman even had her roof carried off while she slept. Although the police might eventually be summoned to settle a conjugal spat, no one would think of calling them in for defense against the *maconheiros*.

Respeito, the native term closest to "honor," normally appeared in the form of a transitive verb, to describe the manner a person treated another, but rarely mutually. In 90 percent of the cases registered in my field notes, the subject of the verb clearly had superior status and "to respect" an inferior meant not cashing in on this advantage.

So, how is it exactly that a vila resident can guarantee respect?

To answer this question, we should take a look at the vila's leading personalities, men whom the *maconheiros* are supposed to respect. Mikika, an authoritarian father of twelve, including several adult boys, is the owner of a small bar. Atanajildo is the owner of the most prosperous general store in the vila. Also, as a junkyard owner, he is the vila's biggest employer. João, a night watchman who hopes to be president of the new resident association, struts up and down the main road with a revolver tucked ostentatiously in his belt. They are all heads of relatively stable households, in possession of several of the conventional marks of prestige. But all this does not explain their importance in the community. There are, for example, storekeepers who have been assaulted five times in a single year; others, such as Atanajildo or João, have never been bothered. The truth is that, aside from conventional prestige, Mikika, Atanajildo, and João have other qualities. First of all, they are all literally big men who, through looks and gestures, make it clear they are not easily pushed around. They let it be known they have guns and wouldn't hesitate to use them.

One would never say that these important men are respected; rather, "they demand respect." In this case, the respectful attitude of the *maconheiros* implies more than a simple abstention of the use of violence; if the process stopped there, nothing would guarantee cohesion of the social fabric. The element that creates an active bond between the *maconheiros* and the vila's leaders is well known to the less powerful residents for it is what they themselves give in exchange for the *maconheiros'* respect: homage. One pays homage to the local leaders by accepting them as mediators between the vila and municipal authorities, by responding to their plea for community works (flattening the road, digging a sewer); Atanajildo's prestige was, for example, considerably increased when he agreed to dig the foundations of a new community center. Paying homage to the *maconheiros* involves a bit more subtlety.

In order to study this aspect of the social code, it would be useful to compare two families that, despite the two heads' similar status (as salaried workers), have completely different relationships with the group of *maconheiros*. Seu Jorge was attacked in broad daylight as he returned home, with his wife on his arm, after receiving his week's pay. This was but one of the many episodes of harassment his family underwent at the hands of the *maconheiros*. Seu Elpídio, on the contrary, can arrive drunk at two in the morning, with his paycheck practically falling from his pocket, and not a soul touches him. One woman's commentary, that "the hoodlums attack Seu Jorge because they're cowards and know he's not a fighting man," only partially explains the issue, since Seu Elpídio is not a fighting man, either.

Here we come to a major observation: vila residents' interactions are regulated by a code of honor in which physical violence and homage are the principal moneys of exchange. Seu Elpídio and the members of his family, like other vila residents who want to live in peace, curry the favor of the *maconheiros*. One may do this by offering small gifts or services. An older resident tells of a time when the *maconheiros* would knock on people's doors in the middle of the night demanding money, but nowadays they request only small services: a drink of water, a plate of food, cigarettes. The repercussions of these little offerings are sized up by local families and most try to integrate themselves into the "circuit of exchange" as soon as possible.

Are these acts of extortion, pure and simple? The situation is not all that simple, for what the *maconheiros* really appear to be after, more than little favors, is public recognition, the validation of a positive self-image. First of all, people do refuse their requests. One old lady shows me where she hid her cigarettes after the boys came by for the fourth time asking for a smoke: "I just told them I was out of them." An old man who doesn't want to lend them his horse simply claims the nag is lame. It is the spirit of the gift (or refusal) that counts. Begrudged offerings bring no benefits whatsoever. Seu Elpídio's wife, when she described how she helped the "poor boys," would always emphasize her non-material gifts. "I give them advice. Some of them claim I do more for them than their own mothers." In all the households which participate in these exchanges, I would regularly hear praises of the local youth: "So and so is a fine person, generous, hard-working." The ultimate importance of all these gestures is summed up by Solange when she states: "I get along well with the *maconheiros*. I have no quarrel with them and I don't put on airs as do some people around here."

In fact, the symbolic value of homage is worth more than many a material gift. The young people, contrary to the leading personalities, enjoy no conventional marks of prestige. Feeling vulnerable, they endeavor to raise their status according to other criteria. What they can offer as their contribution to the circuit of exchange is personal protection. "No one dares touch a hair on the head of Seu Elpídio's girls," brags one young man, "because they know they'd have me to answer to." This sort of relation contributes to the positive self-image of the *maconheiros*. Ironically, it is exactly the constant threat of violence, associated with the young men, that makes their protection—their respect—so valuable.

But the supreme homage that anyone can pay these youth, the ultimate proof of their acceptance, is to permit them access to the girls in the family. Thus, Seu Elpídio's three girls, aged fifteen, twelve, and nine, were in more or less permanent contact with the *maconheiros*. If no romance blossomed between them, it is probably because the girls considered the fellows more as brothers than as lovers. However, Solange, Elpídio's daughter by a previous marriage, who had lived in the vila for a year and a half with her husband and their children, left her husband shortly before the end of my field research to live with a *maconheiro* she had met in her father's house. On the other hand, it is significant that Seu Jorge, victim of constant harassment, keeps his twelve-year-old daughter practically under lock and key at home. A serious sixth-grader (practically the most advanced student in the vila), she never participates in the street-side circles of sociability; nor do the *maconheiros* cross her doorstep. Another woman, a single mother whose teenage daughter was highly educated, a high school student, left the neighborhood within a year, explaining her departure thus: "It's impossible to give a daughter a decent upbringing in such a place."

In their demand for recognition, the young men will not tolerate being ignored as potential husbands. Couples whose children are still very young can enter into the exchange circuit, making symbolic offerings to the gang, without compromising their own upward aspirations. However, families with adolescent girls are obliged to let them circulate in the local "marriage market" lest they want to offend the available bachelors. Since this sort of participation, together with the possibility of creating family ties with a *maconheiro*, put their projects for upward mobility in risk, many couples prefer to leave the vila rather than to capitulate to its "code."

Gossip

In the same way that the word "respect" reveals the role of physical force in the network of symbolic exchanges, another word, heard everywhere in the mouth of women, gives us insight as to the female counterpart of male violence: *fofoca*, or gossip.

People say:

> "So-and-so left the neighborhood because of the fofoca."

> "I don't visit the neighbors because I don't want to get mixed up in the local fofoca."

> "My husband lost his job because of some fofoca his colleague spread about him."

Gossip includes the narratives about the real or imagined behavior of others. It is always seen as negative, designed to harm specific individuals. No one considers himself a gossip (*fofoqueiro*), but everyone agrees, gossip is a constant and all-pervasive presence in the neighborhood.

From the researcher's point of view, gossip has positive functions in this setting: it creates a sort of social history of the group. Thus, the anecdotes about murder, conjugal infidelity, and so on, constitute a sort of historical corpus with which the residents identify. Furthermore, gossip helps define the limits of the group—you don't gossip, after all, about outsiders because they are not submitted to the same norm. To be the object, as well as the perpetrator, of gossip are both ways of being integrated into the group. Handman (1983), in her study of violence and wiliness (*ruse*) in a Greek village, underlines the educational aspect of gossip. Adults do not teach their children morality through any sort of didactic lectures. It is rather through gossip that the young pick up nuances about the group's moral principles. Hannerz (1967), in his study of an urban black community in the United States, suggests that gossip may be an important element in the communication system, especially among the illiterate. It is thus that one discovers the new address of a lost cousin, the whereabouts of old friends, places to avoid, and good deals. Finally, gossip builds and destroys reputations, furnishing information about the local residents. It is here that gossip meets up with honor, for what else is "reputation" if not one's public self-image?

Reputation: Gossip as counterbalance to physical force

Certainly, one's reputation has very serious consequences when up against "external agents." It has great influence on the police reports that decide what to do with a child picked up for vagrancy, or with a teenager on his first arrest—his good reputation may be a deciding factor. Within the vila limits, it also plays a fundamental role. As suggested above, a man's pride depends on public recognition of his courage, virility, and generosity; a woman's pride depends on the recognition of her maternal achievements and housekeeping. To besmirch a person's name, referring to one or another of these attributes, strikes at a person's core. It is as though the words that shape his public image had the magic power to wound him physically.

This perspective brings out a female form of power since, although men have the upper hand in terms of violence, women have the power to make or break a man's reputation. Here, we are not referring to the passive process by which, in certain Mediterranean societies, a woman's virtue is the pivot of her male relatives' honor, but rather to the very active role women play in spreading gossip. Their role is all the more important because, according to masculine dictates, a modest fellow should not toot his own horn. On the contrary, a man is likely to kid about his own defects: his laziness, his wild spending, his irresponsibility—exactly because his wife's (or sister's) role is to contradict him—to affirm he is a hard worker, a generous husband, a responsible father.

Women are supposed to gossip, not men. A gossipy man is looked down upon. The virile form of criticism is through direct confrontation, and woe to the unfortunate fellow who does not have the brawn to back up his insults. For a woman to insult someone stronger, she would either have to be crazy (like an old "witch" who refers to most of her female neighbors as "that whore") or else well protected by influential friends. The wife of the vila's largest store owner, also president of the neighborhood association, is the only woman I ever saw criticize a *maconheiro*—and she had a hunting rifle to back up her insults!

Whereas a man imposes his will though brute strength, a woman imposes hers by manipulating (or threatening to manipulate) public opinion. Moema, distressed by the fact that her husband was hanging out with the *maconheiros*, waged a slur campaign against the local gang. Dora, a betrayed wife dared not criticize her husband, but she did everything she could to mobilize public opinion against her rival. Jane, trying to recover her child who long since was living with a foster mother, set in motion rumors that the foster mother was unloving and incompetent. Ciça whose husband had blackened her eye for the first time in ten years, made a point of showing her bruises to the whole block. Adão, roughed up by his son, did likewise. It is, however, a delicate balance between the gossip of the meek and the potential clout of the strong.

The gossiping woman must not go beyond permitted limits. She can be pretty sure that what she says will reach her victim's ears. Often it is even within a person's design to thus aim indirect insults of more or less recognized origin at an erstwhile enemy—and, in this respect, the local network of communication is most obliging. But, just to play it safe, it is best to play up the inherent vagueness of gossip. A gossip drops hints and lets the public draw its own conclusions. For example, no one will say "So and so is a thief." Rather, they will leave a sentence dangling in the middle: "People say that fellow hangs out with those who...," completing the phrase with a furtive gesture suggesting theft. (Such insinuations, after all, are not necessarily harmful unless they are made around "outsiders" who might call in the police.) One of the gossip's favorite tactics is to damage another person's public image by donning him with a nickname. Contrary to the self-styled nicknames chosen by the young men themselves, these names are always pejorative, not necessarily by their objective contents, but certainly by the mocking tones with which they are applied.

Whereas reputation is important for a man, it is crucial for a woman. Reputation defines the upright citizens of the neighborhood—those who are worthy of being included in the networks of mutual aid and protection. The exclusion from community networks is one of the worst punishments one can inflict on a woman. A cranky old lady who complained incessantly about the "bandits," and who had been more than once to the police with accusations against her neighbors, was branded a witch with the death of several babies to her account. Although feeble and often entirely alone, the neighbors gave her no help; on the contrary, she was the object of daily hassling, theft, and petty violence. Another woman, referred to as "the beast" because of her gossip and lack of sociability, did not benefit from the local information circuits when her husband was arrested for robbery. One of her neighbors explained to me: "I knew that Maria's lawyer would do no good. Everyone knows that lawyer just spends your money and never gets results. But I wasn't going to tell her." Other neighbors expressed similar sentiments: "I knew that Wednesdays they don't let kids in to visit at the Penal Colony [150 km from the city]. I saw she was going to lose her time and money, but too bad for her. After all the dirt she's spread about me, she doesn't deserve my help." When Sara, a seventeen-year-old girl, well into her third pregnancy, was stabbed by her live-in companion, one of her neighbors remarked: "She had it coming. She's a tramp, an alcoholic. I've seen her with ten different fellows in the vacant lot out back." But the real motive for scorn comes at the end of this string of accusations: "Anyhow, she's a thief. She came to grandmother Vera's birthday party and left with the radio. I know because I saw her selling the radio later. I tell you, she's a *sem vergonha* [shameless person]."

There exist common moral principles that are not linked to individual personal pride. I already mentioned the inviolability of children and pregnant women. Death is also respected. When a woman let her husband be buried as an indigent, without a coffin, everyone was profoundly shocked. Only then did they begin saying that "furthermore" she had cheated on her elderly husband for years. When Salete expelled her husband from the house, everyone deemed her act fully justified: after all, he had committed outrage (*desaforo*), going out to celebrate carnival the day after his child's death. But even these transgressions against general principles incur no more than temporary disapproval. Hence, the young people who have somehow marred their reputation (the boys with a police record, the girls with sexual promiscuity) are not necessarily considered morally polluted. People will say, "He erred, but at the bottom of his heart, he's a good lad," or, "She strayed [*se despistou*], but now she's on the right path [*endireitou*]."

Besides murder, the only act that seems to provoke general condemnation, serious and durable enough to make people leave the vila, is theft between friends. The professional thieves make a point of not plying their trade in the neighborhood. True, the *maconheiros* do not exclude their neighbors as potential victims, but they make a distinction between the well-integrated residents and those who are fair game. During my last visit to the vila, I ran into some of the "lads" hot on the track of a friend who had robbed one of the community's "respectable" matrons at gunpoint. ("And what's more, she had her baby in her lap!") A thief such as Sara will not necessarily be pursued in the same manner, for to ruin her reputation, thereby excluding her from the networks of support and protection, may be punishment enough.

For the sociable woman (uma *pessoa dada,* or "who is given," loosely translated, "who gives of himself"), a good reputation represents general protection and discouragement of potential aggressors. In one episode Regina the *louca* found a shirt cast aside or forgotten at the water spigot, and tried first to sell then to give the item to Elisete. Elisete stubbornly refused even the idea of a gift: "No, I don't know where it comes from. People will say I stole it and then I'll be finished here." Elisete, about the same age and social condition as Sara, has never had serious problems of aggression in the vila. She explained how, despite being an "outsider" (with no blood relations in the vila), she was well accepted: "If anyone insults me, I don't answer. It's not easy, but I lower my head and it blows over." Constantly singing the praises of her friends and neighbors for their generosity, Elisete is considered a person *dada*; as a result, (as she herself assures me), she is respected.

It is rare that anyone considers a man *dado*. Men don't need such qualities. Theoretically, they are strong enough to dispense the need to cultivate the good grace of others. Women take care (*eu me cuido*) because "the worst thing in the world is to be talked about [*falada*]." The concern about maintaining one's reputation and avoiding gossip both appear to be typical of the weak—those without physical force.

Gossip among equals

The weak use gossip to manipulate those who might otherwise have the upper hand and thereby assure minimum protection. Used against an equal, however, gossip becomes an instrument of attack—the challenge to a duel in which the stakes are all on self-esteem. Where there is rivalry between near-equals, there is gossip. This rivalry is especially obvious between neighbors when one of them is unable to repay some service or borrowed goods. Elisete, for example, complained about the joking insults Dione murmured each time she walked past her house, adding, "Just think! I used to be her best friend, crossing town to pick up milk for her daughters when she was in the pits. And now, this is how she repays me!" Any sort of extra good fortune may set off jealous gossip: if a couple appears to be getting along too well, if a person receives more than her share of visits from the anthropologist! Vera managed to buy a new refrigerator, sofa and television; the woman living next door lets me know that, of course, it must all be stolen goods. The Catholic sister who occasionally visits the area brings Gloria a pile of used clothes for her children; the neighbors remark that Gloria's last baby was born more than a year after she'd separated from her husband.

Gossip is an equalizer; it is the instrument of those who feel inferior and consider they can only raise their own status by denigrating the status of others. In fact, it is not so much a matter of rising above others, but rather refusing to be lower than they are. By this token, the lower one goes on the socio-economic hierarchy, the more vulnerable people feel. The norms of global society frequently end up thwarting the satisfaction gleaned from the local code of honor. A woman may be extremely *dada*, with all the personal virtues admired by the community, but it's her neighbor who has the TV. One week a woman will be admired for having a nice little house and a wily husband; the next week, her prestige has gone up in smoke, with the arrest of her husband. One might manage to feed the children by begging or working as a cleaning lady, but in both cases it is at the price of daily humiliations inflicted by the "bourgeois." It is as though an apparent well-being were constantly undermined by the moral criticisms of the dominant class. One afternoon, arriving upon a scene of conjugal discord, I saw this morality poke its way into an ironic exchange of insults. The woman scolded her husband as a "down-at-the heels" indigent (*chinelão*); he shot back by calling her a beggar (*esmoleira*).

Final Remarks

For centuries now, the privileged classes have oscillated, in their discourse about the poor, between compassion and condemnation. Too often the customs of our native poor are deemed worthy of interest solely for practical purposes—to plan educational intervention and to "help them reform their habits." With rare exceptions (wherein we manage some "distance" thanks to ethnic or historical differences), we seldom recognize any distinctive cultural traits among the urban poor. When such distinctiveness is detected, it is normally interpreted as a degenerate or pathological form of our own social organization. With relative facility, we manage to picture promiscuity, violence, and exotic family forms as elements of a cultural system well adapted to the ecological necessities of faraway tribes. People close to home are, on the other hand, threatening. To consider their "deviant" behavior as somehow logical, and even creative, is to endanger our own system of values. In past years, researchers have demystified the state's "disciplining" of the urban poor (Donzelot 1977, Meyer 1978), but seldom have they spelled out exactly *what* is being disciplined, that is, *alternative* cultural dynamics. The concept of honor forces us to think precisely about this—the symbolic exchange and internal coherence of a non-hegemonic code of values.

The reader may be prompted to ask, "And so, after all, does it work or not? This system of auto-regulation—does it manage to spread power around and satisfy the needs of personal pride for everyone?" The answer is, "Of course not." The majority of men feel more or less chronic frustration because they are unable to support their wives and children on what they earn. Most women have known moments of great distress as they go through temporary or permanent separation from their husbands. No social code could resolve the concrete problems of misery, nor soften the anguish that sends so many people to psychiatric hospitals. Let us say simply that, in the Vila do Cachorro Sentado, the people have established norms which, theoretically, each and every one has the possibility of living up to; they share an "alternative" moral code which maintains some sort of order and manages to guarantee a minimum of personal satisfaction. By discrediting or eliminating the non-conformists, the code selects "integrated" individuals. If this "counternorm" is constantly menaced, invaded and even broken by dominant society, at least it exists.

If now one inquires which direction the winds of change will take this population, the perspectives are even less reassuring. Little by little, as in nineteenth-century Europe (see Faure 1977), the city is being "hygienized." (Poverty is not eradicated, it is simply sent to distant locals where it will not bother the middle classes). Obliged to leave their present *cour des miracles*, the residents of the Vila do Cachorro Sentado, will probably be propelled toward distant working-class suburbs. Far from their bourgeois clients (and victims), incapable of recreating a territorial group and rejected by the "worthy poor," it may well be that these people see their system of regulation crumble and that physical violence, with no symbolic retainer walls, falls upon the handiest victims—the working poor.

References

Donzelot, Jacques. (1977). *La police des familles*. Paris: Editions de Minuit.

Faure, Arlette. (1977). Classes malpropres et classes dangereuses: quelques remarques à propos de chiffoniers parisiens au XIXe siècle et de leurs cités. In *L'Haleine des faubourgs. Recherches* 29: 79–103.

Handman, M.E. (1983). *La violence et le ruse*. Paris: EDISUD.

Hannerz, Ulf. (1969). *Soulside*. New York: Columbia University Press.

Meyer, P. (1978). *L'enfant et la raison d'état*. Paris: Editions de Seuil.

Pitt-Rivers, Julian Alfred. (1977). *The Fate of Shechem: or, The politics of sex: Essays in the anthropology of the Mediterranean*. Cambridge: Cambridge University Press.

Chapter XI

Reprimand and Respect, Love and Fear, in Experiences of Violence in Colombia

Myriam Jimeno

Violence as Lived Experience

A good deal of thought regarding violence in Colombia assumes that the intensity and frequency of violent actions lead to indifference or, further, assume its incorporation in daily life by way of the cultural acceptance of violence. These assumptions overlook the social relationships and cultural meanings present in acts of violence. A certain normative bias clouds violence by excluding the matrix of meanings which allow actors to overcome their suffering, and which guide their daily actions. A certain fatalism ascribes the extreme and cruel aspects of acts of violence to "Colombian culture." Diverse forms of violence are thus converted into one, *violence*, the product of a macabre tendency in Colombians. It then becomes extremely difficult to understand the mechanisms behind individual expressions of violence, and to identify common threads among them.

Everything in this approach points to confusion of the explanations of violent events provided by actors, and the cultural and psychological mechanisms used to overcome suffering, with indifference and habit. This is probably due to close proximity with the phenomenon and to the enormous impact that acts of violence can have on the conscience of individuals. Analysts, just like cultural natives, move jointly with their referential systems, so that external cultural complexes are not easily perceptible, according to Lévi-Strauss (1983). But in this case it is not a matter of distance and contrast, whereby others are traveling on different roads at different speeds, but of precisely the opposite: we are so involved we cannot focus. If we distance ourselves from the most common stereotypes seeking to explain violence in Colombia as social pathology (rooted in history or other features of our make-up), and if we likewise distance ourselves from a certain fascination with reaffirming Colombia as a violent nation, then we may advance in understanding the violence which effectively strikes at us daily.

Society and culture create conditions, such as the need to continue working, which help mitigate critical situations and provide new tasks and goals for people. It also reminds us that the need to understand the meaning of life, its organization, and the significance of social actions "do not disappear under horrible conditions" (Peacock 1986).

An inquiry into the events regarded as experiences of violence by individuals from low-income sectors of Bogotá, and on the ways in which they explained them, was conducted between 1993 and 1994. This paper summarizes the results of the Estudio Exploratorio de Comportamientos Asociados a la Violencia [Exploratory Study of Behaviors Related to Violence], conducted jointly by the author and Drs. Ismael Roldán (psychiatrist), David Ospina (Ph.D. in statistics), Luis Eduardo Jaramillo (psychiatrist), Jose Manuel Calvo (psychiatrist), professors of Universidad Nacional de Colombia, and Sonia Chaparro (anthropologist) (Jimeno 1993). Research was supported by the Universidad

Nacional, COLCIENCIAS, and ACAC. The goal was to understand the dynamics involved in these events, the interpersonal relationships present, the psycho-cultural points of reference, and their relationship to specific institutional configurations. The methodology sought to understand the psycho-cultural significance of experiences of violence for a low-income urban population, rather than focusing only on cases of extreme violence.

Violence was understood as a social fact that discriminates between scenarios, chain-event situations, relationships, actors, and cultural apprenticeship. Thus there are people, beliefs, values, expectations, forms of communication, and individual and institutional actions that are specifically associated with violence. Violence is therefore not an inexorable factum which has always hounded us; it becomes possible to recognize its expressions and to locate critical areas, critical actors, critical relationships and perceptions, and eventually to act upon them. If violence is a specific form of interaction between individuals and groups in specific environmental contexts, characterized by the intent to harm others, we can relate its occurrence to certain elements of the cultural orientation and social organization.

As with other forms of human interaction, violence may be seen as the oneness of situations comprising a series of observable events, cognitive cultural frameworks which assign meaning, and the specific motivations of social actors (see Gibbs 1986; Barth 1992; Bateson 1991). Thus, violent interaction is produced where socio-environmental settings, circumstantial structures providing the opportunity or direction for violent interaction, and culturally constructed cognitive complexes, converge.

Socio-structural or psychological factors cannot monopolize the explanatory power in violent interactions. They are not reduced to social needs, psychological disturbances, or access to material goods, power or prestige. More than understanding violence as an abstract notion, the goal is to characterize experiences of violence in their specificity and particularity. Identifying the distinctive features of specific forms of violence, and the physical, cognitive and emotional contexts associated with them, makes it possible to discover common traits and to identify the elements which structure them.

Situations of Violence

The majority of the individuals studied (264 adults over age fourteen) were women living in Bogotá for over five years. Recent decades brought them significant changes: reduced illiteracy, a drop in the number of formal marriages, fewer children per couple, a decline in religious observances, and greater numbers of women employed outside the home. Many of the women migrated to Bogotá, especially from eastern Colombia (62%), in pursuit of greater economic and educational opportunities. Considerable residential mobility in the city, weak networks of support and social integration, low levels of income (minimum $150 monthly in 1996) and high unemployment were noteworthy. Four out of every five individuals have lived in several neighborhoods, and almost half do not own a home. A third are non-professional independent workers, and the majority do not have fixed monthly salaries and are not covered by social security. Eighty percent did not complete high school.

Focusing on what takes place at home, half of the men and 44% of the women admitted to abuse in their original homes and among them, 13% reported brutal punishments. In over 76% of the abuse cases the victims were children. These individuals cited varying circumstantial reasons for the violence they encountered, but it is interesting to note that in 37% of the cases, they could not point to a clear motive: "I don't know; I can't understand; For no reason." Next in line were disobedience and failure to perform assigned chores. Together, these three factors covered 80% of the responses. Other circumstantial reasons cited were seeing forbidden friends or lovers, leaving the house without permission, consumption of alcohol by perpetrators of abuse, and lack of control by the latter, whether drunk or not.

Regarding possible reasons for the behavior of offenders, these were mainly related to the fact that they had been abused, were short-tempered or ill (22%), ignorant or jealous (21%), or "because that was the way one was reprimanded then" (16%).

Seventy-two percent of the married women stated they had been abused by their spouses. Eighty-three percent of the men between 18 and 49 endured most of their experiences of violence outside the home, while women from the same age group were mainly attacked at home (55%). Although the offender was known to 48% of the male and 63% of the female victims, only 38% of the men and 47% of the women sought assistance from the police.

Forty-eight percent of adults experienced at least one hold-up, 57% of these being males. Eighteen percent regarded hold-ups as the most significant act of violence taking place outside the home. However, it is noteworthy that the second most significant response (15%) regarding major acts of violence outside the home mentioned terrorist attacks and bombs, events in no way affecting respondents personally. As prominent experiences of violence outside the home, women referred to cases reported by the media (18%), especially television. Surely this relates to the number of housewives among the respondents (43%). This category places them more continuously in touch with radio and television, but above all points to a significant responsiveness to events taking place in Colombian society.

Another aspect of street violence is directly related to abuse by authorities. Again, it is men who are affected the most. More than half of them reported abuse by authorities, especially by the police, the army, and traffic police, and to a lesser degree by teachers, the clergy, and their superiors. Only 10% of the females felt likewise. On the whole, it may be stated that one out of every three individuals experienced abuse by authorities.

Hospital care (70%), education (65%), and the church (52%) were the only three institutions deserving the confidence of significant numbers of individuals. Institutionalized justice produced results almost as devastating as those for the police and politicians (over 80% distrust). In general, over half of those who suffered significant abuse at home failed to report their aggressors. The same occurred with sexual abuse cases (14%), half of which went unreported, even though the perpetrators were relatives or acquaintances of the victims in 70% of the cases.

One-fifth of the respondents (18%) referred to hold-ups as the principal experience of violence outside the home, but four out of every ten brought up the attacks and bombings which took place in Colombia in recent years. The storming of the Palace of Justice, and television reports of violent events, such as massacres, were especially mentioned. Little mention was made of the violent period of the fifties, even if the majority knew of it one way or another, given their age bracket. On the other hand, cases of torture, kidnapping, and extortion were hardly taken into account, with the exception of a few cases broadcast by the media.

In contrast with the above, when narrating their life histories, respondents identified principally their own direct experiences or those affecting relatives and friends. The first responses may be influenced by televised dramatizations of acts of aggression. Given the relative isolation of this sector of society, especially housewives, television has probably played a significant role in the construction of representational models of violence and in the creation of images about violent acts. This may result in a polarized view of society and a simplification of its conflicts. However, it is possible that the research instrument itself may induce a change in the conceptual field, from the social to the personal.

Further, what becomes generally evident is a cognitive distinction between instrumental violence, as in burglaries and hold-ups, and emotional violence, where feelings and relationships determine the course of action. This is the case for quarrels and national acts of violence such as massacres and homicide attempts. Delinquent violence does not seem to be as meaningful nor as oppressive as personalized, emotional violence, especially for women. Certain institutional agents, most notably the police, are even personalized and blamed for a number of wrong doings such as depraved and brutal acts, corruption, bribes, and "clientelism."

Delinquent violence remits to a view of society as an abstract entity which one must endure, whereas emotional violence is the result of interpersonal relationships. The recurrent phrase among respondents, "I fear no one because I have problems with no one," alludes to this distinction, and to a notion on the origin of meaningful violence in personal confrontations. A recurring reason many did not participate in neighborhood activities was "to avoid getting into trouble," a possible result of being close to one's neighbors. Another manifestation lies in people's comments about a victim of non-delinquent violence, when they state, "surely there's a reason." Delinquent violence in society is somehow regarded as inevitable—that is, all societies are assumed to be that way.

That is why a large portion (half) did not consider Colombia to be a dangerous nation, even though many had experienced hold-ups and other forms of street violence. The other half believed it dangerous to live in Colombia because of its violence and insecurity, but only a small percentage preferred to live elsewhere, and basically for other reasons. Those who considered the nation to be violent tended to personalize this in representatives of institutional authority, who were then blamed for the state of things. In all cases, fearful individuals lacking or distrusting institutional means of protection were seen as defenseless and orphaned in the face of conflict and its dangerous consequences. They should therefore take precautions, permanently preventing and avoiding situations that could lead to violence. This, in turn, feeds passivity and inhibits individuals from reporting acts of violence and from aiding victims.

In sum, Colombians clearly identify experiences of violence and classify them according to their significance in their own lives as well as in social life. They are not indifferent to violence, and it is not an acceptable pattern of behavior. They attribute violence, as a painful experience, to a variety of circumstantial reasons related to the life conditions and characteristics of aggressors and victims themselves, in this way creating the possibility for understanding and overcoming it. Although a large number have been victimized by domestic and street violence, they single out certain experiences as the most relevant, and link them to broader features of Colombian society. But in contrast to the analysts, they do not view this society as more violent than others.

Meanings in Reprimand and Respect, Love and Fear

Experiences are layered with meanings. Notions of abuse and violence are useful to designate certain repertoires of social behavior. For those interviewed, these concepts are not so vague as to become inoperative in daily life, nor are they so blurred they cannot be used to make conceptual and moral distinctions. For some, both notions, abuse and violence, are similar or identical and interchangeable, while for the majority they are basically distinguished by the intensity and social situation of the facts. Violence tends to be associated more with murder and extreme physical aggression, and often designates acts that take place outside the home involving serious injuries. Abuse summarizes experiences lived at home, childhood and personal histories characterized by blows, beatings, and hands placed over sources of fire. Whether differentiated or assimilated, both notions refer to interactions where there is a clear intent to harm others, and include an explicit value component. This moral dimension sanctions the actors of violent deeds even as there is an attempt to discover reasons for their behavior in certain of the internal or external circumstances of the individuals involved.

An important group of respondents (almost half) described their own childhood as hostile and abounding in suffering due to parental abuse. When child abuse was confronted with the description of current moods, a significant relationship was found between being abused as a child and describing oneself as an adult who is often nervous or sad. There is also a close statistical relationship between the description of the mood, admitting the need to commit abuse in the current home, and having been abused as a child. Feelings of sadness, distrust, and loss of control thus seem to take root in the violent conditions of family life. In spite of the fact that child abuse meant suffering and injuries to all respondents, some of them attribute it to special conditions such as stress due to poverty and scarcity, infidelity, disobedience, or drinking. Others point to attributes of the aggressors themselves: irritable, nervous, short-tempered, mean, unpredictable. Both, however, coincide on the shared notion of the need for correction or reprimand, given the paternal/maternal need to maintain control of family life and instill patterns of behavior. In the most extreme cases, however, victims clearly feel that the abuse exceeded this purpose and even had a destructive intent. The whole cultural complex indicates that family life is perceived as vulnerable, threatened by disorder and disrespect for authority. In this context, parental reprimands act as means of prevention; perhaps individuals are also perceived in the same way, always prone to exceeding their limits.

The notion of seeking to "correct" individuals also has a significant emotional effect. Reprimanding is closely linked to the notion of the "respect" primarily owed parents and secondarily to the male spouse. This permits a better understanding of the contradiction manifested by the majority of the abused, who judged their experience as painful, even unfair, without clear motives, but who nevertheless felt that there was fondness in the relationship, and that the intention to reprimand was what moved the parents. Reprimand and respect act precisely as mediation mechanisms, as mitigating factors that help individuals understand experiences that seriously question the love and concern of parents towards their children. Excesses are therefore seen as deviations from the intent to reprimand, due to circumstantial or personal reasons. In this context, abuse is blamed on ignorance (the view of the majority), drinking, nervousness or anger, or even on the belief that "that was the way one was reprimanded then." All these reasons become protective screens for the victims. Acceptance of the intent to reprimand gives rise to respect, which in no way morally legitimates the use of violence, but which permits the experience to be integrated under an essentially ambivalent code. Hence respect appears as the reason behind violent interactions and hides as its cognitive product. Respect is simultaneously love and fear, and in the memory of the abused, they are intertwined, yet contradictory.

A smaller segment of the sample, however, recognized a destructive intent in abuse, and blamed it on lack of affection. Behind abuse they saw hatred, animosity, and jealousy. Parents loathed their children for their sex, attitude, or their relation with the other parent or stepparent, or were jealous of their qualities or position in the family. Here the painful experience is more crude and simple in the minds of respondents, but some continue to question the reason for this hatred. Also, a few within the group favored the use of violent punishment when reprimanding, and openly justified it (see Montañez 1996).

The privileged settings for violent interactions at home are those where social control of the family unit is at play. Both manifest and potential behavior matters for the intent to regulate. A considerable number of cases of abuse took place for no apparent reason. Sometimes it was linked to situations where control of the family unit was challenged in very subtle ways, for example with minor tardiness in returning home, slightly rude answers, or even small gestures of disrespect. In the dynamics of violent interactions, obedience and its opposite, disobedience, are central. As a result, apparently trivial acts judged as disrespectful to parents or spouses unleash excessive reactions such as complaints or questions about the conduct of the parent or spouse. Obedience is expected in cases of excessive chores and absurd commands, as are strict compliance with established time frames and consulting about relationships outside the home; one does not challenge the exercise of domestic control with gestures, words, acts or omissions, but rather one explicitly indicates submission.

"Reprimanding" operates as a cognitive interpretation of the ultimate purpose of the offender, and as such, guides the perceptions of specific interactions. For its part, "respect" points to the behavior of abuse victims, inhibiting their answers—but at the same time providing a broad value framework with which to judge relationships with parents and between spouses. Both inform and structure the situation. Anger, fear and sadness, associated with the situations and present in their effects, are modeled in a tense and relative way on the reprimand-respect cognitive complex. "Reprimand" and "respect" guide (punctuate in Bateson's terms, 1991) the dynamics of interactions in situations of violence, in a game of actions and responses.

Now, a still-incipient generation change was detected in the use of the reprimand-respect complex as justification for the use of violence at home. Brutal punishments were suffered mainly by respondents over the age of 30, whereas among the young there was greater influence of a referential system that disapproves of brutal punishments and recognizes the right of children not to be abused. Some of the respondents see this change as confusing, as they now have doubts, not previously considered, about the punishment of children and parental rights. Some even attributed this change to delinquency and violence in society: "Well, since you can no longer correct them..." For the majority, these changes in the reference pattern are experienced ambiguously. On the one hand, the majority regarded dialogue as the proper means to solve interpersonal conflicts at home. On the other hand, although only a few justified the use of violence in reprimanding, many employ it at home, sometimes without motive, and don't see themselves as abusers. The victim's condition as the target of abuse is easily recognized, whereas that of the offender tries to conceal itself, not only due to social sanctions but mainly because of a still inadequate use of alternate methods of correction. The broader cognitive framework points to a model for interpersonal relations between the members of a group with unequal positions (parents-children, male-female). It thus constructs a larger concept with which to grasp domestic personal experience as well as a wide range of relations with others, especially those liable to end in open conflict.

Experiences, Situations, Representations

It would be fitting to ask: What is the relationship between the lack of credibility, distrust, and the illegitimacy of authority figures, institutions and violence in Colombia? The lack of credibility and distrust of relationships in social life prepare the ground for acts of violence. These are not provoked immediately, in direct relationship. They are nurtured through fear, distrust, and apprehension in social life, especially in relation to authorities (people and the institutions which represent them). When they confront eventual or effective conflict situations, individuals thus feel defenseless and alone. This is why many flee from that which, in their view, might confront them with possible conflict escalation. They avoid daily interactions such as the ones of the neighborhood, refuse to react to delinquent or other acts of violence witnessed or known about, and remain passive.

Why do crime witnesses remain silent? Why do officials complain about "lack of cooperation with justice"? Is this lack of cooperation similar in other nations? Aren't fearful silence and passivity the result of distrust of authority, and powerful allies of increased forms of violence? Aren't they means of adapting to social life conditions in Colombia? Wouldn't a certain ambivalence towards those who infringe norms—something which is widespread in Colombia—have to do with the notion that authorities fail to transmit regulations clearly, fail to sanction everyone fairly, and, on the contrary, are circumstantial, bribable, and bendable? Besides, reporting transgressions is not only useless but also potentially dangerous, as the reaction of authorities is unpredictable. Does this not open the door to impunity in general, an impunity that in turn reinforces extremely violent groups? Are not passivity, distrust, and fear adaptive in this social context?

On the other hand, it is known that fear can also induce attacks. Resorting to violence means anticipating an attack by another. Given the failure or disinterest on the part of authorities to mediate in conflicts, attacks can become a defensive and protective mechanism, as does resorting to private forms of "justice," usually based on violence. Why is it that special private "justice" groups are flourishing today in Colombia, if not because authorities are not trustworthy or credible? Evidently once conflict starts it takes on its own dynamics and tends to feed on and reinforce itself. As a means, violence subjects and devours the ends for which it is used.

In conclusion, it doesn't seem true that witnessing and suffering acts of violence makes Colombians, at least those of low income in the principal cities, insensitive to violence or unable to distinguish it from other social relationships. On the contrary, they draw subtle distinctions, they recognize the ones experienced at home or in the streets, and are moved by the suffering of others. They are hardly indifferent to the acts of violence they have suffered themselves, or to those witnessed on television. Rather, they are affected by the fact that violence and crime, as ruptures of and affronts to the collective conscience, as Durkheim (1893) would have it, are not sanctioned adequately by institutions.

It may be said that in the Colombian case, the frailty of power is the other side of arbitrary authority, and violence prospers in its shadow. In the experiences and conceptions of respondents, in the synthesis of environmental and perceptive complexes, legitimate authority is not recognized because it does not mediate in aggressive situations. Instead, it makes an obscure and ambivalent use of violence itself. This is recognized as might, as external coercion, and as a prerogative of the individual—hence the personal origin attributed to meaningful violence. In this sense, the absence of the state or its weakness is not the reasons for which authorities are not recognized. The absence of the state forms part of the social aggregate through which authority reaffirms itself using authoritarianism, at home, on the streets, and in society at large. This is why authority, at least for the sector which was studied, is unable to transcend and secure profound legitimacy.

In this social context, the psychological tensions resulting from lack of work, low income, privations, long working hours, and those generated by social inequality, all permit credible justifications for acts of violence at home and away from home. Under these conditions, intimidation or anticipated attacks, or on the contrary, passivity and avoidance, could become adaptive mechanisms. Learning to handle conflicts sets the pattern for dealing with future interactions, where a self-reinforced circle of aggression connects violent responses to self-defensive ones.

Family life is perceived as a fragile entity. Its members are on the verge of disorder, and authority must reaffirm itself with the use of force in anticipation of disrespect. Its means are reprimand and respect. As emotionally dense, cognitive constructions, they explain painful experiences. Victims are offered a guide for action and understanding that helps them face and overcome their suffering. But its ambivalent nature, composed of fear and love, weakens credibility and compliance with authority. Does this conception of family life extend to social life as a whole? The evidence points in this direction.

In varying ritual and secular forms, social systems reiterate that acceptance of the social order goes far beyond obedience, as their permanence is based on this (Fortes and Evans-Pritchard 1979: 100). Ideological validation, the art of theatricality, as Balandier (1994) calls it, is not a simple subordination mechanism or instrumental resource. Instead, the very diverse staging means represent the society that is governed. They also represent its capacity to deal with disorder and with the conflict inherent to human relations. Failed validation becomes a crack between individuals and their social environment, and is an invitation to violence.

References

Balandier, Georges. (1994). *El poder en escenas: De la representación del poder al poder de la representación*. Barcelona: Editorial Paidós.

Barth, Frederick. (1992). Towards greater naturalism in conceptualizing societies. In *Conceptualizing Society*, edited by Adam Kuper. London and New York: Routledge.

Bateson, Gregory. (1991). *Pasos hacia una ecología de la mente: Una aproximación revolucionaria a la autocomprensión del hombre*. Buenos Aires: Planeta.

Durkheim, Emile. (1893/1993). *La división del trabajo social*. México City: Colofón.

Fortes, Meyer, and E. E. Evans-Pritchard. (1979). Sistemas políticos Africanos. Introducción. In *Antropología Política*, edited by José Llobera. Barcelona: Anagrama.

Gibbs, John J. (1986). Situational correlates of aggression. In *Violent Transactions: The Limits of Personality*, edited by Anne Campbell and John Gibbs, pp. 107–249. Oxford: Basil Blackwell Ltd.

Jimeno, Myriam. (1993). *Conflicto social y violencia, notas para una discusión*. Memorias del Simposio Conflicto Social en America Latina, VI Congreso de Antropología en Colombia, IFEA-Sociedad Antropológica de Colombia, Bogotá.

Lévi-Straus, Claude. (1983). *Le Regard éloigné*. Paris: Plon.

Ministerio de Salud, Centro Nacional de Consultoría. (1993). *Estudio Nacional de Salud Mental y Consumo de Sustancias Psicoactivas*. Informe Preliminar presentado a la División de Comportamiento Humano por Yolanda Torres de Galvis, Colombia.

Ministerio de Salud, División de Comportamiento Humano. (1993). *Estudio Nacional de Salud Mental y Consumo de Sustancias Psicoactivas: Santafé de Bogotá*. Resumen Ejecutivo realizado por el Centro Nacional de Consultoría Ltda, Colombia.

Montañez, Sonia Liliana. (1996). *Maltrato infantil y castigo físico*. Trabajo para optar por el título de antropóloga, Programa Curricular de Antropología, Universidad Nacional de Colombia, Bogotá, September.

Peacock, James. (1986). *The Anthropological Lens: Harsh Light, Soft Focus*. Cambridge: Cambridge University Press.

Personería de Santafé de Bogotá, D.C. (1994). *Estadísticas de muertes violentas y presuntamente violentas: Julio de 1992 a julio de 1994*. Santefé de Bogotá: Divulgación y Prensa División de Informática.

Policía Nacional: Sudirección de Policía Judicial e Investigacion. (1994). *Criminalidad 1993, tendencia delincuencial: Primer trimestre de 1994*.

Chapter XII

The Paradox of Politeness

Dov Cohen and Joe Vandello

Violence and friendliness are usually thought to be opposites. Congeniality, hospitality, openness, and warmth are often assumed to preclude aggression and mayhem. What is frequently missed, however, is how often these two polar opposites seem to go together. The paradox of politeness is that violence and friendliness are *not* opposing forces. Rather, in many cultures, these two forces work together and reinforce each other, creating societies where what is on the surface is vastly different from what is occurring underneath.

Violence, or the threat of violence, can create a society where friendliness, congeniality, and politeness are the norm. And, as we will show, these norms for politeness and anger-suppression can in turn foster violence by driving conflict below the surface, depriving people of the opportunities to work out their differences, and ultimately leading to a full blown explosion when one person has gone too far. Our own empirical research has focused on the U.S. South, but we start by reviewing anthropological work showing that the same processes may occur elsewhere around the world.

Politeness around the World

The world over, one of the major preconditions for producing a violent society is the lack of a state or central authority to intervene in conflicts (Daly and Wilson, 1988; Pitt-Rivers, 1968). This seems to square well with the Hobbesian view of humanity, where, in the absence of a state, a war of all against all ensues and people's lives are "brutal, nasty, and short" (Hobbes, 1957/1651; see also discussions by Colson 1975: 32).

Yet, despite the theoretical predictions and the empirical evidence showing high rates of violence in such cultures, anthropologists who survey societies with minimal government often find a world where everyday life is marked by friendliness, congeniality, and helpful interdependence. To Westerners who assume that people's acts are or should follow from their personal feelings, such a world seems quite surprising (Miller 1984). But it should not be. People are often quite friendly because of what they fear below the surface. As Elizabeth Colson (1975) wrote,

> We listen to informants' fears and to their tales of violence . . . and we diagnose a world of warring factions, of feud, of frequent acts of aggression. . . . We look around us, however, and we find people apparently behaving with kindness, generosity, and forbearance, avoiding disputes and sharing resources, tolerant of each other's foibles. What we may miss is the connection between the two sets of social facts: the beliefs are related to the behavior. . . . [I]t should therefore be no surprise to us if some people live in what appears to be a Rousseauian paradise because they take a Hobbesian view of their situation: they walk softly because they

believe it necessary not to offend others whom they regard as dangerous. (1975: 37).

This pattern is found in a great many traditional, interdependent societies in Asia, the Mediterranean, and Africa. That is, people in such societies tend to be "extraordinarily afraid of each other and afraid of supernatural beings...(Thus, they) may act in extremely polite, gracious, or generous fashion, but these social acts may or may not entail corresponding personal feelings of love, liking, or trust" (Fiske, Markus, Kitayama, and Nisbett 1997: 115). People are generous "despite or because of" their belief that "family members, friends and neighbors are envious, malicious, or greedy," and will do harm to them (Fiske et al. 1997: 115–116).

From classical Greek civilization where "hospitality must be offered and must be accepted" to many contemporary societies, people give and give graciously because they fear the enmity and anger of others (see Gould 1973: 91, 88). As one Tonga informant explained, "It is not safe to deny (others). The only thing to do is to give" (Colson 1975: 47–49).

People in such societies try to prevent violence because they believe long spirals of revenge will result from single acts of aggression. Thus, they try to avoid the triggering incidents that can bring on catastrophic blood feuds. These practices lead to a strong emphasis on being slow to anger, to being a "quiet man," or to having thick skin—"seven thumbs thick" in the case of the Iroquois Indians—so that uncontrollable conflicts do not begin unnecessarily (Colson 1975: p. 41). Such extreme emphasis on conflict avoidance can be seen among the Inuit around Point Barrow, where "revenge cycles within the community were . . . greatly feared. Several informants remember fellow villagers, hysterical after the death of a loved one, being physically held down by kinsmen who repeated over and over again, 'Don't kill anyone, don't kill anyone; if you kill somebody their relatives will kill us all'" (Hennigh 1972: 90). Thus, as in many other societies, there is "peace in the feud" or rather the threat of feud (Colson 1975: 43; Gluckman 1955).

Here it is extremely important to note that there is some debate over just how much violence really exists in such societies. That is, whether people in these societies actually experience much violence or whether they live in the fear of violence that will probably never come is a matter of some contention (see review by Colson 1975). But there are two points to be made. The first is that even if violence in the form of physical aggression rarely occurs, it certainly is a psychological fact that people live with in their everyday lives. Whether it is force or the threat of force that is keeping people in line, the theme of violence (actual or implied) is regulating behavior.

The second point is that quantitative studies demonstrate that, for at least some of these societies, actual violence is incredibly high. For example, the traditional !Kung San "have been immortalized by anthropologists as 'the gentle people'" (Daly and Wilson 1988: 224). Yet, they have a homicide rate over a 50-year period of 29 per 100,000 per year (Lee 1979). To put this in perspective, it would mean that the !Kung San have a rate of homicide three times higher than the U.S. average and have homicide figures comparable to those of Chicago, New York, and Los Angeles. Revenge among the !Kung San is also not an idle threat. "If a killing occurred it was more likely than not be followed by a retaliatory killing; 15 of the 22 homicides were events in blood feuds" (Lee 1979: 392).

Even more striking are the Gebusi of lowland New Guinea. Despite their strong emphasis on friendliness and "good company," they have a homicide rate that has been "conservatively calculated to have been at least 568 per 100,000 per annum (e.g., over 50 times the current U.S. rate of killing from all sources)" (Knauft 1985: 2). Their homicide rate is "among the highest reported for any human society" and, indeed, almost one-third of all adult deaths between 1940 and 1982 were products of violence (Knauft 1985: 2). In Knauft's analysis of Gebusi violence, he describes how "good company" and violence are inextricably bound together. Further, his research suggests not only how violence can enforce a norm of congeniality but also how persistent congeniality may actually feed a cycle of violence. That is the part of the process we turn to next.

Keeping Conflict Hidden

Gebusi are an exuberant, warm, and friendly people. Their pervasive spirit is one of collective good will and camaraderie, and their very word for culture (*kogwayay*) is also their concept of "good company." Good company is the *sine qua non* of daily social life and is also the theme of the Gebusi's major gatherings—ritual feasts, spirit seances, and the telling of narratives. Good company effectively informs relations not only between kinsmen or coresidents but between community members at large. The dominant ethos is one of self-effacement, easy humor, and friendly deference. . . . In many respects, their communal and noncompetitive spirit of amity is indeed idyllic (Knauft 1985: 1–2).

Yet, there is a suggestion that such behavior can create its own problems. As conflicts are driven under the surface, grievances build up and they may culminate in an accusation of sorcery. This is a very serious thing in Gebusi society as sorcerers can be killed, beaten, burned, "clubbed over the head," "shot with arrows," and occasionally, eaten (Knauft 1985: 102,105). As Knauft wrote,

It might even be argued that, far from fending off aggressiveness, Gebusi violence is predicated on Gebusi good company, and on the extended conflict avoidance this orientation entails. With antagonisms ignored and denied for long periods of time, they could be expected to build up until they are triggered in a culturally legitimated context where violence is normatively sanctioned—namely a sorcery attribution following a sickness death. Hostility in this setting is all the more severe for having been previously unexpressed, and may serve as a legitimate means of displacing or making manifest antagonisms from many sources and/or from many people. . . . What ultimately results is juxtaposition of pervasive good company with occasional but extreme violence (Knauft 1985: 79).

There are Freudian psychodynamic explanations for this type of pattern—namely that hostility becomes repressed, pressurized because it is held down, and then ultimately explodes out like a shaken-up can of soda pop. But there are also more strategic and "rational" reasons why such a pattern of repressed conflict and sudden explosion might occur.

The economist Thomas Schelling (1978) has described many conflicts as amounting to coordination games. That is, if two parties are in a conflict, they must somehow signal to each other what will be tolerated and what constitutes an unacceptable act of aggression that calls for retaliation. This understanding must be arrived at either through acknowledging the natural boundaries of the situation or through subtle or overt communication about where the "line in the sand" lies. This communication can take the form of veiled threats, calculated bluffs, biting humor, verbal jousts, or overt warnings. However, in cultures with extreme emphases on politeness and congeniality, many of these avenues are cut off. These techniques are not part of the "cultural tool kit" that people have for resolving conflicts. And thus, a forced friendliness keeps people from telling others to back off and it keeps issues under the surface—until it is too late and one party has crossed over the line or passed the point of no return.

Further, the problem is especially acute in cultures that have stringent norms for politeness *and* violence. In such cultures, anger or hostility is not something to be taken lightly. Thus, anger may not often be expressed; but when it is expressed, *it means something* and both parties know it. It therefore becomes extremely dangerous to let even a little hostility leak out prematurely. The other person may take this as a sign that the conflict is about to become violent and may thus race to strike the first blow. Aside from participants being *unable* to signal their hostility because they don't have the behavioral repertoire to do so, they may also strategically and consciously choose to inhibit their hostility until they are ready to go into a full blown attack. For both strategic and "cultural tool kit" reasons—as well as for psychodynamic ones—politeness, hospitality, and violence may go together in many cultures.

Southern Hospitality

Our own research has shown that these patterns of conflict suppression and explosion can be found here in the U.S. South: That is, conflicts are often driven under the surface and then ultimately explode in an incident that might have been avoided if the offending behavior had been checked in time. This notion is embodied in the old expression that "a southerner is courteous and friendly...until he is mad enough to kill" (Wilson 1989: 635). In a similar vein, folk wisdom holds that Appalachian men are "slower to anger or panic, but absolutely without reason or mercy once the fat was in the fire" (Thompson 1966: 172).

Honor and violence in the South. Our previous work using attitude surveys and lab experiments has shown that white U.S. southerners hold to a version of a *culture of honor* stance, in which insults, threats, and affronts must be punished with violence (Nisbett and Cohen 1996). Historically this has been true, and it is still true today (Fischer 1989; McWhiney 1988).

In opinion surveys, contemporary white southerners are far more likely than their northern counterparts to endorse one person hitting, and in some extreme cases, shooting, another person for a variety of offenses—from insulting words to physical affronts or attacks (Cohen and Nisbett 1994). And in lab studies, we have shown that white male southerners act out these aggressive tendencies when provoked. In a series of three experiments, we invited subjects to the lab and had them insulted by a confederate who was actually working with us. Subjects were walking down a long narrow hallway when our confederate, who was working at a file cabinet, slammed the file drawer shut, rudely bumped into the subject, and then called him an "asshole" after the collision. The effect of this insult was profoundly different for southerners and northerners in our study. In response to the insult, southerners became far more angry, whereas northerners tended to be far more amused. Southerners also became more cognitively primed for aggression after the insult (as shown by their more violent completion of a written scenario), and they acted out their aggressive feelings in subsequent meetings with others and in physical challenge situations. Perhaps most surprisingly, southerners responded to the insult *physiologically* in a different way than northerners did. Whereas northerners seemed to be unaffected by the insult, southerners showed dramatic increases in their levels of cortisol (a hormone associated with stress and arousal) and testosterone (a hormone associated with aggressiveness and competition) after being insulted (Cohen, Nisbett, Bowdle, and Schwarz 1996).

However, these lab experiments tell us only about one type of conflict—that is, a conflict that begins with a single direct and unambiguous insult. In a more recent study, we examined the process by which politeness norms and aggression norms work together and feed off each other as conflicts escalate over time. In this study, we wanted to expose white male northerners and southerners to a series of irritations and annoyances from another person and see how they dealt with the conflict as it progressed.

Conflict over time. We had northern and southern subjects come to the lab and participate in what they thought was a simulated "art therapy" session. For this session, they were to draw a series of pictures from their childhood using crayons, ostensibly to promote relaxation and get "in touch with their inner child." As they were doing this, however, another subject (actually a confederate of ours) began to annoy the subject while the two were left alone.

The provocations from the confederate were all mild (unlike like the unequivocal "asshole" insult above), though definitely meant to irritate. For example, the confederate would repeatedly wad up his drawings and throw them away, missing the trash can and hitting the subject instead. Or he would repeatedly call the subject "Slick." Or he would steal the subject's crayons. Or he would comment negatively on the subject's drawings. The question was: how would northerners and southerners handle this situation?

Relevant predictions derive from the different cultural styles of the regions. Northern culture does not have the South's emphasis on graciousness and politeness. Indeed, the reaction many southerners have to the North is that it is exceptionally rude. ("Conversation in New York, Roy Reed has written, is 'hurled stones'" (Reed 1986: 70)). And conversely, the reaction many northerners have to the South is that it is claustrophobic and "phony" (see De Lisser 1996; Nethaway 1996). However, even if it's not at this extreme level, many will agree that in manners lies "one great remaining (North-South) difference" (Reed 1986: 68–69).

In our experiment, northerners should do more to head off a conflict in the beginning and be more up front about their hostility at first, but then they should eventually level off, never letting their anger go completely "over the top." Southerners, on the other hand, should play it cool, staying polite and expressing little emotion; and then when some critical point has been reached, they should be more likely to express intense anger or explode.

Consistent with predictions, people from the two regions did handle our confederate differently. Northerners were more likely to respond to the provocation in the beginning with expressions of hostility and more likely to be confrontational (as rated by our confederate and by an experimenter who watched on a video feed in another room). However, when they probably realized their warnings did little or no good, they leveled out. About halfway through the study, northern anger and conflict behavior plateaued.

Southerners showed a distinctly different response. Through the first part of the experiment, they showed little or no reaction to the annoying confederate, betraying no hostile affect. At some critical point, however, things changed. About half way through the experiment, southern anger and conflict behavior ratcheted up quickly and dramatically. Though they began the study absorbing the annoyances stoically, they ended the experiment with expressions of anger and conflict that were far more intense, unpredictable, and hostile than northerners had ever shown. These patterns were born out in statistical tests that examined how people from the North vs. South differed in the *absolute levels* of anger shown over time, the *rate of change* in anger shown over time, and the *maximum upward jump* in anger and conflict behavior from one point in time to another (Cohen and Vandello 1997).

Politeness and homicide rates. In addition to the lab study data, we have some correlational evidence suggesting that this process of anger suppression and explosion occurs in the real world as well. The evidence derives from the following logic: If it is true that in a culture of honor, politeness norms are going to drive conflicts underground only to have them explode later, then it should be the case that where southern society is more polite, there will also be more incidents of lethal violence. For places without a culture of honor (in this case, the North), this should not be the case.

To test this prediction, ideally we would have data on the politeness of various cities. Unfortunately, such a data set does not exist, but there is something close. Levine and colleagues have collected data on how friendly and helpful various cities are. They looked at such things as United Way contributions per capita as well as examined how helpful people were when experimenters dropped pens on the street, requested change for a quarter, and posed as blind people needing aid crossing the street. They found, not surprisingly, that the South was the most helpful region of the country (Levine, Martinez, Brase, and Sorensen 1994).

Perhaps more interesting for the present purposes, however, is what helpfulness was associated with in the southern vs. non-southern regions of the United States. We merged Levine's data with data about white male homicide offenders, age 15 to 39, in the corresponding counties. As one might expect, in the North, the friendlier a place was, the less lethal argument- and brawl-related violence it had, whereas in the South, the effect was slightly in the opposite direction. In the South, more polite places actually had slightly *more* argument- and brawl-related homicides (Cohen et al. 1997). The statistical interaction held when we controlled for factors such as income, size of the metro area, and percent non-Latino white. Importantly, this pattern was true only for argument-and brawl-related violence (which are likely to center on insults, conflicts, and affronts and thus involve the processes of anger suppression and explosion described above). The interaction did not hold for felony-related homicides, that is, homicides committed in the context of another felony such as robbery or burglary. In both the South and the Nonsouth, more helpfulness and friendliness was associated with less felony-related homicide.

Dispute Resolution: Forgiving and Forgetting

Forgiving. How do disputes ultimately get resolved in a culture of honor generally, and in the southern culture of honor, in particular? Our lab study provided data bearing on this issue. In this study, after all the provocations ended, but *before* subjects were debriefed about the experiment and the confederate's role in it, the confederate attempted to apologize to the subject. He went over to the subject, attempted to shake hands with him, and apologized for his actions. Our confederate then rated how much the subject seemed to accept and forgive him.

For both northerners and southerners, the degree to which the subject accepted the apology depended greatly on how the subject himself had acted as he experienced the provocations. But the specific patterns for northern and southern subjects were opposite. Northerners who had stayed calm during the experiment were likely to accept the subject's apology and be rated as forgiving. Northerners who had "blown up" during the course of the study, however, were obviously quite mad. They were far less likely to accept the apology and were also less likely to even shake the confederate's hand when he offered it.

For southerners, the reverse was true. Southerners who stayed calm during the experiment seemed to still hold a grudge, and they were less likely to accept the confederate's apology and shake his hand. Southerners who had blown up, however, were actually *more* likely to accept the apology and forgive the confederate rather than staying angry. It was as if southerners were following a cultural script that went something like: "You were a jerk. I blew up at you. Let's shake hands and call it even."

Forgetting. This was not just a short term phenomena, either. Six months later, we mailed a set of pictures to subjects who had been in our experiment and asked them to identify the person who had provoked them in the study. Classic psychological theory informs predictions here. The "Zeigarnik effect" shows that people's memory for unresolved or uncompleted tasks is better than their memory for completed ones (Zeigarnik 1935). After a task has been completed, people can cognitively put it away and forget about it. If it has not been completed, it is still quite accessible and alive in our minds. This effect technically has its pedigree from social psychology but it has its roots in Freudian psychology, which argues that it is our unresolved conflicts that keep coming to the surface and bedeviling us.

With this long-term memory data, the same interaction occurred as with the hand shaking and forgiveness data. Few people forgot the person who had done this to them six months earlier. Yet, those who did were a) northerners who had stayed calm and b) southerners who had blown up. It appears that the people who had most resolved the conflict and put the incident behind them were the ones who had solved the problem according to their culturally appropriate scripts. Northerners who had cognitively explained away the incident and stayed calm as the provocations happened in the lab were more likely to forget about the incident than were northerners who had blown up. In contrast, southerners who had blown up were more likely to forget than were southerners who had stayed calm and not vented their anger. The interaction pattern was statistically significant.

Extreme caution is necessary in interpreting these results. The number of people classified as "blowing up" was kept extremely small because we wanted to put people in this category only if they had truly expressed their anger and not if they were merely working themselves up to an explosion. Specifically, we only classified a subject as "blowing up" if a) his anger scores were in the top 20 percent for the last time period or b) we had to stop the experiment. Thus, cell sizes in the "blow up" conditions (usually about 5 per cell, depending on the measure) were small, and extreme tentativeness in interpretation is appropriate. Nevertheless, the handshake data, apology data, and forgetting data all hint that the social and psychological conflict resolution scripts for northerners ("ignore it") and southerners ("express your anger") can be dramatically different.

As an aside, such information may be quite useful for people doing violence prevention work. These results suggest that there may only be true forgiving and forgetting for people in southern culture (and perhaps other cultures of honor) if two conditions are met: (1) the aggrieved party must have had some opportunity to express his anger, and (2) the provoking party must ask for forgiveness. These are tricky things because first, the expression of anger must be channeled into some appropriate and nonharmful avenue if violence is to be avoided; and second, the provoking party must be persuaded to ask for forgiveness, an act that may be seen as humiliating.

Yet there is some hope. In many classic cultures of honor, there is a strong tradition of the *suppliant*. If a person asks for forgiveness and performs the rituals in the right way, he *must* be forgiven (Gould 1973). In classical Greek culture, custom dictated that the suppliant was to indicate his submission to the other (by touching the other's hands, knees or chin), at which point the other was to raise him up and restore him to honor. The reciprocal nature of this honoring was extremely important. Thus, the paradox: through a "ritual procedure which enacts the total abdication of any such claim" to honor, a person's honor is given back to him (Gould 1973: 94).

To violate the expectation of reciprocity and mistreat the suppliant was a serious offense that could draw the anger of Zeus (protector of suppliants) or other men. In fact, classics scholar John Gould noted, two cases of such mistreatment "played a dominant role in the diplomatic propaganda of the Spartans and Athenians on the eve of the Peloponnesian War" (Gould 1973: 74). Respect for the ritual of supplication and honor for the suppliant was considered extremely important and not something which could be violated.

All this is not simply ancient history. There are parallel rituals among groups such as the Bedouin, the Tonga, and the Tswana today (Gould 1973: 101). And—if our lab results are any indication—perhaps some version of this supplication ritual holds in the U.S. South: southerners who have expressed themselves may also be bound by the code of honor to accept the apologies of those who ask for it correctly.

Trade-offs and Possible Worlds

Two final issues must be raised before this topic is left. The first has to do with the trade-offs that violence entails. The second has to do with multiple equilibria and the many different ways cultures can solve the problems that confront them.

Regarding the first point, from a northern ethnocentric perspective, it would seem that the trade-off of greater violence in return for more politeness is not a good thing. However, it is far from clear that everyone would assent to this. In the Old South, in fact, the practice of dueling was defended on the grounds that it encouraged greater civility. Thus, it has been written that, "When a man knows that he is to be held accountable for his want of courtesy, he is not so apt to indulge in abuse. In this way dueling produces a greater courtesy in society and a higher refinement" (Kibler 1946, cited in McWhiney 1988). Even today in the United States, where a recent *U.S. News and World Report* poll found that "9 out of 10 Americans consider incivility a serious national problem," traces of this sort of reasoning can be found (Morris 1997: 15). For example, Jeffrey Snyder, who is an activist for a more armed populace, noted that

> Regarding . . . our society's general level of aggressiveness and disregard for rules, you may wish to consider Robert Heinlein's famous dictum that 'An armed society is a polite society.' Knowing that one's fellow citizens are armed, greater care is naturally taken not to give offense. (Will 1993: 93).

Whereas the homicide rates of the South can be between two and four times greater than those of the North, the chance of dying by homicide is still quite small for most people (Nisbett and Cohen 1996). So to some, it may be a reasonable trade-off to exchange a slightly greater risk of violence for more politeness, civility, respect among people, and friendliness in our everyday lives. Further, possessing a sense of honor may in itself be a psychological good that justifies facing a slightly greater risk of physical violence. Indeed, there is more than one way to read research on North-South cultural differences. That is,

> Northern men are spineless wimps with no honor. They will not defend themselves, their women, or their culture, assuming they have a culture. . . . The South's sense of honor is the underpinning of southern courtesy and hospitality. An iron fist in a velvet glove. (Nethaway 1996: G5)

And some people may like it that way.

Violence has a different meaning for people in different societies (Cohen and Vandello 1997). Among the Gebusi, "violence is not seen as a threat to good company, but as a means of reaffirming it" by ridding the community of those who cause trouble (Knauft 1985: 79). In a similar vein, one famous explanation for southern violence holds that, "In the South, there's just more folks who need killing" (Wright 1997: 64). Obviously this is a somewhat sardonic statement of the view in its most extreme form. But in its toned-down version, there are quite a few people who would agree that sometimes violence can be appropriate medicine, and that in the case of children, some of them just "need" a "good hard" spanking (see Cohen and Nisbett 1994: 563). As John Reed wrote, many southerners "actually don't see much of the violence around them, don't register it as 'lawlessness,' because it isn't 'lawless.' It is *lawful* violence, in the sociological if not the legal sense: more-or-less predictable, more-or-less expected, (and in consequence) more-or-less taken for granted" (Reed 1981: 12, emphasis added). In this context, violence is conceived of as a legitimate and often necessary tool for restoring order, justice, and goodness in the world (Blumenthal, Kahn, Andrews, and Head 1972; Cohen and Vandello 1997; Fischer 1989: p. 765).

Other worlds. It is far from clear, however, that a satisfactory trade-off of more violence for more civility had to emerge. We have presented the argument that violence and "good company" or violence and friendliness inevitably go together like yin and yang, subtly reinforcing each other. But just because congeniality and violence go together in *some* societies, it does not mean that they do so in *all* societies. That is, there may be multiple equilibria for a culture that finds itself in the Hobbesian dilemma. One equilibrium point is for a culture to settle on norms of politeness and conflict avoidance so that the underlying threat of force is rarely realized. But another equilibrium point for a culture to settle on is for people to adopt an "aggressive" deterrence model where they advertise their willingness and desire to engage in violence instantaneously. The strategy here is to let it be known how fierce you are, how "crazy" you are, how much "nerve" you have, and how ready to seek out conflict you seem. And indeed, many cultures of honor the world over embody some version of this opposing stance in which people look for chances to fight.

For example, Campbell's description of Mediterranean herders bears this out when he notes how youths will deliberately start quarrels to prove themselves (Campbell 1965). Hunter S. Thompson's account of the code of the Hell's Angels makes a similar point about their bullying behavior; The Angels, he wrote,

> . . . have a belief in total retaliation for any offense or insult. . . . Their claim that they don't start trouble is probably true more often than not, but their idea of provocation is dangerously broad, and one of their main difficulties is that almost nobody else seems to understand it. Yet they have a very simple rule of thumb; in any argument a fellow Angel is *always right. To disagree with a Hell's Angel is to be wrong—and to persist in being wrong is an open challenge* (Thompson 1966: 65, emphasis added).

Similarly, in American inner cities, some members of the so-called "street culture" adopt a parallel position.

> In street culture, especially among young people, respect is viewed as almost an external entity that is hard-won but easily lost, and so must constantly be guarded. . . . The person whose very appearance—including his clothing, demeanor, and way of moving—deters transgressions feels that he may possess, and may be considered by others to possess, a measure of respect. With the right amount of respect, for instance, he can avoid "being bothered" in public (Anderson 1994: 82).

Thus, some members of this culture react with aggression to things that "might seem petty to middle class people (maintaining eye contact for too long, for example)", or some may go on the offensive and try to show "nerve," which is displayed when someone "takes another person's possessions (the more valuable the better), 'messes with' someone's woman, throws the first punch, 'gets in someone's face,' or pulls the trigger" (Anderson 1994: 82, 92). Because doing these aggressive acts is so dangerous or life-threatening, the perpetrator is showing how tough he is and this "helps build a reputation that works to prevent future challenges" (Anderson 1994: 92).

These are the rules of the street, and when people are in public, they must play by them. Definitely, this is a dissatisfying solution, and the vast majority of people in the inner city are unhappy with it (Anderson 1994). But it is one equilibrium point that a culture of honor can settle on. In Prisoner's Dilemma games, a norm for cooperation and positive reciprocity can be an evolutionarily stable strategy, but the opposing norm for everyone defecting can also be quite stable (Axelrod 1984). And this latter strategy seems to be the equilibrium point that the culture of honor in parts of our inner cities has settled on, as people adopt a norm for defection (that is, violence or taking the offensive) as a viable alternative in an uncertain and unsafe world. Perhaps the work of political scientist Robert Axelrod or economists Timur Kuran (1995) and Thomas Schelling (1978) can help in finding ways to move from one stable culture of honor equilibrium point to another, or perhaps it can suggest ways for making respect a commodity that can be gained through things other than violence. Doubtless the respect through violence formula is tied up with having few other economic or social ways to gain status in mainstream society, and thus violence may not be reduced until this issue is addressed (Anderson 1994; Wilson 1987). But that is another, deeper matter altogether.

About Gender. Perhaps one of the most fascinating topics in cultural psychology is the way many different and coherent cultural realities are possible. Again, in considering cultures of honor, there are a number of different roles women play in such cultures. This deserves a much longer treatment, but it is briefly mentioned here to support the general point about many diverse, plausible cultural models.

We usually associate cultures of honor with hypermasculine and hence also hyperfeminine roles. Consistent with this is the mythology of the southern belle. The belle is "the fragile, dewy, just-opened bloom of the southern female: flirtatious but sexually innocent, bright but not too deep, beautiful as a statue or painting or porcelain, but like each risky to touch" (Jones 1989: 1527).

However, whereas some cultures strongly mark off the masculine and the feminine, there are other cultures of honor where the women are every bit as tough as the men and actually perform some of its violence (see discussions by Anderson 1994; Fischer 1989, especially page 770; McWhiney 1988; Miller and Sperry 1987; Nisbett and Cohen 1996; Reed 1986). For example, in the Mediterranean, women "routinely carry out some sorts of homicide, for example, the stoning to death of women believed to be unfaithful" (Nisbett and Cohen 1996: 87). Or in today's inner cities, "increasingly teenage girls are mimicking the boys and trying to have their own version of 'manhood'...including posturing, abusive language, and the use of violence to resolve disputes" (Anderson 1994: 92).

Even within a given culture, a diversity of subtypes can exist. In the South, there is the southern belle. But there is also the "good old girl." She is "a tomboy who could drive a car and outshoot a man...(but) who could also blow you away when she put on a pink cotton dress" (McGee 1983, quoted in Reed 1986). *Within* as well as *between* individuals, culture can stress male versus female distinctions, or culture can reconcile potential "contradictions" such as extreme femininity and extreme masculinity into a coherent whole (see discussions by Bem 1975; Heilbrun 1973). Perhaps this state of affairs was best expressed for parts of the South by former Governor Ann Richards, who noted that in Texas, "Everyone has to prove their masculinity—especially women" (Nisbett and Cohen 1996: 88). This is a perfectly coherent statement in some cultures of honor and a perfectly incoherent one in others. Again, the highly variable role that women play in cultures of honor around the world is an excellent topic for future research, and it is sure to tell us about the many ways in which different forces within a cultural system can interact, modify, and sustain each other in a meaningful way.

Cultural Wholes. Returning to the more limited focus of this chapter, it is clear that there are multiple equilibria and multiple manifestations of the culture of honor stance. Why people in a given culture settle on one "solution" to their collective situation and not on another is a matter for speculation. However, the more general point must be made: Cultures are not like tinker-toys. They cannot be disassembled into their parts and understood as "pieces" isolated from the whole. Rather, cultures are coherent wholes whose parts and whose subsystems constantly interact, influence, and reinforce each other in a dynamic way (see also Shweder 1993; Triandis 1994).

This lesson is illustrated in the way the yin and yang forces of politeness and violence work together in many societies as described above. And the lesson is probably equally true in other societies with the opposite pattern, where violence and everyday belligerence go together hand in hand. Within a given society, these cultural forces sustain each other, and importantly, they are in turn sustained by *other* forces and subsystems within that culture which make meaning of everyday life, social interaction, and people's conceptions of themselves and the world.

The broad point is that a culture is a dynamic system that fits together into a coherent whole. And the genius of culture is that it can reconcile potential opposites, in this case, friendliness and aggression for many of the societies described above. There is no single formula for how societies must be put together or for what cultural syndrome *must* go with what other cultural syndrome. There are many combinations which can be made to "make sense." Thus, it is important to understand how the forces within a society interact, sustain, and are reconciled with each other; and it is important to remember that, through the integrating power of human culture, multiple coherent worlds and multiple coherent meaning systems are possible.

References

Anderson, E. (1994). The code of the streets. *Atlantic Monthly* 5: 81–94.

Axelrod, Robert. (1984). *The Evolution of Cooperation*. New York: Basic Books.

Bem, S. L. (1975). Sex-role adaptability: One consequence of psychological androgyny. *Journal of Personality and Social Psychology* 31: 634–643.

Blumenthal, M. D., R. L. Kahn, F. M. Andrews, and K. B. Head. (1972). *Justifying Violence: Attitudes of American Men*. Ann Arbor, Michigan: Institute for Social Research.

Campbell, J. K. (1965). Honor and the devil. *Honour and Shame: The Values of Mediterranean Society*. Edited by J. G. Peristiany. London: Weidenfeld and Nicolson.

Cohen, Dov, and R. E. Nisbett. (1994). Self-protection and the culture of honor: Explaining southern violence. *Personality and Social Psychology Bulletin* 20: 551–567.

Cohen, Dov, R. E. Nisbett, B. F. Bowdle, and N. Schwarz. (1996). Insult, aggression, and the southern culture of honor: An "experimental ethnography." *Journal of Personality and Social Psychology* 70: 945–960.

Cohen, Dov, and Joe Vandello. (1997). Meanings of violence. Unpublished manuscript, University of Illinois.

Colson, Elizabeth. (1975). *Tradition and Contract*. Chicago: Aldine.

Daly, Martin, and Margo Wilson. (1988). *Homicide*. Hawthorne, New York Aldine De Gruyter.

De Lisser, E. (1996). Culture clash: Northern charm and southern efficiency. *The Wall Street Journal* (29 October 1996: A1, A14).

Fischer, D. H. (1989). *Albion's Seed*. New York: Oxford University Press.

Fiske, A. P., H. Markus, S. Kitayama, and R. E. Nisbett. (1997). The cultural matrix of social psychology. Unpublished manuscript, University of Michigan.

Gluckman, Max. (1955). *Custom and Conflict in Africa*. Oxford: Basil Blackwell.

Gould, John P. (1973). Hiketeia. *The Journal of Hellenic Studies* 43: 74–103.

Heilbrun, C. G. (1973). *Toward a Recognition of Androgyny*. New York: Knopf.

Hennigh, L. (1972). You have to be a good lawyer to be an Eskimo. *Proceedings of the American Ethnological Society* 1971: 89–109. Seattle: University of Washington Press.

Hobbes, Thomas. (1957/1651). *Leviathan*. Edited by Michael Oakeshott. Oxford: Oxford University Press.

Jones, A. G. (1989). Belles and ladies. *Encyclopedia of Southern Culture*, edited by C. R. Reagan and W. Ferris, pp. 1527–1530. Chapel Hill: University of North Carolina Press.

Knauft, Bruce M. (1985). *Good Company and Violence*. Berkeley: University of California Press.

Kuran, Timur. (1995). *Private Truths, Public Lies*. Cambridge: Harvard University Press.

Lee, R. B. (1979). *The !Kung San*. Cambridge: Cambridge University Press.

Levine, R. V., T. S. Martinez, G. Brase, and K. Sorensen. (1994). Helping in 36 U.S. cities. *Journal of Personality and Social Psychology* 67: 69–82.

McGee, M. G. (1983). Prime-time Dixie: Television's view of a "simple" South. *Journal of American Culture* 6: 100–109.

McWhiney, Grady. (1988). *Cracker Culture*. Tuscaloosa: University of Alabama Press.

Miller, J. (1984). Culture and the development of everyday social explanation. *Journal of Personality and Social Psychology* 46: 961–978.

Miller, P., and L. L. Sperry. (1987). The socialization of anger and aggression. *Merrill-Palmer Quarterly* 33: 1–31.

Morris, D. (1997). The civility wars. *Utne Reader* (March–April 1997): 15–16.

Nethaway, R. (1996). Southern white men on honor. *The Orlando Sentinel*, 28 July 1996, G5.

Nisbett, R. E., and Dov Cohen. (1996). *Culture of honor*. Boulder, Colorado: Westview Press.

Pitt-Rivers, Julian Alfred. (1968). Honor. *International Encyclopedia of the Social Sciences,* edited by David Sills, pp. 503–511. New York: Macmillan.

Reed, J. S. (1981). Below the Smith and Wesson line: Reflections on southern violence. *Perspectives on the American South: An Annual Review of Society, Politics, and Culture*, edited by M. Black and J. S. Reed, pp. 9–22. New York: Cordon and Breach Science Publications.

———. (1986). *Southern Folk Plain and Fancy*. Athens, Georgia: University of Georgia Press.

Schelling, Thomas C. (1966). *The Strategy of Conflict*. New York: Oxford University Press.

———. (1978). *Micromotives and Macrobehavior*. New York: W. W. Norton and Company.

Shweder, Richard. (1993). "Why do men barbeque?" and other postmodern ironies of growing up in the decade of ethnicity. *Daedalus* 122 (Winter 1993): 279–308.

Thompson, Hunter S. (1966). *Hell's Angels: A Strange and Terrible Saga*. New York: Ballantine Books.

Triandis, H. C. (1994). *Culture and Social Behavior*. New York: McGraw-Hill.

Will, G. F. (1993). Are we a "nation of cowards?" *Newsweek* (15 November 1993): 93–94.

Wilson, C. R. (1989). Manners. *Encyclopedia of Southern Culture*, edited by C. R. Wilson and W. Ferris, pp. 634–637. Chapel Hill: University of North Carolina Press.

Wilson, W. J. (1987). *The Truly Disadvantaged*. Chicago: University of Chicago Press.

Wright, J. D. (1997). A matter of respect. *Reason* (February 1997): 62–64.

Zeigarnik, B. V. (1935). On finished and unfinished tasks. *A Dynamic Theory of Personality*, edited by K. Lewin, pp. 300–314. New York: McGraw-Hill.

Part Three

Institutional Architectures Mediating and Memorializing Violence

Besides the family, almost every other societal institution figures in the cultural shaping of violence. Law and order function to check violence, ideally, but both policing and soldiering are sites for the socialization of forceful violence, not just for prevention of or for defense against violence. Politics impacts all other institutions, including the legal, by being increasingly implicated in their constitution and regulation. Politics also articulates interests beyond the local and even beyond the nation-state, through practices often lacking in transparency. Such issues tend to be spatially expansive-unto-global and temporally infinitely recursive, such as the situations examined in these chapters.

Chapter XIII

Violence by the Book: Redefining the Legitimate Use of Force in Municipal Policing

Stephen J. Lutes and Michael J. Sullivan

Introduction

> The American policeman regards himself as the embodiment of society's legitimate power of violence. When in uniform, he carries a billy-club, he wears an ammunition belt and a holster with a gun in it, his handcuffs dangle from the belt, he frequently sports a crash helmet, and he carries mace and other incapacitating chemicals. The tools of his trade are instruments of violence (Chambliss and Seidman 1971: 274).

Aggression and violence probably mean about the same thing to most people, but dictionary definitions say that the former indicates commencing an attack, an assault, an invasion, or more generally, hostile actions not necessarily involving the use of physical force, while the latter means physical force exerted for the purpose of violating, damaging, or abusing. We tend to conceptualize the origins and functions of aggressive or violent behavior in similar ways, too. Theories range along the traditional nature-nurture continuum and attribute aggression and violence to variable individual genetic predispositions, a natural response to certain stressful stimuli, to socialization, or to a combination of these factors (e.g., Myers 1993).

Our look at police violence and police uses of force policies will show considerable evidence to suggest that both are very much shaped by historical, social, and cultural contexts. So much diversity in types and frequency of "legal force" by police or analogous social actors exists that we are compelled to admit significant social and cultural mediation of whatever else may be going on when violence is wrought. Police use of force policies also varies between jurisdictions and across time, and so does the extent to which actual practices conform to formal policies, randomly deviate from the norm, or suggest covert shaping by informal policies.

Today, use of force incidents in the United States often precipitate controversy. These responses are no less socially and culturally patterned than is the police violence. But it has not always been so. The following paper uses local, historical, and cross-cultural data to consider how the cultural shaping of violence employed legally by police officers, primarily in the City and County of San Francisco, has responded to trends in other areas of social-cultural organization, especially to political and legal trends, particularly those involving civil rights and increasing cultural and social diversity. We shall see conflict at all levels, between police and citizens, between groups of citizens, between institutions, within bodies of policy, and between cultural imperatives.

Our perspective on lawful violent behavior starts from Bohannan's concept of legal systems as doubly institutionalized norms and customs and in terms of what he labels "colonial law." Bohannan (1967: 51–52) considered colonial law to be the result of a peculiar and passing situation characterized by a unicentric power system controlling populations with two or more distinct legal cultures. For him, the defining traits of colonial law are a "systematic misunderstanding" between the two cultures within the single power system, with constant revolutionary proclivities resulting from what is, at best, a "working misunderstanding." Bohannan distinguishes the contradictions or disjunctions of colonial law from problems of "phase" which seem to be similar in nature and outcome but are more properly characteristic of modern, unitary municipal systems of law:

> A legal culture, for the present purposes, is that which is subscribed to (whether they know anything about it or not, and whether they act within it or "agree" with it or not) by the people of society . . . Municipal systems, of the sort studied by most jurists, deal with a single legal culture with a unicentric power system. Subcultures in such a society may create vast problems of law's being out of phase with the customs and mores of parts of the society, but is a problem of phase.

There are implicity evolutionary assumptions in Bohannan's typology, for example when he (1967: 52) relegates the colonial pattern to the dustbin of history and observes:

> We are only now far enough removed from colonies—now that they are obsolete—to begin a thorough examination of the effect that colonial powers had, via such a system, on the legal systems of the countries in which they were found.

Police agencies are a part of our legal system, and the system is organized along classic bureaucratic lines (e.g., Weber 1964: 329–341). Particular bureaucracies can be looked at as institutions with the usual array of structural-functional features such as charter, rules, staff, and the like. Neither real bureaucratic organizations nor the extent of bureaucratization of some aspect of human life are unchanging or constant. Recent trends in our legal system and institutions run toward increased bureaucratic complexity and increased applicability to a growing list of human relations. For example:

> The transition of nineteenth-century civil law systems into the twentieth century is closely tied to the transformation of liberal laissez-faire governments into modern social welfare states with planned or regulated economies . . .the gradual shift away from nineteenth-century liberalism and the market economy has meant a shift in emphasis from private or civil law to public law. . . . The legal order has begun increasingly to take on the characteristics of a bureaucratic, or administrative order (Glendon, Gordon, and Osakwe 1982: 47).

Both in relation to legal institutions and other formal or intentional groupings, we explore the occurrence and effects of two varieties of bureaucratic organization: mock bureaucracy (Gouldner 1964) and the administered community (e.g., Kushner 1973). The first is conceptualized as an explicitly pathological or dysfunctional condition of affected organizations, the second implicitly so, at least, due to an assumed decoupling effect whereby various societal subgroups are estranged not only from meaningful participation in governance and control over relations of production, but also lose much of their autonomy over their neighborhoods, child-rearing and education practices, and many other "intimate" activities that traditionally were regulated mostly by custom as interpreted within a local group.

Concurrent with these changes has been an elaboration of and increased ideological and practical focus on persons' rights to due process of law and freedom from unreasonable search or seizure and cruel or unusual punishment. What is unreasonable or cruel or unusual are in particular not static concepts and have been changing or vacillating a great deal over the last five decades. We propose, in general, that the dominant legal cultural perspective has tended to shift towards opposition to corporal punishment in sentencing and use of force in law enforcement.

The changes discussed above reflect a movement to bring equality to the legal standing and treatment of persons as individuals. At the same time, increased immigration, and perhaps internal differentiation (e.g., Green 1981), have resulted in growing cultural and social diversity, especially with the surge of immigration after the early 1970s and changes in the cultural and socio-economic composition and background of new arrivals. We have recently attempted to deal legally with groups in much the same way that we have dealt with individuals. Treatment of immigrant groups-qua-groups, and of newly incorporated peoples (e.g., the Chamorros of Guam after the island's acquisition from Spain), has in many ways paralleled the treatment of our indigenous Indian populations with shifts in policy and practice that emphasize separation (e.g., exclusion in enclaves), coercive assimilation, restoration or recognition of special groups status, and termination of special groups statuses previously restored or recognized (Spicer 1980: 178–195). The current dominant philosophy seems to promote policies tolerant of multiculturalism, cultural pluralism, or general diversity. Because the political discussions and debates on both sides of the issue tend to be venomous and muddled, it is sometimes difficult to guess what someone who supports or opposes multiculturalist policies has in mind.

If police violence and reactions to it are mostly dependent variables shaped by culture and social context, some cultural and social variables identified above are, in our thinking, at the root of what has been going on in the world of police-violence-as-public-issue, and the product is probably somewhat indicative of what is to be expected if this community of trends persists.

The Legal and Social Definition of Police in the United States

Much of any definition of police officers is legally codified; peace officers are one of the very few specific types of person to be legally defined in such detail and differentiated from the rest of the population (e.g., citizens or civilians), primarily by a grant of authority to do things that would otherwise be illegal.

Despite the extensive codification of police powers, considerable official and public ambiguity attaches to definition of the role. One can argue that a lot of the ambiguity is a matter of design. Although American police officers are not held to very strict standards of conduct, the standards are operationally defined and qualified such that the applicability of the standards to actual incidents can often be determined only after much wrangling.

Consider the official name and definition of the job. Section 830 of the California Penal Code defines "Peace Officer" (note the difference between the title and public perceptions regarding the job's essential attributes) as, "Any person who comes within the provisions of this chapter and who otherwise meets all standards imposed by law is a peace officer, and notwithstanding any other provision of law, no person other those designated in this chapter is a peace officer." There follows a long list of types of peace officers and cross-references, then Section 830.1 defining the peace officer's scope of authority to include any place in the state:

> (1) As to any public offense committed or which there is probable cause to believe has been committed within the political subdivision which employs the peace officer.

> (2) Where the peace officer has the prior consent of the chief of police, or person authorized by him or her to give consent, if the place is within a city or of the sheriff, or person authorized by him or her to give consent if the place is within a county.

> (3) As to any public offense committed or which there is probable cause to believe has been committed in the peace officer's presence, and with respect to which there is immediate danger to person or property, or of the escape of the perpetrator of the offense.

This is a pretty broad scope of authority, with more than a little ambiguity as to what constitutes, for example, immediate danger or probable cause. Probable cause is procedurally defined in California Penal Code, Section 991, i.e., defined in a manner consistent with our common law tradition that has developed, unlike civil law traditions, "with its obsession with facts and concrete situations, and its disdain for generalization and systematization" (Glendon, Gordon, and Osakwe 1982: 46). Immediate danger is not defined in the Code, its presence or absence is determined by weighing facts and concrete situations using the same kind of process required to determine probable cause.

Despite the label of "peace officer," it seems certain that the general public as well most police single out the use of coercive force as the defining characteristic of the job. The force has to be used in a legal or legitimate way, the definition of which contains as many shades of gray as the peace officer's scope of work. Because the duty of the officer is generally constructed as maintaining the peace and responding to public offenses, it follows that they are expected to intervene as necessary and to direct, arrest, or detain persons as required—required here means for the most parts as determined by the individual officer (cf. Davis 1975: 164–165), acting with probable cause, in response to the dictates of an immediate situation. Persons are required by law not to resist arrest by a police officer (California Penal Code, Section 834a) and this is generally (but, recently, not always) interpreted to include even a situation where the arrest may not be lawful. Boundaries on the police officer's use of force to effect an arrest are defined in the most general terms in the Code:

> An arrest is made by an actual restraint of the person, or by submission to the custody of an officer. The person arrested may be subjected to such restraint as is reasonable for his arrest and detention (California Penal Code, Section 835).

> Any peace officer who has reasonable cause to believe that the person to be arrested has committed a public offense may use reasonable force to effect the arrest, to prevent escape or to overcome resistance. A peace officer who makes or attempts to make an arrest need not retreat or desist

from his efforts by reason of the resistance or threatened resistance of the person being arrested; nor shall such officer be deemed an aggressor or lose his right to self-defense by the use of reasonable force to effect the arrest or to prevent escape or to overcome resistance (California Penal Code, Section 835a).

When the arrest is being made by an officer under the authority of a warrant, after information of the intention to make the arrest, if the person to be arrested either flees or forcibly resists, the officer may use all necessary means to effect the arrest (California Penal Code, Section 843).

With a few notable exceptions, such as the labor movement earlier in this century, this language, or similar wording, for many years seemed to work throughout the United States, wasn't seriously scrutinized, and caused little or no grief for police, courts, or the vast majority of Americans. The second sentence in Penal Code Section 835 was introduced around 1957 in California, but it is only a minor reworking of the sixth of Sir Robert Peel's nine principles of policing, which holds that legitimate force is the minimum force necessary to secure the observance of the law or restore order. Sir Robert introduced his principles in the late 1820s as part of his drive to reform English policing so that the occupation no longer served "to prostitute the useful employment of a thief-taker to the procuring of both public and private rewards, at the shameful and shocking price of innocent blood." British discontent with the practices of thief-takers, at that time, was associated with sweeping changes in the political economy of England as it became fully embroiled in the industrial revolution's dislocation (often unwillingly) of a mostly rural labor force, and as it became truly a colonial empire on which the sun never set.

Sir Robert's need to make certain that police use of force was legitimate and reasonable was directly related to a common perception that as matters stood it was often neither one nor the other. That is, in large measure, it was a response to potentially revolutionary proclivities on the part of an increasing mass of citizens who viewed current practices as strictly in the interest of a distant and uncaring upper class. It seems that, in England, a consensus about reasonableness was arrived at fairly early and persisted until quite recent times. In America, no such general agreement developed and the concept's greatest utility may be its ambiguity. As noted by Chambliss and Seidman (1971: 275–276) in a discussion of Wisconsin's equivalent Penal Code 835:

> The norms which define the permissible use of violence by a policeman are appropriate to the purposes for which he is given instruments of violence. He is permitted to use force either to effectuate the official purpose of taking certain categories of criminals into custody or preventing certain sorts of crimes, or to defend himself. The law provides, however, that he use only the minimum amount of force necessary to effectuate these purpose. . . .The critical question concerning the content of these norms, of course, is the word "reasonable." . . . More frequently . . . the word "reasonable" is used to mark a normative concept. It is used by courts and legislatures to cover a variety of cases too wide for precise definition.

Not so long ago, police and the public in the most of the United States typically understood legitimate or reasonable force to include elements of punishment as well as apprehension, and the use of lethal force to apprehend suspects did not draw much criticism either. Due process wasn't much on people's minds, and where the courts differed too much from public sentiment on an issue, the courts could be openly disregarded and even blamed for forcing nonjudical if not extralegal solutions to criminal behavior, as occurs in the posters advertising a reward "Dead or Alive" for apprehension of accused transgressors.

Neither police nor police stations today are equipped with, for example, bamboo splinters, iron maidens, acid vats, or whipping posts, but it should be recalled that flogging was practiced in England as late as 1948 and was still legal in some southern U.S. states in the middle 1960s (Symons 1966: 31). "Cruel and unusual" punishments are a matter of socially and culturally contingent definition, and historical shifts are not necessarily unidirectional. The recent reappearance of castration (chemical and otherwise) and chain gangs as possible or real means of crime prevention and punishment suggest just how contingent the definition of cruel and unusual may be. We currently like our force to be clean, as non-intrusive of the body as possible, and as painless as circumstances allow, even if it is lethal force. Our society thus limits the types of force police can use to guns, impact weapons like batons, incapacitating but non-lethal chemical sprays, and bodily force—and also tries to limit the extent to which these can be used, demanding that only a reasonable amount of force be used, and that only when necessary.

Changes in the legal system and police work being wrought by external social forces and statutory law do not always manifest themselves in the Penal Code itself, although, for example, use of both "him" and "her" in Penal Code Section 830.1 to describe a police chief could not have been considered necessary or descriptive of possibly factual states of affairs until very few years ago. With a few exceptions, the General Orders developed in individual police jurisdictions often respond to local rulings and sentiments. Again, in line with our common law tradition, whether or not local definitions, police, and decisions can stand legal muster are matters that can be and increasingly are adjudicated in local, state, and federal courts on a case-by-case basis.

In court, the normative concepts of reasonable or necessary conduct as applied to any citizen, including police officers, are examined in the light of admissible evidence, and what is "admissible" also masks a normative concept. Evidence codes in the United States allow for the exclusion of evidence if, in the opinion of the court and subject to judicial review, there is, e.g., "probability that its admission will (a) necessitate undue consumption of time or (b) create substantial danger of undue prejudice, or of confusing the issues, or of misleading the jury" (California Evidence Code, Section 352). Rothstein (1981: 6) sees "distrust of the jury as the basis of much evidence law."

These remarks briefly describe the controversial status of police power, especially that involving the use of violent or coercive force, in the United States today. They are meant to show also that our common law tradition is predicated on the existence of some uniformity in and acceptance of norms applied by the public to human conduct and judgment, and to indicate certain conditions destructive of normative uniformity that have developed in our society over the past several decades. In the following section we describe "police" powers in a number of other societies and times, and consider what anthropologists and other scholars have been able to infer based on knowledge of this broader cultural and historical context. Finally we examine changes regarding police use of force that have occurred in a specific local U.S. jurisdiction during the last thirty years.

The Cultural Dimension of Violence as a Reasonable, Legitimate, or Effective Response to Public Offenses

The really fundamental sine qua non of law in any society—primitive or civilized—is the legitimate use or physical coercion by a socially authorized agent. Truly, as Jhering emphasized, . . . "A legal rule without coercion is a fire that does not burn, a light that does not shine." . . . There are, of course, as many forms of coercion as there are forms of power. Of these, only certain methods and forms are legal. . . .The essentials of legal coercion are general social acceptance of the application of physical power, in threat or in fact, by a privileged party, for a legitimate cause, in a legitimate way, and at a legitimate time. This distinguishes the sanction of law from that of other social rules (Hoebel 1972: 26–27).

The systematic and impersonal application of force in the maintenance of individual rights and in the public interest is the central substance of law... (Redfield 1967: 14).

Most discussions in this country about the legitimate use of force by persons who exercise police powers really have to do with examples where the violence used as a means of coercion is an acceptable form inappropriately or excessively applied. Allegations of physical torture involving police officers and the use of unacceptable means of violence appear to be relatively rare. The usual terms employed are unnecessary force, excessive force, police brutality, and, on occasion, physical or psychological torture. Their terms have somewhat different meanings and different people may use the same term with very different meanings. To understand how "normal" or legitimate police violence is culturally shaped and defined, it is useful first to distinguish the types of violence that are acceptable and formal/informal rules, if any, defining the types of person and circumstances against whom various forms of violence can be used. Although all societies seem to have rules, there is clearly much cross-cultural variability on what kinds of violence are acceptable and what the rules for proper violence are, as the following examples attempt to show.

There was once a strong "lawless" man among the Ellery Creek band of Australian aborigines. He intimidated everyone and nobody individually dared to confront him with his crimes. According to Hoebel (1972: 305):

It was not until the warriors of three communities (one his own) were convened under a leader who got them together that action was taken. They agreed on his death. But even with this mustering of force it was not done by them directly. The women were "ordered" to lure him into the bush, engage him in intercourse, seize him, and kill him. They did it with a vengeance. His own mother-in-law snared him in the sexual embrace. Then he was pounced on by the rest of the females who attacked him with their digging sticks. (from here Hoebel quotes Roheim, 1942)

"First they pushed his eyes out and then they poked the heavy sticks right through his body, through his nostrils, through his head, etc., until they killed him."

As gruesome as that may sound, much more "civilized" peoples can be much more "savage":

> More primitive prison systems employed more obviously barbaric methods. Torture was common practice in the Far East, and to extract admissions from suspects Indian and Oriental police used a variety of methods, including the use of hot oil in the ears and nose, slivers of bamboo pushed under the nails, the use of the bastinado to break knee and ankle joints, and confinement in a cell containing quicklime (Symons 1966: 31).

And, also suggestive of cultural continuity despite increasing modernity is the following:

> In 1980, officers in Bhagalpur police station in India held as many as 30 suspected dacoits (bandits) on the floor and put out their eyes with sharpened bicycle spokes and acid. . . .The incident was confirmed by the chief minister of the Bihar state, as well as by the prime minister . . .who publicly promised a thorough investigation (Bayley 1995: 262).

The thorough investigation was in all likelihood intended to pleasure adherents of official ideology, much of which is imported and of recent Western vintage, and it probably concluded without practical issue, because:

> ...the public may excuse in the police what it would excuse in itself. It may, in face, expect from the police what it would expect in itself. Both public and police frequently blur the distinction between arresting and punishing... (Bayley 1995: 272).

"Primitive" and "barbaric" used to describe means of legitimate coercion used by other peoples, both today and in earlier times, invoke moral and/or evolutionary assumptions that are themselves products of particular times, cultures, and societies. What these and several following examples indicate is only that the types of violence employed are limited by the physical/technical means available, and, as regards, an increasing number of potential of means, by preferences for or against different ways of inflicting bodily harm. It is difficult to provide an objective basis for thinking that jabbing sticks through a person's body is somehow less reasonable or primitive or barbaric than pouring hot oil in one's nose or ears, or that it is less reasonable or more primitive or barbaric than putting out one's eyes with bicycle spokes and acid.

Inuit (Eskimo) traditionally limited legitimate use of force in the settlement of all but the most egregious public offenses to boxing or wrestling contests, or song duels, carried out by the disputants in the company of onlookers; although death might result from the wrestling matches, it doesn't seem to have been an expected outcome (Hoebel 1972: 92–93). The only violence exercised by a privileged party is that involving lethal force, usually but not always in response to multiple homicides, and the methods of choice seem limited to "steel, thong, or shot" (Hoebel 1972: 89). A case is reported where a man known to have killed many other Inuit was taken into custody by white traders:

> The man had been publicly whipped by the whaling captains at Herschel on injunction of the local missionary, because he had exposed a baby to die. All the Eskimos had reacted with disgust to such unheard-of punishment,

for, to their mind, "to whip a man does not cure him" (Hoebel 1972: 89–90).

Back at the other end of the scale of social complexity, "torture" by Japanese police authorities is said to have:

> ...included prolonged isolation, lack or privacy, interrupted sleep, complete dependence on custodial staff, even for permission to wash or lie down, lights kept on all night, and irregular and unannounced interrogations. Force seems rarely to have been applied, but it was often threatened (Bayley 1995: 263).

The point of the examples thus far is to show that the forms legitimate violence can take are numerous and not necessarily associated with any developmental or moral continuum. Much of the force used in the examples cited above would today be called cruel and unusual or "torture," by most Western Europeans and North Americans, but even that definition, we have suggested, is quirky, historically and culturally contingent, and so subject to changes that could go either way. Consider the transformation going on in Britain, for example, in light of the thirty-year-old statement by Banton (in Skolnick 1996):

> In Edinburgh . . .violence means to a policeman, I suspect, either fists or stones, or at the worst, assault with sticks or iron bars. It does not mean guns or knives.

British police generally did not escalate to the means of violence and even their abuse of force followed Banton's description:

> Richard Culley, a seventeen-year-old black youth, was attending the Putney Common fun-fair with his sister in May 1983 when British police officers grabbed him and took him between two trailers where he was thrown on the ground and beaten. His allegations were denied by the police until a man came forward with photos... (Bayley 1995: 261).

But times and police responses had changed sufficiently such that two years later it was clear that police expectations going into an incident were very different from 1966:

> In Britain, five-year-old John Shorthouse was shot by a West Midland's police officer during an armed raid in 1985 on his parents' home. Although a crown court found the constable who shot the child not guilty, one officer was admonished and three others "given advice" by the chief constable concerning poor planning and execution of the raid (Bayley 1995: 264).

In England, then, shooting has gone from being a form of intragroup violence considered by nearly everyone to be beyond the pale to one that is increasingly, albeit reluctantly, used in response to changing social conditions, including cultural diversity through large scale immigration, and normative standards.

Like most Western police violence we hear of, the abuses and changes in British force remains constrained and is limited to fire arms, club, or other impact weapons, chemical aerosols, or bodily force involving hands and feet. In the case of the Rodney King beating, for example, there was considerable dispute about whether or not the kinds and extent of force used was legitimate. Note that the much-viewed use of the electric stun device was often portrayed as something verging on, if not in fact being, torture. Had police poured boiling oil into his nose and ears, or even used a cutting instrument, there can be no doubt that even the original Simi Valley jury would have overwhelmingly found the officers guilty of excessive force and worse, regardless of what King might have done. So, the issue wasn't so much whether specific means of inflicting pain were acceptable, but rather whether they were used in an appropriate manner at a reasonable level. Even in Western societies, broadly defined, what constitutes an appropriate manner of applying acceptable force differs considerably between and within societies.

> Analysis of data collected in Jamaica, Brazil, and Argentina suggests that police shootings are being used as a form of "social control" . . . So common are shootings by the police in Brazil that some officers are identified in the media as the "Pistoleiros." In addition, Brazil's notorious "death squads," in which off-duty police are believed to participate, have operated for years, their presumed intent being to deter criminal activity by repeat offenders (Bayley 1995: 264).

At best, it seems that condemnation of such actions occurs only after particularly brutal killings, such as those of children or nuns, and it is difficult to find convincing evidence that such behavior by police is broadly unacceptable to most people in most socioeconomic strata, as policy, except on a case-by-case basis.

San Francisco is a volatile city when it comes to issues of police violence. Over the past quarter century the authors have observed firsthand a number of marked changes in how the public and various branches of government generally react to police cases involving the use of force. The changes are politically controversial at every level of society and government. Behind these changes are newsworthy incidents, where police misconduct is the immediate issue, and a host of political and legal maneuvers that follow. The differing sides can interpret the same events to be victories for human, civil, or group rights or harbingers of social disintegration and catastrophe. The positions of actual people cover a broader spectrum of possibilities, but from the imagery and action one knows there is a real social unrest and political venom involved. The literature on police violence documents an entrenched social problem that has existed since the 1960s (e.g., Lipset 1974; Locke 1995: 133).

During the entire time, it has been acknowledged that social and political problems related to acts of police coercion are tied to several other intractable issues. Frequently the literature presents a case for declining legitimacy, where civil authority in general and police authority in particular are no longer accepted by broad segments of the citizenry.

The anthropological concepts of ethnocentrism and cultural relativity are used by anthropologists in such settings, it seems, mostly to identify sources of cultural misunderstanding and conflict that result in physical violence. This is similar to the way it is used in the domestic literature by non-anthropologists. We take a different approach here in order to look at culture as something that shapes police violence and shapes public perception of the "legitimacy" of such acts. In the police brutality genre, significant work has been done by sociologists on the troublesome normative dimension of laws, including analyses of the normative assumptions contained in statutes governing police use of physical coercion (e.g., Chambliss and Seidman 1971: 275–276). But typically the focus in most recent research avoids qualitative and holistic styles of inquiry in order to achieve tightly focused, fundable, hypothesis-testing approaches.

Ethnocentrism and cultural relativity are used in the literature as "root causes" of socially patterned intolerance and misunderstanding, but are not often employed as analytical concepts per se. The lack of well-developed ethnographic and comparative traditions limits the concepts' use, partly because culture-based concepts seem almost to require an ethnographic or "community study" type approach to yield thick descriptions rather than superficial or very narrow spectrum data on cultural systems. The other major empirical schools in police violence research have nevertheless demonstrated beyond dispute that it is socially and culturally patterned and linked to other important and emotionally charged issues, i.e., problems associated with race, ethnicity, and gender in particular, and those involving human and civil rights and the philosophy of multiculturalism in general.

Our discussion has bounced between macro- and micro-level considerations, because the issue of police violence is intimately bound up with these and other events occurring in the United States and abroad. In the United States, issues of race, ethnicity, multiculturalism, and institutional legitimacy are paramount. This has not always been the case in America and, today, while many other countries have the same problems, their importance is often eclipsed by other issues that are relatively less pressing for us—such as establishing the basic institutions necessary to create a civil order and securing a social and political environment where considerations of basic human and civil rights can begin.

References

Bayley, David. (1995). Police brutality abroad. In *And Justice for All: Understanding and Controlling Police Abuse of Force*, edited by David Geller and Hans Toch. Washington, D.C.: Police Executive Research Forum.

Bohannan, Paul. (1967). The differing realms of the law. In *Law and Warfare*, edited by Paul Bohannan. Garden City: Natural History Press.

Chambliss, William J., and Robert B. Seidman. (1971). *Law, Order, and Power*. Reading: Addison Wesley.

Davis, Kenneth Culp. (1975). *Police Discretion*. St. Paul: West Publishing Company.

Glendon, Mary, Michael Gordon, and Christopher Osakwe. (1982). *Comparative Legal Traditions*. St. Paul: West Publishing Company.

Gouldner, Alvin. (1964). *Patterns of Industrial Bureaucracy*. New York: The Free Press.

Green, Vera M. (1981). Blacks in the United States: The creation of an enduring people? In *Persistent Peoples*. George Pierre Castile and Gilbert Kushner, editors, pp. xv–xxii. Tucson: University of Arizona Press.

Hoebel, E. Adamson. (1972/1954). *The Law of Primitive Man*. New York: Atheneum Press.

Kushner, Gilbert. (1973). *Immigrants from India in Israel: Planned Change in an Administered Community*. Tuscon: University of Arizona Press.

Lipset, Seymour M. (1974). Why cops hate liberals—and vice versa. In *The Police Community*, edited by Jack Goldsmith and Sharon S. Goldsmith, pp. 183–196. Pacific Palisades: Palisades Publishers.

Locke, Hubert G. (1995). The color of law and the issue of color: Race and the abuse of police power. In *And Justice for All: Understanding and Controlling Police Abuse of Force*, edited by William A. Geller and Hans Toch, pp. 133–150. Washington, D.C.: Police Executive Research Forum.

Myers, David. (1993). *Social Psychology*. New York: McGraw Hill.

Redfield, Robert. (1967). Primitive law. In *Law and Warfare*, edited by Paul Bohannan. Garden City: Natural History Press.

Rothstein, Paul. (1981). *Evidence*. St. Paul: West Publishing Company.

Skolnick, Jerome. (1966). *Justice Without Trial: Law Enforcement in Democratic Society*. New York: John Wiley and Sons, Inc.

Spicer, Edward. (1980). *The American Indians*. London: Belknap Press.

Symons, Julian. (1966). *A Pictorial History of Crime*. New York: Bonanza Books.

Weber, Max. (1964/1947). *The Theory of Social and Economic Organization*, edited by Talcott Parsons. New York: Macmillan Free Press.

Chapter XIV

Fortunes of War: From Primitive Warfare to Nuclear Policy in Anthropological Thought

Barton C. Hacker

Anthropologists have regularly revised their viewpoints about the cultural meaning of war and peace since the late nineteenth century. For the discipline's formative years, from the last half of the nineteenth century through the first quarter of the twentieth, war and military institutions fit well into the social evolutionary paradigm that dominated all the social sciences. That changed after the First World War as structural-functionalism displaced social evolutionism. Functional explanations of war achieved some currency during the 1940s and 1950s, but they remained isolated, individual statements rather than contributions to the development of a coherent field. The anthropology of war emerged as a recognizable subfield only in the late 1960s, partly in response to Vietnam. Sociobiology, which also rose to prominence in the 1960s, likewise made war a central concern. At the same time, a revived social evolutionism stimulated new interest in military institutions. The archaeology of war followed a generation later, stimulated at least in part by the turn of the century's ethnic wars.

Although Plato's *Republic* (1945 [c. 350 BCE]) and Aristotle's *Politics* (1946 [c. 340 BCE]) had anciently recognized the central role of military institutions in the state, the modern version of that idea emerged from eighteenth-century reflections on the secular bases of human society and the fundamental importance of social (including military) institutions. Enlightenment social philosophers regularly noticed that the rise of military institutions appeared to link the origins of war with the origins of the social order (Hacker 1993: 2–4; Hacker 1994). But what they observed, chiefly in passing, about the foundational importance of military institutions became a major theme in nineteenth-century social thought.

Through most of the nineteenth century, anthropology remained merely part of a largely undifferentiated and historically oriented social science (Ross 1991). Its central paradigm was social evolution, in which military institutions played a decisive role (Anderson 1990). Military institutions occupied the very center of Herbert Spencer's immensely influential social evolutionism based on ethnography and historical sociology rather than myth or philosophy (Spencer 1876–1896). Social Darwinism owed more to Spencer than to its namesake (Oldroyd 1980: chapters 16–17; Bowler 1984: chapter 10; Bannister 1979; Russett 1976: chapter 4; Clark 1984). His work underpinned a wide range of late nineteenth- and early twentieth-century conflict sociologies (Becker and Barnes 1961: chapter 19; Sorokin 1928: chapter 6; Aho 1975), some explicitly linking social Darwinism to warfare (Crook 1994).

Military institutions also held vital roles in Max Weber's unfinished and posthumously published masterwork of comparative historical sociology, *Economy and Society* (1968). Weber, who died in 1920, was a serious economic historian whose theory sprang from systematic analysis (Frank 1976); Spencer, in contrast, tended to rely on selected ethnographic and historical example (Carneiro 1967). Spencer was not, however, Weber's primary rival. It was Karl Marx, whose social theory Weber devoted his greatest efforts to amplify (Zeitlin 1968, chapter 11; Collins 1974, 1986; Vitkin 1981). Like Weber's *Economy and Society*, Marx's masterpiece, *Capital* (1906), had remained unfinished at his death in 1883 and his *Grundrisse* (1973 [1939]) had not even been intended for publication (Oakley 1983). Unlike Marx, Weber insisted on paying explicit attention to material means of social functions other than production, violence among them. "Separation of the warrior from the means of warfare" seemed to Weber no less significant than separation of the worker from the means of production, "the concentration of the means of warfare in the hands of the warlord" as freighted with meaning as the concentration of the means of production in the hands of the capitalist (Weber 1968: 2: 1155).

Marx had noticed the military origins of discipline (Marx 1906, chapter 13), which became a subject of Weber's close study. Vital to the social order, discipline was the key to shifting the basis of social action from charisma to bureaucracy, from ephemeral enthusiasm to stable routine, from passion to reason (Weber 1968, chapter 14. 3. 1). And it began with the army. "Military discipline gives birth to all discipline," Weber (1968: 2: 1155) asserted. "It has always in some way affected the structure of the state, the economy, and possibly the family." The barracks-like men's houses widespread among pre-state societies maintained warriors apart from family, and it was this so-called warrior communism that accounted for such allegedly pristine social phenomena as universal promiscuity, marriage by capture, or matriarchy (Weber 1968: 2: 1153-1154).

By the end of the nineteenth century, the idea that government ultimately originated in military institutions had become widely accepted. Some believed with Spencer that militarism declined as industrialism advanced; others shared the social Darwinist view that military institutions still dominated social evolution. Even those who rejected war as a positive good could still allow it as a necessary role in civilized life. Either way, virtually no one questioned the historical primacy of military institutions. "All state organization was originally military organization, organization for war," commented one of Germany's most eminent historians, Otto Hintze (Simon 1968; Gerhard 1970) in a 1906 Dresden lecture. "This can be regarded as an assured result of comparative history" (Hintze 1975: 181).

A decade later in England, R. R. Marett (1920 [1915]: 36) in his presidential address to the Folk-lore Society about "War and Savagery" termed it "a commonplace of anthropology that at a certain stage of evolution . . . war is [read: military institutions are] a prime civilizing agency." To the extent that a field discernable as the anthropology of war existed in the half-century before the First World War, however, it comprised catalogues of weapons arranged to demonstrate a hypothetical cultural evolution. This quite exactly describes the first article actually to carry the title "Primitive Warfare," originally published serially from 1867 to 1869 in a British military journal by A. H. Lane-Fox Pitt-Rivers (1906). The field might indeed better be termed the anthropology of weapons.

The World War inaugurated dramatic changes in every aspect of culture and society, not least in intellectual life (Winter et al. 2000). Revulsion against the experience of war fed into disciplinary reactions against the excesses of social evolutionism to sharply reduce the study of war (Becker and Barnes 1961: chapter 20; Hawthorn 1976: chapter 8). Social science fragmented into separate disciplines, each stressing a more narrowly conceived scientism focused on structure, function, and behavior (Anderson 1990, Moore 1978). When war again forced itself on the attention of social scientists in the 1940s, their structural-functional approach contrasted sharply with the evolutionary orientation of such thinking before and during the First World War (Benedict 1946, 1959 [1939]; Malinowski 1941; Childe 1941; Swanton 1943). Conceptually, war displaced the military as the social institution to be studied by anthropologists and other social scientists (Mead 1940, Clarkson and Cochran 1941, Bernard 1944). The new approach also enjoyed significant government support during World War II (Dower 1986).

Through the 1940s and 1950s, even into the early 1960s, however, the anthropology of war never attained any clear identity as a field of study in its own right. As they had for decades, war or weapons usually appeared as a topic in ethnographic studies (LaBarre 1948, Duff 1952, Lewis 1955, Cunnison 1959) or might briefly cross the pages of a general survey (Hoebel 1949, Jacobs and Stern 1952, Bates 1955, La Barre 1955, Honigman 1959). Diligent readers could find published accounts of indigenous warfare as formerly practiced in such widely scattered regions as the Great Plains (Newcomb 1950, Smith 1951, Secoy 1953), the Pacific Northwest (Swadesh 1948, Codere 1950), or the desert Southwest (Stewart 1947, Spicer 1950, Woodbury 1958) of North America, in South America (Fernandes 1949, 1952), Africa (Jeffries 1956, Evans-Pritchard 1957), or Oceania (Tippett 1958, Glasse 1959). Functional explanations competed with psychological explanations of warfare among particular non-state peoples (Murphy 1957, 1958; Wilson 1958), and more general discussions of warfare appeared occasionally in the journals (Pear 1948, Schneider 1950, Hobhouse 1956, LeVine 1961, Leeds 1963). None of this came together in an anthropology of war.

That began changing in the 1960s, stimulated at least in part by the trauma of Vietnam. Two substantial anthologies of previously published material appeared in the mid-1960s (Bramson and Goethals 1964; Bohannon 1967), but the crucial event was an unprecedented plenary symposium at the 1967 meeting of the American Anthropological Association, which became a book the following year. Edited by Morton Fried, Marvin Harris, and Robert Murphy, *War: The Anthropology of Armed Conflict and Aggression* (1968) helped define the anthropology of war as a distinct subfield.

Strongly reinforcing that definition in 1971 was the second edition of Harry Holbert Turney-High's study of *Primitive War*, a book scarcely noticed in its first edition two decades earlier (Rapoport 1971). Anthropologists had also largely ignored a still earlier (and less polemical) argument for a qualitatively distinct "Primitive War" in Quincy Wright's otherwise influential *Study of War* (1942); its 1965 edition attracted little notice either. Wright was a jurist and political scientist, of course, while Turney-High was an anthropologist, which may explain why their work received such different receptions.

Turney-High argued strongly for the priority of organization over weaponry in determining the course and outcome of war. He also forcefully insisted that "primitive warfare" differed qualitatively from "civilized warfare," although his assumption that then-current U. S. Army doctrine somehow represented the last word on military correctness seemed odd for an anthropologist (Turney-High 1971/1949, 1981). Notwithstanding the book's highly polemical tone and other flaws that have largely vitiated its latter-day relevance, it clearly played a major role in launching the anthropology of war (Roland 1991).

Another factor in forming the anthropology of war was the reopening of highland New Guinea for ethnographic fieldwork, scarcely begun before interrupted by World

War Two (Watson 1964: 1-2). Anthropologists for the first time in recent memory could observe nearly pristine primitive warfare and a series of field reports in the late 1960s and 1970s did much to provide the anthropology of war with a more persuasive empirical basis (Rappaport 1967, Gardner 1968, Koch 1974, Vayda 1976, Hallpike 1977, Meggitt 1977; cf. Puma 1987). Functional approaches of various kinds dominated the emergent anthropology of war, all viewing war as a product chiefly of culture, despite evidence of its ubiquity (Otterbein 1970, Harrison 1973, Divale 1973, Nettleship et al. 1975). That war is chiefly a product of culture, not genes or human nature, has remained the dominant anthropological viewpoint (Ferguson 1984, Ferguson and Farragher 1988, Robarchek 1989, Haas 1990a, Knauft 1991; Reyna and Downs 1994).

To others, the ubiquity of war suggested a genetic basis for weaponry and killing, an idea popularized by Robert Ardrey in *African Genesis* (1961) and several later books (Ardrey 1966, 1970, 1976). Popularizers with better credentials than Ardrey, such as Konrad Lorenz (1966) and Desmond Morris (1967, 1969), reinforced the claim. They rediscovered the social Darwinist view, as Greta Jones (1980: 174) phrased it, "of the essential unchanging character of the structure of human society showing how its natural basis reflected war, acquisitiveness, property, aggression and inferiority of the female."

In the 1970s, the more or less popular treatises written by scientists in the new field of sociobiology, most notably Edward O. Wilson (1975, chapter 27; 1978, chapter 5), usually included a chapter that argued from innate human aggressiveness to explain the origins of war (Barash 1979, chapter 6; Alcock 1979, chapter 13; Eibl-Eibesfeldt 1979). With few exceptions, anthropologists and other social scientists sharply criticized sociobiology's implied or overt reductionism (Montagu 1968, 1976; Alland 1972, chapter 6; Bock 1980; Howell and Willis 1989; Hunter 1991). Accordingly, sociobiological claims, if not entirely withdrawn, became muted or at least more nuanced (Hinde 1992, Howe 1992, van der Dennen and Falger 1990, van der Dennen 1991, cf. Morris 1983, chapter 7).

More recently, the same claims that genes determine a wide variety of social and cultural behavior, including warfare, have been reasserted (admittedly minus some of the worst sociobiological excesses) under the rubric of evolutionary psychology (Barkow et al. 1992, Plotkin 1998, Buss 1999). Although most of the "evidence" drawn from nonprimate behavioral studies has been expunged, evolutionary psychology remains no less suspect than sociobiology (Wilson 1994, Dusek 1999).

Questionable or not, the supposed genetic basis for war attracted the interest of some anthropologists. Archaeological evidence for prehistoric death by artifact became all too easily transmuted into evidence for war (rather than, say, murder), ambiguous rock drawings into evidence for armies (Tiger 1969, chapter 4; 1993; Holloway 1974; Chagnon and Irons 1979; Shaw 1985; Shaw and Wong 1989; Manson and Wrangham 1991). For the most part, however, before the mid-1990s few archaeologists gave much thought to just how one might identify war as distinct from other forms of violence in the archaeological record, or what record military organization might leave, and the conclusions were by no means clear-cut (Roper 1969, 1975; Behrens 1978; Vencl 1984, 1991; Tkaczuk and Vivian 1989; Haas 1990b).

Such concerns remained unresolved through what Roberta Gilchrist (2003: 1) described as the mid-1990s "explosion of interest in the archaeology of warfare." Just as the Vietnam War stimulated the emergence of the anthropology of war, the moral impact of the late twentieth century's bloody ethnic wars may have influenced the rise of the archaeology of war (Vankilde 2003). The specific catalyst was the 1996 publication of *War before Civilization*, Lawrence J. Keeley's polemical assessment of archaeology's unwarranted pacification of the past. Neither Keeley nor some of those who followed in his footsteps seemed much concerned with distinguishing war from other forms of violent behavior in the archaeological record (Martin and Frayer 1997, Carman and Redmond 1997, Walker 2001). Yet the distinction matters, as a recent exchange between political scientist Azar Gat (2000a, b) and anthropologist R. Brian Ferguson (2000) in the pages of *Anthropological Quarterly* clearly demonstrates.

The Gat-Ferguson argument falters upon their failure to address the qualitative differences between warfare and other forms of individual or intergroup violence. People may have always fought with each other, but war belongs to complex societies. As H. S. Harrison (1929: 9), the curator of London's Horniman Museum and Library, long ago observed in his handbook of the museum's weapons collection, "fighting has its roots in defensive rather than offensive instincts, whilst warfare proper is a refinement of civilisation." Exactly when war began has evoked a range of answers from modern scholars, but many share the view that at some point 10,000 and 5,000 years before the present a new kind of violent human interaction emerged, qualitatively different from past forms of violent behavior. The origin of war was a historic event, not part of the human condition (Dawson 1999, Kelly 2000; Thorpe 2003).

War has also attracted growing interest from historical archaeologists. Documentary evidence, even if indirect, allows them to finesse the problems of identifying warlike remains. They can determine when they have found a battlefield (Scott et al. 1989, Fiorato et al. 2000) or another manifestation of military presence (Cocroft 2000, Hill and Wileman 2001). The study of twentieth-century military structures on the land has lately become an especially lively enterprise, emphasizing the World Wars and the Cold War (Foot 2000, Schofield et al. 2002, Dobinson 2003, Cocroft and Thomas 2003). Anthropological and sociobiological attempts to account for war simply reflected another facet of the long-running and inconclusive debate over nurture versus nature as primary determinants of human behavior (Cravens 1978; Degler 1991, Dawson 1996). In a sense, it hardly mattered whether war was a function of sociocultural imperatives or an expression of innate human biology. Both sides took war as a central human activity, widespread though seemingly maladaptive, and assumed that what needed explaining was fighting and killing. Neither paid much attention to the more significant topic of military organization and its consequences.

The 1960s saw a third approach to the problem of war that sidestepped the nature-nurture debate and focused on institutions. Modern political anthropology developed around the question of the origin of the state (Service 1985). It made war a dependent variable, the product of social organization, specifically military institutions. This had been one of the central themes of nineteenth-century social evolutionism, which also enjoyed a new lease on life. Three important books reopened the old question and forcefully stated a modern case for social evolution. Elman Service laid the groundwork with a textbook of case studies first published in 1962 (with several later editions): *Primitive Social Organization*. His later monograph, *Origins of the State and Civilization* (1975), addressed the question more directly. Meanwhile Morton Fried in 1968 published *The*

Evolution of Political Society. Although neither Service nor Fried made war a crucial factor, both addressed war as a central topic in social evolution.

Robert Carneiro became the key figure in moving military institutions back to center stage when he gave coercion the starring role in state formation. "A Theory of the Origin of the State" appeared in 1970, though its thesis had been foreshadowed in an earlier, less widely noticed article (Carneiro 1961). Drawing on a wealth of anthropological and archaeological data, he persuasively argued that only in circumstances that allowed conquest through armed force could states be formed. Carneiro's thesis has been immensely influential (Roscoe and Graber 1988) and he has continued to expand his views (Carneiro 1992, 1994). Other anthropologists have followed his lead in discussing the general problem (Webb 1970; Webster 1975; Lewis 1981; Haas 1982; Cohen 1984, Redmond 1998), but also in studying the role of armies in specific instances of state formation, especially in Africa (Law 1980; Roberts 1980a; Siran 1980; Barnes and Ben-Amos 1983; Tymowski 1981, 1987).

Carneiro (2003) has lately published a critical history of evolutionism in cultural anthropology and contributed to a recent reappraisal of Herbert Spencer's work (Caneiro and Perrin 2002). That Spencer's sociocultural evolutionism strongly influenced Carneiro's thinking emerges clearly from Carneiro's 1967 edition of Herbert Spencer for modern readers. The same seems true of Stanislav Andreski (1969), who also edited Spencer for moderns. Despite its conventional tagging as sociology, Andreski's 1954 study of *Military Organization and Society* rests squarely in the comparative, sociocultural evolutionary tradition that antedated the First World War. Like Turney-High's *Primitive War*, Andreski's book received little notice when first published. Its real impact upon the social sciences—sociology, political science, and history, as well as anthropology—followed the publication of a second edition (1968), and even more its appearance in paperback three years later.

By the 1970s the nascent field of ethnohistory began to meld findings from the anthropology of war and political anthropology. The seminal work was Jack Goody's 1971 essay on *Technology, Tradition and the State in Africa.* Following Max Weber, he argued that any attempt to understand society demanded paying attention not only to the material means of production (as Marx advocated) but also to the material means of other social functions, violence among them. Discussing nineteenth-century state formation in the Sudan, Goody (1971) explicitly addressed "Polity and the Means of Destruction," a theme others found persuasive (Smaldone 1977, Roberts 1980b, Winzeler 1981).

Ethnographers also noticed that armed force was not limited to state formation. In due course, some began to infringe on sociological territory with studies of civilized military institutions, most notably in pursuing the ethnography of nuclear decision-making and other aspects of military-technological policy in late twentieth-century America (Mandelbaum 1984, Rubinstein and Foster 1988, Turner and Pitt 1989, Gusterson 1996).

Anthropological approaches to war have taken three tacks. Anthropologists of war mostly address the warlike activities of non-state and pre-state peoples as observed in the field. This has always posed problems, for a number of reasons. The rise of fieldwork as a professional rite of passage coincided with the growing efforts of colonial powers to suppress primitive warriors. And, as we have learned in recent years, the practice of war among non-state peoples has never been observed in a truly pristine environment (Ferguson and Whitehead 1992). Military influence, if not direct pressure, from states almost certainly distorted normal practices beyond all recognition.

Sociobiologists claim to find war springing from human genes. In its extreme position, the argument is ludicrous, leading some to equate ant and human societies (O'Connell 1995, chapter 2; cf. Topoff 1984). Moderation, however, still leaves war as an expression of innate human aggression. There may, in fact, be some case to be made for a genetic component in human warfare. People are, after all, capable of bellicose behavior. But bellicosity, although it may be an asset for warriors, only hampers soldiers, whose primary virtues are discipline and obedience. However uncomfortable the terminology has become in recent decades, primitive warfare really is distinct from civilized warfare, and the difference between bellicosity and obedience is crucial.

Social evolutionists have been most consistent in recognizing the enduring influence of military activity on social organization. In the discourse of social evolution, war tends to be peripheral to the central inquiry, which concerns military institutions. Unfortunately, social evolutionists regularly attempt to use the term "militarism" neutrally to label normal military activities and organization. In doing so, they neglect the term's pejorative connotations and the studies that have identified militarism as an aberration of the military order (Vagts 1959, Berghahn 1982).

Military institutions are species of social institutions, patterned social relationships between individuals and groups that organize and control the achievement of enduring social purposes. Unlike more commonly recognized social institutions present in all human societies, military institutions exist only in those that have attained state or near-state organization; indeed, they have shaped the state from its origins at the dawn of history. The social purposes they serve center on wielding coercive force toward several ends: warding external threats, seizing resources, quelling internal dissent. Military institutions comprise more than uniformed men. Ultimately, they encompass the state itself and their influence pervades the entire social system (Hacker 1994).

Social scientists have too often failed to acknowledge, perhaps even to recognize, the distinction between the social action of war and the social structure of military institutions. Distinguishing clearly between war, even war conceived as a social institution, and military institutions is essential. Armies are complex, hierarchal, and disciplined social organizations of soldiers, not ephemeral gatherings of more-or-less independent warriors. And the kind of war fought by armies is qualitatively different from the other kinds of inter-group conflict that has sometimes been termed primitive war. "War," in short, labels several very different activities and our language betrays us when we unthinkingly apply the same word to all.

The issue is not merely the impact of a specific war or wars, or even of war in general. That war serves as potent cause of change is an old idea. But war is also sporadic, making it difficult to discern as a shaper of development. Thus war appeared as a natural catastrophe or divine retribution, an agent of social disruption rather than a motor for social change. Military institutions, in contrast, are powerful and persistent social structures. As major nexuses of social values, ideas, and interests, they clearly play large and constant historical roles.

But social scientists seldom grant the subject the attention its importance merits. Antiwar or antimilitarist sentiments, rather than spurring efforts to understand the evil, instead seem chiefly to evoke revulsion and to condone, if not to justify, ignorance. War will not go away because we deny its existence, but we may be able to do something about it if we learn enough about the social, especially military, institutions from which it derives.

References

Aho, James Alfred. (1975). *German Realpolitik and American Sociology: An Inquiry into the Sources and Political Significance of the Sociology of Conflict*. Lewisburg, Pennsylvania: Bucknell University Press; London: Associated University Presses.

Alcock, John. (1979). *Animal Behavior: An Evolutionary Approach*. 2nd edition. Sunderland, Massachusetts: Sinauer Associates.

Alland, Alexander, Jr. (1972). *The Human Imperative*. New York: Columbia University Press.

Anderson, Stephen K. (1990). *Social Evolutionism: A Critical History*. Oxford: Basil Blackwell.

Andreski, Stanislav. (1954). *Military Organization and Society*. London: Routledge and Kegan Paul.

———. (1968). *Military Organization and Society*. 2nd edition. Berkeley: University of California Press.

———, editor. (1969). *Principles of Sociology*, by Herbert Spencer. Hamden, Connecticut: Archon Books.

Ardrey, Robert. (1961). *African Genesis: A Personal Investigation into the Animal Origins and Nature of Man*. New York: Atheneum.

———. (1966). *The Territorial Imperative: A Personal Inquiry into the Animal Origins of Property and Nations*. New York: Atheneum.

———. (1970). *The Social Contract: A Personal Inquiry into the Evolutionary Sources of Order and Disorder*. New York: Atheneum.

———. (1976). *The Hunting Hypothesis: A Personal Conclusion Concerning the Evolutionary Nature of Man*. New York: Atheneum.

Aristotle. (1946). *The Politics of Aristotle*. Translated by Ernest Barker. London: Oxford University Press.

Bannister, Robert C. (1979). *Social Darwinism: Science and Myth in Anglo-American Thought*. Philadelphia: Temple University Press.

Barash, David. (1979). *The Whisperings Within*. New York: Harper and Row.

Barkow, Jerome H., Leda Cosmides, and John Tooby, editors. (1992). *The Adapted Mind: Evolutionary Psychology and the Generation of Culture*. New York: Oxford University Press.

Barnes, Sandra J., and Paula Ben-Amos. (1983). Benin, Oyo, and Dahomey: Warfare, state building, and the sacralization of iron in West African history. *Expedition* 25 (Winter): 5–14.

Bates, Marston. (1955). *The Prevalence of People*. New York: Charles Scribner's Sons.

Becker, Howard, and Harry Elmer Barnes. (1961). *Social Thought from Lore to Science: A History and Interpretation of Man's Ideas about Life with His Fellows*. 3rd edition, 3 volumes. New York: Dover.

Behrens, Hermann W. (1978). Der Kampf in Steinzeit (Ein Diskussionbeitrag vom Aspekt des Prähistorikers). *Mitteilungen der Anthropologischen Gesellschaft in Wien* 108: 1–7.

Benedict, Ruth. (1946). *The Chrysanthemum and the Sword: Patterns of Japanese Culture.* Boston: Houghton Mifflin.

———. (1959 [1939]). The natural history of war. In *An Anthropologist at Work: Writings of Ruth Benedict,* edited by Margaret Mead, pp. 369–382. Boston: Houghton Mifflin.

Berghahn, Volker R. (1982). *Militarism: The History of an International Debate, 1861–1979.* New York: St. Martin's Press.

Bernard, L. L. (1944). *War and Its Causes.* New York: Holt.

Bock, Kenneth. (1980). *Human Nature and History: A Response to Sociobiology.* New York: Columbia University Press.

Bohannon, Paul, editor. (1967). *Law and Warfare: Studies in the Anthropology of Conflict.* Garden City, New York: Natural History Press, for the American Museum of Natural History.

Bowler, Peter J. (1984). *Evolution: The History of an Idea.* Berkeley: University of California Press.

Bramson, Leon, and George W. Goethals, editors. (1964). *War: Studies from Psychology, Sociology, Anthropology.* New York: Basic Books.

Buss, David M. (1999). *Evolutionary Psychology: The New Science of the Mind.* Boston: Allyn and Bacon.

Carman, John, and Elsa L. Redmond, editors. (1997). *Material Harm: Archaeological Studies of War and Violence.* Glasgow: Cruithne Press.

Carneiro, Robert L. (1961). Slash-and-burn cultivation among the Kuikuru and its implications for cultural development in the Amazon Basin. In *The Evolution of Horticultural Systems in Native South America: Causes and Consequences, a Symposium,* edited by Johannes Wilbert, pp. 47–65. *Antropológica* (Caracas), supplement 2:

———, editor. (1967). *The Evolution of Society: Selections from Herbert Spencer's "Principles of Sociology."* Chicago: University of Chicago Press.

———. (1970). A theory of the origin of the state. *Science* 169: 733–738.

———. (1992). The role of warfare in political evolution: Past results and future projections. In *Effects of War on Society,* edited by Giorgio Ausenda, pp. 87–102. San Marino: AIEP Editore, for the Center for Interdisciplinary Research on Social Stress.

———. (1994). War and peace: Alternating realities in human history. In *Studying War: Anthropological Perspectives,* edited by Stephen P. Reyna and R. E. Downs, pp. 3–27. Langhorne, Pennsylvania: Gordon and Breach.

———. (2003). *Evolutionism in Cultural Anthropology: A Critical History.* Boulder, Colorado: Westview Press.

Carneiro, Robert L., and Robert G. Perrin. (2002). Herbert Spencer's *Principles of Sociology*: A centennial retrospective and appraisal. *Annals of Science* 59: 221–261.

Chagnon, Napoleon A., and William Irons, editors. (1979). *Evolutionary Biology and Human Social Behavior: An Anthropological Perspective.* North Scituate, Massachusetts: Duxbury Press.

Childe, V. Gordon. (1941). War in prehistoric societies. *Sociological Review* 33: 126–138.

Clark, Linda L. (1984). *Social Darwinism in France*. University: University of Alabama Press.

Clarkson, Jesse D., and Thomas C. Cochran, editors. (1941). *War as a Social Institution: The Historian's Perspective*. New York: Columbia University Press.

Cocroft, Wayne D. (2000). *Dangerous Energy: The Archaeology of Gunpowder and Military Explosives Manufacture*. Swindon: English Heritage.

Cocroft, Wayne D., and Roger Thomas, editors. (2003). *Cold War: Building for Nuclear Confrontation*. Swindon: English Heritage.

Codere, Helen. (1950). *Fighting with Property: A Study of Kwakiutl Potlatching and Warfare, 1792–1930*. Monographs of the American Ethnological Society 18. Seattle: University of Washington Press.

Cohen, Ronald. (1984). Warfare and state formation: Wars make states and states make wars. In *Warfare, Culture, and Environment*, edited by R. Brian Ferguson, pp. 329–359. Orlando, Florida: Academic Press.

Collins, Randall. (1974). The empirical validity of the conflict tradition. *Theory and Society* 1: 147–178.

———. (1986). *Weberian Sociological Theory*. Cambridge: Cambridge University Press.

Cravens, Hamilton. (1978). *The Triumph of Evolution: American Scientists and the Heredity-Environment Controversy, 1900–1941*. Philadelphia: University of Pennsylvania Press.

Crook, Paul. (1994). *Darwinism, War and History: The Debate over the Biology of War from the "Origin of Species" to the First World War*. Cambridge: Cambridge University Press.

Cunnison, Ian. (1959). *The Luapula Peoples of Northern Nigeria: Custom and History in Tribal Politics*. Manchester: Manchester University Press, for the Rhodes-Livingstone Institute, Northern Rhodesia.

Dawson, Doyne. (1996). The origins of war: Biological and anthropological theories. *History and Theory* 35/1: 1–28.

———. (1999). Evolutionary theory and group selection: The question of warfare. *History and Theory* 38/4: 79–100.

Degler, Carl N. (1991). *In Search of Human Nature: The Decline and Revival of Darwinism in American Social Thought*. New York: Oxford University Press.

Divale, William Tulio. (1973). *Warfare in Primitive Societies: A Bibliography*. Santa Barbara, California: ABC-Clio.

Dobinson, Colin. (2003). *Building Radar*. London: Methuen, for English Heritage.

Dower, John W. (1986). *War without Mercy: Race and Power in the Pacific War*. New York: Pantheon Books.

Duff, Wilson. (1952). *The Upper Stalo Indians, of the Fraser Valley, British Columbia*. Victoria: British Columbia Provincial Museum.

Dusek, R. Valentine. (1999). Sociobiology sanitized: Evolutionary psychology and gene selectionism debates. *Science as Culture* 8.2: 129–170.

Eibl-Eibesfeldt, Irenäus. (1979). *The Biology of Peace and War: Man, Animals, and Aggression*. New York: Viking.

Evans-Pritchard, E. E. (1957). Zande Warfare. *Anthropos* 52: 239–262.

Ferguson, R. Brian, editor. (1984). *Warfare, Culture, and Environment*. Orlando, Florida: Academic Press.

———. (2000). On evolved motivations for war. *Anthropological Quarterly* 73: 159–164.

Ferguson, R. Brian, and Leslie E. Farragher. (1988). *The Anthropology of War: A Bibliography*. New York: Harry Frank Guggenheim Foundation.

Ferguson, R. Brian, and Neil L. Whitehead, editors. (1992). *War in the Tribal Zone: Expanding States and Indigenous Warfare*. Santa Fe, New Mexico: School of American Research Press.

Fernandes, Florestan. (1949). A análise funcionalista da guerra: possibilidades de aplicação à sociedade tupinambá. Ensaio de análise crítica da contribuição etnográfica dos cronistas para o estudo sociológico da guerra entre populaçãos aborigenes do Brasil quinhentista e seiscentista. *Revista do Museu Paulista*, new series 3: 7–128.

———. (1952). A função social da guerra na sociedade tupinambá. *Revista do Museu Paulista*, new series 6: 1–425.

Fiorato, Veronica, Anthea Boylston, and Christopehr Knüsel, editors. (2000). *Blood Red Roses: The Archaeology of a Mass Grave from the Battle of Towton AD 1461*. Oxford: Oxbow Books.

Foot, William. (2000). Landscape of war. *British Archaeology* no. 54.

Frank, R. I. (1976). Translator's introduction. In *The Agrarian Sociology of Ancient Civilizations*, by Max Weber, 7–33. Atlantic Highlands, New Jersey: Humanities Press.

Fried, Morton H. (1968). *The Evolution of Political Society: An Essay in Political Anthropology*. New York: Random House.

Fried, Morton H., Marvin Harris, and Robert Murphy, editors. (1968). *War: The Anthropology of Armed Conflict and Aggression*. Garden City, New York: Doubleday.

Gardner, Robert, and Karl G. Heider. (1968). *Gardens of War: Life and Death in the New Guinea Stone Age*. New York: Random House.

Gat, Azar. (2000a). The human motivational complex: Evolutionary theory and the causes of hunter-gatherer fighting, part II: Proximate, subordinate, and derivative causes. *Anthropological Quarterly* 73: 74–88.

———. (2000b). Reply to Ferguson. *Anthropological Quarterly* 73: 165–168.

Gerhard, Dietrich. (1970). Otto Hintze: His work and his significance in historiography. *Central European History* 3: 17–48.

Gilchrist, Roberta. (2003). Introduction: Towards a social archaeology of warfare. *World Archaeology* 35: 1–6.

Glasse, Robert M. (1959). Revenge and redress among the Huli: A preliminary account. *Mankind* 5: 273–289.

Goody, Jack. (1971). *Technology, Tradition, and the State in Africa*. London: Oxford University Press.

Gusterson, Hugh. (1996). *Nuclear Rites: A Weapons Laboratory at the End of the Cold War*. Berkeley: University of California Press.

Haas, Jonathan. (1982). *The Evolution of the Prehistoric State*. New York: Columbia University Press.

———, editor. (1990a). *The Anthropology of War*. Cambridge: Cambridge University Press.

————. (1990b). Warfare and the evolution of tribal politics in the prehistoric South-west. In *The Anthropology of War*, edited by Jonathan Haas, pp. 171–189. Cambridge: Cambridge University Press.

Hacker, Barton C. (1993). Military institutions and social order: Transformations of Western thought since the Enlightenment. *War and Society* 11: 1–23.

————. (1994). Military institutions, weapons, and social change: Toward a new history of military technology. *Technology and Culture* 35: 768–834.

Hallpike, C. R. (1977). *Bloodshed and Vengeance in the Papuan Mountains: The Generation of Conflict in Tauade Society*. Oxford: Clarendon Press.

Harrison, H. S. (1929). *War and the Chase: A Handbook of the Collection of Weapons of Savage, Barbaric, and Civilised Peoples*. The Horniman Museum and Library. 2nd edition. London: London County Council.

Harrison, Robert. (1973). *Warfare*. Basic Concepts in Anthropology. Minneapolis: Burgess.

Hawthorn, Geoffrey. (1976). *Enlightenment and Despair: A History of Sociology*. Cambridge: Cambridge University Press.

Hill, Paul, and Julie Wileman. (2001). *Landscapes of War: The Archaeology of Aggression and Defence*. Stroud, England: Tempus.

Hinde, Robert A. (1992). Aggression and the institution of war. In *The Institution of War*, edited by Robert A. Hinde, pp. 1–8. New York: St. Martin's Press.

Hintze, Otto. (1975 [1906]). Military organization and the organization of the state. Lecture at the Gehe Stiftung, Dresden. In *The Historical Essays of Otto Hintze*, edited by Felix Gilbert with Robert M. Berdahl, pp. 180–215. New York: Oxford University Press.

Hobhouse, Leonard T. (1956). The simplest peoples, part II: Peace and order among the simplest peoples. *British Journal of Sociology* 7: 96–119.

Hoebel, E. Adamson. (1949). *Man in the Primitive World: An Introduction to Anthropology*. New York: MacGraw-Hill.

Holloway, Ralph L., editor. (1974). *Primate Aggression, Territoriality, and Xenophobia: A Comparative Perspective*. New York: Academic Press.

Honigman, John J. (1959). *The World of Man*. New York: Harper and Row.

Howe, Henry, et al. (1992). The rhetoric of sociobiology. *Social Epistemology* 6: 107–240.

Howell, Signe, and Roy Willis, editors. (1989). *Societies at Peace: Anthropological Perspectives*. London: Routledge.

Hunter, Anne E., editor. (1991). *Genes and Gender VI. On Peace, War, and Gender: A Challenge to Genetic Explanations*. New York: Feminist Press.

Jacobs, Melville, and Bernhard J. Stern. (1952). *General Anthropology*. 2nd edition. New York: Barnes and Noble.

Jeffries, M. D. W. (1956). Ibo warfare. *Man* 56: 77–79.

Jones, Greta. (1980). *Social Darwinism and English Thought: The Interaction between Biological and Social Theory*. Sussex, England: Harvester Press; Atlantic Highlands, New Jersey: Humanities Press.

Keeley, Lawrence H. (1996). *War before Civilization*. New York: Oxford University Press.

Kelly, Raymond C. (2000). *Warless Societies and the Origin of War*. Ann Arbor: University of Michigan Press.

Knauft, Bruce M. (1991). Violence and sociability in human evolution. *Current Anthropology* 32: 391–428.

Koch, Klaus-Friedrich. (1974). *War and Peace in Jalémó: The Management of Conflict in Highland New Guinea*. Cambridge: Harvard University Press.

La Barre, Weston. (1948). *The Aymara Indians of the Lake Titicaca Plateau, Bolivia*. American Anthropological Association, Memoir 68.

La Barre, Weston. (1955). *The Human Animal*. Chicago: University of Chicago Press.

Law, Robin. (1980). *The Horse in West African History: The Role of the Horse in the Societies of Pre-Colonial West Africa*. Oxford: Oxford University Press.

Leeds, Anthony. (1963). The functions of war. In *Violence and War: With Clinical Studies*, edited by Jules H. Masserman, pp. 69–82. New York and London: Grune & Stratton.

LeVine, Robert A. (1961). Anthropology and the study of conflict: An introduction. *Journal of Conflict Resolution* 5: 3–15.

Lewis, Herbert S. (1981). Warfare and the origin of the state: Another formulation. In *The Study of the State*, edited by Henri J. M. Claessen and Peter Skalník, pp. 201–221. The Hague: Mouton.

Lewis, I. M. (1955). *Peoples of the Horn of Africa: Somali, Afar and Saho*. Ethnographic Survey of Africa, North-Eastern Africa, part 1. London: International African Institute.

Lorenz, Konrad. (1966). *On Aggression*. Translated by Marjorie Kerr Wilson. New York: Harcourt, Brace & World.

Malinowski, Bronislaw. (1941). An anthropological analysis of war. *American Journal of Sociology* 46: 521–550.

Mandelbaum, David G. (1984). Anthropology for the nuclear age. *Bulletin of the Atomic Scientists* 40 (June/July): 11–15.

Manson, Joseph H., and Richard W. Wrangham. (1991). Intergroup aggression in chimpanzees and humans. *Current Anthropology* 32: 369–390.

Marett, R. R. (1920 [1915]). War and savagery. Presidential address to the Folk-lore Society. In *Psychology and Folk-lore*, by R. R. Marett, pp. 27–48. London: Methuen.

Martin, Debra L., and David W. Frayer, editors. (1997). *Troubled Times: Violence and Warfare in the Past*. Amsterdam: Gordon and Breach.

Marx, Karl. (1906). *Capital: A Critique of Political Economy, vol. 1: The Process of Capitalist Production*. Translated by Samuel Moore and Edward Aveling from the 3d German edition, edited by Frederick Engels. Revised by Ernest Untermann according to the 4th German edition. Chicago: Charles H. Kerr.

———. (1973 [1939]). *Grundrisse: Foundations of the Critique of Political Economy*. Translated by Martin Nicolaus. New York: Random House.

Mead, Margaret. (1940). Warfare is only an invention—not a biological necessity. *Asia* 40: 402–405.

Meggitt, Mervyn. (1977). *Blood Is Their Argument: Warfare among the Mae Enga of the New Guinea Highlands*. Palo Alto, California: Mayfield.

Montagu, M. F. Ashley, editor. (1968). *Man and Aggression*. London: Oxford University Press.

————. (1976). *The Nature of Human Aggression*. Oxford: Oxford University Press.

Moore, Wilbert E. (1978). Functionalism. In *A History of Sociological Analysis*, edited by Tom Bottomore and Robert Nisbet, pp. 321–361. New York: Basic Books.

Morris, Desmond. (1967). *The Naked Ape: A Zoologist's Study of the Human Animal*. New York: McGraw-Hill.

————. (1969). *The Human Zoo*. New York: McGraw-Hill.

Morris, Richard. (1983). *Evolution and Human Nature*. New York: Seaview/Putnam.

Murphy, Robert F. (1957). Intergroup hostility and social cohesion. *American Anthropologist* 59: 1018–1035.

————. (1958). Reply to Wilson. *American Anthropologist* 60: 1196–1199.

Nettleship, Martin A., R. Dale Givens, and Anderson Nettleship, editors. (1975). *War: Its Causes and Correlates*. The Hague: Mouton.

Newcomb, W. W., Jr. (1950). A re-examination of the causes of Plains warfare. *American Anthropologist* 52: 317–330.

Oakley, Allen. (1983). *The Making of Marx's Critical Theory: A Bibliographical Analysis*. London: Routledge.

O'Connell, Robert L. (1995). *Ride of the Second Horseman: The Birth and Death of War*. New York: Oxford University Press.

Oldroyd, D. R. (1980). *Darwinian Impacts: An Introduction to the Darwinian Revolution*. Atlantic Highlands, New Jersey: Humanities Press.

Otterbein, Keith F. (1970). *The Evolution of War: A Cross-Cultural Study*. Philadelphia: HRAF Press.

Pear, T. H. (1948). Peace, war, and culture-patterns. *John Rylands Library Bulletin* 31: 120–147.

Pitt-Rivers, A. H. Lane-Fox. (1906 [1867-1869]). Primitive warfare. *Journal of the Royal United Service Institution* 11–13. Reprinted in *Pitt-Rivers, The Evolution of Culture, and Other Essays*, edited by J. L. Myres, pp. 45–185. Oxford: Oxford University Press.

Plato. (1945). *The Republic of Plato*. Translated by Francis MacDonald Cornford. New York: Oxford University Press.

Plotkin, Henry. (1998). *Evolution in Mind: An Introduction to Evolutionary Psychology*. Cambridge: Harvard University Press.

Puma, Edward Li. (1987). War in the New Guinea Highlands: Theory and ethnography in conflict. In *Dominance, Aggression and War*, edited by Diane McGuinness, pp. 180–196. New York: Paragon House.

Rapoport, David C. (1971). Foreword. In *Primitive War: Its Practice and Concepts*, by Harry Holbert Turney-High, pp. v–xi. 2nd edition. Columbia: University of South Carolina Press.

Rappaport, Roy A. (1967). *Pigs for the Ancestors: Ritual in the Ecology of a New Guinea People*. New Haven: Yale University Press.

Redmond, Elsa M., editor. (1998). *Chiefdoms and Chieftaincy in the Americas*. Gainesville: University Press of Florida.

Reyna, Stephen P., and R. E. Downs, editors. (1994). *Studying War: Anthropological Perspectives*. Langhorne, Pennsylvania: Gordon and Breach.

Robarchek, Clayton A. (1989). Primitive warfare and the ratomorphic image of mankind. *American Anthropologist* 91: 903–920.

Roberts, Richard L. (1980a). Production and reproduction of warrior states: Segu Bambara and Segu Tokolor, c. 1712–1890. *International Journal of African Studies* 13: 389–419.

———. (1980b). Warfare, technology, and the state. *Canadian Journal of African Studies* 14: 334–340.

Roland, Alex. (1991). Introduction. In *Primitive War: Its Practice and Concepts*, by Harry Holbert Turney-High, pp. vii–xi. 2nd edition, 3rd printing. Columbia: University of South Carolina Press.

Roper, Marilyn Keyes. (1969). A survey of the evidence of intrahuman killing in the Pleistocene. *Current Anthropology* 10: 427–459.

———. (1975). Evidence of warfare in the Near East from 10,000–4,300 B.C. In *War: Its Causes and Correlates*, edited by Martin A. Nettleship, R. Dale Givens, and Anderson Nettleship, pp. 299–343. The Hague: Mouton.

Roscoe, Paul B., and Robert B. Graber, editors. (1988). Circumscription and the evolution of society. *American Behavioral Scientist* 31: 403–511.

Ross, Dorothy. (1991). *The Origins of American Social Science*. Cambridge: Cambridge University Press.

Rubinstein, Robert A., and Mary LeCron Foster, editors. (1988). *The Social Dynamics of Peace and Conflict: Culture in International Security*. Boulder, Colorado: Westview Press.

Russett, Cynthia Eagle. (1976). *Darwin in America: The Intellectual Response, 1865–1912*. San Francisco: W. H. Freeman.

Schneider, Joseph. (1950). Primitive warfare: A methodological note. *American Sociological Review* 15: 772–777.

Schofield, John, William Gray Johnson, and Colleen M. Beck, editors. (2002). *Matériel Culture: The Archaeology of Twentieth Century Conflict*. London: Routledge.

Scott, Douglas D., Richard A. Fox, Jr., Melissa A. Connor, and Dick Harmon. (1989). *Archaeological Perspectives on the Battle of Little Big Horn*. Norman: University of Oklahoma Press.

Secoy, Frank Raymond. (1953). *Changing Military Patterns on the Great Plains (17th Century through Early 19th Century)*. Monographs of the American Ethnological Society 21. Locust Valley, New York: J. J. Augustin.

Service, Elman R. (1962). *Primitive Social Organization: An Evolutionary Perspective*. New York: Random House.

———. (1975). *Origins of the State and Civilization: The Process of Cultural Evolution*. New York: W. W. Norton.

———. (1985). *A Century of Controversy: Ethnological Issues from 1860 to 1960*. Orlando, Florida: Academic Press.

Shaw, R. Paul. (1985). Humanity's propensity for warfare: A sociobiological perspective. *Canadian Review of Sociology and Anthropology* 22: 158–183.

Shaw, R. Paul, and Yuwa Wong. (1989). *Genetic Seeds of Warfare: Evolution, Nationalism, and Patriotism*. Boston: Unwin Hyman.

Simon, W. M. (1968). Power and responsibility: Otto Hintze's place in German historiography. In *The Responsibility of Power: Historical Essays in Honor of Hajo Holborn*, edited by Leonard Krieger and Fritz Stern, pp. 215–237. Garden City, New York: Doubleday.

Siran, Jean-Louis. (1980). Emergence et dissolution des principautés guerrières vouté. *Société des Africanistes, Journal* 50: 25–57.

Smaldone, Joseph P. (1977). *Warfare in the Sokoto Caliphate: Historical and Sociological Perspectives*. Cambridge: Cambridge University Press.

Smith,. Marian W. (1951). American Indian warfare. *Transactions of the New York Academy of Sciences*, 2nd series, 13: 348–365.

Sorokin, Pitirim A. (1928). *Contemporary Sociological Theories: Through the First Quarter of the Twentieth Century*. New York: Harper.

Spencer, Herbert (1876–1896). *Principles of Sociology*. 3 volumes. New York: D. Appleton.

Spicer, Edward H. (1950). The military orientation of Yaqui culture. In *For the Dean: Essays in Anthropology in Honor of Byron Cummings on His Eighty-ninth Birthday, September 20, 1950*, edited by Erik K. Reed and Dale S. King, pp. 171–188. Tucson: Hohokam Museums Association; Santa Fe: Southwestern Monuments Association.

Stewart, Kenneth M. (1947). Mohave warfare. *Southwestern Journal of Anthropology* 3: 257–278.

Swadesh, M. (1948). Motivations in Nootka warfare. *Southwestern Journal of Anthropology* 4: 76–93.

Swanton, John R. (1943). *Are Wars Inevitable?* War Background Studies 12. Washington: Smithsonian Institution.

Thorpe, I. J. N. (2003). Anthropology, archaeology, and the origin of warfare. *World Archaeology* 35: 145–165.

Tiger, Lionel. (1969). *Men in Groups*. New York: Random House.

―――. (1993). Biological antecedents of human aggression. In *Primate Social Conflict*, edited by William A. Mason and Sally P. Mendoza, pp. 373–386. Albany: State University of New York Press.

Tippett, A. R. (1958). The nature and social function of Fijian war (focus—1739–1846). *Transactions and Proceedings of the Fiji Society* 5: 137–55.

Tkaczuk, Diana Claire, and Brian C. Vivian, editors. (1989). *Cultures in Conflict: Current Archaeological Perspectives*. Calgary: Archaeological Society of Calgary.

Topoff, Howard. (1984). Social organization of raiding and emigrations in army ants. *Advances in the Study of Behavior* 14: 81–126.

Turner, Paul R., and David Pitt, editors. (1989). *The Anthropology of War and Peace: Perspectives on the Nuclear Age*. Granby, Massachusetts: Bergin and Garvey.

Turney-High, Harry Holbert. (1971/1949). *Primitive War: Its Practice and Concepts*. Columbia: University of South Carolina Press.

―――. (1981). *The Military: The Theory of Land Warfare as Behavioral Science*. West Hanover, Massachusetts: Christopher.

Tymowski, Michal. (1981). The army and the formation of the states of West Africa in the nineteenth century: The cases of Kenedugu and Samori State. In *The Study of the State*, edited by Henri J. M. Claessen and Peter Skalník, pp. 427–442. The Hague: Mouton.

―――. (1987). *L'Armée et la formation des états en Afrique occidentale au XIXe siècle—essai de comparaison: L'État de Samori et le Kenedougou*. Warsaw: Wydawnictwa Uniwersystetu Warszawskiego.

Vagts, Alfred. (1959). *A History of Militarism, Civilian and Military*. Revised edition. London: Hollis and Carter.

van der Dennen, Johan M. G. (1991). Studies of conflict. In *The Sociobiological Imagination*, edited by Mary Maxwell, pp. 223–241. Albany: State University of New York Press.

van der Dennan, Johan M. G., and Vincent S. E. Falger, editors. (1990). *Sociobiology and Conflict: Evolutionary Perspectives on Competition, Cooperation, Violence and Warfare*. London: Chapman and Hall.

Vandkilde, Helle. (2003). Commemorative tales: Archaeological responses to modern myth, politics, and war. *World Archaeology*. 35: 126–144.

Vayda, Andrew P. (1976). *War in Ecological Perspective: Persistence, Change, and Adaptive Processes in Three Oceanian Societies*. New York and London: Plenum Press.

Vencl, Slavomil. (1984). War and warfare in archaeology. Translated by Petr Charvát. *Journal of Anthropological Archaeology* 3: 116–132.

———. (1991). Interprétation des blessures causées par les armes au Mésolithique. *L'Anthropologie* (Paris) 95: 219–228.

Vitkin, Mikhail A. (1981). Marx and Weber on the primary state. In *The Study of the State*, edited by Henri J. M. Claessen and Peter Skalník, pp. 443–454 The Hague: Mouton.

Walker, Phillip L. (2001). A bioarchaeological perspective on the history of violence. *Annual Review of Anthropology* 30: 573–595.

Watson, James B. (1964). Anthropology in the New Guinea Highlands. In *New Guinea: The Central Highlands*, edited by James B. Watson, pp. 1–19. *American Anthropologist* Special Publication, vol. 66, number 4, part 2.

Webb, Malcolm C. (1970). The flag follows trade: An essay on the necessary interaction of military and commercial factors in state formation. In *Ancient Civilizations and Trade*, edited by Jeremy A. Sabloff and C. C. Lamberg-Karlovsky, pp. 155–209. Albuquerque: University of New Mexico Press.

Weber, Max. (1968). *Economy and Society: An Outline of Interpretive Sociology*. Edited by Guenther Roth and Claus Wittich. Translated by Ephraim Fischoff, et al. 2 volumes. New York: Bedminster Press.

Webster, David. (1975). Warfare and the evolution of the state: A reconsideration. *American Antiquity* 40: 464–470.

Wilson, David Sloan. (1994). Adaptive genetic variation and human evolutionary psychology. *Ethology and Sociobiology* 15: 219–235.

Wilson, Edward O. (1975). *Sociobiology: The New Synthesis*. Cambridge: Harvard University Press.

———. (1978). *On Human Nature*. Cambridge: Harvard University Press.

Wilson, H. Clyde. (1958). Regarding the causes of Mundurucú warfare. *American Anthropologist* 60: 1193–1196.

Winter, Jay, Geoffrey Parker, and Mary R. Habeck, editors. (2000). *The Great War and the Twentieth Century*. New Haven and London: Yale University Press.

Winzeler, Robert L. (1981). The study of the Southeast Asian state. In *The Study of the State*, edited by Henri J. M. Claessen and Peter Skalník, pp. 455-467. The Hague: Mouton.

Woodbury, Richard B. (1958). A reconsideration of Pueblo warfare in the Southwest U.S. *Proceedings of the International Congress of Americanists* 33, part 2: 24–33.

Wright, Quincy. (1942). *A Study of War.* 2 volumes. Chicago: University of Chicago Press.

———. (1965). *A Study of War.* 2nd edition, with corrections. 2 volumes in 1. Chicago: University of Chicago Press.

Zeitlin, Irving M. (1968). *Ideology and the Development of Sociological Theory.* Englewood Cliffs, New Jersey: Prentice-Hall.

Chapter XV

Combat, Emotions, and the "Enemy": Metaphors of Soldiering in a Unit of Israeli Infantry Reserves

Eyal Ben-Ari

Cognitive Models of Soldiering

This paper explores the central assumptions about, and images of, "conflict," the "enemy," and the "use of military force" that characterize the thinking and reasoning of members of an elite battalion of Israeli infantry reserves. My aim is to uncover the assumptions, images, and interpretive schemes that ground common sense military knowledge. By "common sense" I do not mean that this knowledge is simplistic, nor do I imply that it is unimportant. Rather, these terms refer to the unquestioned knowledge that "everyone knows," to what Geertz (1988) has termed the "of-courseness" of common sense understandings. These models are of great importance because they are the basic points of reference for "what we are" and "what we are trying to do," through which military reality is constructed.

Seen against the background of previous studies, my project suggests a subtle shift in focus, from military "traditions" to one on the culture of military organizations. The advantages of such a shift rest in widening the subjects of military-related research to hitherto little explored areas, such as how military knowledge is organized and used. Based on a number of years of participant observation (I was an officer in this unit), this study is basically ethnographic in its approach.

The study of cultures or "meaning systems" has long been one of the primary subjects of anthropological inquiry. I will use analytical tools of cognitive anthropology, which begins its inquiry by asking what one needs to know in order to function as a member of one's social group. This school of thought came to stand for a view of culture as "shared knowledge": what people must *know* in order to act as they do, make things they make, and interpret their experiences in distinctive ways (Quinn and Holland 1987: 4). Since the early 1980s cognitive anthropology has begun to inquire about "cultural" or "folk" models—those taken-for-granted models of the world that are widely shared by members of a society, and that represent and explain the way the "world" (or parts of the world) is ordered. These models—which predicate certain simplified causal chains and may be characterized by contradictions—serve pragmatic purposes such as describing, explaining, or justifying the tangible, the probable, and the experiential (Keesing 1987: 374).

Accordingly I suggest that an examination of the "folk" models—the metaphors, reasonings, and propositions—that officers and soldiers in this battalion use in order to "make sense" of what they do and who they are, may be a good entry into the meaning soldiering holds for them. And furthermore, that this kind of analysis may lead us to understand how concepts like "conflict," "force," or "the enemy" are part of the causal schemes posited by these models. My aim is thus one of reconstructing the cultural understandings of military life in this unit of infantry soldiers.

The Unit

The battalion—a few hundred men (there are no women in this battalion)—belongs to one of the army's elite infantry brigades, yet it is an organization that is made up exclusively of reservists, or *miluim-nicks* (literally, people who fill in the gap). These soldiers and officers had volunteered for one of the crack infantry forces during their compulsory term of service and upon completion of that term were assigned to our unit. By law every man who has completed compulsory service can be mobilized (until the age of fifty) for a yearly stint of up to forty-two days. In reality, units like this battalion are usually called up twice a year and often for longer periods. I am a staff officer, an adjutant (*shalish*). I have been in this noncombatant support role for most of my army career.

Like many reserve units in the Israel Defense Forces (IDF), the general atmosphere in the battalion tends towards the informal and the familiar. While there is a clear divide between officers (or senior non-commissioned officers, NCOs, fulfilling officer roles) and the enlisted men, rank is de-emphasized, and everyone (including the unit's commander) is called by his name or nickname. All of us serve under similar general conditions: the same beds and barracks, the same food and canteen services, similar clothes and equipment, and approximately the same kind of furloughs.

The battalion is an "organic" unit (*yechida organit*). Organizationally this implies (1) a framework characterized by a permanent membership and role structure, and, (2) that upon mobilization, the entire battalion will be recruited. Socially this term implies a military force characterized by relatively high cohesion, overlapping primary groups, and a certain sense of a shared past. The unit trains at least once a year and its senior commanders are proud of the high level of competence shown during these maneuvers. While the battalion carries out a variety of military tasks, recently it had been deployed at Mount Hermon where Israel, Lebanon, and Syria meet.

The Model of Combat

The unit (battalion) is a machine

The main metaphor used by officers and soldiers in talking about the battalion is that of a machine. In analytical terms, this metaphor maps the characteristics of a machine onto those of a military unit. It is not surprising, because analyses of the military have long underscored its claim to professional competence: the management of violence (Lang 1979: 29). The notion "management of violence" alerts us to the fact that underlying modern military structures are shared beliefs about the *organization* of violence.

The following excerpt from Yoel, a former commander of the battalion, illustrates this point.

> Your mission (*mesima*) is to build a framework that will be able to immediately undertake any task assigned to it and that it will perform that mission with a minimum of casualties. Your responsibility is that things will go smoothly in this framework and this would include the capability of one company commander to replace another. This means that there will be

the smallest number of snags as possible in the way of the framework so it can continue to function as a framework.

This short passage consists in a string of metaphoric mappings: the smoothness and efficiency of the unit's performance, the activation of the battalion, or the interchangeability of parts are all qualities we assume (or know) that machines have. Likewise, in the same interview, Yoel goes on to stress that different parts of the unit have different prices attached to them, again not unlike the different prices of the various parts of a machine:

> I don't think it would be good for the battalion commander to be the first to go [get killed], because of the price this would entail. Not the moral price, but the price in terms of the functioning of the framework. When he goes, the chance that the system will continue to go on working won't be very high.

When we talk of organizations as machines (Morgan 1986: 22), we often have in mind a state of orderly (mechanical) relations between clearly defined parts. In technical terms, the machine is the source domain, while the military unit is the target domain. Because we usually have a more extensive knowledge of the source domain—machines—the use of the metaphor illuminates certain characteristics of the target domain—in our case the battalion.

Tasks undertaken by the service company were often referred to by the deputy battalion commander as "finished products," and in appraising the caliber of soldiers it is not uncommon to hear of "product quality" or "product description." Commanders often speak of a squad or a platoon "in the cartridge" (*makhsanit*) to refer to a unit kept in readiness for an assigned mission. Correspondingly, in referring to himself before a combat patrol on the border with Lebanon, one company commander said, half jokingly: "If I don't come out, don't worry, there are plenty of spare parts [*sper*, literally spare tires] around." Finally during a training exercise the battalion commander was explicit about the replacement of one commander by the next should the first one be "finished."

The Israeli military's use of the verb "to operate" (*letaf'el*) serves as another example. This verb is used as a continuum stretching from equipment to men: thus one can say to operate light and heavy firearms, APCs (armored personnel carriers), individual soldiers, squads, teams, platoons, companies, and battalions. Moreover, this term is used referring to people only in the context of the army.

But why is the image of a machine so prevalent? The reasons not only lie in the development of modern armies and the historical association between the military and large-scale industrialization. I would argue that the continuing currency of this metaphor has to do with the fact that in our societies, properties of machines are so apprehensible to humans [following Quinn and Holland (1987: 28)]. The metaphor (image-schema in their terms) of machines, allows many of the attributes and dynamics of the unit and its parts (actual as well as desired) to be conceptualized in terms of the tangible qualities of machines, or of the processes in which machines are used to process or manufacture goods and services. To reiterate, the metaphor of machine is a dispassionate composite image of efficiency and rationality (men, equipment and drills), coordination and synchronization (times, places and activities), and distinctions and categorizations (of units and subunits, and of authority structure).

The unit (battalion) as brain

Yet arguing that the primary metaphor used in regard to the unit is that of a machine, a mechanical instrument designed to carry out tasks, is still too simple. In the interview I held with Yoel (a highly successful director of a manufacturing firm), he often used other terms that, while grounded in the language of management, sounded somehow different. For example, he spoke of such matters as "acquiring managerial skills," "building a system of working relations," or of "management wisdom." I began to comprehend the significance of this terminology when I reread another part of the interview during which we discussed the resemblance between running a business and commanding an army battalion:

> Now in terms of thinking and planning. In both places [business and the army] you make decisions, it's your role as commander or manager if you're looking for the commonalities. Now you can't plan anything if you can't define the situation—the conditions of the environment (*matsav hateva*). Now here you call it intelligence and there you call it market research. It's the same thing . . . Now it's true in the army, that you won't send someone [without real directions], sort of like "go over there somewhere there is a *wadi*," so it's the same in business. Policymaking in both places is the same. You have to set the parameters: price, number of agents, advertizing budget. In marketing these things are your ammunition. Now in the army you say, "wait a minute what have I got here, point targets, area targets? infantry, armor?"—you even choose the types of ammunition in the part called fire-plan.

In general terms, Yoel is talking about the relationship between organizations and their environment. More specifically, he is discussing the planning and reactive capacities of the battalion to uncertain and changing circumstances. The metaphor governing this passage may be clarified against the background of a very common negative label applied to some soldiers and officers within the Israel Defense Forces.

This rather standard term is the derogatory "*rosh katan,*" which literally means "small head." Closely associated terms are "pinhead" (*rosh sika*), or the humorous "tweezers head" (*rosh pintseta*) (implying a crown small enough to be picked up with tweezers), or "small lightbulb head" (*rosh natznatz*). These terms usually refer to soldiers who are considered somewhat "lower grade"—whether mediocre, inept, or unwilling—and who lack motivation or are disillusioned with army life. The prime grievance against these soldiers is their unwillingness to take on responsibilities and their apathy. The contrasting category is a "big head" (*rosh gadol*), which is used to characterize people with initiative, drive, and a sense of enterprise. Here the related terms include "thinking" (*chashiva*), "using one's head" (*haph'alat rosh*), "judgment" (*shikul da'at*), or "operating the brain" (*haph'alat moach*). The essential metaphor at work here, although it is not one used explicitly by the men, is of "unit as brain," or "unit as mind." By this assertion I mean the likening of certain military activities to the information processing and reactive capabilities of the human brain or mind (Morgan 1986: 81).

This metaphor is related to the machine metaphor. The mechanistic approach is well suited to conditions characterized by straightforward tasks and a stable environment, i.e., circumstances in which machines work well (Morgan 1986: 34). Conversely, mechanistic approaches are restricted to their adaptability and their potential for "robotic" compliance. Thus, organizations need the capability of scanning and sensing changes in the environment, and then reacting to these changes. The greater the uncertainty the more difficult it is to program and routinize by preplanning a response (Morgan 1986: 82).

There are a number of examples of the unit as brain metaphor. The first instance is taken from an interview with Itai, the battalion's deputy commander. We were having a conversation about what he looks for in military service:

> Where do the interesting things begin? When the field (*shetach*) creates problems that are unexpected, and you have to meet those problems with your own initiative.

Corollaries of this view are found in expressions commanders use such as "creativity in managing," "problem solving," or "meeting challenges is like solving crossword puzzles." Moreover, when officers on all levels talked of accepting "smart comments" from soldiers, they seemed to be stressing the need for a basic openness to suggestions about the operation of the unit in a changing environment.

One of the most common phrases used to appraise troops and commanders is their "ability to think beyond their organizational slot or box" (*mishbetset*). This concise expression captures a desired ability to comprehend the general picture within which the unit is operating (i.e., the environment), to process information relevant to concrete action, and to act beyond the dictates of one's role (in the machine or in the bureaucracy). While I have very little comparative data on this point, I would suggest that to a greater degree than in other armies, the IDF's elite combat units encourage every person to have more initiative. The IDF expects troops to be open and innovative to a greater degree than in other armed forces (Moshe Lissak, personal communication).

Yet for all the stress on innovation and thinking, the brain metaphor is subordinated to the metaphor of machine. This is evident in the following two excerpts. The first is from the exchange with the deputy battalion commander:

> If you don't give the company commanders the limiting framework, and if you don't give them a degree of independence, then you lose any output you can produce from them.

The second passage is from an extended talk with Ehud, commander of C company:

> I don't get up in the morning and give an order here and an order there: "This is what and how I want things!" I think about things and when I send someone I explain why it's important that he do that thing. This goes on until the stage where I say, "OK, this is, after all, the army. I've explained until now, and from this moment on, what I say is an order."

The implication of such statements appears to be that creativity and innovation are welcome so long as they represent contributions to the greater efficiency of the military machine. The outcome is a situation where units are populated by resourceful and ingenious people who contribute (and are encouraged to contribute) to the innovative and multifaceted quality of their military units.

Combat, Survival, and the Rhetoric of Emotional Control

My analysis does not stray far from rather conventional examinations of organizations. This is because there are many such frameworks—in the business world or in the public sector, for example—which may be marked by the use of such a mixture of metaphors. In order to understand what distinguishes military organizations, there is a need to take into account the *kind* of environment wherein units like this battalion are supposed to function, namely, combat. The dimension of combat reveals the distinctiveness and the strength of military metaphors.

What kind of experience is combat? In the stark words of various soldiers, combat is a matter of "survival," a situation of "meeting danger," or "a game you just can't lose." This kind of imagery is not atypical of the depiction of combat in any modern army. The scene of the actual firefight with the enemy is generally one of utter chaos and confusion. In this situation the soldier not only confronts the imminent danger of loss of life, and perhaps more frightening, the loss of limb, he also witnesses combat wounds and death suffered by others (Moskos 1988: 5). Closely related to this experience are the more "routine" stresses of combat existence: the weight of the pack and the equipment, the taste and quality (or lack) of food and water, loss of sleep and often difficult weather conditions. There is also a constant and gnawing sense of uncertainty not only about all of these material things, but also about the unfolding action on the battlefield (what has often been termed the "fog" of war) (Keegan 1976: 47).

In the context of the IDF, one of the most common terms used to describe the situation of combat is *lachats*. The literal translation into English is pressure, but the Hebrew includes all of the synonyms and connotation of this English word: stress, anxiety, strain, or tension. It is at this juncture in which the "machine" and "brain" metaphors of military performance meet the highly stressful situation of combat that an entire "rhetoric of emotional control" emerges. Furthermore, this emotional control, within and later without the combat situation, comes to figure in a key model or scenario of military performance. Finally, this model is then used in order to evaluate soldiers and actions, and to interpret new situations.

In the combat situation, emotions—intermingling and externally triggered emotions—take on prime importance for soldiers and commanders. In these circumstances, fear, apprehension, dread and at times exhilaration blend together, and issue forth within oneself *because* of the external situation. The problem becomes one of agency: Who will be master? Situation or person, circumstances or (because this is such a male thing) man? Furthermore, in the military context issues of control of or by the situation (via emotions) are related to the overall aims of the unit (the fighting machine) that are performing actions in order to change the environment. For example, destruction of personnel and equipment, securing advantageous positions, or simply holding ground. Because emotions may impede or hinder the performance of military tasks—they must be overcome, channeled, and above all controlled.

This may become clearer by means of a distinction made in regard to emotions. Lutz (1990) describes a lack of control of emotions in American culture—and I would argue that by extension in most middle-class cultures in the West—leading to uncontrolled action: "running wild" or "boiling over," for example. In her words (1990: 72), the metaphor of control implies something that otherwise would be out of control, something wild and unruly, a threat to order. This type of argument has been put forward by Katz (1990) in her study of U.S. army drill sergeants. She found that for these men the prime danger of emotionality is lack of control or uncontrolled behavior, which would prove to be an obstacle to military performance.

Under certain situations such as combat, the understood danger is not only wild, untamed, or frenzied behavior but in a curious way the very opposite: lack of action or paralysis. This aspect of uncontrolled behavior is very often implied in being "pressured" in combat. Here the image seems to be one of physical pressure on one's limbs and body that impedes intended, forceful and effective action. The image of external forces operating on all or parts of one's physical form well fits the logic of causation in this folk model of emotions where an external situation influences emotions which then impede action.

It is on the basis of this kind of reasoning, for example, that so much of military psychotherapy has focused on the debilitating effects of combat rather than on treating a variety of uncontrolled behaviors. Shell shock and battle fatigue are expressed in terms of lack of action or lack of control over one's body, therefore hindering military performance. The very terms "combat reactions" and "functional debilitation" capture the notion of the soldier's involuntary response to the firefight in terms of inability to contribute to the military effort.

A Key Schema: Combat

In the shift of focus from the individual to the cultural level, we may benefit by asking about the kind of cultural expectations the peak experiences in combat engender.

Such a schema can be understood as one centered around the term "cool performance" (*kor ruach*), a phrase that encapsulates emotional control in the service of military missions. This Hebrew term is used most often in appraising performance under "pressure." The literal meaning of *kor ruach* is "cool" or "cold spirit" but it refers to the ability to act with poise and composure under trying circumstances, specifically the ability for such things as control of breath and voice while talking, giving orders smoothly, thinking clearly, reacting quickly, or even controlling one's limbs or countenance (no grimacing, for example). A closely related term is *dvekut bamesima*, which strictly speaking means "cemented" or "glued" to one's mission, but carries the connotation of carrying out one's assigned mission *despite* all of the difficulties of the combat situation. Perhaps an English equivalent of this latter term is "sticking to one's guns" during an enemy attack. Essentially, what is important in "cool spirit" is the self-control needed to master a situation.

We are now in a position to formulate the "folk" model of combat: Combat is a threatening situation of extreme stress and uncertainty (the chaos or "fog" of battle) in which units (combinations of soldiers, lethal equipment, and drills) under the command of officers perform their assigned tasks by mastering their emotions. The four main elements of this scenario are: situation, unit, command, and emotion. The individual soldier is the juncture through which the four elements are expressed. He undertakes actions derived from membership in a machine-like organization, and masters emotions precipitated by actions dictated by his commander under extremely stressful circumstances.

The knowledge of the soldier is organized—grounded and formulated—in terms of the combat schema. The cognitive operation is one of matching things such as "activating" mortars, "successful hits," or "conditions of pressure" with the main elements of the schema that is available to members of Israeli military culture. Moreover, while the combat model is relatively uncomplicated, it is comprised of more complex schemas and metaphors like the activation of mortars (men-machine-drills) or conditions of pressure (the uncertainty of battle triggering tangled emotions). Finally, given this schema it becomes apparent why experiences can become the "apex," the ultimate test of soldiering. While this kind of understanding should be obvious, it is our task to explain just how this obviousness is organized.

I will illustrate how the combat scenario is used in regard to a variety of military matters through the following examples.

Evaluating soldiers: Professionalism

The first example deals with the "ideal" or "good" soldiers. The following is a passage from Ehud's interview (commander C company). Like most of the officers in the battalion, Ehud formulates his answer in terms of military "professionalism":

> A good soldier is one whose equipment is in order. He has his webb gear in order . . . He has all he needs: magazines, canteens, water in the canteens; his specialized equipment, like if he carries a communications rig then he has all of the antennas (short and long), that they are secured to the rig . . . If he carries a light mortar then he has the proper ammo in order . . . Always to be meticulous about the weapons being clean, oiled . . . This is one side of being a professional soldier. The other side is that he be able to perform all of the drills like the right kind of movement, quietly and with control. Also basic discipline: not to talk while on the move, not to smoke, to move quickly, not to gripe, not to be afraid of water, and not be afraid of the sun, and not to be afraid of puddles and not of dunes. All of these things make a good infantry soldier.

While this picture of an exemplary soldier may apply to any situation (small and large scale exercises or patrols, for example), his desired traits and qualities are derived from the basic combat schema. The criteria for judging whether a certain person deserves or does not deserve to be labeled or categorized as a "professional" are derived from the combat schema. In other words, the underlying systematicity of this portrayal is based on relating the machine metaphor to the metaphor of emotional control, and through this relation to military actions.

The next excerpt does not concern an ideal soldier but one that Omer, commander of the support company, had under his command during the *intifada*:

> He is a constant talker, he jabbers away constantly (*kashkeshan peraee*). But the reasons for throwing him out were not related to that but to his being irresponsible. He's the type where you can't anticipate his reactions: you go to a village and he suddenly begins to run after someone, and he'll disappear into some alley and he won't even think about the fact that he's endangering himself and that everyone has to look for him. Simply irresponsible . . . So I decided to get rid of him. He is excitable, has a higher level of excitability than others.

Here the link between responsibility, reliability, and self-control is more explicit. In this case, two criteria derived from the basic scenario—emotional control and endangering situation—are used to evaluate soldiers in a threatening situation. The appraisal and justification are carried out by pointing to how the schema or scenario of "proper" action has been disrupted. In terms of the cognitive operation that takes place here we see how through gauging whether a specific case corresponds to the sequence of events and behavior posited in the prototypical scenario, military knowledge is extended to the new circumstances of the intifada.

The scenario can also be used in self-evaluation. The following words are from an interview with an ex-soldier. After many years of service in the support company, he had become a driver and was explaining the advantages he brought with him to his new role:

> I'm just trying to think of an engagement (*hitaklut*). In terms of my past, I was in three wars and I hope I haven't changed in terms of my ability not to run away. I don't really know. You would have to try me again now, but I begin from the assumption that a driver who has worked in a canteen all of his life and never experienced pressure, never had a tough experience like being under fire, will behave differently in a critical situation. Here (patrolling Israel's northern borders) the minute we find ourselves in an engagement I find myself a fighting soldier (*lochem*, literally "warrior") and I have to man the machine gun.

By contrasting himself to other soldiers who have not been in battle, the driver's self-evaluation is also an assertion of his greater military importance. Here again, combat is the test—in our terms *the* criterion—of true soldiership.

Similar reasoning based on the model of combat is used in regard to prescriptions for behavior. For example, soldiers are constantly being exhorted to restrain themselves in use of ammunition during exercises, or not to go wild with their guns (*lo lehishtolel*) during combat patrols, the intifada, maneuvers, or proof firing. In one summing up session to a battalion exercise, the commander of the brigade (an officer belonging to the permanent force) commented about the machine gunners' performance:

> You carried out your missions well, but (pardon the words) every once in a while you seemed to be reaching an orgasm while firing. You neglected to take into account the situation like the fact that if this were a real battle you would be exposing yourself to enemy fire. Don't leave your senses because you can get killed.

Emotional control is thus figuratively linked to survival and to performance.

Trust and survival: Evaluating commanders

A scenario depicts different (albeit overlapping and complementary) roles for soldiers and for commanders (primarily but not only officers). Of the rank-and-file combatant, a minimum amount of courage is expected, as well as a capacity to control fear in the face of danger, discomfort, pain, or misfortune. However, much more is expected of a leader: more composure, additional competence, greater self-control, and an ability to lead by inspiration, by example (Boene 1990: 31). Thus soldiers use two criteria derived from the combat schema to evaluate their commanders: professionalism (the machine and brain metaphors) and emotional control. The following is an example from an interview with Noam, a veteran NCO, who is now a clerk. Speaking about the ideal officer, he said:

> Yes, well, his professionalism (*miktso'iut*): like how he moves the forces, how he navigates. If it's a commander who can't find his way then you don't like being with him. I mean that in the end if your commander, and especially the company commander, is not professional then your feeling is not good, insecure. Because you know that you may have to go out with him to war one day, a very bad feeling. We had one platoon commander like that with us in Lebanon. He was a nice guy but not very good professionally and in the end he was thrown out . . . I wouldn't go with someone like that to war, I wouldn't be calm (*lev shaket*, literally, with a calm heart) like I was with Omri or Nimrod (two former battalion commanders), people that you feel are professional and know how to manage, and know how to give clear orders, and who will get you out of there alive.

The ability to impart or inspire a feeling of security among commanders' (overwhelmingly officers) troops is a theme that repeatedly surfaced in the interviews. This was often linked to the professionalism of commanders. For example, one soldier spoke of his feeling of security when his commander gave orders in a smooth way, without mistakes, blocks of communication, or hesitation. Similarly, a machine gunner articulated these same themes:

> Do you remember Eran? He is cool (*kar*) and gives his troops a feeling of security. This is especially important when you're under pressure. During these kind of periods, it's especially important that someone give you confidence (*bitachon*, also "security"), will calm you and direct you. Do you remember how Eran was in the ambush we laid and waited until the terrorists were only a few meters from us before opening fire?

These kinds of statements are comprehensible to others because they assume the underlying schema of combat.

Officers are clearly aware of the criteria soldiers use in appraising their performance as commanders. Consequently they often attempt to answer the expectations of the lower ranks in a conscious and intentional manner through what may be termed a military "presentation of self." Accordingly, officers told me that they often felt that in stressful situations there arose a need to give the impression, through the tactical use of emotion, of being in control (Bailey 1983). At the base of their reasoning was the assumption that the example of emotional control in circumstances marked by pressure was a means to show their leadership by infusing the stressful situation with a greater measure of certainty and security and therefore influencing the emotions of the troops under their command. The following is from a discussion with a former company commander:

> The professionalism of the company commander is very important for soldiers. They can tell you that you're a son of a bitch but if you're professional then it's OK . . . It has a lot to do with [interpersonal] politics: How he [the company commander] presents himself and what he does.

> Like whether he's insecure or he shows that he is in charge is all a matter of politics, a sort of eternal example for action. If he shows that he's in charge in a forceful way the soldiers begin to accept all he says.

Another officer once observed that he was rather proud of himself and his self-control, despite the fact that he was never really calm about matters (*af pa'am lo shaket*):

> I never get angry, do I? I try not to get emotional and to give orders in a clear way . . . Take the way to speak on the communications net: think before you talk. Don't start yapping away and get suddenly stuck. Think and then give orders shortly and curtly.

Given the various criteria derived from the schema of combat, it may now be more than clear how new members of the unit are appraised. Gathering a large amount of information on each new arrival (be he a soldier or an officer) is unnecessary. All one needs to do is check for a small number of characteristics in terms of the potential performance of the new member under conditions of battle. Thus, all one has to say about a new officer is that he is someone who is liable to be pressured easily (*lachtsan*), for a whole set of connotations rooted in our scenario to be understood. Along these lines, when looking at a new platoon commander briefing his troops, commanding them in an exercise, or simply making sure that they are on time for some activity, the company or battalion commanders may be running a sort of mental simulation model of how the new officer would behave under combat conditions. A few rather simple clues from his behavior are used as a basis for this judgment.

The advantage of the shared cultural model lies in its facilitating communication: experiences, appraisals, or prescriptions can be rapidly communicated to other people *because* they are formulated according to the conventions of the cultural model. The price of this cognitive economy however, is some rigidity in interpreting the world and a certain slowness in recognizing or learning new models. While the shared schema of soldiering allows one to discuss and communicate about a highly complex world in manageable terms, the schema may impede the understanding and the ability to react to novel situations.

Enemies

The images, metaphors, and categories of "enemies" are also derived from the key model of combat. On one level, metaphors used in regard to one or one's unit are also used in regard to the enemy. The machine metaphor is probably the most obvious in this regard. In briefings, planning meetings, or any field orders, the enemy is treated in terms of the equipment-men-drills complex. The number and quality of the opposing forces are analyzed as well as the type of ammunition, support groups, or typical drills which characterize them. Similarly, in any situation the problem is usually one of simply finding the right means (*emtsa'im*) to treat (*letapel*, literally "handle") the enemy.

Although these kinds of definitions and categorizations are related to a dehumanization of the enemy, they do not express a demonization of the opposing forces. Antagonists become objects or series of objects: so many targets to be hit, obstacles to be destroyed, or articles to be taken into account in the threatening environment. This language of objectification also allows one to understand the neutral language used to talk about "interaction" with the enemy: engagement (*maga*), incident (*eru'a*), or skirmish (*hitaklut*). For example, the issue is often deciding upon the right force composition, tactics, and ammunition for countering the perceived threat.

This "objectification" is different from the dehumanization of enemy forces that went on in the American army during World War II and in the American Marine Corps during the Vietnam War, if Eisenhart (1975) and Shatan (1977) are to be believed. In the elite reserves of the IDF, there is almost no organizational propagation of a view in which enemy forces are turned into "evil" groups toward which some kind of special treatment should be accorded. This situation stands in stark contrast to the American forces where one finds an almost obligatory demonization of the enemy and his portrayal as the foe of civilization and as the opponent of progress.

Another categorization of the enemy is derived from the element of threatening situation in the combat schema: Here the criterion is the seriousness of the threat enemies pose to oneself, to one's unit, and to the performance of both. Thus enemies are arranged along a gradation of significance: regular armies, professional Palestinian fighters, knife wielders, Molotov cocktail and stone throwers, tire burners, and all the way to "just" civilians demonstrating. The point is simply that the criterion derived from the key scenario allows the unit's soldiers to categorize and place different kinds of opposing foes on an ordered continuum.

The upshot of this categorization is threefold. First, position on the continuum is related to different types of treatment accorded to the enemy (for example, shooting versus arresting, or wearing protective gear or not). Second, the continuum is used as a measure of the importance of a specific kind of activity: the more dangerous, the more threatening, the more important. Thus, during those mislabeled periods of peacetime, a stint along the international borders opposite regular armies or professional fighters is more serious and important. Third, the importance of the mission is related in turn to the prestige of the individual or the unit in the army and in Israeli society in general. For example, patrols along the borders are more prestigious than patrols that occupied territories among civilians.

The treatment of civilians, in turn, is related to the emotional control required of soldiers. Take the following instance from a briefing by Ehud, commander of C company during the intifada:

> So our missions define our activities [patrols and keeping roads free of stones and roadblocks]. This means we don't come in contact with them too much, this means not to go wild with live ammunition. Don't shoot plastic bullets. We don't usually fire. We will not anger them (*nitgareh*), won't throw anything at them.

Conversely, hitting, pushing, or shooting—more generally labeled as using "undue force" against—civilians is considered an aberration. It is an aberration not just because of the basic humanity or human values of the soldiers. No less importantly, these are aberrations because they indicate a lack of professionalism. Thus, using "undue force" demonstrates a lack of control and an inability to master oneself and the situation.

Eran (deputy of the support company) said of firing plastic bullets at Palestinians:

> There was once when I shot two plastic bullets and this was my greatest failure during the last five years. I made a mistake in going into the village

and then I had to shoot two bullets in order to get out of there. It is a mistake to shoot live ammunition of any kind; it shows lack of control and there is no need to put your finger on the trigger.

The following words are from the meeting held to conclude a stint in the territories. Ari the battalion commander is speaking:

> I know of only two accidents (*takalot*) of opening fire during this stint. One was the guy who fired in the air, and the other was the soldier that fired during that night. I hope these were only irregularities (*kharigot*) . . . I don't think this should satisfy us because it still happens to us. As commanders these things keep happening and the responsibility is on us.

These acts are exceptions, and an understanding of the organizational implication of the aforementioned rationale is the following: Inept, non-professional soldiers are labeled as some "ill-fitting" or "malfunctioning" parts of the unit (under the unit as machine metaphor). This necessitates that a commander replaces them so that the company or battalion is able to continue to perform. Because there is so much stress involved in making the humans fit the requirements of a mechanical organization, there is less necessity to reflect about the place of the machine in the wider environment.

Conclusion

Let me begin with a story. As my fieldwork progressed, and as I occasionally discussed my project with soldiers and officers, some men joked with me about feeling that I could somehow "peer into their minds." By these mild jibes, I take it, these men commented about the fact that I had somehow come to understand and to explicitly formulate their doubts and reasonings. Perhaps they seemed to be wary of my "magical power" as an anthropologist, a power akin to the one psychologists have in the popular mind. From an analytical point of view, these kinds of reactions could be taken as an indicator of the validity of my findings; my discussions were a sort of "natural experiment" in which I verified my interpretations.

Of course, I could not and was not peering into their minds (I still can't). Rather I attempted to look systematically at the publicly shared symbols (naturally occurring metaphors, images, or even comments) they (and I myself) use to give meaning to military life. Beyond using my own native intuitions and perceptions, I attempted to systematically uncover the means (again, the words, tropes, and imagery) through which these men represent themselves to themselves and to others. As an anthropologist, I did not analyze doctrinal knowledge (of strategy or of tactics), let alone the expertise needed in drills and exercises.

Rather, I aimed to uncover the meanings of soldiering and commanding as they are expressed and used in the everyday lives—in a taken-for-granted, common sense manner—of troops and commanders. I did this by systematizing these meanings, and by formulating them in terms of a number of basic models by which they are organized. Thus, I have traced out and exemplified a way of looking at military knowledge and at the way such concepts as "combat," "soldiering," and the "enemy" are predicated on certain models which organize military knowledge.

References

Bailey, F.G. (1983). *The Tactical Uses of Passion: An Essay on Power, Reason, and Reality*. Ithaca: Cornell University Press.

Boene, Bernard. (1990). How unique should the military be? A review of representative literature and outline of synthetic formulation. *European Journal of Sociology* 31.1: 3–59.

Eisenhart, R. Wayne. (1975). You can't hack it little girl: A discussion of the covert psychological agenda of modern combat training. *Journal of Social Issues* 31.4: 13–23.

Geertz, Clifford. (1987). *Works and Lives: The Anthropologist as Author*. Stanford: Stanford University Press.

Katz, Pearl. (1990). Emotional metaphors, socialization, and roles of drill sergeants. *Ethos* 18: 457–80.

Keegan, John. (1976). *The Face of Battle*. New York: Vintage Books.

Keesing, Roger M. (1987). Models, "folk" and "cultural": Paradigms regained? In *Cultural Models in Language and Thought*, edited by Dorothy Holland and Naomi Quinn, pp. 369–393. Cambridge: Cambridge University Press.

Lang, Kurt. (1972). *Military Institutions and the Sociology of Law*. Beverley Hills: Sage.

Lutz, Catherine A. (1990). Engendered emotion: gender, power, and the rhetoric of emotional control in American discourse. *Language and the Politics of Emotion*, edited by Catherine A. Lutz and Lila Abu-Lughod, pp. 69–91. Cambridge: Cambridge University Press.

Morgan, Gareth. (1986). *Images of Organization*. Beverly Hills: Sage.

Moskos, Charles C. (1988). *Soldiers and Sociology*. United States Army Research Institute for the Behavioral and Social Sciences. Government Publishing House.

Quinn, Naomi, and Dorothy Holland. (1987). Culture and cognition. In *Cultural Models in Language and Thought*, edited by Dorothy Holland and Naomi Quinn, pp. 3–40. Cambridge: Cambridge University Press.

Shatan, Chaim F. (1977). Bogus manhood, bogus honor: Surrender and transfiguration in the United States Marine Corps. *Psychoanalytic Review* 64: 586–610.

Chapter XVI

Being Broken in the Marines: The Social Construction of Belonging in the U.S. Marine Corps

Rhonda J. Moore

> The more signs of a victim an individual bears, the more
> likely he is to attract disaster.
> —Girard 1986:26
>
> "Pain is good. Extreme pain is extremely good."
> —Anonymous MCRD, USMC, 1991

This chapter is about how an organization, the U.S. Marine Corps, by the use of "minor violence" in the form of controlled abuse perpetrated on the bodies and the psyches of civilian men and women, transforms these men and women into the kinds of Marines who ultimately form different conceptions of pain than they had as civilians. Psychological and physical pain become transformed from something worthy of complaint and concern to something that is at best ignored, at worst worthy of contempt. Thus, it is the case that in becoming "broken," a civilian has not made the crucial transformation to Marine precisely because he has failed to change his conception of pain. Moreover, in boot camp it is becoming "fully broken" rather than "half-broken" (i.e., broken just enough to be built back up) that spells failure in the Marine Corps.

This paper further documents the extent to which this initial redefinition of the meaning of pain, both psychological and physical, carries over into the culture of the regular infantry regiments. For it is the case that Marine Corps boot camp is predicated on an "infantry assumption" more than any other Military Occupational Specialty the Marines offer. Recruits spend thirteen weeks in boot camp, with an additional four weeks in Infantry Training Regiment, and are thereafter defined as Basic Marine Riflemen (hence the crossed rifles on all Marine Corps chevrons from lance corporal on up). Thus, the question becomes: If Marine Corps boot camp, for a ritually laden thirteen-week period, inculcates a particular view of pain and suffering into neophyte Marines, how does that culture carry over into infantry regiments? It will be seen that pain and suffering will continue to be something to be ignored, and if not likewise ignored by the Marine, he, not the pain, will be held in contempt. It is that unfortunate state of affairs that will spell the difference between being broken and not being broken. It will be shown that there seems to be a distinction made between incapacitating injury and merely painful injury in defining a Marine as "broken."

Send in the Marines

This ethnographic study of the cultural management of and ability to endure pain in the U.S. Marine Corps was carried out over a period of two and one-half years (1992–1994) at three different field sites in the United States. Among other things, I explored what it means to be physically and emotionally "broken" in such an organization which places a primacy on physical prowess, performance, and the ability to bear pain—just in order to belong and achieve membership, as a man or woman, and for the organizational mission.

> Also, the Marines make no secret of breaking a young man down. That was stated explicitly to us the day we hit San Diego. The first thing to go was hair. After the haircut (so fast and so rough, our scalps were bleeding from the electric clippers), we were obviously all alike. And no one was allowed to use any personal pronouns when a DI (drill instructor) was present. "Sir, the private wishes to speak to the drill instructor, sir!" (Anonymous ex-Marine, 2003)

When I interviewed Lance Corporal "Hays" over several sessions, he eventually told me how his own earlier personal experiences with physical injury potentially compromised the mission of the Corps. He was unable to physically perform, and to a certain degree blamed himself for the persistence of his injury. His self-blame for physical injury had both emotional and mental components. Three operations and several months of physical therapy later, he talked with me about his attempts to finish boot camp. However, due to his physical injuries, Hays often spoke about being recycled if he did not heal after his most recent operation.

Connell (1990), among others, has argued that there has been very little work that actively explores the processes through which masculinity is socially constructed. There is even less research exploring the relationships between masculinity, femininity, and the enduring of pain in the U.S. Marine Corps. The USMC presents a fascinating case study of the manner in which the social construction of gender and its relationship to pain gets "played out" on the terrain of identities, emotions, and bodies—specifically what it means and how it feels to be both physically and emotionally "broken" in the most socially conservative of the U.S. military organizations.

Infantrymen (both injured and non-injured) in the U.S. Marines subscribe to a culture where the bearing of pain is expected and normalized within the following contexts: through the socialization to become a Marine, in training for the mission, and through an intense personal and organizational experience of transformation of the body, emotions, identity, and mind. The cultural context of physical injury for injured enlisted infantrymen represents a space where both masculine and Marine identity are continuously challenged and renegotiated.

Understanding Marines

Though members of the USMC are usually self-selected volunteers, there is also a cultural process of socialization that all Marines must endure. Marines are made, broken, and reformed in the following ways: through physical exertion; value change; training through the harnessing of emotion; acceptance of personal and professional challenges; rank and organizational connection at the expense of personal disconnection; and an intense pursuit of trained physical perfection and sacrifice. This process of socialization and reformation is part of the history of the organization. The Marine Corps is strewn with dramatic stories of heroes who gave their all for the Corps.

Joan Borysenko (1987) in her book *Minding the Body, Mending the Mind* has reasoned that "men in general are less accustomed to recognizing their emotional states than women since in many families men are rewarded for hiding their feelings—appearing strong and imperturbable" (Borysenko 1987: 164). While this might be true in some instances, it is not necessarily the case in the Marines. Organizational expectations and the organizational culture play a significant role in the appropriateness of certain kinds of emotional expression.

Some of the men in these accounts describe the feelings of being "pumped up" because they were able to run after having sustained a severe stress fracture. Others describe the lack of feeling and emotional sensations after witnessing and participating in particular types of pain-giving and war. And still others articulate their feelings of shame and inadequacy over not being able to physically perform. They felt that they had let their buddies down. Many did not feel as if they were really full Marines. Thus the context of the Corps, with its strong emphasis on masculinity, male Marines, and infantrymen in particular, are expected to stoically bear the pain and appear strong for their buddies and for the mission.

A Question of Value

The ability to endure pain is culturally shaped. In western culture, this ability is often defined in terms of a cognitive state of being in control of one's mind. That control is in turn exerted over one's emotional, spiritual, and physical realities. Because of the cultural expectations for enduring pain in this organization, the Marine Corps embodies a shifting sense of history and a transformation of the self which occurs at the levels of thoughts, bodies and emotions. Male Marines in particular are defined in part by their relationship to pain.

In the context of being a Marine, and an infantryman in particular, embracing and enduring pain supposedly makes one stronger, a better "man," a better member or team player. Bearing pain is a given, in regards to the mission, and the definition of both the organizational and individual self as a Marine. Echoing Connell (1990), masculinity is not inherent in the male body. In fact, if the body is very much at odds with the social definition, there is trouble (Connell 1990: 89). In the USMC, the experience of being in the Marines is to some degree a controlled reality, in a total institution, mediated by an organizational culture, which is at odds with persistent physical injury. And the ability to endure is one exceptionally important parameter of how reality and masculinity are culturally constructed in the USMC.

The value placed on bearing pain is dependent on any number of cultural variables. The construction of pain is shaped by: (1) a willingness to risk and to endure; (2) the pursuit of excellence and the motivation to improve performance; (3) the desire to distinguish oneself, and finally; (4) the individual's ability to endure pain and to value a particular activity for the sheer fun of it. In my research on the USMC, I found that Marines show that they value the organization by expressing an absence of conflict over the giving of the self, a driving commitment and loyalty to the Corps, and the ability to bear and sustain injury, discomfort, and trauma for their peers and for the mission. Leckie has argued that it is the ability to sacrifice the self for the mission:

> It is sacrifice that answers the interminable argument about peace and war. But sacrifice says: "not the blood of your brother, my friend—your blood." That is why women weep when their men go off to war. They do not weep

for their victims, they weep for them as victim. That is why, with the immortal insight of mankind, there are gay songs and colorful bands to send them off—to fortify their failing hearts, not to quicken their lust for blood. That is why there are no glorious living, but only glorious dead. Heroes turn traitor, warriors age and grow soft—but a victim is changeless, sacrifice is eternal (Leckie 1992: 294).

Marines are judged not only in terms of their ability to sacrifice the self for the mission. They are also judged by an absence of conflict over this sacrifice of the self. Here, I define value in terms of the conflicts over one's personal values versus the values of the organization.

This culture of pain has different facets in the sense that belonging and acceptance are based on one's ability to sacrifice oneself for the organizational mission. This is fine if one remains uninjured. But what happens to those individuals who fail? I found that another reality co-existed in the USMC. This identity was opposed to the image of the marine who could endure the pain. Here, the construction of an identity based on "being broken" became one of the main vehicles used by Marines (who were uninjured) to describe the status, physical (bodily), and mental capacities of those individuals who occupied a somewhat complex liminal state of being, yet not being, and not belonging in the USMC.

Being Broken

I first heard the term "broken" in 1992 when I interviewed a major about his perceptions of his injured enlisted infantrymen, as well as their potential for recovery. Other officers and non-commissioned officers had told me that he had failed to get promoted, and that was why he had taken over as their primary officer. It would probably be his last assignment before he was retired from the Corps.

Rank, reputation, and promotion are a reflection of what the person is, as well as an assessment of character in terms of what the organization thinks of the particular marine, how it values, rewards (or punishes), and respects him. One could argue that being in command of these "broken Marines" mirrored his now devalued status, showing that he was also on his way out. In a sense, he was also being recycled (for whatever reason, or he was being punished, since he had failed to be promoted).

However, in retrospect, I doubt that he recognized any similarities between the "broken Marine" under his authority, and his own social and physical displacement. After all, he could assume that his lack of promotion (as an officer) reflected an entirely different process of marking—one, such as downsizing, which was not necessarily seen as permanently discrediting. He described the situation for his Marines:

MS (Officer): Oh those Marines (laughs), why they are just broken.

RJM (Me): What is that? Broken? What does that mean?

MS: It means that they are badly injured, and they will probably be recycled out of here. Some are in so much pain, and some (low voice) go crazy, in boot camp for example (pause) the mind just snaps (snaps his fingers), they just won't heal and they are no good. Some are sent home, like those there (points to a building) are mentally broken, they just went crazy in boot camp, (points) and they have to be separated immediately (sighs) and they will be sent home, to wherever they are from.

RJM: What will happen to them and what is recycling? Do you mean like trash or cans?

MS: Yeah (laughs), and who knows what will happen to them, it's not their fault that they couldn't take it, look, some get disability, and some are ruined, it is sad I guess but it happens, like that (snaps his fingers). Someone who you thought could take it gets broken and then he is probably outta here, you know, and as for recycling, yeah, they are separated and then they are sent home, or wherever they belong.

And unfortunately, they are not alone.

Other Stigmatized Identities

Being broken is a metaphor for not belonging, lacking social power or being seen as marginal. Injured enlisted infantrymen are not alone in this process. Indeed, the metaphor and reality of being perceived to be broken certainly affects other members of this organization in different ways: injured enlisted infantrymen weren't the only ones so-labeled. Other individuals who were stigmatized in this manner were women, gays and lesbians, and finally those individuals (male or female) who were overweight.

Marines have names for everything or anyone that does not fit, things or people they do not value, things that are stigmatized or reflect an organizational taboo, or those things (or individuals) who fail to conform to the organizational standard. Goffman has used the term "stigma" to define an attribute that is deeply discrediting (Goffman 1963: 3). Stigmas are not discrediting in themselves. Rather they exist in relation to other things, other people and other meanings. "An attribute that stigmatizes one type of possessor can confirm the usualness or the normalcy of the other, and therefore nothing is discreditable as a thing in itself" (Goffman 1963: 3).

The stigma, or mark, may or may not be permanently discrediting. It is based on some variant of the following: the duration of the stigma, whether or not the stigmatized individual can overcome the stigma and become socially accepted as normal. Following Goffman, Jones et al. (1984) have added that the mark is only "potentially discrediting" and commonly becomes permanent when it is linked through attributional processes. Only then are certain dispositions seen as deviant. Over time, however, the discredit becomes more consequential when the deviant dispositions are devalued, judged to be persistent, and occur long beyond a specified time frame. As a consequence the stigma becomes an "essential" part of the marked person's identity (Jones et al. 1984: 6–7; Goffman 1963).

Markings or stigma as such may or may not be physical. In this particular research the cultural and institutional process of marking begins with physical injury and possible disability. As such, labels, markings, or stigmas do make a difference, since once such marking or label is applied, further information regarding the marine is guided by these connotations.

This cultural process of naming defines belonging by distinguishing or discriminating between those who belong and those who do not. Susan Sontag (1979: 25) expands about how distinctions are created. She maintains, for example, that illnesses such as cancer also serve to "flush out" an otherwise obscure identity. The creation of such distinctions not only confirms the existence of an identity, but also confers identity through the creation of distinctions based on race, sex, and physical ability.

Marines who are overweight are called "fat" Marines, or "diet privates." The standard says that Marines cannot be fat. No one wants to take orders from a "fat Marine." They are not respected, they are not models, and they are out of control. No one wants to take orders from someone who is out of control. For another example, all Marines are green, but black Marines are sometimes referred to as "dark green Marines."

One Marine, Private First Class "Jones," states:

> I was a diet private. I had to lose weight. Half glass of milk, plain salad, no dessert, so you can lose weight. Sure it was physically tough, I am not a runner . . .

Yet another explicit example of labeling is the case of women Marines. Out of the context of race or weight, all male Marines are simply called "Marines." Being called by the title of "Marine" confers a particular type of belonging, maleness, and Marine-ness as social identity, and personal status. However, Marines who are female are always called "Women Marines," or "WMs." Their title, according to Williams (1989), is always capitalized, drawing a distinction between women and men. One WM, Sergeant "Sharp," states:

> Women Marines make up only about 5% of the organization. Because of this you are always scrutinized and your reputation is based on perceptions of how you carry yourself. Like if you are wearing something too tight, well these perceptions drive people to think things. I guess it drives me to be that much more of a lady.

In addition, when a Woman Marine marries a Marine, even if she has more time in the Corps, she is referred to as Mrs. X rather than her rank if she is in the company of her husband's peers, in contrast to the situation at her place of work. In yet another example, a Sergeant "Ellen Jones" claims

> I had to lose five pounds, and sure, five pounds shouldn't matter, but here it does. Everyone knows that I am overweight. People tease me (pause) but I think they think that I am out of control and no one wants to take orders from an out-of-control woman.

In her landmark study on women and men in nontraditional occupations, Williams (1989) found that the Marine Corps (as an organization) carries an image of masculine toughness and discipline, a preoccupation with masculine symbols, such as guns and muscles, a sense of pride and honor, and a kind of phobia about non-warlike and feminine sentiments, such as gentleness and love (Smelser in Williams 1989: ix). But these are just a few examples of how differences are created through a systematic marking of difference in an organization where physical conformity and maleness are the norm, certain bodily norms are valued, and any further deviations from the norm will be activated and named at any given moment.

Still Different . . . Still Men . . . and Still Broken

Still, the brokenness of an injured enlisted infantryman is different than other forms of brokenness in this organization. It is different in that it refers to a unique process of social blame and the conferring of social value and identity. On the other hand, the possibility of women serving in the infantry was seen as undesirable. Women simply do not belong and the possibility of their inclusion is resented; they could break the tradition of the all-male infantry. Injured enlisted infantrymen are uniquely broken because they are men. In this regard, the injured infantryman's injury causes a conflict that is eventually internalized if the injury persists. If he heals, he still has organizational potential for inclusion and belonging. A real "man" can and will heal. On the other hand, failure to heal is always an individual Marine's fault. It is his fault for not belonging since the organization is rarely at fault for its mismanagement of identities and bodies. Instead, the "man" couldn't cut it. He was not a real Marine.

The cultural contexts through which particular stigmas become activated are linked to the foundations of the cultural meanings of both the body and identity. In the Corps, the expectation of performance and the perfectibility of both the identity and the body are historically positioned as sites that define organizational belonging, a healthy and organizationally defined masculine self that relies on organizational ideals of "normalized identities and bodies" that perform under extreme pressure. This does not mean that the internalization of the stigma was not resisted. Indeed, these injured Marines told me that they often tried to resist when other Marines, namely their peers, labeled them and treated them as if they were less, that is, broken.

Pain, a multidimensional and multifactorial experience, is also a discursive practice that produces specific types of subjectivity in the USMC. I kept asking questions about what belonging meant to these young injured men. Did it mean that they received no respect? If this was the case, what did a lack of respect imply to them? Many of the young men I interviewed revealed that they no longer felt like they really belonged in the USMC. Despite having completed and graduated from boot camp, or having spent significant time (often two or three years or more in the fleet), many told me that they often felt that they were not full Marines: that is, that they were not treated with the full respect accorded to members who did not have persistent injuries.

Being an enlisted infantryman in the USMC is not merely a single-minded pursuit of systemic and ritualized violence instigated (at least in part) by the nation, or passively endured by the recruit. Beyond this, the cultural discourses about bearing forms of acute pain and stress nurtures a subjectivity whereby the Marines come to understand themselves, as selves and as Marines.

Some Conclusions

This paper has argued that men who sustain serious physical trauma that persists and gets in the way of their job performance are perceived as not belonging because of their inability to endure the pain of being a Marine. And over time these injured enlisted infantrymen are labeled and stigmatized for their inability to perform. Then they are recycled or let go from the organization. This process of being seen as broken occurs in a variety of ways, and depends on the social, political, and economic contexts which informs the particular experience with pain. Thus it is always important to examine a marine's position in a field of social relations in order to grasp his experience with pain (Rosaldo 1989, 1993; Kan 1989).

Being injured in an organization that places primacy on the ability to physically perform causes a crisis in the individual's identity. These individuals make sacrifices to belong all the time. And some are more extreme than others. And all know when they do not belong and why. Their understandings of the pain experience and its relationship to processes of social stigma and labeling reflect an insight into an organizational culture and structure which is intolerant to persistent pain and injury (especially if the trauma was not sustained on the battlefield). It also reflects an intense labeling process. In effect, Marines who are physically or emotionally "broken" during boot camp or soon after they are in the fleet might not heal, might never be fixed, and consequently cannot be reformed or remade. This metaphor of "broken" serves to raise doubts amongst one's peers—those who do belong, who are "normal," who without physical or emotional injury are "unbroken." They are the rightful members having earned the right to identity and belonging.

References

Borysenko, Joan. (1987). *Minding the Body, Mending the Mind.* New York: Bantam New Age Books.

Connell, Robert W. (1990). An iron man: The body and some contradictions of hegemonic masculinity. In *Sport, Men and Gender Order: Critical Feminist Perspectives*, edited by Messner and Sabo. Champaign, Illinois: Human Kinetics Press.

Girard, René. (1986). *The Scapegoat.* Translated from the French (*Le bouc emissaire*; Paris: B. Grassnet, 1982, by Yvonne Freccero. Baltimore: Johns Hopkins University Press.

Goffman, Erving. (1963). *Stigma: Notes on the Management of Spoiled Identity.* New Jersey: Englewood-Cliffs.

Jones, Edwards E., et al. (1984). *Social Stigma: The Psychology of Marked Relationships.* New York: W.H. Freeman.

Kan, Sergei. (1989). *Symbolic Immortality: The Tlingit Potlach of the Nineteenth Century.* Washington, D.C.: Smithsonian Institution Press.

Leckie, Roger. (1992). *Helmet for My Pillow.* New York: Warner Books.

Rosaldo, Renato. (1989). *Culture and Truth: the Remaking of Social Analysis.* Boston: Beacon Press.

———. (1993). Notes towards a critique of patriarchy from a male subject position. Manuscript, Department of Anthropology, Stanford University.

Sontag, Susan. (1979). *Illness as Metaphor.* New York: Vintage.

Williams, Christine L. (1989). *Gender Differences at Work: Women and Men in Nontraditional Occupations.* Berkeley: University of California Press.

Chapter XVII

Epistemic Violence, Smear Campaigns, and Hit Lists: Disappearing the Palestinians

Nada Elia

> "What are the words you do not yet have? What do you need to say?"
> —Audre Lorde (1984), "The Transformation of Silence"
>
> "But if I didn't name myself Palestinian, who would?"
> —Suheir Hammad (1996), *Drops of This Story*

I welcome every new multicultural anthology, every new leftist journal, with pleasure that borders on masochism: my voracious appetite for readings that celebrate difference remains unsatiated, my enthusiastic desire for a greater knowledge of the plight of the underdog is soon disenchanted, as I note once again, with ever greater pain, the absence of a whole people from the list of the world's oppressed natives, the dispossessed, and the targets of ethnic cleansing. Why are we not there, not considered as worthy of inclusion as other colonized, exploited and/or under-represented peoples? Why is it that the U.S. left, which eagerly supports and promotes concepts such as indigenous people's rights, self-sufficiency, self-representation, and self-determination, has not produced so much as a bumper sticker denouncing our dispossession? Why isn't our suffering acknowledged; why are we not listed among the wretched of the Earth?

I am a subaltern, a pariah, a member of a people the liberal left cannot accommodate. The Western dominant discourse, both left and right, has so obliterated my existence that, although I am Semitic, I am never the referent in the expression "anti-Semitic" (Elia 1998; I will excerpt from this article throughout).

In this essay, I examine the epistemic violence operative in U.S. culture that allows for the disappearance of a whole people, the Palestinians, whose plight has been rendered so invisible that, to millions of Americans, they are, at best, no more than a highly abstract concept—not a suffering people, but a problem. Without suggesting that physical violence is a minor aspect of the plight of the Palestinian people, I focus here on only one facet of our condition, the linguistic oppression that daily subjects us to ethnic cleansing, to a denial not only of our civil and political rights, but of our very identity. We are allowed to function in society; we may even thrive financially and academically. However, with the exception of the extremely few, the necessary "tokens" who shoulder the heavy and homogenizing burden of representation, we do not have the privilege to claim our identity.

A well-wishing friend who knew I was on the job market advised me: "Get the job first, and then tell them you're Palestinian. If you absolutely have to."

Whoever said silence is golden was a hypocrite, preaching the opposite of what they were engaging in, engaging in what they were preaching against. From that patronizing position, they were able to preserve their privileges, including that of speaking for others, representing them.

Our silence does not protect us, it directly benefits our oppressors.

Today, members of non-hegemonic social groups know that the improvement of their circumstances is contingent upon rendering their problems visible. Yet it would be naive to assume that visibility alone is the solution, rather than a venue for airing the problem, a sine qua non for the cure. And visibility comes at a high cost. Visibility, the foothold that non-hegemonic groups seek to achieve, is generally met by gigantic counter-attacks from the right, which still constitutes the dominant discourse. It is quite revealing of this culture's mood that books such as Alan Bloom's *The Closing of the American Mind* and Dinesh d'Souza's *Illiberal Education: The Politics of Race and Sex on Campus*, demonizing feminism and multiculturalism, are best-sellers, purchased by individuals who would never themselves consider going to college, yet rejoice in the attacks on challenges to the canon. Martin Bernal's *Black Athena: The Afroasiatic Roots of Classical Civilization*, or Ngugi wa Thiong'o's *Barrel of a Pen* remain as marginalized as the people they seek to empower.

When it comes to the Palestinians, however, both the right and left discourses conflate to efface signs of the suffering of that people. Thus we find that narratives that perpetuate the image of Palestinians as murderers (such as the movie *Raid on Entebbe*) are popular successes, feeding mainstream discourse. However, those which depict the Palestinian suffering are not necessarily welcome by the left, and even there remain marginalized, the purview of the few.

The very few.

On the whole, the U.S. liberals and leftist intellectuals seem incapable of moving beyond the Zionist meta-narrative which equates being Jewish with being oppressed. While they celebrate the collapse of the binary with regards to other discourses, they have proven resistant to ambivalence when it comes to the Middle East. As Europe's "others," the Ashkenazim are posited at the opposite end of the East/West, Oppressed/Oppressor binary. The voices of anyone residing East of those European Jews are too distant—the voices of the Native Palestinians are muffled. Critics of Zionism are labeled anti-Semitic, (self-hating if they happen to be Jewish), a stigma that silences its bearers, denying them the very right to defend their position. Among the numerous linguistic achievements of the Zionist meta-narrative is the ease with which the charge of anti-Semitism becomes an indictment, a final verdict—the accusation becomes a conviction as soon as it is articulated. [For a lengthy discussion of the hegemonic Zionist discourse, see Edward Said's *The Question of Palestine*, particularly chapter 2, "Zionism from the Standpoint of its Victims;" Ella Shohats' "Sephardim in Israel: Zionism from the Standpoint of its Jewish Victims," in *Social Text*, 19/20 (Fall 1988); and Nada Elia, "Affirming Life, Inscribing the Intifada," in *Radical Philosophy Review*, 1998]

The journal *Diaspora* was pressured for featuring the displacement of non-Jews (such as Palestinians and Armenians), and the word "Holocaust" is apparently the monopoly of the Jews, not to be used for the genocide of Native Americans or other victims of ethnic cleansing. Delegitimized by the left, the plight of the Palestinians is pushed into subaltern status. Attacks on feminism have been vocally criticized by the left, the smear campaigns against pro-Palestinian intellectuals have gone relatively unanswered. Said's *The Question of Palestine*, a volume in the trilogy which includes the groundbreaking *Orientalism*, was turned down by two publishing houses before being picked up by Random House. Yet one must keep in mind how rigorous his scholarship must be, for it to be published at all.

Years ago, I had a button on my backpack that read "Support the Intifada, End the Occupation." A Jewish colleague in women's studies asked me, "What occupation?"

A startling cultural moment in the late 1980s was the appearance on American television of Hanan Ashrawi, an articulate Palestinian woman who shattered the stereotype of the uneducated, submissive, veiled Arab female. The American media must have secretly rejoiced when Ashrawi became openly critical of the Palestinian Authority—rather than comment on the tribulations and labor pains of a fledgling not-yet-state, they could now prove to their spectators that Ashrawi was, after all, not representative of her people. Ashrawi becomes the odd one out, the few who abuse their power are more "typical" of that uncivilized people, the Palestinians.

Similarly, academics who do not fit the stereotype of thick-featured, thick-accented, emotional and cantankerous speakers are forever reminded that they may not/do not speak for the Palestinians, for are they not, after all, Western-educated intellectuals? To be "other," to be Palestinian, is deemed a fixed entity. In his essay "The Other Question," Homi Bhabha (1996) argues that a stereotype "impedes the circulation and articulation of the signifier 'race' as anything other than its fixity as racism. We already know that blacks are licentious, Asiatics duplicitous." To which we must add "Palestinians are depraved murderers." In keeping with the culture of the Hyperreal, where the illusion has greater currency than reality, all those who do not fit the stereotype of "The Palestinian" are denied authenticity, and the suicide bomber becomes the sole representative of his/her people. Yet nobody would suggest that Buchi Emecheta is not Nigerian, Ama Ata Aidoo not Ghanaian, although both write in English, and the first left Nigeria for England when she was sixteen, while the latter has resided in many European countries and in the United States.

And language continues its pernicious operation. Every Palestinian act of violence is termed terrorism, every Israeli massacre is presented as reprisal, or the isolated act of a crazed individual. Thus Dr. Baruch Goldstein, who machine-gunned praying men and boys at Hebron's Ibrahimi Mosque, killing twenty-nine, and setting off riots during which many more were killed, is a "crazed individual." What about Rabbi Ya'acov Perin, who at Goldstein's funeral, at which he declared him a martyr, claimed that "One million Arabs are not worth a Jewish fingernail?"* What about the Jews who daily visit Goldstein's grave, now a national shrine at Kiryat Arba?** Each and every one an isolated crazed individual? [*Cited (deemed "fit to print") in the New York Times, February 28, 1994. **See Washington Report on Middle East Affairs, XVI, 1 (June/July 1997) page 3.]

In *Of Grammatology*, Jacques Derrida writes that a deleted word always leaves a trace behind, that the crossing out never completely obliterates a sign (1967/1976). But to be deleted, a symbol has first to be inscribed. In the United States, the press, the liberal intelligentsia, and the academic community combine to ensure that the Palestinian sign is never allowed to fully impress itself before it can be deleted, crossed out, leaving if only the slightest trace. Those exceptional individuals who have managed to achieve academic and media prominence have been subjected to vicious smear campaigns ranging from character assassination to scholarly delegitimization.

Professor Edward Said was placed on the Jewish Defense League hit list after the murder of Meir Kahane. How many people know that fact? How many denounced it?

Visibility requires courage, even as it is essential for survival. Yet passing is, clearly, the most painful choice, for it is a denial of one's social identity when the ill is always already social. Passing is social suicide. More dangerously for one's collective group, passing reinforces the dominant discourse, for it allows for the preservation of the stereotype. And passing raises the question, physical death, or spiritual death? If denying your Palestinian identity reduces the risk of harassment, should you "come out"? And what if spiritual death is the first step towards your final annihilation, your physical death? What if everybody, except for yourself, benefits from your silence, your spiritual death? Are you not contributing to it, by denying who you are?

Our silence does not protect us. Other genocides make the news, ours goes undenounced. By failing to represent us, language annihilates us.

"But if I didn't name myself Palestinian, who would?" asks a weary Suheir Hammad in the autobiographical *Drops of This Story*. Hammad, who grew up in Brooklyn, recounts an episode sadly familiar to numerous Palestinian-Americans: "I stood up in class one day and let my teacher know I was Palestinian, and that we did exist as a nation, as a people" (1996: 60). But the teacher was relentless:

> What did you say? Pakistani? Which one of your parents is black? . . .
>
> *I'm Palestinian. I'd have to point it out on the map (the region, not the name).*
>
> Oh, you're Israeli! Did any of your family survive the holocaust?
>
> *Reply that my people were living through their own holocaust.*

Teachers would challenge me:

> There's no such place as Palestine. Where is it on the map?
>
> Why do you people make so much trouble? Don't you know what the Jews have been through? (1996: 73)

All entrance into culture requires language, and language, or rather a venue for language, is denied us. As victims of epistemic violence, we have no ready venue to articulate and inscribe our oppression. Language betrays us, perniciously pushing us not to the margins, but off the page, outside the text. The scope of suffering, poverty, hunger, disease, unemployment, and despair among Palestinians is comparable to that of the Jews during the Third Reich; standards of living in the West Bank and Gaza Strip, already very low prior to the Oslo Accord, declined by seventy percent inside of four years (Amos 1997). But reports of the misery of Palestinians rarely make the news in the United States, and will certainly not catalyze nation-wide denunciation and relief efforts.

In Israel, where the reality of human bodies cannot be overlooked, where flesh and blood litter the streets, the Palestinian presence is dealt with, with a monstrous military apparatus. Two continents away, it is sufficient to manipulate the words and images that are supposed to "bring" that distant land to us, and the flesh and blood are forgotten, pushed off the text.

Language is political. Words allow us to tell lies, to create an illusion that takes hold of our minds, which in turn attempts, often successfully, to take hold of matter. Golda Meir, who claimed in 1969 that "There are no Palestinians. These are Southern Syrians," remains unshaken on her pedestal. Yet the left is unforgiving of other political leaders whose statements are not nearly as outrageous. When language is not within reach, semiotic utterances can still break the silence, affirming life.

It is vital for Palestinians and their supporters to break the hegemonic discourse by denouncing the misrepresentative binary.

Words allow us to tell lies, something the dominant discourse has historically done. In occupied Algeria, the French fumigated tribes that had taken shelter in caves, and reported to the metropolis on their "pacification efforts." The European settlers in Australia spoke of the success of their "assimilation projects"—which the Aborigines termed the "annihilation plan." And today's Zionist meta-narrative, by suggesting that Jews are the sole occupants of the margins of hegemonic discourse, is annihilating the Palestinian presence.

European Jews, the Ashkenazim, are the victims of European anti-Semitism, and Zionism, the call for a "return" to Eretz Israel, started among them. Ninety percent of the Ashkenazim still live outside of Israel, and their denunciation of racism and discrimination does not address the plight of the victims of anti-Semitism in the Middle East. Maybe when the left realizes there is a whole people "East" of the Jews, and that Zionism as an ideology and movement for the empowerment of European Jews has created problems of a magnitude comparable to that of the (Jewish) holocaust, we will finally be able to address solutions for both Jews and Palestinians. Until then, the Palestinians will keep on being violated, will keep on screaming, hoping to break through hegemonic discourse.

When language is not within reach, semiotic utterances still can break the silence, affirming life.

References

Amos, D. (1997). Report on "All Things Considered," October 17, 1997. National Public Radio.

Bernal, Martin. (1987). *Black Athena: The Afroasiatic Roots of Classical Civilization*. New Brunswick: Rutgers University Press.

Bhabha, Homi K. (1996). The other question. *Contemporary Postcolonial Theory*, edited by Padmini Mongia, pp. 37–45. New York: Saint Martin's Press. First published in *Screen* 24.6 (1983): 18–36.

Bloom, Alan. (1987). *The Closing of the American Mind*. New York: Simon and Schuster.

Derrida, Jacques. (1976). *Of Grammatology*. Translated from the French (*De la grammatologie*, 1967) by Gayatri Chakravorty Spivak. Baltimore: John Hopkins University Press.

d'Souza, Dinesh. (1991). *Illiberal Education: The Politics of Race and Sex on Campus*. New York: Free Press.

Elia, Nada. (1998). Affirming life, inscribing the Intifada. *Radical Philosophy Review* 1:1.

Hammad, Suheir. (1996). *Drops of This Story*. New York: Harlem River Press.

Lorde, Audre. (1984). The transformation of silence into language and action. *Sister Outsider: Essays and Speeches*, pp. 110–113. Freedom, California: Crossing Press.

Ngugi wa Thiong'o. (1983). *Barrel of a Pen: Resistance to Repression in Neocolonial Kenya*. Trenton, New Jersey: Africa World Press.

Said, Edward W. (1978). *Orientalism*. New York: Pantheon Books.

———. (1980). *The Question of Palestine*. New York: Random House.

Chapter XVIII

Violence Within and Against the Pacific

Katerina Teaiwa

Picture: Moruroa, Fagataufa, Kalama, Nauru, Enewetak, Bougainville, Ko'olawe, Kwajalein, Bikini, Rongelap, Kiritimati, Monte Bello, Banaba, Kanaky, Emu, Vatukoula, Maralinga, Woomera. Pieces of Oceania ruptured, fractured, blown up and left wounded or dying. The land, the sea blown to smithereens to save other lives, perhaps...

In the Pacific, many of us are still trying to decolonize politically and intellectually. Our work is often personal even when the language is "objective." In this paper, my criticism of certain forms of violence in the Pacific is emotive. So where must the process of decolonization begin? With remembering Bougainville's "discovery" of the sexually uninhibited noble savages of Tahiti in 1768? With the settlement of Samoa "and other questions" between the British and Germans in 1899 (Daws 1980: 1, Silverman 1971: 94)? What about Albert Ellis' British flag on Banaba in 1900 (Ellis 1935), or the U.N. creation of the United States "Trust Territories" in Micronesia after World War II? Or with the introduction of the notion that land could be traded, bought and sold, physically re-shaped, or given away to foreigners?

In indigenous epistemology, "land" often includes the people and their culture, the ecology and surrounding ocean. The land and ocean live, breathe and remember. Like many indigenous populations, island communities conventionally have a spiritual connection to every rock, plant, animal and phenomenon of nature; this is where gods and goddesses reside. In Kiribati tradition, Nei Tituabine is the giant ray and Tabakea is the turtle; in Hawai'i, Pele is the volcano and Hi'iaka is the forest; in old Samoa, Saveasi'uleo is the eel, O le Fe'e is the octopus; and to Polynesians, the Ocean is Moana Nui. When Europeans came to the Pacific with all their "superior" tools and ideas, these spiritual attitudes towards nature became suppressed. With Christianity and modernity, Europeans and Americans disrupted, problematized, poked holes in, and altered the land and sea, and for some islanders the deities died violent deaths.

When I refer to "Pacific Islanders," I am speaking of Chandra Mohanty's reformulations of Benedict Anderson's "imagined community," including peoples bound by their location within an ocean of colonial religious, economic, and political histories (1991: 4). Our experiences of colonial dominance are as diverse as are our particular cultures and languages, but we all share a common continental misperception as inhabitants of "Paradise."

Mohanty's premise for describing "imagined communities" is based on groups which share the potential for political alliances. The penetrating influence of colonialism across Oceania provides such a potential. I do not wish to claim an absolute similarity of experience or attitude for Pacific Islanders, but what we also share is a lack of attention from the international academic community who find more urgent sites of oppression elsewhere. In addition, what many indigenous peoples of the Pacific share, within and without the intellectual realm, is a basic relationship with the land and ocean as a source of life and spirituality (even among those who have completely converted to capitalism and Christianity) and a struggle to live with the encroaching modernity in a meaningful and strategic mode. I speak of violence within the Pacific, then, from a position at which these commonalities intersect.

We do not need a dictionary to understand that violence means destruction, pain, harm, and suffering. We are appalled at the violence in Bosnia, Somalia, Los Angeles, and Haiti—and then remember that there are wonderful places like Hawai'i, Fiji, and Tahiti with swaying palm trees and hula dancers. As France detonates weapons of mass destruction in the heart of a coral atoll, we—in and beyond the Pacific who have access to television—still dream of and find console in *South Pacific, Mutiny on the Bounty*, and *Green Day's* hula dancers on MTV's *Alternative Nation*.

If an external force drastically alters people's lives causing pain and suffering, it is violence. The "cultural context" of violence does not simply indicate the ways in which violence is played out within and between different ethnic groups or individuals. It could also describe the diverse and highly specific cultural experiences of external (though I admit the boundary implied by the word "external" is not clearcut in some cases) violence, and here, that violence generated by the environment-altering activities of colonial powers in the Pacific—today, specifically, mining and nuclear testing. Such activities have impacted the lives of islanders for decades; the disruption goes on to precipitate "domestic" warfare, dispute, depression, deprivation, dispossession, dislocation, and degradation of health, culture, economy, and society. In all cases the rhetoric used to obfuscate the harmful effects of mining and nuclear testing is that of "paradise," "development," "progress," "growth," and "security"—in reality, not ours but theirs.

Today, many islanders, along with the rest of the world, tend to see the manufactured Pacific Paradise and not the Pacific reality. Today, we islanders also watch MTV and eat or desire McDonald's hamburgers and drive Toyota Landcruisers. Well, at least some of "us" do—power is not restricted to Euro/American elites, but belongs to indigenous ones too. One only has to find out what's happened in Tahiti, Fiji, Papua New Guinea, New Caledonia, Aotearoa/New Zealand, and even everyone's favorite paradise, Hawai'i, to comprehend that violence foments here at the physical, spiritual, and psychological levels. The root of this chaos is the colonial alteration of island life. Ironically, the Pacific is anything but peaceful.

In social science, there is the notion of structural violence, which manifests itself at the institutional social level, and physical violence, where people actually harm each other. I do not distinguish between structural and physical violence—pain is pain. The international community is often quick to acknowledge the latter form of violence: you can always find war and torture in the media. You can also find widespread concern about human rights, women's rights, and animal rights within non-governmental organizations. However, it is rare that the Pacific is included in any category of these concerns (although the United Nations is fully aware of our struggles). Continental audiences seem to bypass problems in the Pacific altogether, because this is supposed to be an idyllic place. Although the 1995 French nuclear testing incidents in Tahiti were televised across the world, many of my friends in California, Oregon, and Washington still hadn't heard anything about them. My concern is not that everyone should know everything about islanders, but that we put a stop to the exclusion of Oceania from the realm of "reality," including grim reality.

Popular notions of islanders remain forever static to the media and its publics. In the film *The Fifth Element,* 300 years into the future, we still see hula dancers and lei bearers as a significant part of the recreational experience. Paradise simply cannot exist without ocean, beaches, smiling and dancing natives; and while "culture-less" people in the First World develop, the rest of us are held back by our adherence to indigenous identities. Everywhere else but here in the Pacific, our existence relies on the assumption that all is well—unchanging, relaxing, slow, comfortable. The penetrating activities of powerful colonial and neocolonial actors also relies on the "fact" that Pacific peoples are geographically and demographically small in size and number. This is supposed to justify nuclear testing, mining and development in the islands. We're still the last frontier for an ambitious capitalism and militarism.

Many people do not know or care about current problems in Oceania because it's not a wise marketing or patriotic move to broadcast such facts; the countries responsible can hide behind their saintly international and domestic images to distract their citizenry. However, it's okay to let people know, decades after-the-fact, that the United States nuclear testing activities displaced, dispossessed, and dislocated thousands of Marshall islanders. Since Americans subscribe to the notion that they are not physically or psychologically (but perhaps slightly morally) responsible for past wrongs, such news today is sad but irrelevant. For indigenous people, who do not amputate themselves from their ancestors, past wrongs are very much alive in present life discourses and experiences. The image of Ebeye atoll comes to mind—7,000 relocated Bikini and Rongelap Islanders living on 67 acres, the most densely populated area in the Pacific, described by some as a "biological time bomb." Undoubtedly, Marshall islanders are still suffering from the activities of the American military. For example, in 1963 a polio epidemic left 190 people paralyzed in the unsanitary conditions of Ebeye. In recent years, the suicide rate has been more than twice that of the United States (Weingartner 1991: 21). I certainly wouldn't say that the violence in these islands is over.

The military governor of the Marshall Islands had explained to Bikini Islanders that their home was needed to contribute to the ending of all wars on earth; it was the will of God. How ironic that most islanders and Americans now share this same God. The islanders must have felt so proud that something belonging to them was needed for the greater good of humankind—and it was, the bikini bathing suit was and continues to be a hit sensation (Teaiwa, T. 1994: 89). Bikini Islanders agreed to be absent from their homes for a short time, but 50 years later, they are scattered throughout the Marshalls. In 1954, with winds blowing towards the east islands, the device code-named "Bravo" was detonated and radioactive ash fell on Rongelap Islanders. They weren't evacuated for three days, and by 1985, 77% of all Rongelapese who were under 10 in 1954 had developed major tumours (Weingartner 1991:20). Bravo, "Bravo"!

We should turn to less depressing matters, to desirable worldly items now available to us like wine and cheese, perfume and designer labels, *An American in Paris* and *Gigi.* Ah Paris! The center of high culture and high colonialism. The French Government has done more than their share of violence in the Pacific. Ever since the establishment of the "Centre d'Experimentations du Pacifique," French Polynesia has been slowly turned into a nuclear and welfare state hostage. Whether they liked it or not, Tahitians, as French citizens, were obliged to provide a testing ground for nuclear weapons which their colonial masters considered essential for the security of France as a world power (Finney 1992: 67). Another sacrifice for the "greater good"?

How did the Tahitians go from being the toast of Paris in the 1770s, to the nuclear-radiated natives of the 20th century? Two centuries after Europe decided that the noble savage is ignoble, the modern world promotes the original romantic notions of Polynesia, and even a nuclear bomb cannot make us see that life in Tahiti is not always romantic. There have been three major civil uprisings in Papeete, and the French government still hangs onto these islands long after colonialism has become unfashionable in the rest of the world.

Violence in the Pacific includes everything from French colonialism to tourism marketing—the results are enduring for indigenous peoples. The fact that many Tahitian lives are kept going by French monetary subsidies is not always a positive thing for them: for some it is an oppressive situation—politically, economically, and biologically (as the nuclear tests have shown us). Many Tahitians bravely resist the French denial of their autonomy, but dependency is a hard thing to shake off. Of course, not all islanders criticize development, or aid, for that matter. Many, in fact, accept the idea that cash economies are inevitable and they must follow the examples or directions set by First World nations. However, we all carry a thread of suspicion for modernity. Whether or not we act on this feeling politically and economically, is different. Pondering over, analyzing, and contesting the influences of imperialism and capitalism—influences already woven into our practice and ideology—is a luxury reserved mostly for social science university students. But the concerns do surface in different ways—from our insistence at doing things on "Pacific time," to our poetry, art, music and dance. I will never forget performing an anti-nuclear *tamure* (Tahitian dance) aboard the Greenpeace ship *Rainbow Warrior II* just days before it was violently boarded by French commandos in the waters surrounding Moruroa atoll.

Why has the Pacific been militarized by countries like the U.S.A. and France? Why would they extend their violence into the Pacific? Among other things, the ocean is a veritable gold mine of resources. From its sheer size and "lack" of land or "significant" habitation, the Pacific is the perfect place to exploit. There is, or was, in some places, an abundance of mineral deposits. Bauxite, nickel, copper, gold, phosphate, cobalt, and sulfides are just a few of the geological resources housed by the Pacific. If they haven't already blown it up, powerful countries could mine these minerals for themselves—and some already have (Weingartner 1991: 17).

Britain, which did its own fair share of nuclear testing in Australia and at Kiritimati Island, also participated in massive mining projects which practically drained the land out from beneath Islanders. My sister, Teresia, once said, "agriculture isn't in our blood, but our blood is in agriculture." The physical land of our ancestral home, Banaba, was mined and shipped off to England, Australia, and New Zealand to provide cheap fertilizer for their farmers. In Banaban culture, blood was land and kinship was constructed on its exchange (Teaiwa, T. 1995:10, Silverman 1971). However, it was our misfortune that our island was made entirely of phosphate. The destruction of Banaba by the British Phosphate Mining Companies has produced a dislocated, dispossessed (but necessarily creative) group of islanders on Rabi Island in Fiji. To say that we are still struggling to figure out our place in Fiji society and the world in general is an understatement. Banabans have experienced exploitation, confusion, and cultural degradation at the physical, psychological, economic, and political levels over the past century. Like Marshall Islanders and Tahitians, Banabans gave up their island to provide agricultural security (sustenance) for colonial governments and foreign populations.

Many of the environmentally and spiritually destructive activities carried out in our region have been justified by the agents of development and growth. Do we really need radioactive fish and phosphate graves in exchange for money and technology in order to grow and feel good about ourselves? In *Sustainable Development or Malignant Growth,* Atu Emberson-Bain writes, "as a general rule, mining in the Pacific has proved to be one of the most destructive and unsustainable forms of foreign-initiated development" (1994). She describes the suffering of Bougainvillians, in the Northern Solomon Islands, as a result of Australian Colonial copper mining on their land; 3,000 deaths, the wiping out of 6,000 village homes, and the torture and murder of hundreds of innocent people mark the movement of this once peaceful community to armed revolution (Emberson-Bain 1994: 94).

Emerson-Bain goes on to say: "Traditional Pacific values have no parallel in Western capitalist notions of land as an alienable and disposable material commodity. Land is crucial to physical survival; it is central to the reproduction of traditional social relations; and it has a spiritual value that enshrines a sacred link between the dead (ancestors) and the living" (1994: 96). Those used to living in contrived suburbs or concrete high-rise apartments, cannot imagine the emotion and anxiety associated with losing a traditional habitat to foreign exploiters. The land and ocean are everything to islanders; destroying it invites retaliation or indigenous cultural recession. The current violence in Bougainville between indigenous rebels and the Papua New Guinea army, is perhaps more literal than the Banaban and Marshall Island cases, but it is definitely in reaction to the initial appropriation of indigenous land by outsiders for monetary exploitation. Hundreds of people have lost their lives in this war; the state of health and education in Bougainville has been in ruins for almost a decade. There is also severe warfare, armed resistance, and indigenous persecution in West Papua/Irian Jaya which is connected to Indonesian and American exploitation of land through mining and logging. The international media afford little attention to the wars in this Pacific region.

Conventionally, violence is defined as physical force, injury by distortion, infringement or profanation, discordance and undue alteration. Colonialism, together with economic and military imperialism, has infringed upon Pacific lives, profaning the earth and distorting or altering the physical and spiritual fabric of Pacific lives leaving behind much discord. Such force violates *te kainga* (ancestral land—Gilbertese, Tongan) and drains our *wairua* (spiritual force—Maori) and our *mana* (power—Polynesian). Pacific people continue to struggle with and resist this specter of violence in creative and strategic ways.

References

Daws, Gavan. (1980). *A Dream of Islands: Voyages of Self Discovery in the South Seas.* New York: Norton.

Ellis, Albert Fuller. (1935). *Ocean Island and Nauru: Their Story.* Sydney, Australia: Angus and Robertson.

Emberson-Bain, Atu. (1994). De-romancing the stones: Gender, environment and mining in the Pacific. *Sustainable Development or Malignant Growth,* edited by Atu Emberson-Bain. Suva, Fiji: Marama Publications.

Finney, Ben. (1992). Nuclear hostages. In *From Sea to Space.* Honolulu: University of Hawai'i Press.

Mohanty, Chandra Talpade, Ann Russo, and Lourdes Torres, editors. (1991). *Third World Women and the Politics of Feminism.* Bloomington: Indiana University Press.

Silverman, Martin G. (1971). *Disconcerting Issue: Meaning and Struggle in a Resettled Pacific Community.* Chicago: University of Chicago Press.

Teaiwa, Teresia K. (1994). Bikinis and Other S/Pacific N/Oceans. *The Contemporary Pacific Journal* (Spring 1994): 87.

———. (1995). *yaqona/yagoqu:* contested roots and routes of a displaced native. Pacific History Conference, December 1995.

Weingartner, Erich. (1991). *The Pacific: Nuclear Testing and Minorities,* A Minority Rights Group Report, Britain, January 1991.

Chapter XIX

Liberation, De-liberations, and Stallings, or, Is the "Post"-here Yet?

Nada Elia

This article was completed before the United States' recent invasion of Iraq, and does not therefore discuss the Iraqi situation. Yet it is obvious that, in the aftermath of a Western invasion and occupation, even a people such as the Iraqis, with a long history of secularism, will revert to religious fervor, especially when they are designated as "religious others" by a fundamentalist Christian juggernaut.

What follows must not be construed as a statement of support for the institution of veiling. I do not wear the veil; I deplore and condemn the murder of unveiled women by fundamentalist zealots. Yet because of the seemingly endless demonization of Islam in the West, I seek to highlight the motivations of contemporary women who, exercising their own agency, willingly veil themselves. More than a reclamation of a villified sign, veiling today, when done voluntarily, illustrates how minuscule the space of dissent becomes, as postcolonial nationalist fervor and anti-Western feelings are collapsed into one another.

Anxious to see Zimbabwe abandon the last vestiges of its former inclination towards socialism, the World Bank in 1992 successfully initiated the imposition of a token tuition fee in all schools of the famine-stricken African country. Nominal as the fee was, it nevertheless constituted a burden to the poorest families, who responded by sending only boys to classes. As a result, little girls turned to prostitution in order to secure basic food offered their male siblings at school.

The Western reinforcement of women's oppression, presented as aid to an ailing nation, is nothing new. This essay examines how colonial powers, over the last two centuries, have helped exacerbate women's circumstances in the Middle East, pushing some to a total rejection of all things Western. Specifically, I will look at these women whose lifestyle today reveals how the European powers actually cemented sexism while supposedly working to promote democracy. The denunciation of colonialism's impact on the status of women in the Arab world is aptly summed up by Moroccan sociologist Fatima Mernissi, who writes that: "Th[e] idea of France as a 'modernizing' force is a colonial fantasy, since the French protectorate actually helped bring about an astonishing consolidation of traditions and breathed new life into existing hierarchies and inequalities" (1987: 153).

Looking at the titles of various studies of contemporary Middle Eastern women, the novice may be misled into believing the issue of Arab women's oppression is a simple one, conveniently summed up in one word, "Islam." But well-intentioned as some of the studies of Arab women have been, they are guilty of a major oversight: Arab women today are as much a part of the Muslim world as they are part of the postcolonial reality, and they have been oppressed by the predominantly-Christian West no less than by the mostly-Muslim Middle East. And just like their male compatriots, their ordeal did not end with the ousting of the occupying forces. Hence, the image of Islam as the foremost, unmitigated factor of women's oppression and alienation in the Middle East today must be redressed. And the West should also be credited for the harm it inflicted on the female half of the Muslim peoples stripped of their basic human and political rights for over a century.

Colonialism and dishonesty go hand in hand. The Western European imperial powers have attempted to justify their exploitation of foreign lands and labor that were not theirs in terms of (mostly Christian) charity and benevolence. Those countries that do not go so far as to claim their dominion over another land constituted unmitigated altruism will nevertheless argue that they contributed to the advancement of the occupied nation, by helping to "modernize" it. That this is a blatant lie is obvious today, as the postcolonial world exhibits its industrial, financial, and organizational weaknesses, and backwardness. Again, blaming these problems on the "neo-colonial elite" is delusory, for the very existence of this class is itself a legacy of colonialism.

Britain, for example, claimed that it was colonizing the world in the name of the Three Cs: Commerce, Civilization, and Christianity. But while Commerce benefited the "queen-size" pockets, it impoverished all natives who did not service the Western institutions. And whereas Civilizations, old as humanity, existed in the Indian subcontinent, Africa, and pre-conquest North America, these were either subjected to a systematic effort at eradication, or brought to a standstill by the British forces. As for Christianity, the system of belief predicating love, charity, tolerance, humility, and total disregard of all things material, the occupiers were too far removed from it to be in any position to exercise rather than merely preach it.

France did not claim that its expansionism was motivated by a desire to spread the word of the Christian god. At no point during its 132-year occupation of predominantly Muslim North Africa did it actively seek to convert the subject populations to Christianity. Although official documents that are only now coming to light reveal that France was trying to rid its metropolitan territories of undesirables, and hoping to avoid agrarian bankruptcy by exploiting lands more fertile than the European, the reason given for the French colonization of North Africa was a desire to "civilize" (read "create new markets") the otherwise deprived ("untapped") parts of the world. As with British imperialism, this *mission civilisatrice* proved ultimately counterproductive, because North Africa, suspicious of all things French, held on as best it could to its pre-occupation ways, thus inevitably falling behind, at least when measured against the Western linear pattern of history and development.

Because the French in North Africa governed the colonies solely for their own benefit, their departure left the new nations in a shambles, presenting the national leaders with an immense challenge. In many ways, it can be argued that the standard of living in North Africa today is very little different from what it was prior to the 1830 European conquest, i.e., prior to the Industrial Age. In other words, numerous aspects of today's postcolonial world are, anachronistically, pre-colonial. This is particularly true with regard to women's circumstances. But more so, one can hypothesize that, left to themselves, Muslim communities in various parts of the Arab world would have dropped the hijab, recognizing it for the obsolete handicap that it is. The hijab is the traditional openair dress for women in the harsh desert environment where Islam first appeared, not unlike the flowing robes and headscarf some men still wear today, especially if they live in rural areas or work outdoors, while others, sitting behind desks in air-conditioned offices, prefer the European business suit. No one would suggest these men renounced Islam when they donned their first pair of trousers. Similarly, women would not necessarily be renouncing Islam if they wore jeans and a T-shirt. After all, the *Qur'an* merely suggests modest dress, not a shroud:

> Tell the believing women to lower their eyes,
> guard their private parts, and not display their charms
> except what is apparent outwardly,
> and cover their bosoms with their veils,
> and not to show their finery
> except to their husbands or their fathers or fathers-in-law (*Qur'an* XXIV: 31).

Twentieth-century Islam has interpreted numerous *suras* to fit contemporary life, going so far as to allow for the establishment of interest-free banks and oil cartels. It is plausible that, were it not for foreign intervention, the *sura* recommending modesty would also have been adapted to allow for non-constrictive dress. After all, if "private parts" referred to one's face, men too would be veiled, in compliance with the *Qur'an* (XXIV: 31, but also XXIII: 7), which implies that these parts are the genital organs, since a man must also only show them to his spouse:

> The true believers will be successful,
> Who are humble in their service,
> Who shun all frivolities,
> Who strive for betterment;
> And those who guard their private parts
> Except from their wives and maids they have married (*Qur'an* XXIII: 2–7).

Colonialism, however, left a lasting impression in the Arab world, and overcoming it at times meant the indiscriminate rejection of ideas associated with the former oppressor. Among the more advertised claims of the imperial project was the "emancipation" of Arab women, hence the suspicion with which the newly independent nations viewed gender equality. "Women and their role [became] a stick with which the West could beat the East," writes Malti-Douglas (1991: 151). "When the West left, the pain-inflicting stick was discarded, rather than the causes behind its brandishing."

But the Western powers were themselves engaging in an oppressive system, not just as imperial nations, but because of the inherent sexism in their denunciation of Arab oppression of women. Thus they scarcely ever discussed gender issues as far as the role of Arab women in political life was concerned. Rather, they concentrated both their theoretical work and empirical observations on women's autonomy and control in the domestic sphere—the kitchen and the bedroom. It is no coincidence that in occupied Algeria, schooling was mandatory for young boys, but optional and frequently unavailable for girls. But more, the French administration did not even attempt to ban polygamy, a practice which could easily be rendered illegal, and which most Europeans viewed as unequivocally oppressive for women.

Similarly, the empirical example the French authorities provided was totally phallocentric: the administrators were men, their spouses domestic creatures. French men were also in control of all of the intellectual spheres: the academic disciplines, philosophy and science, the media, the presses and publishing houses, and the research foundations, in addition to the economic sector, the factories, the industries, and trading. The French co-lonial administration also took away from Arab women certain legal rights they had prior to their country's occupation. In particular, France did not allow land ownership by women, and many propertied Arab women had their land taken away from them to be registered in the name of their male next of kin. This Western intervention catapulted the feminization of poverty and its correlative, women's economic dependence on men. In cultures where women seldom enter the professional working sector, this dependence acquires critical dimensions.

In North Africa, the sexism of the European colonizer also manifested itself in chil-dren's education: schooling was compulsory for boys, with both the boy and his father going to jail for three days, and paying a heavy fine, if the young one played truant. But nothing of the sort applied to girls. Thus, by not making school mandatory for girls, the French allowed for a generation of uneducated women, in a culture where literacy for all children had been highly valued. The North Africans were holding on, as best they could, to their "independent," i.e., pre-colonial, traditions and cultures, and keeping young girls at home was one of the few legal options now available to them. Kabyle poet Fadhma Amrouche, born in 1882, explains that educated Kabyle women were viewed with suspicion by their clansmembers, because education could be obtained only in French schools. The North Africans' reluctance to educate their children in French schools is understandable, when one considers what the children were taught. Amrouche recalls:

> I was top in French history, but I hated geography—I could never remember all the Departments and Districts, whereas I can still remember in detail all the kings of France, who married whom, who succeeded whom, and all about the French revolution and the Napoleonic era. I loved French, except when I had to explain proverbs and maxims (1968/1989: 16–17).

The boys, on the other hand, could receive either secular (the official designation for French) or Qur'anic education, so long as they went to school. Ironically, the young North African girls may have been witness to French ways in their schools but, in most cases, they did not live them. Racial segregation prevailed within the schools, where the daughters of colonists had separate dormitories and dining halls. (From my own experi-ence as an Arab girl in a French-run school, I recall sitting at the same dining hall table as my European classmates, but being served different food. My friend Florence ate chicken, as I tried to avoid the weevils in my stock-flavored crushed wheat.) This segre-gation alienated the young girls, making them marginal to both their native culture and that of the colonizer. Thus Amrouche explains that, when the French closed her school, she found herself short-changed and ill-equipped, at the age of fifteen, for the life await-ing her in her native village. Her bitterness resulted in a conscious rejection of her French training and education:

> From that day I tried to rid myself of the veneer of civilisation that I had acquired and not even think about it. Since the Roumis [Arabic for "foreigners"] had rejected us, I resolved to become a Kabyle again. I told my mother she must show me how to do all her work about the house, so that I could help her (1986/1989: 30). I did not want to think of my past life

any more, since I had to forget that I had been educated. I was determined to do my best about this (1968/1989: 32).

Colonial occupation, thus, harmed Arab women in numerous ways. It stripped them of rights they enjoyed under Islam. It failed to provide a valid model for equality, while promoting emancipation. And it aggravated Arab men, who were eager to recover "their ways" following liberation, the long desired and fought-for departure of the foreign occupier. Arab men, however, were less eager to surrender gains secured under colonialism, namely the land that belonged to their mothers, wives, or sisters. Even today, the Western "help" offered needy African countries favors a continuation of sexism.

Another illustration of contemporary Western aggravation of Middle Eastern sexism is evident from the choice of nations the United States supports (invariably the more conservative ones, where polygamy remains legal, and women cannot drive), and those it opposes (which are the ones that actively promote gender equality). Ramla Khalidi and Judith Tucker confront and aptly address Western hypocrisy, as they write that the colonial powers:

> . . . argued that the oppression of women justified colonial intervention, and that the imperial project would elevate women to the standards of equality putatively present in northern Europe. The debatable sincerity and validity of these claims aside, the linking of gender issues to Western intervention and the invocation of Western standards to which all must aspire left a bitter legacy of mistrust (1992: 2).

Thus the European presence subverted the possibility of discarding the *hijab,* for in the minds of the colonized Arabs, a bare-faced woman was Western, or Westernized, i.e., precisely what they were seeking independence from. In *A Dying Colonialism*, his study of the Algerian revolution, Frantz Fanon observed:

> Servants under the threat of being fired, poor women dragged from their homes, prostitutes, were brought to the public square and symbolically unveiled to the cries of "Vive L'Algerie française!" Before this new offensive old reactions reappeared. Spontaneously and without being told, the Algerian women who had long since dropped the veil once again donned the haik, thus affirming that it was not true that woman liberated herself at the invitation of France and of General de Gaulle (1965: 62).

Motivated by similar feelings, Muslim women in Lebanon in the 1990s started donning the veil in a gesture of defiance to the West. In fact, the greater the foreign influence had been felt in the daily life of the occupied peoples, the more radical was the call for a "return to the roots." In Algeria, the French sought to obliterate the native culture. And as I write this, almost half a century after independence, Islamic fundamentalism is taking Algeria by storm. Similarly, in Iran, where the much-hated Shah, whose mere existence depended on subservience to the West, had banned the veil in 1936, Islamic fundamentalism has secured its hold on the country, and seeks to "liberate" the rest of Muslim Asia of the visible traces of Western influence. The fact that it does so with Western weapons does not appear to bother the Muslim brethren. It is the face of the *gharbzadegi,* or Westernized woman favored by the Pahlavi administration, that has come to symbolize the effects of imperialism and moral corruption.

In Lebanon, where the mandate favored the Christian segment of the population, women are wearing the veil to demonstrate both their rejection of the French-inspired undemocratic constitution, and their allegiance to Iran, symbol of anti-West feelings. Shortly after independence, the Lebanese government officially relinquished matters of personal status to the country's religious authorities, in a move destined to maintain the sectarian balance of power that favored the Christian ruling elite. Today, thanks to the French-inspired constitution, Muslim women have fewer rights than their Christian women fellow-citizens. Blaming the Islamic Republic, or Ayatollah Khomeini, for the reactionary turn of events in the Middle East since the ousting of the Shah is simply not enough. Had the West not made itself so unpopular there, Islam would not be so indiscriminate in its rejection of (most) things that can be associated with it. And, historically speaking, the first unveiled women that the alienated Iranians and pauperized North Africans saw in the twentieth century were European women, the consenting companions of their oppressors. The oppressed were not going to let their own wives remind them of the misery they experienced under colonialism, if they could help it at all. And they could, thanks to the *Qur'an* and its recommendation that women guard their "private parts."

Yet the Arab women who wish to navigate the twenty-first century as veiled creatures, determined to conceal all traces of foreign influence, are anachronistically holding on to a past long gone. For as we look at both form and contents as far as our veiled sisters are concerned, we fail to see how they differ from their precolonial great-grandmothers. Indeed, it seems that the greater the colonial influence on their everyday lives had been, the less they will let it show, when everything and everyone else around them has changed.

Clearly, emulating the West has never helped Middle Eastern women, nor is it likely to begin doing so now. Yet allowing a hatred of the West control one's life is no less oppressive. Instead, a totally independent look at how Muslim societies should treat all their members is needed, lest liberation turn to de-liberation. For there is no turning back, only stallings and unfortunate delays.

References

Amrouche, Fadhma. (1989). *My Life Story*. Translated from the French (*L'histoire de ma vie*. Paris: Maspero, 1968) by Dorothy S. Blair. London: Women's Press.

Fanon, Frantz. (1965). *A Dying Colonialism*. Translated from the French by Haakon Chevalier. New York: Grove.

Khalidi, Ramla, and Judith Tucker. (1992). *Women's Rights in the Arab World*, a special MERIP (Middle East Research and Investigation project) publication. Washington, D.C.: MERIP.

Malti-Douglas, Fedwa. (1991). *Woman's Body, Woman's Word: Gender and Discourse in Arabo-Islamic Writing*. New Jersey: Princeton University Press.

Mernissi, Fatima. (1987). *Beyond The Veil: Male-Female Dynamics in Modern Muslim Society*. Revised edition. Bloomington: Indiana University Press. First published, Cambridge: Schenkman, 1975.

◆ **Part Four**

Escalating Ecologies of Perturbation

Once upon a time, humans did not have to contend with violence beyond the hearth and their face-to-face community. Certainly, humans have had a long history and prehistory of ignoring the long-term impacts of their own practices, in society and on the landscape. When those systems did not kick back within a single generation, it was easier to ignore surpluses of population, depletions of resources, and the atrocities of impersonal violence through torture and devastation. These chapters consider the recent past and ponder bleak futures—so bleak that even tentative interventions might be better than none.

Chapter XX

Violence in Madura:
The Interplay of Resource, Culture, and History

Glenn Smith

Introducing Carok

Since early colonial times, the Madurese have been seen as a coarse and violent people, their character exemplified by *carok*, an attack motivated by a dispute over women or property. The historical role of the Madurese in the Netherlands East Indies helps situate the relationship between this violent ascribed behavior and cultural factors. Today, despite laws aimed at curbing anti-social behavior and denials that carok persists, various forms of violence continue to provide avenues for individual justice. An analysis of recent cases suggests that personal, family, and social pressures play a part in sustaining high levels of violence, as do cultural perceptions of shame and guilt. However, in continuity with the past, institutional, ecological, and economic factors remain of fundamental importance. This chapter draws on fieldwork in Madura in 1995–1996 funded by the Fyssen Foundation (see Smith 1997).

Carok is defined by Kiliaan (1904–1905) as "fighting with a sharp weapon" (*atòkar ngangghúj sandjhata tadjhem*). The word is also used to describe a match where the players exchange winning and losing streaks, money which changes hands, and bouts of artistic martial arts (probably *pencak silat*) held at the turn of the century at Marengan, near Sumenep (*carok Marengan*), in which combatants fought with daggers without injury.

Madurese are often referred to by outsiders, and quite often by themselves half-jokingly, as *orang carok*, or "carok people." In distinction to the Malay *amok*, commonly seen as the sudden unleashing of an indiscriminate attack (Winzeler 1990), carok is usually a premeditated settling of scores that targets a perceived wrongdoer, or, in the case of a feud, his family, but it can also describe acts of self-defense. Historically, carok has been known to take the form of a formal scheduled duel in the presence of witnesses. At variance with the long-standing government policy against violent crimes, informants in Saronggi (Sumenep District) recount that carok combatants before World War II signed up at the local police station, thus insuring that decorum would be respected during the bout. The image of carok as a duel is dramatized by newspaper accounts and by at least one full-length film, *Carok!* The duel notion is also perpetuated by village accounts and oral history of prolonged bouts between similarly armed protagonists protected by amulets. Today, carok is usually a surprise attack, often from behind, with the victim quite often unarmed. As with Malay amok, carok has usually been viewed through a lens provided by the popular press, hearsay, and anecdotes gathered in casual discussions of folk character. The term has come to denote virtually any attack or homicide by persons of Madurese extraction, be they on the island, in East Java, or elsewhere in Indonesia. The aim of this paper is to review historical sources and introduce data from recent cases to correct some misconceptions, and more importantly, to get at the interplay of past and present, structural and social forces in Madurese violence.

Madura as Garrison and Tax Base

Recent historical work paints a portrait of a people subject to oppressive taxation, an ever-present danger of military conscription, and nonexistent or arbitrary rule of law, all compounded by marginal natural resources (Jonge 1993). The hardships endured by the Madurese peasantry quite often went beyond those endured by other Indonesian groups.

Beginning when Madurese retainers aided in routing the Mogul invasion in 1293, Madura was to provide soldiers for overseas expeditions under the auspices of indigenous princes and the Dutch colonial power. In 1677, rebellious Madurese liberated the island, only to come under the rule of the Dutch East India Company between 1705 and 1743. This new status left the Madurese principalities with a new degree of independence and security vis-à-vis Java, but in time meant increasingly burdensome obligations and growing isolation from the outside world.

By the eighteenth century, the Dutch had realized the value of Madurese troops who could be counted on as loyal, brave, and ruthless allies in putting down revolts by Javanese, Chinese, Balinese, and other subjects (Smith 1997). Madurese mercenaries were to see action many times from 1742 until their last mission in 1923 to suppress a railway strike in Java. The role played by the Madurese in colonial armies would not only have a lasting effect on the reputation of their society as a whole, but would also have ramifications on the welfare of the island. "Voluntary" conscription was voluntary only in theory, and the threat of forced conscription caused many eligible men to flee the island to Java. One source cited military conscription in the early nineteenth century as partly responsible for effecting a one-third decrease in Madura's population in the space of a mere six years (Smith 1997).

Subordination to the Dutch provided protection from the Javanese, but the price was an obligation to provide soldiers, tribute, and goods at below market value. Since Madura's forests were insignificant to the Dutch, and the area suitable for rice cultivation small, the colonial government sought other items of value that were available locally, either free or for prices well under market value. When compulsorily delivered produce was resold, the government could often reap profits of 300 to 400 percent (Smith 1997).

With opium, gambling, and other highly profitable sources of revenue controlled by the colonial power, regents could only turn to the peasantry to meet the deliveries imposed on them. All irrigated land (*sawah*) was under the control of the regent. Part was given as salary fields for the regent's lower officials and servants, and part was share-cropped out on behalf of the regent. Peasants held hereditary rights to dry fields (*tegal*) as long as they paid their taxes. The most important of these were a poll tax, the proceeds of which went to the regent himself, and a land tax, much of which was distributed in appanage. In time, a growing parasitic class of nobility, appanage-holders, and village chiefs developed. The system proliferated in pyramidal fashion in the eighteenth century as tax farmers from the towns delegated their rights to representatives. Nothing prevented the latter from adding taxes of their own or farming out their rights to local tax farmers (Jonge 1986). Villagers also made yearly offerings to guardians of sacred tombs (*bhuju'*).

Resources and Violence

The growing numbers of people who could claim from the peasants rights to portions of their production, not to mention a variety of unpaid services from roadwork to fodder collection, was matched by galloping population growth—according to one source Madura's population doubled four times between 1799 and 1895 (Touwen-Bouwsma 1977) despite massive migration to Java. Even allowing for differences in census coverage over this period, whatever increase there was further intensified pressures on resources. Madura was never to become self-sufficient in foodstuffs or even firewood.

No serious efforts were made until the early twentieth century to inquire into the welfare of the common Madurese. As long as soldiers and contingencies were forthcoming on demand, the colonial authorities saw no need to meddle in the affairs of the three regencies; on the contrary, the regents could count on their help to put down any eventual rebellion. The island became more and more isolated from the social and economic forces affecting Java. The tendency to rely on individual justice or self-help—already encouraged by the spatial separation of individual family units or household clusters (*taneyan*) in the middle of their fields, in contrast to the Javanese pattern of concentrated village groupings—could only develop further with mistrust of officials and outsiders. While one of the most diversified tax-collection and labor-service structures in the Netherlands East Indies functioned in Madura, reports increasingly spoke of unexplained murder. Madura's rudimentary judicial system was ill prepared to cope with the violence, even after a law was passed in 1864 to confiscate publicly displayed weapons. The murder rate for Sumenep was estimated in 1871 at 42.7 per 100,000 people, but an estimate for the entire island in 1860 arrives at a figure of 222 (calculations based on Jonge 1993:9). Historical sources are vague as to the motives for these killings, but one can assume that they were often triggered by disputes over valued resources. It would not seem far-fetched to suggest that the combination of squeezing the Madurese economically while tolerating if not encouraging their ferocity in battle could go some way towards ingraining the behavioral patterns for which they were to become notorious.

Shame and the Value of Women in Contemporary Madura

While much has changed in the institutional structure of the island (Indonesian independence in 1945 and Madura's integration into Indonesia in 1950, bureaucratic expansion of the courts in the towns and police and military posts down to the subdistrict and village level), rural Madurese in many areas still rely on self-help before they submit to the rule of law or turn to local or religious structures for conflict resolution. In some areas where, until recently, violence was endemic, heads of Koranic schools and other religious leaders have significantly reduced violence through their influence and their ability to act as mediators. Yet, although violent crimes are less prevalent today than they were in colonial times, the Indonesian legal system has had only partial success in curbing carok, notwithstanding the occasional denial by urban elites that carok still exists. A "culture of violent solutions" (Elias 1997) seems to persist, not because the Madurese are inherently violent, but because structural, economic, and social pressures still provide an environment where violence is perceived to be one of the few means available for resolving certain problems.

In examining contemporary carok, we may get a more tangible idea of the conditions likely to trigger violence and the dynamics of confrontations. There are several key idioms that are used to explain and justify violent action. The most important of these are shame (*todus*), anger (*ghighir* or *dhuka*), fear (*tako'*), and revenge (*balessan*). Evoked alone or in combinations, they give emotional expression to conflicts that are often material in nature.

One opinion of colonial observers still heard today is that Madurese violence results from disputes over "insignificant" matters. A carok case in 1994, still much discussed in judicial circles, originated out of the cutting of kite strings, and, one year later, escalated to multiple manslaughter.

In this case, the past history of rivalry between the families, and the succession of events between the kite incidents and the killings would of course have to be elucidated before any judgment can be made concerning the motives involved. Rarely is such information inscribed in court records, but we must assume these issues were taken into consideration by the judges. Even kites could have been enough to warrant such a reckless act of vengeance. Kite flying is a competitive sport in Madura (opponents even glue crushed glass to their lines and try to cut each other's strings), thus disputes over kites may be expected to break out from time to time as they do in other Madurese pastimes like bull racing or card playing. Other incidents probably built on the enemy relationship (*amosowan*) that had developed between the two families regularly trying each other's self-esteem. The word for enemy, *moso*, also denotes an opponent in a game or sport. As in many other societies placing a high value on personal honor, one cannot afford to appear weak in the eyes of one's enemies (Kiefer 1972). The twenty-year sentence imposed in this case ranks among the longest applied in Madura for carok.

Everyone today who has any familiarity with carok is in agreement that the most common motive is advances toward another man's wife, whether or not adultery occurs. When conflicts over affronts to the honor of female kin (broken engagements, malicious rumors, and the like) are included, then conflicts involving women account for slightly over half of the carok cases examined. Although most townspeople and many educated village youths claim that they would not seek revenge in such situations, most rural men would feel extreme anger (*ghighir* or *dhuka*) and public humiliation. For many, even the hint of infidelity or rumors of the same are cause for action.

Protagonists evoke shame (*todus*) to explain reluctance to seek arbitration by village or religious leaders. Fear of letting on to the enemy that one is actively planning retribution is another reason cited for keeping an affair under wraps. Variations on the saying popularized in the writings of the Madurese poet K. H. Zawawi Imron, "better white bones than white eyes" (*ango'an potéa tolang étémbhang potè mata*) serve to justify violence to counter shame. Likewise, many justify carok by what they see as cardinal rules of Islam forbidding violations of Islam itself, another person's property, or another man's wife.

Sentimental love, expressed in Madurese as love (*tresna*), compassion (*neser*), and sexual desire (*cinta*) provide reasons enough to defend the honor of one's wife or, for a few, entice another's, since "your wife is where you hang your heart" ("liver" for the Madurese). Among Indonesian societies, Madurese society is noted for placing an especially high value on a woman's sexuality within marriage (Niehof 1985), which for a woman usually occurs soon after menarche. Numerous potions (for which the Madurese are famous), incense, and treatments are used to enhance a woman's attractiveness to her husband. Compassion, desire, and sexuality are also the basic themes in Madurese theatre, danced-singing, and songs that accompany gamelan or oboe (*saronen*) music (Bouvier 1994). The virtually total male control over the portrayal of Madurese women in performing arts means that the most extreme images of female sexuality, desire, and behavior can be used if necessary to please audiences. To what extent these images can lead to adultery and indirectly to violence is uncertain; in recent years Islamic teachers and their students have had success in reducing the impact of some popular art by suggesting as much. Although sexuality is highly valued, premarital experimentation is strictly forbidden. Madurese see no contradiction here, but do suggest that the immaturity of partners in arranged marriages creates situations where adultery and carok can arise.

Women are fought over to save social face and for sentimental feelings but also because day-to-day existence becomes unmanageable for a man without his partner. Shame is a "key idiom" (Kiefer 1972:55) that may be evoked in substitution for more material interests. A man who loses his wife for whatever reason becomes a dependent. He will have to move in with family or have female kin come cook his meals and do other gender specific tasks. He loses income from her trading and her labor power, the loss of either often meaning the difference between outright poverty and just getting by.

One who has defeated his wife's lover, or suspected lover, will not necessarily divorce her. If he must go to jail, he will need her to take care of his house, fields, and children, as well as bring him supplemental food and tobacco in jail. The question of what actually happened can be left for later, and is usually forgotten. As long as there is a possibility that nothing happened, that becomes the story. Not surprisingly, it is said that a man will have a difficult time finding a new wife if he has gained a reputation for losing one. A few generations back, it is said, a man could not marry in some villages if he had never engaged in carok. Wives or others sometimes goad a reluctant man into taking action to redress a wrong by questioning his masculinity. A few recent cases demonstrate this; perhaps in other cases outside pressure is hidden to avoid implicating close ones.

Other causes that can lead to carok include misunderstandings of various kinds (such as encounters on paths at night where one or both parties fear attack), and disputes over interests that are more obviously material. Disputes over small (but for poor Madurese, significant) amounts of money, or over land boundaries, irrigation water, and animal fodder are examples of valued resources for which many rural Madurese are prepared to fight and risk their lives over. Whatever the costs involved, they have to be weighed against the consequences of inaction.

Unpaid debts can lead to violence because the lender feels shame in calling in a debt, and the borrower feels shame at being unable to pay or in being late in reimbursing. When accounts are settled, careful calculations and exhaustive discussions assure the parties that all debts are paid (*lonas*), and that the borrower has not forgotten a debt that the lender is too ashamed to remind him of. The fear of course is that this oversight could fuel latent hostility. In unusual instances the use of paid scapegoats and contract killers may come into the picture; in one documented case the issue was to revenge a death blamed on witchcraft by a traditional healer (*dhukon*).

Rumors occur often enough, though proof of wrongdoing is sometimes sought if this will not alert the suspected offender. One individual who was certain that his child had been killed by a rival through black magic declared that he would trap him one day by sending someone to seek his services. If his enemy agreed to provide black magic, this would be proof enough to authorize his execution.

The Limits of Deterrence

That the prospect of jail and financial ruin can act as deterrent factors is demonstrated by the many cases in which an attacker merely wanted "to teach a lesson," particularly in carok attacks over women. Jail sentences for murder range from four to twenty years. The accused must often sell cattle to pay fines or bribes to affect the outcome of the trial or free family members imprisoned as witnesses. Fear of jail, further impoverishment, or physical injury all act as deterrents (although letting it be known that one "almost committed carok" can also be a cheap way of saving face). The word fear (*tako '*) is used to describe fear of police and judicial sanctions, fear of powers an enemy might possess, but never fear of the enemy himself. The degree of deterrence is open to question, however, where faith in the police and judicial system is less than total.

More than one subdistrict police station is known for carrying out or encouraging summary killings of petty thieves. A significant number of convictions are overturned on appeal, on the basis of insufficient proof or a determination that the confessions were extracted under police coercion. While police brutality during questioning is common, many believe that acquittals on appeal are due to judicial corruption. The usual reasoning is that acquittal must come from higher courts to prevent reprisals on local judicial authorities by families of the victims. The perceptions that irregularities exist no doubt affect the cost-benefit calculations for protagonists, blunting whatever deterrent effect the law might have.

The Future of Carok

On the resource end of the scale of contributing factors, tobacco cash cropping has transformed the economy and the landscape in East Madura. Spreading from south-central Madura, the expansion of cultivated area over the last fifteen years has stimulated extensive land clearing and intensified pressure on land, fodder and especially water resources. Since 1990, machine pumping from wells and reservoirs for watering tobacco has further extended cultivation and created new conflicts between upstream and downstream farmers and between pump owners and their clients.

However, since 1990, there have been profound generational changes in the leadership of a number of villages due to new government requirements that all village chiefs be conversant in the national language, Indonesian. Sons of former village chiefs or neighborhood heads have come into their offices with considerably more formal education than their fathers, and a greater willingness to interact with the subdistrict apparatus, including police and military. In some areas, curbing the activities of thieves (or at least forcing them to limit their operations to outside the village) has reduced one major source of conflict and carok. In one village, long considered the nest of thieves of the Sumenep district, a corrupt village head was replaced in 1990 by his son, who immediately embarked on a vigorous mission to clean up his village. He and his aides have since broken up many violent disputes in progress, and brought the sides to sit down and iron out their differences. As an example of a discernable trend, it provides some hope that a new generation of leaders can find effective local forms of conflict resolution.

References

Bouvier, Hélène. (1994). *La matière des émotions: Les arts du temps et du spectacle dans la société madouraise (Indonésie)*. Paris: École Française d'Extrême-Orient.

Elias, Robert. (1997). A culture of violent solutions. In *The Web of Violence: From Interpersonal to Global*, edited by. J. Turpin and L. R. Kurtz, pp. 117–147. Urbana and Chicago: University of Illinois Press.

Jonge, Huub de. (1986). Heyday and demise of the apanage system in Sumenep (Madura). *Papers of the Fourth Indonesian-Dutch History Conference, volume 1*, edited by. S. Kartodirdjo, pp. 241–269. Yogyakarta: Gadjah Mada University Press.

———. (1993). Gewelddadige eigenrichting op Madura. In *Liber Amicorum Moh. Koesnoe*, edited by H. Slaats, pp. 1–15. Surabaya, Indonesia: Airlangga University Press.

Kiefer, Thomas M. (1972). *The Tausug: Violence and Law in a Philippine Moslem Society*. New York: Holt, Rinehart and Winston.

Kiliaan, H. N. (1904–1905). *Madoereesche-Nederlandsch Woordenboek*. Leiden: E. J. Brill.

Niehof, Anke. (1985). *Women and Fertility in Madura*. Leiden: Rijksuniversiteit.

Smith, Glenn. (1997). Carok violence in Madura: From historical conditions to contemporary manifestations. *Folk-Journal of the Danish Ethnographic Society* 39:57–75.

Touwen-Bouwsma, Elly. (1977). *De barisanoganisatie van Madura*. M.A. thesis in Anthropology. Amsterdam: Vrije Universiteit.

Winzeler, Robert. (1990). Amok: Historical, psychological, and cultural perspectives. In *Emotions of Culture: A Malay Perspective*, edited by W. J. Karim, pp. 96–122. Singapore: Oxford University Press.

Chapter XXI

Ambivalent Exchanges: The Violence of *Patronazgo* in the Upper Amazon

Bartholomew Dean

Why is it that the leaders of one indigenous society—the Urarina of Peruvian Amazonia—rely on violent discursive formations when talking about debt peonage, even though coercive violence is not a primary aspect of this form of labor recruitment as practiced today? In exploring the reasons behind why violence figures so prominently in the stories that Urarina headmen tell about their exchange relations with outsiders, this paper evaluates local conceptualizations of alterity and the appeal to the fears of the "natural" brutality of others. Narratives of debt peonage are rife with images of brutal labor bosses (*patrones*) and hoarding, asocial *mestizos* counterpoised by representations of the beatific, generous and hardworking Urarina.

Instead of hiving off the cultural or performative dimensions of violence from the instrumental domain of power, violence is interpreted here, "as a narrated form of symbolic exchange" (George 1996: 2). Violence, as Pareto noted, "is not to be confused with force" (1966: 135). In its narrative form, debt peonage is articulated through a common vocabulary of referents which binds its participants from distinct economic groups, in this case, traders, labor bosses, and indigenous peoples. I refer to the narrativized intimidation and social compulsion associated with extractive mercantilism and patron-clientilism as *patronazgo*. Characterized by vertical ties of mutual interdependence, patronazgo is a variation of a broader and more generalized pattern of patron-clientilism found throughout South America.

In areas of the Upper Amazon where patronazgo is operative, one notes the presence of a symbolic web of mutually defining representations and relations. Cultural identity in these regions is bound not merely by ethnicity, gender or class, but rather by a shared vocabulary of authority, power and violence that conjoin indigenous peoples, mestizo peasants, and labor bosses in a "culture of terror" and "space of death" corresponding to the atrocities associated with unbridled frontier economies, such as the rubber "boom" (Taussig 1991; see also Brown and Fernandez 1991: 99; Maybury-Lewis 1997: 5–6). By serving as part of a larger rhetoric of control and domination, European myths about indigenous savagery have traditionally played an important role in the formation of the Upper Amazon's "culture of terror." But instead of evaluating the significance of European elaborations of the "natural" savagery of native peoples, this paper explores indigenous narratives associated with the mobilization of a "culture of terror." After outlining the historical record of debt-peonage, enslavement and violence perpetuated against the Urarina, I scrutinize patronazgo tales as instances of indigenous leaders making sense of their presence in a broader network of labor and market relations. Yet this essay goes beyond interpreting Urarina narratives simply in terms of the creation of localized cultural meanings. I show how Urarina headmen recount myths to substantiate their own claims to power, which I argue are couched in terms of appeals to fear, and threats of retaliatory violence.

Violent Exchanges: The Urarina Peoples and Habilitación

Numbering between 4,000 and 6,000, the Urarina are a semi-nomadic hunting and horticultural society inhabiting a swath of Peru's lowland tropical rain forest known as the Chambira Basin (Dean 1992). In the Urarina's geographically isolated homeland, labor relations remain mercantilistic. Non-Urarina traders act as agents of supra-local exchange by advancing trade goods, and by receiving in return, timber, food crops, and specialized commodities like peccary hides, sarsaparilla, and *leche caspi* latex (*Couma macrocarpa*) extracted from the forest.

The current system of debt-peonage—or what is called colloquially in Peruvian Amazonia as *habilitación*—is a living legacy of the rubber boom. Starting well over a century ago, rubber companies, patrones, and itinerant traders (*regatones*) began mobilizing local labor-power through the system of habilitación that, in essence, "was an extension and intensification of pre-existing feudal relations" (Chibnik 1994: 40). In the Upper Amazon, the familiar system of *compadrazgo/padrinazgo* or ritual compeership, coupled with local labor-bosses and traders' virtual monopoly of cargo transport and credit, has long ensured the viability of inequitable forms of exchange.

In Peruvian Amazonia the rubber boom was facilitated through the system of habilitación that mobilized "a long chain of debtors and creditors" (Gray 1996: 222). During the height of the rubber bonanza (circa 1870–1915), the large commercial houses of Amazonian frontier towns like Iquitos and Manaus would supply credit and goods to intermediaries, who in turn would advance manufactured goods to local rubber-tappers and their labor-bosses. Debts were then repaid with rubber.

Urarina oral history suggests long and enduring relationships with traders, intermediaries and other classes of extractive entrepreneurs. Elderly informants confirmed reports that a small number of families from Iquitos established control over the flow of goods in and out of the Chambira watershed during the rubber boom (see Castillo 1958, Quintana 1948, Kramer 1979). As the rubber trade expanded in importance in Amazonia, "the control of chiefs became increasingly important to those traders who monopolized the Indian commerce" (Murphy 1978: 122). Typically, merchants and labor bosses in regions such as the Tapajos Valley in Brazil and Peru's Chambira Basin appointed their indigenous trading partners as government functionaries in the emergent local civil hierarchy. In the Chambira watershed, the office of *teniente gobernador* or deputy governor was created, while in the Tapajos, the office of *capitão* or captain was established. Besides relying on *teniente gobernadores* (who have usually acted both as local police and as judges), patrones working in the Chambira have counted on non-Urarina overseers—or what the Urarina euphemistically call "caretakers" (*cuidadores* or *acarabelladá*)—to enforce their will.

At the beginning of the last century, the Urarina from the lower stretches of the Chambira River were preyed upon by ruthless labor recruiters during the dreaded *correrías*, or slave raids. Some Urarina ended up as "virtual slaves" on feudalistic estates dotted along the Marañón river (Kramer 1979: 15; cf. Chibnik 1994: 41). The

Urarina responded by disbanding and escaping to the far reaches of the Chambira Basin's headwaters (Kramer 1979: 52–3). Throughout the first half of that century, a number of patrón-controlled *fundos*, or agro-extractive estates, thrived in the Chambira. The fundo is a type of Amazonian commercial estate owned and operated by a labor boss—a *patrón*—who recruits local labor-power throughout the system of *habilitación* (Chibnik 1994: 38; Gow 1991: 93–94). Traders and *patrones* regularly lived for years on end among local Chambira communities, and in so doing contributed to miscegenation and cultural hybridity. Throughout Peruvian Amazonia, "*patrones* (have) entered into multiple sexual unions with women living on their fundos" (Chibnik 1994: 46).

The system of habilitación continued to flourish in the Chambira Basin until at least the 1970s, when the "traditional" system of patron-clientilism began its decline. Currently, the pace of social change on the Chambira, like elsewhere in Amazonia, has quickened (Nugent 1981: 71; see Brown 1993; Conklin and Graham 1995; Knauft 1997). The structure of patron-clientilism is being strained by the expansion of competitive mercantilism (petty patrones, small-scale traders or *comerciantes*, and others); the intensification of class distinctions based on access to land, labor, and capital; the spread of literacy; and the slow but perceptible growth in "urbanward" migration (Odicio Egoavil 1992). Nevertheless, goods advanced on credit continue to create relations of indebtedness, and in so doing reinforce local hierarchies of power animated by social relations of violence. While Urarina labor relations with patrones and the region's fundos are variable and defy simple classification, they all share similar elements of performative intimidation and social subjugation mediated through extractive mercantilism.

The Urarina's lengthy historical experience of the violence of extractive mercantilism—including, forced labor conscription, rape, disease, concubinage, and abusive treatment at the hands of outsiders—reinforces their survival strategy of political autonomy through seclusion. Many Urarina communities have managed to achieve a degree of relative isolation from recurrent epidemics and the exploitation of their labor-power by continuing to rely on a strategy of flight. Urarina men discontented with their patrón will flee, either by river or along an intricate network of forest trails (*berü*) linking rivers and communities. But the structure of the local labor market, coupled with the Urarina's own demand for industrial commodities, means that there is ultimately no escape: Urarina headmen, acting on behalf of their long house group, eventually enter into unequal exchange relationships with competing patrones and traders.

Urarina oral histories attest to a violent history of forced labor recruitment. Many informants were able to cite actual cases of physical abuse perpetrated by cruel labor bosses. Some Urarina reported episodes of brutal floggings (*bisillá*), while many others had stories to share about unjust confinements in the local stockade (*calaboso*). Yet the Urarina continue as active economic participants in the chain of debt-peonage linking the Chambira River Basin to regional and global markets, given that acquisition of desired trade-goods has become a precondition for subsistence production (Warren 1992: 92). At the local level, unequal exchanges are sustained temporally through continual advances of goods flowing from the traders to the Urarina. Mestizo *patrones* and traders advance relatively inexpensive yet necessary consumer articles—including ammunition, salt, batteries, and a miscellany of medicines, coveted trinkets, and dry goods—to Urarina headmen who in return provide forest goods such as hunted forest game, pelts, timber, and food crops that invariably fetch higher returns in faraway urban markets (Dean and McKinley 1997).

The virtual absence of cash on the Chambira means that the Urarina vigorously seek out relations with traders because it gives them access to commodities (*rikelé*) of unreliable supply, and because it suits their own patterns of barter (Dean 1994; see also Hugh-Jones 1992: 69; Muratorio 1991: 151; Siskind 1977: 170–171). The allure of foreign trade-goods has drawn the Urarina into permanent, albeit episodic exchange relations with outsiders whose behavior is motivated by entrepreneurial desires to profit from indigenous surplus production and forest extraction. In the Chambira watershed, goods—both "domestic" and "foreign"—are significant for they give the Urarina a way for dealing with the politics of identity, particularly in the postcolonial context. Recent scholarship has displayed the extent to which the sphere of consumption and the allure of imported goods are themselves crucial to understanding the multiple ways in which national identities have been "stated, contested, and affirmed in postcolonial Latin America" (Orlove and Bauer 1997: 8). Urarina individuals can convert commodities such as imported shotguns and hunting-dogs into singularized possessions by endowing them with a personal identity.

The Urarina's productive "entanglement" with manufactured and imported items (including dogs) has heightened their dependence on traders who regularly finagle unequal exchanges, often with the aid of tobacco (*mapachu*) and stupefying cane liquor or *aguardiente* (*abaríti*) traded at an exorbitantly inflated rate (see Castillo 1958: 28). Due in part to the barriers of language and literacy, the Urarina are not fully versed in the logics of capitalism. While many Urarina long house settlements now have portable shortwave radios that receive daily broadcasts of market prices in urban centers like Iquitos, this information does not appear to have enabled Urarina producers and consumers to obtain better terms of trade with the area's patrones and regatones. Largely innumerate, the Urarina only partially understand the dominant norms of commercial exchange—including weights and measurements—which puts them at a great disadvantage in the transcultural mercantile context.

In portraying the inequitable exchange relations between the Urarina and mestizo patrones, I do not mean to suggest the absence of any "redeeming" aspects of habilitación. As in other indigenous frontier zones, such as the early nineteenth-century Columbia Plateau region of North America, "the traders' (primary) purpose was to carry on a profitable—and therefore peaceable—trade with Native peoples" (Vibert 1997: 8). In the succinct words of doña Rosita, the middle-aged wife of a prominent trader operating in the Chambira Basin, "we are simply regatones, traveling merchants, we bring trade-goods to the Chambira so that we can make a good living" (*hacer buen negocio*) (field notes, May 1996). Traveling merchants and patrones will occasionally rent space on their boats (*fletar*), dispatch messages (*pasar la voz*), obtain desired manufactured items (*pedidos*), or arrange for the repair of a broken shotgun or chainsaw in Iquitos. They provide limited employment for the Urarina in their agricultural fields as day-laborers (*peones*), as traveling assistants on their boats (*portadores*; *ayudantes*) and as domestic servants (*empleadas*) on their fundos. Urban-based traders and patrones will occasionally provide shelter for those few

Urarina men (many of whom are senior headmen) who make the long and often arduous journey to "the big city."

Obviously, without these additional "benefits" the Urarina would not be nearly as supportive of peonage. Anthropologists working in Amazonia have long underscored the significance of exchange as a mode of action "that is positively valued as much for the social relationship that it establishes as for the opportunity which it offers to acquire material goods" (Henley 1996: 234). According to classical patronage relationships, the Urarina derive the fullest benefits of peonage from exclusive alliances with "benevolent" patrones, rather than from non-preferential participation in the system of debt-peonage (cf. Murphy 1978: 189). The advantage of establishing long-term exchange relations with specific traders or patrones helps to explain the paradox of indigenous peoples' continued and active involvement with individual trading partners—in spite of their bitter criticism of the entire system of habilitación.

The exchange of material goods in Amazonia pales in significance when compared with the importance of the circulation of persons through marriage, or with the circulation of "non-material aspects" of personhood (Henley 1996: 234; see also Viveiros de Castro 1992). In a similar vein, habilitación cannot simply be reduced to the exchange of manufactured goods for forest produce—say mahogany logs for steel axes, or hunted game for cotton cloth or glass beads. Nor can this complex be understood simply in terms of coercive labor recruitment practices. Habilitación relationships encompass many types of circulation, both material and ideological. These multiplex relationships are much more than purely economic transactions; they involve the strategic manipulation of fluid codes of social distinction—many of which are inscribed in mythic praxis—and articulated as chants, songs, adages, legends, and stories.

Discursive Formations and the Violence of Patronazgo

The elaborate oral traditions of the Urarina, along with other historically exploited indigenous peoples of the Upper Amazon illustrate "in painful detail the abuses and mistreatment inflicted on them by the local rubber barons" (Muratorio 1991: 121), labor bosses, and itinerant traders. In the words of one Urarina headman I spoke with following a day of unpaid work in his patrones' garden clearing in the jungle:

> Our patrón gave us our new machetes, these new ones from Colombia [pointing to three shiny new orange handled machetes propped against a nearby log] . . . but we are the ones who sweat in the sun, our hands ache after working all day with our new machetes. The patrones shout and call us 'shimaco' [derogatory label] . . . they only watch us from the cover of shade. When we are finished working, then they will eat from our bowls.

While the Urarina are grievously aware of their vulnerability at the hands of abusive labor-bosses who revile them for being lazy and ignorant "savages," they are also mindful of their own moral "superiority." Urarina political oratory constantly alludes to the value of Urarina community, which headmen discursively frame in diametric opposition to the labor bosses and outside traders' asocial behavior. Invariably, expressions of profound ambivalence emerge from the Urarina's ongoing perception that they, the worthy ones, toil for the unworthy mestizo labor bosses.

Throughout indigenous Amazonia, the most respected orators are those who lead: the elders, the religious diviners, the warriors, and the political chiefs. Urarina male leaders' understandings of debt peonage are routinely expressed in their graphic accounts of commodity flows. Ambivalence figures prominently in their narratives about inter-ethnic exchange that relay a sense of the moral ambiguity of overt symbols of power, such as trade-goods, literacy, and the Spanish language. Urarina headmen purposefully inspire ethical debates by recounting narratives in ways that highlight indecision, promote equivocality, and exploit ambivalence, thus encouraging their listening audience critically to reflect on moral predicaments. Largely alienated from the supra-local circulation and consumption "logics" of the commodities they produce and consume, Urarina headmen elaborate fabulous mythologies inflected with a sense of the inherent violence of debt-peonage (see Appadurai 1992: 48). Regarding the origin of trade-goods and money, Kirina, a mature and powerful Urarina headman, explained to me rather cryptically one late evening during the 1992 rainy season with the following words:

> Kane Kuánra—the creator of our world—sent the Anazairi [mestizos] in canoes to deliver trade-goods and silver coins [*plata*] to us. "Go and deliver these things to the Kachá—the Urarina people" commanded Kuánra [the creator god]. But the Anazairi refused to heed his command. They kept the trade goods instead of giving them to the Urarina. They robbed like a regatón [a river merchant]. Because the Anazairi refused to give the Urarina their trade-goods, today they have everything—they tricked our ancestors.

Kirina's account of the origin of trade goods was recorded during a time when the leader had just returned—with his sons-in-law in tow—to his long house settlement after an extended period of arduous work escorting massive tree boles downstream. His tale of the origin of trade goods was part of a longer series of narratives about patrones Kirina recounted that day to the junior men who had gathered around his hearth platform. Over time I came to realize the importance that narratives describing exchange relations with outsiders play in Urarina political oratory. This point alerted me to the fact that the headmen's discourses of violence are an intimate part of the processes of commemoration, and political engagement that draws them into more encompassing, supra local collectivities that characterize postcolonial states worldwide.

Reference to Urarina male leaders' oral narratives describing labor-bosses, peonage, and imported trade goods helps to situate our understanding of the inherently violent nature of economic and socio-cultural production in the Chambira. While further study of the expressive tropes of metaphor, surreal juxtaposition and metonymy will undoubtedly illustrate how Urarina male leaders and mestizo interlocutors regularly reassign meaning to erstwhile dominant cultural symbols, it is important to note—as Tsing has—that "even distorted or oppositional forms of consciousness can reproduce the contours of power" (1993: 75). On this point, I want to stress that Urarina men's narrative accounts of their experiences with notoriously evil patrones bolster their own image as fearless negotiators, especially with representatives of the alien and dangerous non-indigenous world.

Urarina headmen rely on their reputations for commercial acumen, bravery and munificence in constructing their social networks and public personae that extend well beyond local relations. This, I argue, points to a partial explanation of the conundrum put forth at the outset of this paper. When Urarina headmen recount their cunning flights from avaricious *patrones*, their narratives about commodity peonage are framed by a broad geographic landscape that encompasses distant points, as well as diverse and dangerous experiences with malevolent labor bosses, unfair traders, and malicious enemies.

By recounting stories of violent exchange, Urarina headmen legitimize their own monopoly over access to encounters with "alien" human beings and the trade goods they offer. Successful Urarina leaders have a diverse corpus of myths that celebrate—and thus reify—the retaliatory potential of the *patrones*. By framing the condition of alterity in violent ways, headmen position themselves as the only ones capable of dealing with representatives of national Peruvian society, including (and perhaps most importantly) the traders and labor bosses. A tone of retaliatory vengeance shaped many of the stories I collected from Urarina headmen about their exchange relations with *patrones*. In this regard, *patronazgo* tales mimic reality for they caricature the behavior of the nefarious *patrón*—of whom there are many real life models from which to draw. Particularly common in the Urarina headmen's repertoire of stories about trade and labor relations are vivid accounts of the poisoning of *patrones* with deadly toxins such as *ajá* (*Hura crepitans*) mixed furtively into libations of cassava beer. In the eyes of the Urarina leaders I know, the inhumane behavior of the mestizo labor bosses aligns them with the "undomesticated" Dog Spirits—*Rimae Santú*—and the likes of cannibalistic forest demons (*anekái*) who all refuse to share. This contradiction finds expression in the Urarina's account of the mestizo Dog Spirit, Rimae Santú, a narrative that urges the restriction of the circulation of hunted forest game.

While Urarina leaders can exhibit great disdain, anger, and on occasion even coercive violence against rapacious traders and labor bosses, individual acts of resistance to *habilitación* more commonly take the form of heel-dragging, and only infrequently dramatic outbursts of violence. Particularly efficacious headmen will unleash verbal assaults against unfair traders. Moreover, the Urarina enjoy a regional reputation for having shamans (*kuichá*) among their ranks whose supernatural powers can take revenge against even the most unscrupulous of labor-bosses. *Patrones*' reports confirm mestizo fears of the power of Urarina sorcery. When asked how the Urarina respond to unfair exchanges or abusive treatment, mestizo informants most often cited witchcraft as the Urarina's ultimate sanction.

For their part, the Urarina have resorted sporadically to denouncing grossly unfair *patrones* and traders by relying on the intervention of sympathetic priests, public radio announcements, and more formal, written legal declarations. Seldom has this led to the resolution of egregious cases of injustice and abuse. More commonly, it has simply prevented particularly fraudulent or abusive traders from "doing business" in Urarina territory for a limited period. *Patrones*' options for retaliatory action are somewhat limited given the ease with which the Urarina can retreat from disagreeable encounters or grossly unequal terms of trade.

Urarina headmen engage with the "fronts of national expansion" (Dean 1990) through the violent imagery of the discursive formations I have designated patronazgo. Urarina myths about the origin of trade-goods and narratives about the circulation of commodities position men as the primary interlocutors with the "outside world"—that is, the mestizo world of the Anazairi and the social universe of the Bajkagá, comprising the Urarina's arch rivals—the Jivaroan speaking peoples. The political discourse of retaliatory violence is used instrumentally by headmen to advance their interests during the acquisition and distribution of scarce trade-items.

Although trade goods are earned through collective efforts, the headmen apportion them to various members of the long house. Headmen use their trading relationship with non-Urarina to forge relationships of patronage among their own people, especially their sons-in-law and dependent unmarried females. They employ merchandise to establish additional obligations, or debts within Urarina society itself. On the Chambira, the trader's principal clients become creditors in their own right to other Urarina individuals within their immediate spheres of influence. As such, the debt (*rebeukön*)—symbolized by the exchange of trade-goods—assumes a life of its own. "Debt-servicing" is reproduced internally according to the confines of local political alliances. While Urarina headmen's trading function bolsters their power, their representations of patronazgo have helped to sustain not only the discursive violence accompanying the condition of alterity, but instances of actual violence originating from the demands of the regional extractive economy.

In the Chambira, the shortage of labor-power, coupled with the requirements of the region's extractive economy, has meant that patrones are not particularly interested in immobilizing the local labor force, unless it comes time to repay the debt (see Muratorio 1991: 151, 155; cf. Barclay 1989: 168f.). The patrones do, however, rely on a political strategy of intimidation: they amplify their symbolic and instrumental power over the Urarina by promoting an atmosphere of fear based on the potential threat of military incursions into the Chambira Basin. The rhetorical force of these discursive formations helps to explain why most young Urarina males and many adult men are apprehensive of traveling downstream to the Marañón or Amazon Rivers.

The mobilization of fear in the Chambira Basin is intimately linked to the narrativization of patronazgo. Tales of patronazgo, coupled with the perceived threat of forced conscription, a problem undoubtedly exacerbated over the past decade by the civil war between government forces and the rebel Sendero Luminoso and Movimiento Revolucinario Tupac Amaru groups (e.g., loss of *habeas corpus*), have served to create a "space of terror." During the fifteen years I have known them, many Urarina have regularly expressed apprehension about the possibility (admittedly remote) of press-ganging, and the threat of outside military intervention into their ancestral homelands. Common throughout the Chambira Basin are reports of the patrones—as well as specific Urarina headmen's—illicit use of the regional police force to further their own political and economic interests.

Intense factionalism (which mitigates against the development of strong horizontal ties among and between long house settlements), coupled with the generalized atmosphere of fear not only increases the patrones' leverage over the Urarina, but it also enables those headmen who are fluent in Spanish to wield a considerable degree

of clout vis-à-vis their monolingual brethren. This in turn reinforces Urarina geron-
tocratic tendencies: older men beyond the age of military conscription are more mobile, hence younger men are constrained by their inability to travel beyond the
Chambira, and thus become considerably more dependent on their elders to manage
their commercial transactions.

Patronazgo: Postcolonial Stories of Violent Exchange

Expertise in the various verbal arts—including expressions of satire, ridicule, bur-
lesque parody, and the grotesque—plays an important role in the way indigenous
leaders have responded to the reality of living with extractive entrepreneurs in their
midst. Determining the role that narratives play in constituting society enables us to
discern how imaginary structures are deployed by Urarina headmen to mediate the
internal contradictions accompanying the intrusion of market relations into the vast,
yet geographically isolated Chambira watershed. Recently, Kensinger has argued
persuasively that the Cashinahua of central Peru employ Inka myths as a way of not
only comprehending the identity of nonnative traders, but also for associating with
them (1995: 259). Similarly, stories about Dog Spirits and diabolic patrones enable
Urarina male leaders intellectually to negotiate the presence of merchants and labor
bosses from the outside. In both the Cashinahua and Urarina cases of narrativized
violence, one encounters a rhetoric of brutality animated by a historical context of
real aggression. During fieldwork I collected a number of remarkably similar tales
from headmen about Urarina encounters with representatives of the *"Caguachaí
Patrón,"* recounting the death of the archetypal malevolent patrón, which tales illustrate the influence that participation in the regional extractive economies has had
upon the leader's discourse of retaliatory violence

Patronazgo myths also reference the area's inter-ethnic relations (Urarina—
Mestizo—Cocama—Murato) and can be "read" as a commentary on the profound
influence extractive economies have had on the area. They can also be seen as a reflection of violent inter-ethnic conflict. In many stories, the burden of moral incerti-
tude—and ultimately death—counterpoises the paradox accompanying the Urarina's
mythical transformation from being victims of peonage, to becoming violent, mur-
derous aggressors.

Violent inter-ethnic conflict figures prominently in the story of the Bajkagá,
which stands as a testament to the dangers associated with the condition of alterity.
Yet alterity is central to Urarina notions about the reproduction of the social body.
From the Urarina's perspective, the Bajkagá are alien beings who are necessary for
all of those "purposes in which the symbolic and material interpenetrate" (Henley
1996: 235), such as trade.

Mythopoesis and the Violence of Debt Peonage

Mestizo patrones and traders—whether today or during the rubber boom—have subjected the Urarina to a world for which their prior experiences and corpus of myths
have often proven inadequate to regulate commercial transactions. But this has
hardly prevented Urarina headmen from mobilizing their oral, performative genres
as a means of coping with the changes wrought by outsiders and the world they rep-

resent. The ethnographic record is replete with many instances in which indigenous peoples such as the Urarina, or the Rucuyayas (the Quichua of Ecuador), resort to "irony, mockery, humor, dissimulation, and protest . . . to talk down the patrons or the authorities" (Muratorio 1991: 211). By way of subversive bricolage, Urarina headmen have sought to depict not only "empirical social realities, but to control and change them" (Hill 1993b: 48). The discursive formations associated with habilitación have given the Urarina a means to apprehend the past, and a way to cope with an ever-changing world.

When taken literally, mythical narratives explaining the creation of trade goods, exposing the evil patrón, or demonizing rival peoples are socially consequential because they tell people where they come from, where they are going, and how they ought to live. Mythological narratives are a body of socially constituted "facts" which are themselves the result of specific cultural and historical forces, such as the rubber bonanza and habilitación relationships. Mythical tales of violent exchange give Urarina headmen the intellectual space for the articulation of countervailing tendencies, namely, the ineluctable pull of *immeubles* valuables and the forces of impersonal chattelization characteristic of petty-commodity production and peonage worldwide. The latter tendency, which imperils the ties that connect the living to both the remembered past and the envisioned future, is nullified in the domain of myth, which celebrates the reciprocity of gifting while denouncing the commoditized relations of mercantile exchange (Dean 1994).

In conclusion, my comments about debt peonage and mythopoesis are aimed not as a contribution to the well-established debate over the sociological utility of the gift-commodity polarity. Many recent accounts of exchange (i.e., Dean 1994; Bloch and Perry 1989; Thomas 1991; and Carrier 1992) suggest that the contrast between the polar types of gift and commodity exchanges and sociality is not as consequentialist as many have assumed (e.g., Strathern 1988). Rather, they are offered to further our understanding of how aesthetic and rhetorical practices are embedded within power relations, and the flux of social experience—here, the history of violent exchange associated with habilitación. As "performance events" patronazgo tales function as types of "social and aesthetic exchange that are themselves produced from various logics of social interaction" (Flores 1995: 150). The actual performance, or telling of mythical narratives, enables historical memories not only to persist, but also to evolve over time (Graham 1995: 185). As a form of power, the violent discourses associated with debt peonage produce multiple subjectivities, histories, and identities. The process of mythification, or what Hill sees as "the establishment of cultural continuity through verbal signification," serves as a means for linking contemporary social life to "a remembered past" (1993a: 34; cf. Clastres 1994: 68). For Urarina headmen, the encroaching "outside" world is resisted by engendering society in terms of cultural categories refracted through a mythologized conception of the historical past. However, the Urarina's mythic thought, like other native Amazonian peoples, "does not engulf history but distills from events and individuals, memories and experiences, an ordered set of categories but it does not obliterate its sources from consciousness" (Hugh-Jones 1988: 142).

Elaborate narrative accounts of evil patrones exemplify the Urarina headmen's intensely dialogic and historical understanding of their own violent entanglement in debt peonage and petty-commodity production. Attempts at understanding patterns and processes of "interethnic dependency and conflict" have now become crucial to the analysis of indigenous cultural and social formations in Amazonia (Turner 1993: 11). It is simply no longer tenable to represent indigenous and nonnative peoples of Amazonia as if they constituted completely distinct groups. Urarina headmen's mythical narratives are not only overt expressions of theatricalized brutality, but also part of an ideology that mediates authoritarian power and unequal-exchange relations. The historical experience of habilitación has given Urarina headmen a vocabulary of power and authority that they share with the labor bosses. Violence, fear, and senseless brutality punctuate stories that both mestizo patrones and Urarina headmen tell about one another. Nonetheless, the foundational discourses to which Urarina patronazgo narratives belong consistently emphasize the dialectical interplay between relations of violence, aggressive domination, and those characterized by community and relations of reciprocity.

References

Appadurai, Arjun. (1992). Introduction: commodities and the politics of value. In *The Social Life of Things: Commodities in Cultural Perspective*, edited by Arjun Appadurai, pp. 3–63. Cambridge: Cambridge University Press. First edition 1986.

Barclay, Frederica. (1989). *La Colonia del Perené: capital inglés y economía cafetalera en la configuración de la región de Chachamayo*. Debate Amazonico No. 4. Iquitos: CETA.

Bloch, Maurice, and Jonathan Parry. (1989). Introduction: death and the regeneration of life. In *Death and the Regeneration of Life*, edited by Maurice Bloch and Johnathan Parry, pp.1–44. Cambridge: Cambridge University Press.

Brown, Michael. (1993). Facing the state, facing the world: Amazonia's native leaders and the new politics of identity. *L'Homme* 33: 307–26.

Brown, Michael, and Eduardo Fernández. (1991). *War of Shadows: The Struggle for Utopia in the Peruvian Amazon*. Berkeley: University of California Press.

Carrier, James G. (1992). The gift in theory and practice in Melanesia: A note on the centrality of gift exchange. *Ethnology* 3.2: 185–193.

Castillo, G. (1958). Los shimacos. *Peru Indígena* 16–17: 23–28.

Chibnik, Michael. (1994). *Risky Rivers: The Economics and Politics of Floodplain Farming in Amazonia*. Tucson: University of Arizona Press.

Clastres, Pierre. (1994). *Archeology of Violence*. Translated by J. Herman. *Semiotext(e)*. New York: Columbia University Press.

Conklin, Beth, and Laura Graham. (1995). The shifting middle ground: Amazonian Indians and eco-politics. *American Anthropologist*. 97: 695–710.

Dean, Bartholomew. (1990). The State and the Aguaruna: Frontier Expansion in the Upper Amazon, 1541–1990. M.A. thesis in the Anthropology of Social Change and Development, Harvard University.

——. (1992). Informe socio-económico para la inscripción de la comunidad nativa-Urarina: Santa Beatríz del Pangayacu. Report presented to the Gobierno Regional de Loreto, Secretaria Regional de Asuntos Sociales, Iquitos, Peru. (Ley No 24656-Decreto Supremo No 008-91 TR).

————. (1994). Multiple regimes of value: Unequal exchange and the circulation of Urarina palm-fiber wealth. *Museum Anthropology* 18.1: 3–18.

Dean, Bartholomew, and Michelle McKinley. (1997). Amazonian people's resources initiative: Building partnerships in health, education and social justice. *Cultural Survival Quarterly*. 21.3.

Flores, Richard. (1995). *Los Pastores: History and Performance in the Mexican Shepherd's Play of South Texas*. Washington, D.C.: Smithsonian Institution.

George, Kenneth. (1996). *Showing Signs of Violence: The Cultural Politics of a Twentieth-Century Headhunting Ritual*. Berkeley: University of California Press.

Gow, Peter. (1991). *Of Mixed Blood: Kinship and History in Peruvian Amazonia*. Oxford: Clarendon Press.

Graham, Laura. (1995). *Performing Dreams: Discourses of Immortality Among the Xavante of Central Brazil*. Austin: University of Texas Press.

Gray, Andrew. (1996). *The Arakmbut: Mythology, Spirituality and History*. The Arakmbut of Amazonian Peru, Volume One. Providence, Rhode Island, and Oxford, United Kingdom: Berghahan Books.

Henley, Paul. (1996). Recent themes in the anthropology of Amazonia: History, exchange, alterity. *Bulletin of Latin American Research Review* 15.2: 231–245.

Hill, Jonathan. (1993a). *Keepers of the Scared Chants: The Poetics of Ritual Power in an Amazonian Society*. Tucson: University of Arizona Press.

————. (1993b). Cosmology and situation of contact. In *Cosmology, Value, and Inter-ethnic Contact in South America*, edited by Terrence Turner. South American Indian Studies 9: 46–55. Bennington: Bennington College.

Hugh-Jones, Stephen. (1988). The gun and the bow: Myths of white men and Indians. *L'Homme* 106–107 XXVIII (2–3):138–155.

————. (1992). Yesterday's luxuries, tomorrow's necessities: Business and barter in northwest Amazonia. In *Barter, Exchange, and Value: An Anthropological Approach*, edited by Caroline Humphrey and Steven Hugh-Jones, (pp. 42–74). Cambridge: Cambridge University Press.

Kensinger, Kenneth. (1995). *How Real People Ought To Live: The Cashinahua of Eastern Peru*. Prospects Heights, Illinois: Waveland Press.

Knauft, Bruce. (1997). Gender identity, political economy and modernity in Melanesia and Amazonia. *Journal of the Royal Anthropological Institute. (N.S.)* 3: 233–259.

Kramer, B.J. (1979). Urarina Economy And Society: Tradition And Change. Unpublished Ph.D dissertation, Columbia University.

Maybury-Lewis, David. (1997). *Indigenous Peoples, Ethnic Groups, and the State*. The Cultural Survival Studies in Ethnicity and Change. Boston: Allyn and Bacon.

Muratorio, Blanca. (1991). *The Life and Times of Grandfather Alonso: Culture and History in the Upper Amazon*. New Brunswick: Rutgers University Press.

Murphy, Robert. (1978). *Headhunter's Heritage: Social and Economic Change Among the Mundurucú Indians*. New York: Octagon Books. First published 1960.

Nugent, Stephen. (1981). Amazonia: ecosystem and social system. *MAN (N.S.)* 16.1: 62–74.

Odicio Egoavil, Elmer. (1992). *Perfil demografico de la region Loreto.* Documento Técnico No.1. Iquitos: Instituto de Investigaciones de la Amazonía Peruana.

Orlove, Benjamin, and Arnold Bauer. (1997). Giving importance to imports. In *The Allure of the Foreign: Imported Goods in Postcolonial Latin America,* edited by Benjamin Orlove, pp. 1–29. Ann Arbor: University of Michigan Press.

Pareto, Vilfredo. (1966). Les systèmes socialistes. In *Sociological Writing.* New York: Praeger.

Quintana, José. (1948). *Boletín de las misiones Augustinas.* (Iquitos) 7.6: 271–280.

Siskind, Janet. (1977). *To Hunt in the Morning.* New York: Oxford University Press.

Strathern, Marilyn. (1988). *The Gender of the Gift: Problems with Women and Problems with Society in Melanesia.* Berkeley: University of California Press.

Taussig, Michael. (1991). *Shamanism, Colonialism and the Wild Man.* Chicago: University of Chicago. First edition 1986.

Thomas, Nicholas. (1991). *Entangled Objects: Exchange, Material Culture, and Colonialism in the Pacific.* Cambridge, Massachusetts: Harvard University Press.

Tsing, Anna Lowenhaupt. (1993). *In the Realm of the Diamond Queen: Marginality in an Out-of-the-Way Place.* Princeton: Princeton University Press.

Turner, Terrence. (1993). From cosmology to ideology: Resistance, adaptation and social consciousness among the Kayapo. *Cosmology, Values, and Inter-ethnic Contact in South America. South American Indian Studies* No. 2. Bennington, Vermont: Bennington College.

Vibert, Elizabeth. (1997). *Traders' Tales: Narratives of Cultural Encounters in the Columbia Plateau 1807–1846.* Norman and London: University of Oklahoma Press.

Viveiros de Castro, Eduardo. (1992). *From the Enemy's Point of View: Humanity, and Divinity in an Amazonian Society.* Translated by C. Howard. Chicago: University of Chicago Press.

Warren, Patrizio. (1992). Mercado, escuelas y proteinas: Aspectos históricos, ecológicos y económicos del cambio del modelo de asentamiento entre los Achuar meridionales. *Amazazonía Peruana* 9.21: 73–107.

Chapter XXII

Taiwan's Consumerism, Gangs, and Violence

Charles V. Trappey

Official statistics and news reports show that criminal violence in Taiwan is increasing. This information has led to new debates about the causes of violence as well as to public demonstrations demanding greater social order. Because gang-related violence is increasing as Taiwan moves into a new age of consumerism, an analysis of the factors underlying violence and consumption is called for. This study focuses on how factors of consumption become intertwined with feelings of guilt and shame and how group behavior turns deviant as a result of the need to consume.

This analysis traces Taiwan's transition from a structurally violent past to a vibrant consumer society and proposes factors that contribute to violence on the island. The relationship between consumerism, gangs, and violence is presented in three sections. The first describes the history of Taiwan's structural or war-related violence. The second introduces behavioral violence in a consumer society, where individuals act violently against others in pursuit of instant gratification and power. In the third section, the cultural aspects of Taiwan's behavioral violence are introduced using a mathematical model. The model predicts the likelihood that gang members will commit violent acts and provides a means to explain current trends in gang violence.

The History of Structural Violence

History reveals many episodes of violence in Taiwan where external forces caused widespread structural violence resulting in the deaths of thousands of people. Gilligan (1996) defines structural violence as

> . . . increased rates of death and disability suffered by those who occupy the bottom rungs of society, as contrasted with the relatively lower death rates experienced by those who are above them. Those excess deaths (or at least a demonstrably large portion of them) are a function of class structure; and that structure is itself a product of societies collective human choices, concerning how to distribute the collective wealth of society.

Likewise, Gilligan defines behavioral violence as "non-natural deaths and injuries that are caused by specific behavioral actions of individuals against individuals." Table 1 (Chafee et al. 1969) lists fifteen major episodes of structural violence that occurred when one class fought another over the wealth of Taiwan. Either one class of Chinese has fought another, or Europeans have fought Chinese, or Japanese have fought Chinese, or settlers have fought aborigines. However, most structural violence has resulted from classes of Chinese fighting Chinese (seven events) instead of Europeans fighting Chinese (four events), Europeans fighting Europeans (one event) or Japanese fighting Chinese (three events).

Structural violence remains the largest threat to Taiwan's peace and democratic development. There is significant potential for invasion by mainland China if Taiwan declares independence or if the citizens of Taiwan vote for independence through referendum. Longenecker and Yu (1994) point out that Beijing's "refusal to forswear the use of military force as a means of resolving the Taiwan issue is predicated upon the legitimate right of a sovereign nation to protect the integrity of its territorial boundaries." A future outbreak of structural violence between Taiwan and China can easily surpass all of the structural violence of the past. Both sides of the Taiwan Strait are armed with advanced technology aircraft, naval warships, and missiles. Even nuclear and biological warfare have not been dismissed as a means to "resolve the issue."

The thirteenth, seventeenth, nineteenth, and twentieth centuries had incidents of structural violence leading to greater lawlessness and overall increases in behavioral violence. However, the existing threat of structural violence has little impact on person-to-person violence. Consumerism, changes in family structure, and the emergence of gangs and other sub-cultures appear to have the strongest links to behavioral violence.

Behavioral Violence in a Consumer Society

The yearly household receipts of the Taiwan consumer grew rapidly after martial law was lifted in 1987 (Trappey 1997). With the emergence of democratic liberties and the ensuing liberalization of the economy, average disposable income tripled in eight years. Income rose from $10,000 per year in the 1970s and the 1980s to almost $30,000 per year per household. The income distribution has been, for the most part, evenly distributed across consumer groups. On average, the high-income group, the mid-income group, and the low-income group differ by roughly $4,000 of annual income.

Taiwan holds a special place in the development of modern consumer societies. First, almost every household (over 12 million households in 1997) experienced a tripling of income in fewer than eight years. Second, the differences between classes of income earners remained small as incomes increased, meaning that in a very short period of time, all consumers became equivalently wealthy. The transition from a poor, working class society under martial law to a free and democratic society awash with consumer goods has been structurally non-violent. The rise in income across all families is a major factor underlying Taiwan's relatively low levels of behavioral violence compared to other parts of the world.

Societies plagued with behavioral violence frequently have problems with class or race inequalities, war, corruption, drug and alcohol abuse, and child abuse. Taiwan's behavioral violence does not stem from inequalities, war, or high levels of drug abuse. The premise of this paper is that greed, envy, and the desire for instant gratification and power underlie much of Taiwan's behavioral violence. Organized groups and gang members in particular are the most serious source of violence because their desire for power and money compels the most despicable acts of violence.

Roots of Violence

An article in the *Free China Review* (Liao 1996) reports the Ministry of Justice announcing that "out of the 860 elected county level councilors, approximately one-third has a criminal record or close connections with known underworld figures." Furthermore, the Justice Minister, at a meeting of the European Council of Commerce and Trade, identified the drive for instant gratification, money, and social status as the primary reasons for increases in larceny, mugging, kidnapping, and extortion are increasing. This theme is frequently repeated in newspaper editorials, the speeches of politicians, and the lectures of academics. The high visibility of individual wealth and the prevailing perceptions of power associated with wealth spur the desire for others to seek equal or greater status.

Taiwan's consumers increasingly want to be part of Veblen's (1899/1953: 45) "leisure class," to elevate themselves from mundane positions as laborers to positions of ownership and control. The majority of Taiwanese are entrepreneurial in spirit and work hard to achieve or maintain a position in the leisure class. For example, ordinary citizens have added almost 2,000 registered factories a year over the last forty years to build an industrial base of over 100,000 registered factories. On the down side, rapid industrialization has led to rapid changes in the types of families. As often pointed out, Taiwan is experiencing changes in divorce rates, the motivations for marriage, and the structure and size of families. One of the most dramatic outcomes is the emergence of youth sub-cultures that challenge classical Confucian values and Taiwan's strong work ethic.

Shaw (1994) cites his earlier argument that there is a growing population of Taiwan youth which does not want to work but rather prefers to have fun, to break away from "the only positively sanctioned social identity for youth—the 'good student'—modeled the future-oriented, self-sacrificing, hard-working orientations." If the youth cannot achieve the status of the good student and if the home environment offers no psychological support, then the student can easily drop out and adopt deviant behaviors. Shaw (1994) describes two important youth sub-cultures. Members of one sub-culture called the *kah-a* say that after inhaling glue fumes they like to place lit cigarettes to their skin and watch it burn away. Evidently, the lack of feeling and the inability to feel pain causes fascination and enjoyment. Another sub-culture called the *liuomang* (hoodlums, or entry-level gangsters) ridicule drug use as a "meaningless distraction from the serious business of life such as earning money or cultivating one's status and reputation locally." The liuomang find pleasure in beating up local youths and bullying others into paying them to keep away.

The kah-a's deviant behavior may be linked to feelings of guilt that causes depression, self-punishment, self-sacrifice, martyrdom, and masochism (Gilligan 1996). Thus, the kah-a maintain self-respect by sacrificing their bodies in front of others without crying out in pain. Gilligan also notes that the issue of "respect" is central to the vocabulary of violent criminals and that murders can occur simply because someone "dissed" (disrespected) the criminal. Violent acts also occur when guilt-laden individuals tire of punishing themselves and begin punishing others to alleviate their feelings of guilt. Some university students report being attacked by young kah-a carrying machetes. The reason, simply enough, is that the students "looked at them" and did not show respect.

Gilligan (1996) equates shame as the root cause for selfishness, sadism, and revenge. Gang members feel the greatest shame from not having the power to do or buy the "right" things and from not having status in the community. Shame plays a larger part as a component of Taiwan violence than guilt because of the pervasiveness of gangs relative to kah-a and common criminals. Gangs may be the largest source of shame-related violent behavior, but they are not the only source. Anyone or any group that is willing to pursue wealth at any cost, as a means to cover their shame for being poor or powerless, will likely increase the level of behavioral violence. Since the power to buy whatever one wants whenever one wants instantly alleviates shame, people forego rational opportunities to work their way out of demeaning social positions.

Increases in fatalities related to arson and violation of fire safety ordinances, increases in graft and corruption, increases in assassinations of rivals and enemies, and increases in drug use, game-fixing, prostitution, extortion, and kidnapping are, for the most part, the result of organized gangs in Taiwan. Initial acts of violence occur when the gangs force their way into power or extort money from others. Then a cycle of retaliation begins against those who act to limit the gangs' power and wealth. Random acts of violence, such as drive-by slashings, are frequently the results of juveniles who feel guilty because they failed in school. Psychosis and mental illness also contribute to behavioral violence but this source is believed to be the smallest source of all.

In 1995, the Council of Economic Planning and Development reports roughly seventy-five crimes per 10,000 people (Taiwan Executive Yuan 1996a). The same year, 160,130 crimes were committed by a total of 151,591 criminals (28,524 juveniles), but not all of these cases were violent. In the *Monthly Bulletin of Statistics* (Taiwan Executive Yuan 1996b), of the 170,264 cases known to the police for offenses against the penal code in 1995, 10% were violent crimes. The level of violent crimes doubled between 1994 and 1995 and remained at the same high levels in 1996. The crime wave continues. Although the official statistics were not yet available, at least 14,000 violent crimes were expected for 1996 and over 16,000 for 1997.

Cultural Explanations for Violence

Taiwan has in place many social systems that help to remove "shame-inducing" factors from the environment. For example, the most recent social development is the creation of a universal health care system. Housing policies likewise create a positive social environment and most families can afford to own or rent a home (Taiwan Executive Yuan 1996c). The construction of public libraries, schools, and medical facilities is increasing to meet the needs of society, as is the development of public transportation and the civic infrastructure. On the other hand, work is needed to improve the quality of life on Taiwan, to reduce pollution, and to provide disenfranchised youth with guilt-free career alternatives. Overall though, awareness of pressing social issues continues to grow and politicians are making efforts to better manage public resources. Homelessness and vagrancy is very low and is traditionally resolved within families, leaving religious groups and government organizations as support agencies rather than sources of primary care.

The Ministry of Education has addressed the problems of disenfranchised youth by placing emphasis on skills training for students not entering senior high school. Likewise, academic leaders have called for improvements in the education system that will reduce the stress and guilt associated with going to school. Thus, guilt-based behavioral violence will not be a long-term problem, particularly as new professional trade and service schools are built and as higher paying service careers emerge in the private sector.

More perplexing though is the persistence of shame-induced behavioral violence when so much has been done to provide an equitable social base. As discussed, Taiwan's social system has alleviated many "shame-inducing" factors through the distribution of wealth and the maintenance of health and welfare social programs. The question remains why gangs are becoming more violent as Taiwan becomes a freer and richer consumer society. In general, most people have enough money, most people can get a job, housing is not a problem, the Taiwan family is still strong, and drugs, teenage pregnancy, and divorce are not out of control. So what motivates people to join a gang instead of society? Furthermore, when people join gangs, what makes them so violent?

The Spirituality of Gangs

Kavanaugh (1982: 35) describes violence as a "human interaction commodified," where people are conditioned to relate to others as things, to exploit and manipulate others for self-gratification. He further reasons that

> ...once self-worth is defined in terms of an appropriation, the cultural myth will relentlessly be one of materialism, property, consumption, buying-power, competition, and greater economic exploitation. It is this "gospel" with its valued "givens" which prevent us from seeing, much less responding to, the needs of the nation, the community, the neighbor, even the beseeching person next to us. We perceive objects to be used, enemies to be overcome. We no longer see persons. We see things. And things, like idols, are dead.

Although the relationships between the gang and outsiders frequently assumes a commodity form (deviant consumerism), the relationships within the gang are spiritual (blind faith). A family-like structure and ritual enforces the notion of a "great self" that in turn precludes the individual self (Raguin 1974). Thus, the greater gang-based self easily assumes higher plateaus of materialism without remorse (gang absolution). The critical belief underlying gang spirituality is the absolute ground of the leader.

The Mathematics of Gang Violence

Using Grossman's 1995 formulation for killing-enabling factors in America, a mathematical representation has been fitted to characteristics of gangs in Taiwan. Five categories of factors enabling people to commit violent acts are considered.

These categories are the Demands of Authority (DA), Gang Absolution (GA), the Predisposition toward Violence (PV), the Distance from the Victim (DV), and the Target Attractiveness (TA).

Demands of Authority = Leader's Authority × Demand
Intensity × Leader's Proximity × Perpetrator's Respect

Gang leaders play an influential father-like role, enforce the rules, and recite the history and philosophy of the organization (Leader's Authority = LA). Gang leaders define the boundaries, the rivalries and the levels of violence. Gang leaders demand absolute obedience and instruct other members to punish those who deviate from the spoken demands (Demand Intensity = DI). If the infractions are deemed serious, then the leader may personally murder the offender with other gang members as witnesses. The leader hears all and knows all about the members even when far removed from the scene of the crime (Proximity of Leader = LP). The perpetrator of violence absolutely respects the leader since it is the leader that defines the future status, wealth, and power of the gang members (Perpetrator's Respect = PR).

Gang Absolution = Gang Support × Group Number × Gang
Identification × Gang Proximity

The members of a gang belong to a business organization that acts as surrogate family. As noted by Seagrave (1995), tycoons and gang leaders are sometimes hard to differentiate. The intensity of gang support for killing or for violent acts results from close teamwork in bullying others, showing off, and taking what they want (Gang Support = GS). Anything is right if the gang says it is right or if the leader pronounces the action as right. The number in the group perpetrating violence (Group Number = GN) is not as important as the perpetrator's self-identification with the other perpetrators (Gang Identification = GI). Losing face (status) in front of one or more gang members will bring about intense shame and punishment. Therefore, the proximity of the gang to the scene of the crime will have little impact on the predisposition of the perpetrator(s) to act (Gang Proximity = GP).

Predisposition Toward Violence = Perpetrator Training
× Past Experience × Individual Temperament

Daily exposure to violence is an important factor conditioning the perpetrator for further and greater acts of violence (Perpetrator Training = PT). The media play a conditioning role and easy access to stolen goods, violent films, pornography, prostitutes, drugs, and alcohol supports the corrupting mental environment of the gang. Past injustices experienced in life, such as poverty or child abuse, tend to create a violent disposition (Past Experience = PE). The intensity with which the perpetrator participates in gang consumption rituals and the distance from one's own family define the individual temperament of the perpetrator (Individual Temperament = IT).

Distance from the Victim = Physical Distance × Emotional
Distance × Social Distance

Physical distance is commonly provided by guns and on rare occasions vehicles, but knives are sometimes used to kill, torture, or dismember people (Physical Distance = PD). The emotional distance between victim and assailant can be very close, considering that the island is fairly homogeneous and experiences little race conflict. Leaders may require a member to act against another member regardless of emotional ties (Emotional Distance = ED). A larger part of the equation is the hate and antagonism caused by envy of other people's wealth and power. Unless the gang has evolved into a rich and powerful business organization, the social distance between rich and poor is an important factor stimulating violence (Social Distance = SD).

$$Target\ Attractiveness = \text{Relevance of Victim} \times (\text{Payoff} - \text{Perpetrator's Risk})$$

Taiwan gangs will kill to obtain weapons since weapons are the tools used to instantly satisfy needs. Thus, if a target has a weapon and the target is not a gang member or a police person, then the attractiveness of the target is high. The relevance of the victim is related to political or police pressures, rival gang actions, family ties, or business transactions that impact the gang's welfare and status (Relevance of Victim = RV). The pay-off for violence (Payoff = PO) will be status and ownership of the victims' possessions. The potential for retaliation or the creation of unforeseen situations that endanger the payoff is called the perpetrator's risk (Perpetrator's Risk = PR).

The probability for violence (PV) is formulated as follows:

$$PV = \text{Demands of Authority} \times \text{Gang Absolution} \times \text{Predisposition toward Violence} \times$$
$$\text{Distance from the Victim} \times \text{Target Attractiveness}$$
$$PV = DA \times GA \times PV \times DV \times TA$$

Each sub-factor of the model uses a baseline weight of 1. In Table 2, a sample calculation demonstrates the probability of violence for a gang. The demands for authority and the absolution of fellow gang members are assumed to be extremely influential and therefore increase the likelihood that a gang member acts violently. For this reason, the sub-factor weights selected for the demand intensity, the leader's proximity, the leader's authority, individual respect, and gang support and identity exceed the baseline weight of 1. Furthermore, the stronger the influence of authority and the absolution of the gang, the more attractive is the target (higher payoff). A gang member's predisposition toward violence and the distance from the victim fall below the baseline value if there is a strong spiritual belief (or faith) in the gang and its leader. In summary, the category totals that most strongly influence the outcome are the demands of authority, gang absolution, and the attractiveness of the target. The predisposition of the perpetrators of violence and the distance from the target weakly influence the category totals.

Conclusion

The mathematical model fits the argument that Taiwan gangs have the highest potential for violence during the early stages of formation and during the later stages of maturity and decline. New gangs are extremely dangerous because the initial payoff (e.g., obtaining money and weapons) gives the leader immediate validity and the gang as a whole greater faith in the organization. But if the gang and its members already have money, weapons, political power, and business operations, then the leader's authority is diluted, new targets are not attractive, and the potential for violence is reduced. However, mature gangs become violent again when individual gang members solicit their own following or as society moves to establish law and order. Attempts to break up mature gangs leads to gang warfare, cycles of retaliation, and the internationalization of gangs.

Using the arguments above, Taiwan is experiencing increased gang violence because of the breakup of older gangs by police and because of the emergence of new gangs. Some of the older gang leaders have fled the island, and the Central News Agency (Yang 1997) reports that over 100 gang leaders are hiding in Mainland China. The new gangs that emerge to take their place create the most difficult cases for the police to solve since they have fewer business assets and a very shallow, yet very faithful, network of associates. The new gangs are extremely violent and more frequently engage in kidnapping and murder rather than money laundering, bid-rigging, and game-fixing as do the mature gangs. This is not to say that mature gangs do not commit violent acts, because they do. Rather, the violent acts of mature gangs are frequently acts of retaliation that do not involve the general public (relevance of victim > payoff). New gangs have no bounds about who may be their target as long as the payoff is high (payoff > relevance of the victim). For this reason, the emergence of new gangs poses the greatest threat to citizens and creates the greatest public fear.

The continuing efforts of the Taiwan police to arrest and document gang networks are important means to control gang violence. However, serious threats remain. First, gang leaders living abroad might return in the future or create international networks. Second, little effort has been made to study and profile individuals likely to emerge as new gang leaders. Without knowing the environment and the behaviors that give rise to gang leadership, little can be done to eliminate the growing violence. Finally, Confucius recognized that poverty and a low position in life generates contempt in the eyes of others, but taught that dedication to duty, frugality, and benevolence are the essence of wealth and respectability (Ku 1984). Since too few people are teaching and practicing traditional values, Taiwan's consumerism is defining the public's standards, priorities, and values. As long as conspicuous consumption is valued more than non-conspicuous civic mindedness and hard work, gangs will maintain their spiritual appeal.

References

Chaffee, Aurell, Barth, Cort, Dombrowski, Fasano, Weaver. (1969). *Area Handbook for the Republic of China.* Washington, D.C.: The American University Press.

European Council of Commerce and Trade (ECCT). (1996). *Position Papers 1996/97.* Taipei: ECCT.

Free China Review. (1997).

Gilligan, James. (1996). *Violence, Our Deadly Epidemic and Its Causes.* New York: Grosset/Putnam Books.

Grossman, David. (1995). *On Killing—The Psychological Cost of Learning to Kill in War and Society.* Boston: Little Brown and Company.

Kavanaugh, John F. (1982). *Following Christ in a Consumer Society, The Spirituality of Cultural Resistance.* New York: Orbis Books.

Ku, Hung-ming. (1984). *English Translation of the Analects*. Taipei: Shin Sheng Daily News.

Liao, Cheng-Hao. (1996). Speak loudly and carry a big stick. *Free China Review* 46.11 (November, 1996): 12–14.

Longenecker, David, and T. Yu. (1994). The Beijing-Taipei struggle for international recognition, from the Niger Affair to the U.N. *Asian Survey* 34.5 (May, 1994): 475–488.

Raguin, Yves. (1974). *Buddhism, Sixteen Lessons on Buddhism and Christianity*. Taipei: Ricci Institute for Chinese Studies.

Seagrave, Sterling. (1995). *Lords of the Rim*. New York: Bantam Press.

Shaw, Thomas A. (1994). "We like to have fun," leisure and discovery of the self in Taiwan's "new" middle class. *Modern China, An Interdisciplinary Journal* 20.4 (October, 1994): 416–45.

Taiwan Executive Yuan. (1996a). *Taiwan Statistical Data Book*. Taipei: Council for Planning and Development.

————. (1996b). *Monthly Bulletin of Statistics, Taipei: Directorate-General of Budget, Accounting and Statistics*. 22.10 (1996): 20.

————. (1996c). *Urban and Regional Development Statistics*. Taipei: Urban and Housing Development Department, pp.136–137.

Trappey, Charles V. (1997). The Taiwan retail market. Report AIT-97-203 prepared for the Commercial Section of the American Institute in Taiwan, William Brekke, Chief.

Veblen, Thorstein. (1953/1899). *The Theory of the Leisure Class*. New York: New American Library.

Yang, Danielle. (1997). 100 gang leaders have fled to mainland China: Justice Minister. *Taiwan Headline News*. Taipei: Central News Agency, Wednesday, 12 February 1997.

Table 1. Violent events in Taiwan history

Year	Historical Event	Nature of Violence
1200	Hoklo immigrants from Fujien Province begin to arrive and challenge the Hakka's claims to land.	Fighting between the Hoklo and the Hakka ends with the Hakka being pushed further inland and closer to the aborigines. The Hakkas are attacked by the aborigines in the mountains and the Hoklo in the plains.
1250	Taiwan grows as a base for pirates from China and Japan	Ransacking of ships and lawlessness. The Japanese operate out of present day Kee-lung and the Chinese pirates operate out of Tainan.
1622	The Dutch construct forts in the North and the Spanish construct forts in the South	Colonization of 25,000 Chinese immi-grants by the Europeans.
1642	The Dutch expel the Spanish from Taiwan	Territorial war between two European powers.
1662	Dutch expelled by Chi-nese	Nine-month siege of Fort Zeelandia by a land army of 120,000 and a 12,000-vessel pirate fleet under the control of Koxinga. Koxinga, fleeing the Manchus on the mainland, sets out to eliminate all traces of Dutch rule.
1683	The Manchus capture Taiwan unopposed and a two-century dark age be-gins.	Widespread lawlessness and corruption spreads across Taiwan. Banditry, piracy, and inter-clan feuds create nostalgia for the rule of Koxinga. Fifteen major anti-government rebellions occur until 1850. Settlers continue to rebel against govern-ment officials that amass wealth through extortion.
1842	The British threaten to occupy Taiwan	Two British vessels wreck in a storm off of the eastern coast of Taiwan. All crew members are massacred by tribesmen. Britain threatens to occupy Taiwan in re-taliation. Twenty years later, British trad-ing companies are in place selling opium to the Chinese on Taiwan.
1883	The end of the dark age of the Manchus.	A rebel uprising results in the death of 20,000 of the Emperors soldiers and offi-cials. The Manchus begin political and administrative reforms on the island.

1884	The French attempt to gain control.	The French gain control of Keelung and the Pescadores but abandon the attempt to take the island. The capital is moved from Tainan to Taipei.
1894	Taiwan ceded to Japan	Local Chinese and intellectuals claim Taiwan an independent republic and recognize the suzerainty of China. After a three-day battle, 50,000 armed Taiwanese surrender in Keelung. Skirmishes continue against the Japanese until 1902. From 1907 to 1928, only four serious uprisings against the Japanese. Intermittent warfare with aborigines as railroads are built. Taiwan achieves an overall higher standard of living than mainland China.
1930	The Japanese disarm the aborigines	The aborigines are forced to give up hunting and assimilate. Two hundred elementary schools are built for the aborigines.
1933	China and Japan go to war.	Japan tries to supplant the Chinese language and culture with that of Japan.
1945	Chinese Nationalist forces take over the administration of Taiwan from the Japanese.	Taiwan placed under military rule and political rights postponed. Troops strip Taiwan factories and farms for Nationalist struggle against the Communists in China. The breakdown in public health and the spread of cholera and plague leads to the deterioration of education and public morale.
1947	The 2/28 incident and the beginning of "white terror."	Customs police kill a woman selling cigarettes. A general uprising begins that leads to the death of over 20,000 Taiwanese.
1955	The communists pursue plan to capture Taiwan	The communists Chinese capture Tachen and Nanchi islands and begin attacks on Matsu and Kinmen islands. More than 60,000 shells fall per day on Kinmen until the U.S. Seventh Fleet arrives. Kruschev vows to use nuclear weapons against the United States. if the United States uses nuclear weapons against China.

Table 2. Factor weights for gang violence

Factors	Sub-factor Total	Category Total
Demand of Authority (DA)		2.592
Leader's Authority (LA)	1.5	
Demand Intensity (DI)	1.2	
Leader's Proximity (LP)	1.2	
Perpetrator 's Respect (PR)	1.2	
Gang Absolution (GA)		1.440
Gang Support (GS)	1.2	
Group Number (GN)	1.0	
Gang Identity (GI)	1.2	
Gang Proximity (GP)	1.0	
Predisposition (PV)		0.512
Training (PT)	0.8	
Past Experience (PE)	0.8	
Temperament (IE)	0.8	
Distance (DV)		0.512
Physical Distance (PD)	0.8	
Emotional Distance (ED)	0.8	
Social Distance (SD)	0.8	
Target Attraction (TA)		1.000
Relevance of Victim (RV)	1.0	
Payoff (PO)	2.0	
Perpetrator's Risk (PR)	1.0	
Probability of Violence (PV)		0.978

Chapter XXIII

Intended Social Effects of a Culture of Impunity: The Case of Guatemala

Frank M. Afflitto

Investigating the Investigated

This research addresses the disruption of familial and communal life in Guatemala through the exercise of state-sponsored terrorism. Such terrorism is dependent upon a structural-cultural system of impunity. This culture of fear, violence, and impunity has been responsible for the prolonged disruption of pre-violence patterns of existence and social relations since its systematic inception in the early 1960s. Renewed patterns of adaptive social relations, however, based upon an anti-impunity political resistance, have also been formed. Respondents report that a "coming together" has arisen due to impunity and that the violence has given rise to a culture of survivor communities.

Extensive ethnographic interviewing was conducted with eighty Guatemalans in two field research periods, in 1990 and 1992. The fieldwork was participatory and was conducted utilizing Participatory Action Research (PAR) methodology (see Whyte et al. 1991). Respondents were selected on the basis of shared experiences of violence by state-sanctioned security forces and their death squad allies.

Additionally, respondents were active or peripheral members of Guatemalan "popular" movement organizations at the time of interview. These organizations are non-governmental and mass-based, or populist, in nature, and were formed to address the systematic violence and impunity in Guatemalan society, as well as the consequences in movement members' lives. The great majority of respondents were involved with organizations who were affiliates of the UASP (Unidad y Acción Sindical y Popular; Popular and Trade Union Unity and Action). The social sectors integrated in the UASP, being involved in seeking redress, are members of communities historically subject to targeting by state-sponsored violence. The fight against such violence and impunity has been consistently taken up by all member organizations in that coalition. (Research was sponsored by the Society for the Psychological Study of Social Issues and the School of Social Ecology, University of California at Irvine.)

Perpetration of Violence, Culture of Impunity

The Latin American subcontinent is renowned for the violence that reigns over the daily lives of its citizens (see Blanco Muñoz 1977). This violence, however, "is not totally chaotic and unpredictable" (Huggins 1991: 3). Since the 1960s, in particular, numerous social scientific studies have demonstrated a predominant pattern of state-sanctioned violence against civilian populations throughout much of Latin America.

Guatemala is no stranger to violence, especially that which is "predictable" and organized by the state. Violent social relations in Guatemala have historical roots that date back to the Spanish conquest of Mesoamerica (Figueroa Ibarra 1991; McClintock 1985). Guatemala's most recent civil strife has its roots in a nationalist military revolt of November 1960, and the subsequent formation of an organized insurgent movement. This guerrilla movement, which eventually congealed into the four-group coalition known as the URNG, ostensibly commenced in response to the socio-cultural legacy inherited by a 1954 CIA-sponsored coup that destroyed Guatemala's most democratically elected and "dangerously" non-aligned government during the height of Cold War hysteria. Since that time, the more than 150,000 politically related assassinations and more than 45,000 enforced disappearances have led to the existence of more than 70,000 widows, more than a quarter of a million children without one or both parents, and an estimated one million persons displaced from their home communities. The vast majority of the patterns of violence and their widespread consequences have been consistently attributed to the Guatemalan Army, especially its intelligence division (the G-2), and its extralegal (death squads) and paralegal (military commissioners, civil patrols) counterparts.

Guatemala is world-renowned for the state's use of the disappearance of persons as a weapon of terror. It is described as being the first nation in the Americas to systematically employ the enforced disappearance of persons (Asociación Centroamericana de Familiares de Detenidos-Desaparecidos [ACAFADE] 1991, 1990, 1989), as well as the nation where the verb "to disappear" was originally employed (Simon 1987: 14). Guatemala's disappeared account for 50% or more of all cases in Latin America (Federación Latinoamericana de Familiares de Detenidos-Desaparecidos [FEDEFAM] 1992). In addition to the practice of enforced disappearances, the predominance of phenomena such as extrajudicial execution, mutilation, and torture are highly representative of Guatemala's four-decade reign of terror. The detention of persons by uniformed or "unknown" groups and the subsequent reappearance of highly mutilated corpses in public places have constituted consistent and well-documented patterns of violence in that nation.

Respondent Descriptions of the Perpetration of Violence

In providing a basis for understanding the violence and impunity, respondents describe typical manifestations of state-sponsored terror that have served as foundational life experiences. These are represented by the incidents of extrajudicial execution by state security forces, by enforced disappearance and by torture/mutilation. For example, a Mayan activist in an organization of persons displaced by counterinsurgency campaigns described an Army sweep into his village, whose consequences were the deaths by shooting or torture of his immediate family:

> At six in the evening when military commissioners and the Army, who totaled more than 9,000 men, encircled the village . . . they arrived without saying even one word. They arrived at the houses to machine-gun my family. They killed, principally, my father, who was, like, seventy-four years old. Then they killed my brothers, who were twenty-six years old and . . . the littlest one, who was ten.
>
> Then they began with the women. For example, my mother was not killed with firearms nor knives. They made a sharp, pointed stake from wood. So then, they began to torture her in the stomach. Also, they stuck it into her here in the neck, the eyes and they stuck it into her mouth as well.
>
> So then, what they said to her, or, that's to say, what they asked of my mother was me. Who knows . . . my mother knew that I was inside [the house]. But she negated knowing my whereabouts. "I don't know," she

said. So then, they killed her purely by torture. By kicking her. And they also drew a knife. So then, they cut off her ears, and a piece of her nose . . . while she was alive. So then, my mother, herself . . . I could hear her really well. "What do you men want from us? We are poor people!" And . . . "What is it that you want from us?" And, so, they said to her, "You people are pure guerrillas. You are pure communists. But what we want from you . . . we want your son." That's how they spoke to her. So then, they went to grab her once again, my mother, and . . . she was sixty-four years old.

And then they went to grab my wife. And they did the same thing to her. With the stakes. And she was carrying [across her chest in a blanket-type woven cloth called a rebozo] our little girl who was eight months old. So then, they began to torture her. "Tell us where your husband is. Hand him over and you'll go free," but kicking her repeatedly the whole time. And, because of the stake, lots and lots of blood was flowing from her stomach and from her face as well. When they were giving her those incredible kicks, they did it with our daughter strapped to her as well. And they were pulling on her [wife's] hair, and they would stand them up. So then, they killed her, and when they killed her, because the girl was belly-down on top of my wife, when they stuck the stake into her [wife], they killed the two of them, because they drove the stake into the stomach of the both of them.

And after this assassination, this massacre, they pulled her and they dragged her inside the house and they lit the house on fire. So then, what they wanted to do was . . . in addition to the bullets, in addition to the tortures, was to burn them. I was present. I was inside the house, but they [army] didn't see me.

But when they killed my parents and everything, what I did was to go outside. And they began to shoot all over the place. That's when I was able to escape from their hands, though, in any event, they hit me with gunfire. This was in April of 1982.

Another respondent described the circumstances surrounding the disappearance of her trade unionist son. He was disappeared in a mass sequester of trade unionists in 1980 attributed to the Judicial Police [National Police detective/intelligence corps]. This ladina [mestiza] woman from the capital city stated that "they [CNT-affiliated unionists] were celebrating a memorial ceremony for one [fellow unionist] that they [authorities] had killed and there were twenty-seven in the CNT [office], and there they grabbed them."

Look . . . they [sequesterers] blocked off everything. All the traffic. And they didn't let anyone pass. That's what a woman neighbor says. Because I went down there the moment that that thing was occurring. There were even pools of blood that . . . that they'd extracted from them. I went to another place [Judicial Police headquarters] and yes, they looked for him, and . . . they threatened us! One couldn't arrive there asking questions. We put an attorney on the case. They killed him. I didn't even know what his name was.

As a final example of typical violence reported by respondents, a university student torture survivor described to me his experiences with a plainclothes squad on a city street. He began by stating that he was "walking in the street. It wasn't very late, about 6 p.m."

> They came out and blocked my path . . . some individuals who didn't identify themselves as being from any security force or the authorities, but one knows the entire physiognomy of those types . . . the form in which they express themselves, right? The form in which they dress when they're in civilian clothes.
>
> They started to call me names and they were looking to offend me. But, as I didn't heed them in terms of what they said to me . . . [then came] "Hand over the money that you have!" Right? Which wasn't much but it was what I was carrying at that moment. So then, they continued insulting me, right? And the one that was in charge among them told me to give him my jacket, though I'd already given him my wallet. My documents were there in the wallet. They ripped up my documents. I took off the jacket and, when I was giving it to them, that's when he assaulted me. He stabbed me the first time.
>
> Then, when I covered the part he had just stabbed, he cut me in one of my upper extremities, right? So then, I couldn't get away. So I threw myself to the ground. And there they began to kick me. Two individuals, one grabbing me on each side. Then they began stabbing my lower extremities. After, they said various things to me. I believe [they were] things that I understood, no? That perhaps with this, the lesson would make an impression on me . . . that it was a lesson for me.
>
> They walked away. There I stayed, prone, and soon the firefighters arrived and took me away to a medical assistance center. The police never arrived. Even at the medical center, the police officer on duty didn't ask me for any information or anything. And they weren't grave wounds, like, for killing me, right? But . . . only for leaving me marked for life.

Defining and Understanding Guatemala's Culture of Impunity

Various elements of these acts of violence suffered by these respondents and their family members serve to illustrate the cultural components of impunity that surround them. The Mayan man who first described the extrajudicial executions of his family was confronted by illegal acts perpetrated by legally constituted authorities. When asked why he made no formal complaint about these violent, illegal acts, he responded that "In those years, since it was in '82, they were the most difficult and hard moments. And it was in that moment that they were looking for me as well. And to go make a complaint . . . I would have been captured." Considering what had happened to his parents, brothers, wife, and eight-month old daughter, his perceived guilt would have easily been met by even more spectacular forms of violence.

For the ladina mother of the young trade unionist, being threatened at the headquarters of the suspected sequestering force, and the subsequent assassination of the attorney of the families of the twenty-seven disappeared, provided clear messages that legal redress through the established justice system would be futile. Similarly, for the university student who was attacked and disfigured by members of who he perceived to be a plainclothes security force, the fact that the police neither investigated nor made a report, normal duties in matters of this nature, was a clear indication to him of judicial collusion in the torture perpetrated upon him.

Impunity can be defined as a "freedom from legal sanction or accountability" (McSherry and Molina 1992: 2) for criminal actions. Impunity, in Guatemala, is exercised through several principal mechanisms. The first and most prominent is the terror-via-violence itself, which has traditionally made it impossible to claim one's rights in terms of searching for missing loved ones or in successfully prosecuting torturers and executioners. This element has been termed "political/psychological impunity" (McSherry and Molina 1992: 3).

Another principal element of the Guatemalan impunity, highly related to the evasion of accountability, is the official denial of state-sponsored violence or subsequent cover-ups. Such denial takes place at the highest levels of state activity, even at the level of civilian presidency. One respondent delineated such denial as enacted by the first civilian presidency after more than a decade of open military rule. When the GAM (Mutual Support Group for the Families of the Disappeared) met with then-president Cerezo and requested that he investigate the tens of thousands of disappearances, one respondent described how she asked Cerezo to investigate the sequester and disappearance of her younger sister and four brothers by sixty uniformed security force effectives. The respondent stated that "he said 'Yes, I'm going to look to see if they're there,' he answered me."

> So then, when we went up there [president's office], all of us from GAM, the coordinating committee . . . he told us, "Yes, I'm going to give you the names of those who are still alive. And those who are dead . . . I can't do anything about that."
>
> So, we were left, all of us, with some shred of hope, right? . . . if perhaps the name of one of them [five disappeared siblings] would come out there [on the president's list]. And then it came to be two weeks later, which was the day he was to give us the names, and he denied us everything. And he told us "I never said those words to you."
>
> Even the reporters that were there said they'd written down that he had said that he was going to give us the names [of the disappeared who were still alive]. And at the very hour of truth, he denied everything. And later on, he didn't continue denying us . . . he simply didn't talk to us.

This element in the culture of impunity authors J. Patrice McSherry and Raul Molina (1992: 3) term "strategic impunity," which they define as "active measures taken by state official . . . to derail processes of or demands for truth and justice."

A final element is that of "structural impunity," which consists of "mechanisms and structures, institutionalized . . . in the state that serve to protect those who abuse state power" (McSherry and Molina 1992: 3).

Respondents Describe the Culture of Impunity

Respondents have described two salient elements of impunity that show a pattern of expected and "normative" behavior under the state terror system, delineating and shaping the culture of impunity which confronts their familial and communal lives and structures. These elements are the fear of legal redress for alleged rights violations, generated through the systematic exercise of violence, and the systematic non-prosecution of those perceived as guilty for these violations and acts of violence.

In terms of the fear of legal redress, interview data above have already alluded to this phenomenon, with the assassination of an attorney, the torture/murder of an entire family, and the "voiced secret" of a plainclothes torture squad teaching a "lesson" to a university student activist as examples. [*Un secreto a voces* in Guatemalan Spanish signifies an indirect, yet very real, intention or desire of a party in a dispute.] One respondent with a disappeared son, who involved herself with the Mutual Support Group [GAM] in order to claim her 'right to know' regarding the whereabouts of her son, had been repeatedly and violently harassed by the local Civil Patrol [army-directed village-based counterinsurgency force].

> The Civil Patrols don't stop from threatening me! Since I come here [GAM] they told me that Nineth [group's president] eats people's bones. Only by dead people's bones does she live, they told me, because they [GAM] only take the bones out of the clandestine cemeteries.
>
> And, when I left the village about two weeks ago, they fired three shots near my shack. Not ten meters from my house they fired off three shots! "You're doing things with Nineth!" "Of course . . . I'm going for my son!" "But sooner or later you're going to fall beside your son! First went your son and then . . . you're next!" the chiefs of the Civil Patrol told me. Because now I am scared when I come here [GAM]. If I leave here [capital city] and arrive home in the evening, I fall directly into their hands, because they are controlling the roads [after nightfall].

As respondents report being afraid to claim their rights through legal redress, they have turned to the formation of non-governmental organizations in order to claim those same rights and to press their demands for justice. These organizations serve as parallel legal realms of seeking justice outside the formal legal system through which they have been excluded due to fear and structural inadequacy. These organizations, however, are targets of violence in the same way that those working within the formal legal system are subject to violence for pressing for the domination of a culture of the rule of law over the present culture of impunity.

The systematic non-prosecution of those guilty, whether materially or intellectually, for state-sanctioned terrorist violence, has been a given for decades in the landscape of Guatemalan impunity. "Justice isn't seen as the product of some act, but rather as something that's worth something to someone. So then, justice can't be made, because reality's not applied," stated the brother of a university student who had been found tortured to death and dismembered in a plastic bag thrown in a trash can. This same respondent states that if "justice" is applied at all, "It's applied only to the rich and to those who bribe." A number of my respondents report knowing who has sequestered their family members, disappearing them or torturing and killing them. In the same breath, however, they describe how the possibility of legal redress and the prosecution of the alleged guilty parties, either through litigation or organizationally, is precluded by the wielding of fear-via-state terror.

Social Disruption as Intended Consequence of a Culture of Impunity

It is not difficult to extrapolate from the respondent interview data cited above the disruptive effects of violence on family and community. However, the examination of three major areas of such disruption, representative of the disruptive consequences of the culture of impunity, may help the reader in clarification and categorization of these phenomena. The three areas of (a) the existence of the civil patrols and their use in dividing villages and communities and in bringing them under the counterinsurgency apparatus; (b) the dismembering of families through disappearance and execution; and (c) the social distancing of communities of resistance from communities of complacence are the main disruptive aspects of the counterinsurgency culture.

The "Voluntary" Civil Self-Defense Patrol System: The Bi-Polar World of "Quislings" vs. "Subversives"

As anthropologist Laura Nader (1989: 336) states, and as, apparently, the Guatemalan architects of counterinsurgency understood quite well, "the divided village is more susceptible to external domination." The establishment of the civil patrols in Guatemala during the height of army strategizing for eradication of the URNG's rural/Mayan base is uniquely interesting because it pitted villager against villager in the context of role definitions of who was a "subversive" [i.e., anti-army, pro-"communist"] both inside and outside the local village. While the patrol system demanded that local agriculturalists patrol on twenty-four-hour shifts every third day, or pay someone else to cover their shifts when they were away from home working on coastal plantations, the "voluntary" nature of patrolling came into question with the rise of civilian-led government in 1986.

Once civil patrolling was officially defined as "voluntary," this definition was tested "on the ground" by thousands of villagers tired of military indoctrination sessions and hours of forced labor for the army's benefit while their own agricultural work fell behind. One respondent whom I interviewed was called a guerrilla by local patrollers for exercising his legal right in refusing to patrol. He was left in a latrine hole for eighteen days at a local army base with his wife and young children, all partially submerged in a cesspool of floating human filth the entire time. He was driven out of his community for the second time by the civil patrollers, and threatened with death if he ever returned.

> And when we left there [after the first displacement and relocation years earlier], the army said . . . the military commissioners said that "you have to be in the Civil Patrols." And we had to do it, because if we do not participate in the patrols, they say that we are "subversives." That we are "collaborating" there [in the village]. So then, we don't want these kinds of problems. For that reason, we have to be in the Civil Patrol.
>
> I patrolled, and so did my father [who is sixty-five years old]. And they said that they were "voluntary." But it's not voluntary. Because if we're going to go away to work on a plantation or if we go away for a

> month . . . we have to pay someone to do our rounds. So then, we have to pay. And if we are away two months, we have to pay forty quetzales (about $7.25 at the time). And if we don't earn anything, what are we going to do?
> If we don't pay, they say that we are "guerrillas." That we don't want to patrol. Because the soldiers said, "Do your patrolling! Because, for you all, it's work, so that you can live tranquilly. You all look after your own villages and . . ." All that! So then, that is the problem that we have.

Civil patrollers have not only been identified as some of the worst human rights abusers on the local level, exercising a sort of opportunistic terrorism, having the weapons and army backing through which to attain power at the village level. The patrol system itself is responsible for economic, agricultural, and familial hardship on participants and non-participants alike.

Dismembered Families: Violations of the Right to Life and the Right to "Know"

The enforced disappearance of persons, in particular, has been cited by respondents as responsible for the painful disruption of familial life. Not only do familial roles change, as women are called to take on missing men's roles while continuing on with traditional women's roles within the household. The chronic ambiguity of not knowing the whereabouts of missing loved ones also leaves deep psychological scars on family members, and divides some families along the lines of those who blame the victim, those who actively search, sometimes for years, for disappeared loved ones, translating such a search into organized political activism, and those who advocate within the family for a simple forgetting and "moving on."

One respondent, quite representative of many other families of the disappeared, commented on how "I am now very bad off because of so many sicknesses . . . because, due to my nerves I am very bad off and my head has become numb from so much thinking. My husband and my son . . . [are disappeared] . . . My head's all twisted from so much thinking about them."

"Resisters" vs. "Acceptors": The Unanticipated Political Division of Guatemalan Society

In addition to disruption and division at the village/communal level and the familial level, there exists a consequential disruption of both familial and communal life at the political level. While state-sanctioned terrorism most likely calculated the massive political acquiescence and passivity of society, not all violence survivors addressed their experiences in this way. This often brought discord in both families and communities.

One respondent described the divisions in his community between himself, an organizational member of a group working to find the disappeared, and his neighbors. While his neighbors also have disappeared family members, he reported that they stated to him "Why keep investigating if they are no more?"

> But I'd respond that in the ebb and flow . . . the effort, right? That doesn't move backwards. I feel that when I think that no . . . no, he's not an animal or . . . like we're not going to feel it [the pain of disappearance], right? In

the first place, it's family. And we want to at least know what's up, right? How was the disappearance. And for him [son] we cannot vacillate. If we were to remain vacillating, we'd be lost. That's how I look at it. And another thing . . . that I say these things to my children, as siblings of my son, but they don't get up the courage to join in [the group struggle]. They fear because they hear many things. Many sequesters . . . one has much fear. But more than myself, I say, I am disposed to the fact that something happen to me, because . . . as it's a right, really, perhaps I'll give my life, perhaps not. Yes.

Reaction to Resistance

This chapter has presented the experiences of violence based on a system of impunity of a specific population of Guatemalans residing in that nation. The majority of their initial experiences of violent victimization had taken place under military regimes, while they were interviewed under civilian governments. Death threats, tortures, and related persecutions due to their pro-justice activities, however, had consistently taken place regardless of the regime in power. This fact points to the existence of a culture of impunity and a system of state-sanctioned terrorism that supersedes the existence of any particular elected or coup-implemented political administration.

As a consequence of their experiences of violence and the impunity which impedes the attainment of justice objectives, respondents' lives have been disrupted on many levels. This disruption is evident on an individual psychological level, on a familial level as well as on the community level. The experience of violence and the associated guilt attributed by many fearful members of society to the disappeared and executed for their own misfortunes have left many victimized families ostracized and excluded from wider social participation mirroring pre-violence patterns. This "social exclusion" (Blok 1989:32) has itself become an indelible disruptive force in the lives of many of the respondents. This social exclusionary effect is often heightened when respondents pursue justice through political participation.

A final division, perhaps not initially anticipated by the state terror system, is based on the transformation of violence survivors from victims to political resistors. As Jeffrey A. Sluka (1995: 83) points out, through his anthropological work in the Catholic ghettoes of Northern Ireland, "through the shared or communal experience of repression and pro-state terror, they [activists] have transformed themselves into a culture of resistance." Only time will show if the disruption evident in state terror's consistent operation will continuously fortify the culture of impunity, or whether a culture of resistance will bring Guatemalans sharing commonalities of violence by the state across gender, ethnic, and class lines together.

References

Asociación Centroamericana de Familiares de Detenidos-Desaparecidos (ACAFADE). (1991). *Desaparecidos en Centroamérica 1990* (The Disappeared in Central America 1990). San José, Costa Rica: ACAFADE.
———. (1990). *Desaparecidos en Centroamérica 1989* (The Disappeared in Central America 1989). San José, Costa Rica: ACAFADE.

————. (1989). *Desaparecidos en Centroamérica 1988* (The Disappeared in Central America 1988). San José, Costa Rica: ACAFADE.

Blanco Muñoz, Agustín. (1977). *Latinoamérica la historia violentada* (Latin America The 'Violented' History). Caracas, Venezuela: Universidad Central de Venezuela.

Blok, Anton. (1989). The symbolic vocabulary of public executions. In *History and Power in the Study of Law New Directions in Legal Anthropology*, edited by June Starr and Jane F. Collier, pp. 31–54. Ithaca and London: Cornell University Press.

Federación de Familiares de Detenidos-Desaparecidos (FEDEFAM). (1992). Periodical Bulletin. Caracas, Venezuela: FEDEFAM.

Figueroa Ibarra, Carlos. (1991). *El Recurso del Miedo Ensayo sobre el estado y el terror en Guatemala* (The Recourse to Fear Exposition on the state and terror in Guatemala). San José, Costa Rica: Editorial Universitaria Centroamericana.

Huggins, Martha K. (1991). Introduction: Vigilantism and the State-A Look South and North. In *Vigilantism and the Modern State in Modern Latin America: Essays on Extralegal Violence*, edited by Martha K. Huggins, pp. 1–18. New York: Praeger.

McClintock, Michael. (1985). *The American Connection*, Volume II: *State Terror and Popular Resistance in Guatemala*. London: Zed Books Ltd.

McSherry, J. Patrice, and Raúl Molina Mejía. (1992). Confronting the question of justice in Guatemala. *Social Justice: a Journal of Crime, Conflict and World Order* 19.3: 1–28.

Nader, Laura. (1989). The crown, the colonists and the course of Zapotec village law. In *History and Power in the Study of Law: New Directions in Legal Anthropology*, edited by June Starr and Jane F. Collier, pp. 320–344. Ithaca and London: Cornell University Press.

Nairn, Allan. (1993). The roots of torture: U.S. complicity and the need for change. In *Confronting the Heart of Darkness: An International Symposium on Torture in Guatemala*, edited by Shari Turitz, pp. 4–10. Washington, D.C.: Guatemalan Human Rights Commission/USA.

Simon, Jean-Marie. (1987). *Guatemala Eternal Spring-Eternal Tyranny*. New York and London: W. W. Norton & Company, Inc.

Sluka, Jeffrey A. (1995). Domination, resistance and political culture in Northern Ireland's Catholic-Nationalist ghettos. *Critique of Anthropology* 15.1: 71–102.

Smith, Carol A. (1990). Conclusion: History and revolution in Guatemala. In *Guatemalan Indians and the State*, edited by Carol A. Smith with the assistance of Marilyn M. Moors, pp. 258–285. Austin: University of Texas Press.

Whyte, William Foote, Davydd J. Greenwood, and Peter Lazes. (1991). Participatory action research through practice to science in social research. In *Participatory Action Research*, edited by William Foote Whyte, pp. 19–55. Newbury Park, London and New Delhi: Sage Publications.

Chapter XXIV

Political Violence and the Public Eye

Glen A. Perice

Aristide was president . . . and everyone was talking politics and talking about change in Haiti. The walls were covered with pictures of Aristide and pictures of cocks. These pictures were our way of saying, "We're here. We're behind you, Aristide." And because I painted signs and billboards, because everyone knew I was an artist people came and asked me to paint a cock on the wall in front of my house. I didn't want to do it. I told my mother that I was too scared. She told me not to get involved with the crowds that were talking about Aristide and politics.

Then people came to my house one day with ten dollars to buy paint. They said I had to do it and they said if I didn't do it then I wasn't for Aristide and I should get out of the country. I wanted to yell at them that if I could leave the country, I would. But I was for Aristide too. He was telling those in power that they were criminals which is what everybody said anyway, only he was saying it in crowds of people and on the radio.

So begins the story of my friend Jean-Pierre, with whom I spent much time in Port-au-Prince. I used to visit his house every day. He lived in one room with the rest of his family. There were two metal cots that he and his sister slept on, and three other people slept on cardboard on the floor. His neighbors lived in different rooms of the same house, and to visit Jean-Pierre I had to pass their doors, which were always open. They always said "hello" and asked me what was going on. Jean-Pierre's mother was always worried that I would attract too much attention to her son. One could hear everything that happened on the street outside. There is a sensitivity to what goes on beyond one's household, into the next room, and then into the neighborhood itself. The boundaries are as far as one can hear about things, and hear literally, in the everyday noise of the street.

These days we talk about the gaze of power as if power had eyes, as if it could see. Nothing is more prevalent than the connection between seeing and power, or being seen and subordination to power. Being seen instigates discursive features as well, for to be seen is to be communicated and "known" to those in power. Speaking and seeing are linked by power. "Seeing and speaking are always already completely caught up within power relations which they presuppose and actualize" (Deleuze 1988: 82). Power cannot exist if it does not colonize these two productive social sites of meaning. In cultures of terror, this colonization of identity itself becomes a medium of domination as an individual crosses over into the shadow lands, and sees himself being seen by power, perpetually within the boundaries of power.

When imagining the gaze of power, the mind turns back upon itself and sees itself as subjected to that power. There is a nebulous zone of fantasy, of fear, of paralysis between the I and the self caught in a field of visuality. This shadow zone is seeing ourselves being seen by power. I want to keep this thought in mind as I probe this aspect of power as it rises up in the words of dissidents in Haiti. At the end of this essay I will contrast the visual field of the culture of terror with the Public Eye.

If the strange but now familiar image of the Panopticon looms over us in the post-modern milieu as an icon of terror or an obsessive paranoid delusion, states corner us with the feeling of being seen and mapped by their "security forces" and "intelligence agencies." Since governments have been constituting themselves as separate from their citizens, these citizens have been mapped along boundaries of visuality and information.

> A real subjection is born mechanically from a fictitious relation . . . He who is subjected to a field of visibility and who knows it, assumes responsibility for the constraints of power; he makes them play spontaneously upon himself. (Foucault 1977: 202-203).

In other words, within a relation of visibility the subject becomes subjected to the boundaries of that field. Being "subjected to a field of visibility" does not physically constrain a subject, but the recognition of such ("who knows it") influences the construction of social identity. It is possible to extend the notion of visibility to include any relation of power that locates the subject vis-à-vis certain spatially defined fields.

De Certeau, looking at the Panopticon from the underside, reflects that Foucault over emphasizes the machinery of power (he was famous for that) rather than the formative processes upon the subject:

> This "micro-physics" of power privileges the productive apparatus (which produces the discipline), even though it discerns in "education" a system of "repression." (de Certeau 1984: xiv).

Foucault says that a field of visibility produces the subject of power—and if we follow de Certeau's criticism, we can uncover a hidden assumption in Foucault's discussion of the field of visuality—one must "learn" to see one's self in a field of power. If there is a "system" of repression then there are discursive practices that aid in that repression. Along with violence, one learns to see one's self being seen, through "hearing" stories of terror and violence. Seeing one's self is neither theorizing the self nor to be in direct contact with the I one sees: it is in between. Between the eye and the I is a space of negative identity where political identity is fashioned.

> I painted a beautiful cock . . . People would stop by and stare at it and comment about how good it was. Some American journalists came to take pictures of it. That was because it was not far from the Episcopal Church, where all the famous paintings are inside. It took me two days to complete. Some of my friends came around and brought girls to see it. "He's my friend," they would say. At the time, I felt good about it. That's when I started my sign painting business. But Maurice, my sister's boyfriend, was not happy. He said, "You know you shouldn't do that." He meant that I shouldn't do politics. He was right.

A wave of political violence swept through Haiti after the coup d'état of 1991 that ousted democratically elected President Aristide. Aristide was sent into exile and the popular movement that elevated him to president, Lavalas, was destroyed. Duvalierists once again covered Haiti with a reign of terror and violence. De facto regimes popped up, all under the thumb of the Haitian military. One report on Haiti after the coup d'état of 1991 says:

> . . . the situation of human rights [is] dismal, with no freedoms of speech, assembly, or association. We received testimony that at least one thousand and possibly several thousand people have died in coup-related violence. We saw direct evidence of both intentional and arbitrary killing or wounding of civilians . . . fear grips the population across all social groupings. (The Haiti Commission 1991.)

After the coup, military attachés (those connected with the military, often spies) again became a familiar sight, and the worry about them became a constant theme of people's lives. Who was watching and who was listening? The Haitian military set up roadblocks to check cars on a random basis. Soldiers waited along major roads to question people entering small towns and villages. People dropped out of sight. One acquaintance of mine was never home when I went to his house. No one was home. No neighbors were around. Then he would show up a few days later knocking at my door and say, "I heard you were looking for me." One fellow told me:

> If someone in my neighborhood goes away for a few months and then returns, I don't talk to him until I can find out where he's been and what he was doing. You never know.

People were afraid. The organization of military intelligence whereby the Haitian army gathers information about civilians "[was] not known by the Haitian people, who are its constant victims" (Laguerre 1993: 84).

Prior to Aristide's electoral victory, a wave of violence against Duvalierists took place. The *dechouckaj*, the uprooting, as it is known, was revenge and justice against the violence and terror perpetuated by Duvalerists and the *Makout*. The period of the dechoukaj was very short, a few years, in relation to the decades of terror and violence instigated by both father and son Duvalier and their cronies. It was more spontaneous than organized violence.

In 1992, one year after the coup, I was told a story by a young man (rumored by some people to be a military attache, a spy) who lived near Hinche and whom I often met while waiting for a mail plane to land on a grassy field used for cattle and goat grazing. Also standing around us were soldiers in their uniforms. When the plane landed, the soldiers searched the plane and took whatever they happened to like, or they received payment not to take things. The young man turned to me and asked,

—Are you afraid of zombis?

—No. I'm more afraid of a *chef seksyon*. [rural policeman]

He laughed and paused.

—There is a *boko* [practitioner of magic] who lives around here, just down the road to Pappaye. He and his brother, who is an attaché in Thomond, tried to make a zombi but failed. The strangest thing happened to them.

—What's that?

—When they dug up the zombi he went crazy and started to attack them. The attaché grabbed the shovel and broke the zombi's head. When it was over the attaché was covered with the blood of the zombi. The boko and his brother were both very scared.

—Not so easy to make a zombi.

—Well, now they always carry their guns with them.

"Now they always carry . . ." This story, told to me sometime in October of 1992, speaks of redemption and violence. Resistance is quelled with violence. "Now," the Haitian military is everywhere.

This story is a rumor about power, but it also hints at the power rumors: the contours of power as outlined in the story. It is noteworthy that the *boko* is aligned with the attaché. It is this unity that is called into relief by the story. As the zombi regains his senses, the attaché and boko lose theirs. The fact that the zombi can wake up shows the mediated aspect of power. But we would be wrong to read this story as a mere reflection of political events. This story, like all rumors, is productive, and generates the "movement" of discourse—it "works." Rumors are not located within one person or even one "group" but are traces of the movement itself of social knowledge. Rumors generate mobile boundaries of self, the social matrix, and social knowledge. For when we say that knowledge is implicit in social relations, we are often talking about the effects of rumors. Telling, talking, and listening all become productive sites, not reflections, of power. Rumors interrupt and maintain the flows of everyday banter. They create images of the social world and generate movement of discourse. In this particular rumor, images of the rural police mix with talk of zombi. This is surely different than the anthropological take on zombi as either folk tales or some kind of proto-scientific experiment. The image of the zombi has a social force in everyday talk.

Rumors were and are everywhere. There is the rumor I heard that Jean Claude Duvalier was secretly back in Haiti, the rumor of the two soldiers with their eyes cut out, the rumor that the military from Hinche were going to come and kill everyone in the town where I was sleeping, the rumor that Jean-Pierre's aunt was killed by the military because no one had seen her for months, the rumor that a dead body in the street near the Catholic Cathedral was a Lavalas supporter, the rumor that military spies were following me around. Rumors about deaths, rumors about Aristide supporters maimed and killed, rumors about the ambush of a soldier.

In Haiti, where reliance upon personal contact and word-of-mouth outweighs all other forms of communication, rumors and gossip make the socially real, real (Perice 1994). In hear/say the visual field is formed as a real relation to the speaking subject. It is the rumors of deaths, of disappearances, stories of mutilated bodies, headless bodies, bodies without faces, that recall death. And death is the story of the culture of terror, death becoming the fixating focal point of the subject's subjugation. There were rumors of murdered soldiers as well. Rumors were always spinning about the Haitian military, the habits of the de facto leaders, the American C.I.A., and so on. A rumor, once while I was living in the countryside, that the local military was coming to wipe out everyone in the area, caused some people to leave for a while. Couldn't we say that speaking and seeing are linked in these rumors, not in a cognitive sense, but in a profoundly social sense?

Neighborhoods in Port-au-Prince and in the countryside are public spaces of discourse, discursively bounded, not private properties. People do not cover themselves in the cloak of anonymity; they do not hide in the everyday both nameless and faceless.

People know each other's business, and this is part of the everyday banter. Neighborhoods are places where gossip and rumors flourish and anyone can be the subject of gossip; gossip and rumors are oriented around place as much as around specific people. The "feel" of a neighborhood becomes the stories that one tells and hears about it. The bourgeois public sphere, the space where anonymity is established, and the high walls and spatial enclosures of private property are not part of the everyday experience in the poor areas of Port-au-Prince or the houses in the countryside. It is also the case that Haiti is a society built around networks, whom you know and who knows you is important.

"I came back to my neighborhood," my Haitian friend Steve, living in New York for several years now, told me,

> and everyone still talks to me as if I had never left . . . Everyone knows you and everyone knows your business; in my section of Port-au-Prince they still refer to me by the positions and views I had ten years ago. You can't get away from their talk about you and someone always sees you and tells someone and soon everyone knows your business. The same people live in the same houses, their children keep in touch with the neighborhood even if they move away . . . even in New York I get news of what's happening in this little part of the world from my mother.

When anthropologists talk about social knowledge they are often talking about rumors, gossip, and hearsay as discursive forms that mark the boundaries of self and the social world.

The *New York Times* man in Haiti, Howard French, wrote about a dissident in Haiti named Ferleau who was beaten by police and tried to seek asylum at the U.S. Embassy. The story ended by Ferleau saying:

> If democracy returns to my country in a month or two, perhaps I'll be fine . . . But in Haiti, what is difficult is that everyone knows everyone else, and if you are branded as a militant, eventually you will be crushed. (*The New York Times*, 2 February 1993.)

"Everyone knows everyone else," and this can be used against anyone. Of course, among certain classes, so small, everyone knows everyone else. Is it through the visual field of the culture of terror that the very networks between people become a figure of domination itself? Being named as a subversive means being *seen* around, being *spotted*, being located, being *known*. Ferleau describes a situation where there is a feeling among people that people know each other's business. The very networks so vital for support become utilized by those in power as ways of tracking people down. The very networks and daily routines necessary to sustain one's self become the object of dread, because along any nodal point the state can be *looking*. And that eye will tell someone who will tell someone until ultimately it reaches the ears of power. "Knowing," as Ferleau uses it, is a practice of seeing and power and crucially, revealing. Knowing reveals someone to the state: It is a reflexive function of the culture of terror. People are "known by their positions" as Steve said, or "branded," as Ferleau says, and in normal times this poses problems for people, but it has even more far-reaching consequences in a culture of terror. For at the juncture of the gossip about people, the "public sphere of private life," those who oppose the power of the military or the paramilitary-like forces that prop up de facto regimes, can be used against them. It also means that people will talk about you, *teledjòl* (grape-vine) about who you are or what you have done. Ferleau spells it out in terms of "know-ing," but the implication is that you can be turned in, informed upon. Somewhere, some-one must be connected to an attaché, a Makout or the military. The danger of being spotted is a real and present danger today for many supporters of democracy. The gaze of power becomes instituted within the very spaces one occupies.

If, as Ferleau says, "everyone knows everyone else," this becomes a danger because people can inform on others for a favor, a pittance, or perhaps just to get in good with the local military. In such a situation, acquaintances can easily turn into liabilities. This is the danger of such times when everything is difficult and life itself is hard to come by; any-one may decide to see what a piece of information may get them. I carried on fieldwork in Haiti both before the coup d'état of 1991, and after, and the change in people's atti-tudes was noticeable and understandable. After the coup, people did not establish casual relationships with strangers. People may move from living in the Public Eye of power to becoming that eye—they may move from a position of being seen to being a seer, by turning someone in, lying about someone. Underneath the statement that "everyone knows everyone else," there is the fear of the terrifying possibility that anyone at all can become the eyes (mouths and ears) of power.

> A few weeks after the coup . . . a man came around and asked for the fellow who painted the cock. I was standing right around the corner at the time and my neighbor told him that the fellow he was looking for was out of town. "Too bad," he said, "because if he was here I would kill him with the six bullets in this gun," and he pointed to the gun in his holster. Then he said, "Tonight someone will come and paint over this," and he pointed to the cock. And when two fellows came to paint over it they made all kinds of noise to let everyone know what they were doing.
>
> The next morning there was an ugly brown spot painted over the cock.
>
> All this time I have been scared. I left my street and stayed at friends' around Port-au-Prince. I went home once in a while. But I always kept thinking, if they really wanted to kill me, they could have found me.

The necessary corollary to sight is site: seeing must have a field of vision from which to see. Nothing can be seen without a background and a foreground. Spatial constraints on seeing means that the city becomes a grid in de Certeau's sense of vision and of "shadows." To some extent all spatial routes are grids of power where paths are overde-termined and certain routes charged with narrative meaning. Secret paths can save one time—short-cuts through yards, short-cuts through buildings. In Haiti this "routing" in-volves the imposition of political violence where routes and places inspire the dread and fear, where narratives about people missing and people found infiltrate the streets. Secret paths, safe houses, asylums, anything. These make up the deterritorialized landscape in which one must develop tactics of survival.

In Port-au-Prince walking itself entails risks. Jean-Pierre has a number of places he won't walk. Another friend, Charles, also has places within the rhizome of Port-au-Prince where he will not venture. They have different grids reflecting different concerns, spatial insertions, and political identities. For Jean-Pierre, not up Rue Casserne, never past the Palace guards, go far around the Palace, and never get caught walking anywhere in *cité* Soleil without a definite reason and many friends around you. Walking down the street of the national prison (*Rue Internment*) is permitted during the night when people are out, but not in the day. Never past the house of a known Makout or attaché.

These decisions are perhaps only at first conscious—it is in walking around Port-au-Prince that one senses the feel of the city, of danger zones and places of relief. The city becomes a maze, a series of feelings, tactile swatches of possibilities and dangers. Even loitering in Port-au-Prince is not always safe. Every zone has its Makout and others who watch over these places—especially where there are outdoor markets set up. Just as public discourse was forced into the back alleys of rumor, so too people were often forced to walk the back roads, or to stay at home much of the time, and not to go out at night past a certain time.

The Public Eye in Haiti is the memory of political violence.[1] The Public Eye is an allegorical reference to seeing and remembering. In Haiti it was the moral messianic movement of Lavalas that kept the names of the dead and their memories alive. Aristide's picture was painted on walls throughout Port-au-Prince, as well as pictures of cocks—these were the specular images of the Public Eye in Haiti. The Public Eye is the memory of the dead killed by the military and the Makout. In the stories and rumors of the killings, memories were ignited and fanned.

The absence of anonymity in Haiti is the cultural basis for both the structure of the visual field of power and the Public Eye. As I mentioned, before Aristide's rise to power there was the dechoukaj. Both in Port-au-Prince and in the countryside I heard tales of Duvalierists being chased out and even killed by angry people seeking justice. Many Haitians suffered under the hands of the military and paramilitary forces for years, but they didn't forget who brutalized them. A group called Pa Blye, "Don't Forget," was active in Port-au-Prince after Jean-Claude Duvalier (Baby Doc) was chased out of the country. I interviewed key members of this group before the coup d'état and the group's dissolution. People had kept accounts and revenge in their heads for many years. Some big Makout carried around with them reputations for brutality and violence and these reputations were sometimes their downfall after Duvalier fled the country.

Charles worked hard to get Aristide elected president. He spent many nights explaining Haitian society and culture to me. He worked with community groups in his old neighborhood and organized a medical clinic there. Because of his training in economics and his ability to speak Kreyol, French, and English fluently, he obtained a good job working as a clerk in an agency of the government. After the coup d'état of 1991, he was fired from his job and arrested. After his release, he maintained a low profile and I saw him only once in a great while. Sometimes he complained about the difficulty of keeping out of sight:

> People here know each other's business. I hate to take the bus down here
> . . . someone might see me.

---

1. Most helpful in developing this notion of the Public Eye have been the works of Carlo Sini (1993), Georges Bataille (1987), Michel Foucault (1977), Elias Canetti (1984), and Miguel Angel Austrias (1985). In certain parts of Spain I have been told that the police wear hoods over their faces so as not to be recognized by the Public Eye.

Not only was he afraid because of his work in Lavalas, but after Aristide's victory in the presidential election, he was involved in chasing a Makout out of his old neighborhood. After the coup of 1991, that same Makout returned to the neighborhood to settle the score. Charles knew he was on that Makout's list of enemies.

> I should get a gun and shoot him. Instead, I'll wait till the day that everyone burns him.

Charles once met Jean-Pierre in my room in Port-au-Prince and became obviously nervous. It turned out later that he was afraid to speak around Jean-Pierre because he said that young guys like Jean-Pierre, guys with no future and no political conviction, are dangerous because they become the eyes and ears of the military, the police, or the paramilitary groups such as the Makout. The same fear that gripped Jean-Pierre because of his cock on the wall haunted Charles, a committed activist, but no less subjected to the visual field of power. I was in the strange position of having to defend Jean-Pierre without being able to tell Charles about Jean-Pierre's problems with the Makout, because he asked me not to talk to him about it.

> A few days after Aristide returned . . . to Haiti some people wanted me to paint another cock, in the same place. I said, 'No! God saved me once before.' This time they offered me twenty dollars, but I couldn't spend the money if I was dead, could I?

In Bataille's essay "Eye" (first published in *Documents* 4, 1929), we are informed that shortly before his death the illustrator Grandville had a nightmare of the gigantic eye which flies through the air and chases down a criminal. Bataille explicitly linked this eye to the police and to the expectation of torture: all are bound by the horror and seduction of violence—the seduction of horror. The eye that initially chases down the criminal is the eye that rises out of the unprovoked murder of the victim. This eye is the eye of justice, the imaginary eye of justice that pursues the criminal unto death. Bataille explicitly linked this eye with the expectation of violence. Bataille was interested in the contradiction between the desire for repugnance, for horror. It almost appears that Bataille naturalizes this scopic drive, yet his later essays (especially "The psychological structure of Fascism"), he explicitly links psychology and politics. I have noted in my own way here the clash between the field of visuality of power and the Public Eye to see, to know, and to remember enemies.

The field of visuality of power that will spot Ferleau and track him down is linked to the Public Eye that pursues the Makout, and the Duvalierists, and once in a great while, kills them. From the fall of Jean-Claude Duvalier until the 1991 coup d'état, the Makout were subjected to the magical form of punishment: *Pere Brun*—being burned alive by putting a tire over the victim's head and setting it ablaze. In 1992, Charles told me, in a defiant tone, confirming the existence of the Public Eye,

> We know every Makout in this city. We even knew which church Cedras [General Cedras—Leader of the Haitian Military] was going to a few weeks ago.

Jean-Pierre later told me:

> Now, I want to learn English and . . . leave Haiti. I don't know when, but

there is no life for me here. Aristide has been back and nothing has changed for me. I am studying English for the day I can leave Haiti. I don't want someone to come around looking for me to kill me because I painted a cock on the wall. That is Haiti. It's not for me. Things change here so fast that the president today might be lying dead in the street tomorrow. What chance does someone like me have, someone who is so poor?

I saw Jean-Pierre when the U.S. soldiers were newly stationed around Port-au-Prince, and he was happy to see the Haitian military out of power, but the fear of those days had not left him, and he doubted that he would actively get involved in politics. He was content to work on his art and his English, and find a way to leave the country for the United States.

[Thanks to Steve Coupeau, Kate Stewart, and Donna Plotkin for their insights into and criticisms of the ideas discussed here. Special thanks to Sean Harvey.]

References

Asturias, Miguel Angel. (1985). *El Senor Presidente*, Translated by Frances Partridge. New York: Antheneum.

Battaille, Georges. (1987). *Visions of Excess: Selected Writings, 1927–1939*, edited with an introduction by Alan Stoekl. Translated from the French by Allan Stoekl, Carl R. Lovitt, and Donald M. Leslie, Jr. Minneapolis: University of Minnesota Press.

Canetti, Elias. (1984). *Crowds and Power*, Translated by Carol Stewart. New York: Farrar Straus Giroux.

de Certeau, Michel. (1984). *The Practice of Everyday Life*. Translated by Steve Rendall. Berkeley: University of California Press.

Deleuze, Gilles. (1988). *Foucault*. Translated and edited by Sean Hand. Minneapolis: University of Minnesota Press.

Foucault, Michel. (1977). *Discipline and Punish: The Birth of the Prison*. Translated by Alan Sheridan. London: Allen Lane.

The Haiti Commission for Inquiry into the September 30th Coup; Ramsey Clark et al. (1991).

Lageuerre, Michel. (1993). *The Military and Society in Haiti*. Knoxville: University of Tennessee Press.

The New York Times, 2 February 1993.

Perice, Glen A. (1994). *Rumors and Politics in Haiti*. Ph. D. dissertation in anthropology. University of Texas, Austin.

Sini, Carlo. (1993). *Images of Truth: From Sign to Symbol* (Contemporary Studies in Philosophy and the Human Sciences), translated by Massimo Verdicchio. Atlantic Highlands, N.J.: Humanities Press.

Chapter XXV

Violence as Culture: "Educating" Political Prisoners in Romania

Gila Safran Naveh

Politics, History, and Ethnohistory

This essay examines accounts by former Romanian political prisoners incarcerated in the notorious Piteshti penitentiary for opposing Ceaushescu's communist regime. These victims were subjected systematically to harsh physical and psychological torture aimed at re-shaping their mind and, ultimately, transforming them into torturers devoted body and soul to Ceaushescu's culture of terror.

I show that the accounts of former political prisoners evidences a network of cultural processes, expressed in complex cultural codes, which processes permit a better understanding of how systematically exerted violence can be shaped and codified to become culturally acceptable and then appropriated culturally as "education." The dynamic model of systematic torture used in mind control reveals that ideologies are constituted as cultural sequences of acts, manipulations, seductions, torture, inquests, "mise en scene"—used to destroy the prisoners' previous interpersonal, collective, and familial networks. Finally, I point to the relations of reciprocity between acts of violence and changes in effects that in turn validate the assumption that culturally orchestrated violence can transform any recalcitrant individual into a loyal one. I conclude by showing that this study of the "re-education" of political prisoners in Romania by their inmates and a better understanding of their methods of mind control, may help us begin to formulate a semiotics of cultural violence.

Following the dismantling of Ceaushescu's communist regime, many abused individuals began to seek help to reenter the mainstream Romanian culture. Specifically, former political prisoners of Ceaushescu attempted to achieve some psychic integration, in order be capable to function in the new, post-communist era. In an effort to further our understanding of the long-term effects of traumatic stress and mind control, The Cincinnati Psychoanalytic Institute has initiated a cooperative study (the Psycho-Social and Medical Research Association, PSAMRA, project) that includes therapists from former communist countries.

My own contribution is the close study of reports presented by Romanian therapists, who, like the former political prisoners whom they are currently treating, have lived for a long time under harsh totalitarian rules and have also been culturally imbued with misinformation and fear, as well as with a sense of mistrust of authorities. My approach is guided by the understanding that experience can be represented through a narrative; namely, the interaction between therapists and patients, which commonly takes place in the highly semiotic and ritualized environment of the therapy session, aims to produce a coherent narrative with which the patients can identify (Kohut 1977: 122). To the mental workers, this narrative is a sign that the patients have achieved at least a limited psychic integration, and that they will use this narrative to free themselves from the tyranny of their past incoherence (Freud 1933: 123-4; Peterfreund 1971: 224-45). When the therapeutic event is successful, the narrative, generated over time via a network of complex discursive paths, will function *as* the "patients' experience in prison" and help him/her achieve a desired psychic integration in the present (Vygotsky 1962: 213–53). Interpreting the narratives as circulations of signs permits the further claim that to understand communist cultural hyper-codes, such as "re-education"—a pivotal part in mind control—we need to focus not only on the former prisoners' accounts of their prison experience but consider carefully the native therapist's own story which, by its peculiar slant, reveals the pervasiveness of mind control.

Chronology of Cultural Events and Cultural Shifts

August 23, 1944   Soviet conquest of Romania.

June 1953   Soviet army withdrawal from Romania; Ceaushescu's totalitarianism.

1959   Trial/execution/re-incarceration of Piteshti prisoners.

1961/62   Freeing of former Piteshti prisoners.

1989   Trial and execution of Ceaushescu.

1991/92   Former Piteshti prisoners seek help/psychotherapy by local clinicians; Psychotherapists treat ill subjects/torturers; Psychotherapists identify with torturers; Romanian psychotherapists seek help from researchers.

Young student political inmates in the Piteshti penitentiary were customarily incarcerated and submitted to harsh physical and psychological torture. The treatment of prisoners was so brutal there that it frequently resulted in the death of the tortured inmates. My present work deals specifically with the singularly damaging counter-transferential tendencies surfacing in the treatment of post-traumatic stress patients in Romania, where, presumably, a new culture is being shaped out of the relics of the old one. In this study I focus solely on narratives of the Romanian victims and analyze their narrative production in interviews with the therapist over a period of at least one year. The material is made up largely of notes that have not been previously published; the translations from Romanian are mine.

One of the salient features of my interaction with Romanian mental health workers is the realization that, like the former prisoners, the health/mental workers are still living in relative isolation from the free world, and have been culturally exposed to communism over a period of more than forty years. Moreover, access to Western psychoanalytic know-how and Western psychiatric texts has been and continues to be very difficult. In fact, as reported by Romanian therapists, psychoanalysis and self-psychology are treated with contempt. As a result, the Romanian therapists' collaboration with this project seemed uniquely fortuitous.

Torture and Transference

After Ceashescu's fall from power in Romania and his prompt execution, the surviving inmates of Piteshti prison became increasingly willing to speak up and eventually dared to seek help from the local therapists. Even though the entire apparatus of Ceaushescu's regime seems to be intact in Romania, individuals formerly tortured during communism experience a sense of urgency to regain a healthier sense of self and to acquire some psychological balance by recounting their traumatic experiences during their incarceration in Ceaushescu's communist prisons.

To illuminate the peculiarly strong process of counter-transference in therapists from Romania, which signals a very intense cultural indoctrination in therapists as well, I have concentrated on the codification and the narrativization of the highly stylized methods of mind control in these prisons. Commonly, brainwashing began with intimidation, provocation, and temptation, and ended in the total seduction of the prisoner, and, as result, his acculturation in a culture of terror.

This peculiar seduction via torture aimed to destroy the prisoners' previous interpersonal, collective, and familial networks, shatter completely their previous cultural network. Specifically, communist cultural seduction endeavored to create a *tabula rasa* into which to pour its own ideology. This seduction appears to have been extended to the entire population.

In juxtaposing two accounts I compiled—the narrative of the mental health worker, during the workshop, and that of the patient, generated in the space-time of therapeutic sessions in the office of the therapist—I was able to discern singularly damaging countertransferential tendencies which surfaced in the narratives of the native therapist. These peculiar counter-transferential inclinations and a hyper-identification, usually encountered in situations of high experiential affinity—such as that of Holocaust survivors, patients, and therapists, for example—alert us to the possibility of serious problems in the treatment of post-traumatic stress patients in Eastern Europe by their local mental health workers. The incapability of the therapists to detect and subsequently properly integrate their high level of counter-transference, and their peculiar identification with communist hyper-codes, signal a pathology surfacing frequently in the Romanian therapists' self assessments. This pattern suggests a dangerously close identification between therapist and patient in post-communism, an enmeshing which can prove highly damaging in the analytic process and further, to the cultural integration of the former "brainwashed" citizens.

On a larger scale, by intersecting the narrative path of the therapist with that of the former prisoner, and by systematically illuminating the obscured distortions occurring in therapeutic situations in the aftermath of totalitarianism (see Lifton 1961: 122–135), we may come to understand how to nurture the fragile relationship between patient and therapist operating in cultures that have internalized acculturation methods similar to those used in communist regimes. The delicate patient-therapist relationship—commonly threatened by the usual memory loss of the patient, any resistance, and a sense of shame—seems endangered in cultures of terror. The relationship's fragility is exacerbated by strong undercurrents of a culturally promoted hostility towards "transgressors" and "traitors," as well as by the customary lack of mutual trust, instilled in its citizens, in former communist countries.

In investigating the two narrative paths, we also unveil the circulation of communist cultural hyper-codes, such as "internal unmasking," "external unmasking," "rehabilitation," and "re-education," and, as a result, we understand better the processes which have governed cultural codification in communist Eastern Europe. This new knowledge empowers us to lend a more knowledgeable hand to the treatment of all those traumatized in the process; namely, it compels us to include the therapists who, quite clearly, were also victims of communist cultural indoctrination.

Methodological Approach

The initial workshop was sponsored by the International Society for Traumatic Stress Studies, The Dutch Victims Association, and the Berlin Medical Psychological and Social Association. At the beginning, our group highlighted the psycho-historical events brought on by the rule of communist totalitarian regimes and focused especially on those circumstances which seem to have shaped both the current historical circumstances and the internal psychological world of the patients these clinicians from Eastern European countries are currently treating.

Prior to the workshop, we familiarized ourselves with the history of the respective countries and the specific ways in which totalitarian governments were the source of human trauma. Hence we summarized the historical events of late 1980s and early 1990s preceding the treatment experience of which the former prisoners were part. We also attended to the clinical setting or consultation context in which the therapeutic encounter occurred (i.e., within a developing post-totalitarian clinic, as consultation to informal self-help groups, as part of a research project, or other manner).

During the workshop we focused on the members' personal odyssey since the collapse of the iron curtain. I directed my attention specifically to three particular elements: the unique clinical setting in which Eastern European clinicians have to work relative to the types of problems they encounter, the transference and the counter-transference surfacing during the workshop, and a detailed presentation of at least one case.

The "biological" dictatorship—as the Romanian clinicians call it—has lasted for forty years. Most doctors have no knowledge of psychotherapy and show no interest in it. The staff and the nurses in Romania have a condescending attitude toward psychotherapy as well.

The Association of Former Political Prisoners is located now in Bucharest, where an informal self-help group attempts to generate open discussions. Dr. Cucliciu's and Dr. Manoliu's first attempts to contact them met with intense resistance. Contact with former prisoners of Piteshti was made shortly after they asked for guidelines from our team in Cincinnati.

Patterns in Case Histories

Piteshti is a town near Bucharest where a special penitentiary regime had been set up in 1949. Piteshti prison was reserved for students who belonged to the strongest anti-communist opposition organizations. They all were then about twenty-two to twenty-three years of age. The first patient, Mr. A. seems very friendly and is a shy old man. He began telling that before Piteshti he had very strong morals. The second, also a shy, tired-looking person, is called here Mr. B.

From the texts of the patients and the therapists' accounts, one learns that during the first years of communist regime, when panic was at its height, this prison was used to transform political prisoners into torturers by means of brutal torture and thought control. While in other Romanian prisons the tortured inmates would come out alive and had a fair chance to recover after their experience in the penitentiary, in the Piteshti prison the outcome was very different. The prisoners underwent a process of so called cultural "re-education" and "rehabilitation" and were transformed, by means of brutal torture, into equally ruthless torturers. These culturally construed torturers were expected then to defend a culture of torture and mind control.

Upon their arrival, the prisoners were told to remain in the same position for extremely lengthy periods of time. The only exception was when going to the lavatory. They were not allowed to move even in their sleep. This came to be known as the "position torture."

Torture was both collective and individual. The inmates were submitted first to what was called external unmasking and afterwards to internal unmasking, which was the most difficult. What was called external unmasking began early during the incarceration. Without any preparation at all, small groups of prisoners would be put in a special, large, isolated room where another group was waiting for them. Before long, the latter would suddenly attack and beat the first group with cudgels and belts that had been previously hidden. When all the newcomers would lie on the floor overcome by the torturers, the first group's leader, also called *tzurcanu* (a nickname for the man with the greatest authority and who was wearing a sheepskin cap and overcoat) would make a speech which was invariably formulated as follows: "You are nothing but garbage, bandits, dirty plotters against the glorious working class and the USSR." (We found out that all the former inmates knew the long tirade by heart). Next, he proceeded to establish the prison's rules. The former prisoners claim that there were rules for practically everything. Each prisoner had to sit at the end of his common bed, his hands in his pockets, and look only at the floor at his feet. Even the slightest movement of the eyes, if noticed by the torturers, could result in a brutal beating. Customarily, at least one collective beating took place each day.

The food was distributed by tzurcanu, the chief torturer, and the prisoners were obliged to put their dishes on the floor and eat without using their hands, like a dog. The torturers were frequently pushing the face of the prisoner into the hot soup with their feet while he was attempting to eat. Each prisoner could use the lavatory only once a day, for a few moments only. He would be pulled out after a short while whether he had defecated or not.

Many other humiliating techniques were used there. Each prisoner was regularly beaten and throttled to the point of near death without any explanation being offered. Friends were asked to slap each other. During the night, they could be beaten if they moved while sleeping. At a certain point, they were even forced to eat their own excrement.

After several weeks, even months, of humiliating and cruel treatment, they were asked to put down in writing everything they knew about their "criminal activities." If one attempted to conceal anything, he ran the risk of having another prisoner from the same organization speak up and offer details. The "insincere bandits," as they were called, were beaten severely as part of the external unmasking. Many died during this period because of the torture they were subjected to. The torturers were never reprimanded by the "higher" authorities. Some prisoners were thinking of suicide, but committing suicide was impossible there. The staff of the prison never got involved directly in the process of re-education. The chief torturers were political prisoners themselves.

The following stage in the process of cultural re-education and transformation into a torturer was designated by the name of internal unmasking. The prisoners were put in rooms with other teams of torturers with another leader who would announce the beginning of the "cleansing process." He would repeatedly say, "You are all rotten from tip to toe. All this rottenness must be purified away, or else the working class will crush you" (A said). At a certain point, the prisoners were convinced that similar processes were taking place in all prisons all over the country and a general state of hopelessness would take hold of them. If as Eco claims (1986: 130–132), "reality is the voice that sometimes says 'No,'" in Piteshti, this voice was silenced. The prisoners had no reality testing. In listening to other members' confessions, the former prisoners claim that they began believing that those absurd confessions may actually be true. According to those interviewed, the prisoners were uprooted and taken from reality to another dimension of living in the world.

Soon, they were being asked to speak about their family, education, moral and religious values, and such. They had to "confess" that their father was a rogue, that their mother was a whore and an adulteress and had sex with animals, that studying philosophy or going to church was a foul crime against the interests of the working class, and on and on.

When telling their stories, the prisoners were asked to give the most minute details. If the unmasking seemed incomplete, the prisoners were beaten to near death. The same happened if a prisoner was perceived to be misleading. If, for example, in despair, a prisoner who wished to show his "cooperativeness" with the authorities related how he had intercourse with all the animals on his parents' farm and could not explain how he did it exactly, he was accused of trying to fool the re-education committee.

At a later stage, the prisoners were asked to tell their dreams. When they said that they did not dream, they were beaten, and were told that it was impossible not to have dreams. If they told that they dreamt about an "offensive" practice or desire (such as going to a church, or being a bourgeois prime minister and putting all the communists into jail), they were beaten severely as well. If they said that they dreamt of the sun representing the final victory of the working class they were beaten because they were "caught trying to cheat the re-educators."

In this fashion, the prisoners were put in a continuous double bind and punished without ever being told the rules of re-education, nor the conditions of absolution from punishment. This unrelenting assault on the self was meant to break it down completely and reshape it according to a new ideology, a method of thought reform that does not allow for personal freedom or compromise.

The accounts offered by former prisoners indicate that no one, or almost no one, could resist. The denunciation of the father, the mother, and religion seem the coronation of the process. At a certain point during torture, the tortured individuals were asked whether they would be willing to become torturers. They would have to agree wholeheartedly and tell how they "wished" to become "re-educators." At this point, they were told that their words are not enough, and that their words had to be backed up by their deeds.

The chief torturer, tzurcanu, and the other torturers were hoping for big rewards from the communist government. However, in 1952, when the Russian troops withdrew from the Romanian territory, they were brought to Bucharest and a mock trial took place.

Twenty or more leading re-educators were brought to trial and condemned to death on the spot. All prisoners were charged with plotting against the communist State. Those re-educated in Piteshti were also put to trial and accused of belonging to an anti-communist plot. Between 1952 and 1954 they were sent to another prison and underwent two more years of torture to confess that they were anti-communist fascists who organized the terror in Romanian prisons in order to compromise the communist regime, and that they were being helped by fascist organizations in the West. A small number was condemned to imprisonment for life.

In 1964, all the survivors were set free.

Selected Observations by Dr. Cucliciu

The therapeutic relationship is difficult apparently because of the personal experience, independent of the intellectual and moral quality, of the patient. The main problem Dr. Cucliciu seems to have encountered is related to transference, counter-transference, and projection. During the interviews it was very difficult for both the patient and the physician to tear themselves away from the totalitarian experience. Totalitarianism permeated all human relationships, and mental workers are likely to see it in the complaints, assertions, and accounts of their patients. In Romanian society, totalitarianism survives in society and in mind, and it causes a great deal of social and individual suffering.

A serious scission seems to have occurred in Romanian society that appears to be torn into two. Each faction is overtly blaming the other: those who plead for a radical change are looked upon with suspicion by the "mob" ("why disturb the status quo?"). The mob is looked upon with contempt by the first group. According to Cucliciu, the totalitarian regime's indifference to therapy stems from the belief that the mob is insignificant and its opinion unimportant, therefore, it saw no need to bother with its mental health (1994).

In Cucliciu's opinion—and his claims sparked my interest in the therapist's own account which is very revealing about the processes of codifying and thought control at work in Romania—the clinician must believe that the people play a part in history. The belief that the people's opinion does not count is a false belief, which cannot serve as a proper ground for the therapeutic relationship (still very much in tone with communist slogans).

The courageous steps taken by some therapists derive from a belief that "mob" resides in anyone and inside the clinician as well. If the health worker himself has not attained a sense of stability, he is probably tempted to secure his own position by projecting onto the patients the deficiencies he disowns and by nurturing a secret wish to see them punished. The person who was never interested in social action, who was never a public activist, can hardly become a good therapist in the post-totalitarian world. Cucliciu mentioned that he was very active politically between 1989 and 1990. He admitted that could not separate his political experience from the psychiatric one. They complete each other.

The mental worker claimed that the Piteshti phenomenon could be considered a paradigm for a totalitarian experience. He further said that for him too it was only a potential experience. Yet the nagging question remained, "How would he have reacted under similar circumstances?" He stated that in similar circumstances he might have resisted, because "he felt" and "he understood." He said that this brought him to an impasse about his capacity to understand properly Mr. B.'s experience.

He initiated a special discussion of the central question about becoming a torturer, the patient's avoidance, the mental worker's avoidance, and understanding.

The total torture, the total father, and the total authority—the Molotov complex (provisional name given by the mental worker)—was the continuous symbolic murder of the real father and the destruction of previous values.

The mental worker claimed that a torturer may become an ideal father, a "complete father," who gives everything, controls everything, even the movement of the eyes, the eating of the food, and the sleep; he takes away and gives ideas, memories, and dreams. Each real father gives something and each son seems unsatisfied, at least in his unconscious. Similarly, there is a later ambivalence toward every authority figure, every moral value. Giving something is giving little. Taking everything away is an absolute gift. A total torturer becomes a total father (regression).

This total father, further claimed the health worker, after taking away the faith, plays God. "If someone tried to look at him, the punishment is even harsher," said Mr. B. Tzurcanu was saying repeatedly: "Don't think you will be killed, but you will die when I want you to die."

One night Mr. B was taken aside by the chief torturer. He couldn't forget this episode and thought of it as a unique opportunity. He said to the chief torturer that he is far too much a coward to die. Upon returning to the room, in the "unmasking posture," after having spoken directly to the chief torturer, he felt very close to the torturer, a fearful God-father. At a certain point, the prisoner enters the world seemingly free from contradiction offered by the torturer-father figure. But his former values are not entirely lost, and he had to fight a losing and desperate battle anew. This inner struggle continued, as he had to hit his former friends or fellows in order to show that he got rid of his former values. Regular jailers could not be that innovative—they didn't need to be.

Even in a case when the prisoner could not be transformed, he would nurture a hidden admiration for the torturer, and would not be able to rid himself of guilt.

Of significance is also the behavior of the former prisoner after being freed. Some remained strong collaborators of the political police, others tried to reintegrate their self. Even after forty years they did not resolve their dilemma. The therapist tentatively referred to this as to the "Molotov complex" (Molotov, the son of a noble family, became much like these former prisoners)—sort of symbolic murder of the father and a frenetic destruction of all value attached to him.

Attempts to weaken the prisoners' resistance have been made in other prisons as well, but they were much less violent by comparison with the Piteshti experiment. The point is that the entire population living under such totalitarian pressure is going through an analogous experience, but to a lesser degree.

On the whole, only very few former inmates became partisans of the communist regimes. The others remained secretly attached to totalitarianism, only because they have lived through it for so long. Totalitarianism reached the elite as well. The background upon which a totalitarian regime is imposed is universal; only the experience itself is particular.

Integration of Points Brought Up during Sessions

As related above, the victims mention and health workers reflect on:

(1) Images and feelings about torturers and chief torturer: anger and contempt together with love and admiration.

(2) Life, death, and suicide: the previous idea of heroic and "momentary" death, and then repeatedly living through the real point of death; repeatedly wishing to die in a certain moment of the torture, and then wanting to survive it at any price.

(3) Family and sex: instincts and fantasies replacing real life events (very difficult to express or avoided; analogous difficulties for the therapist).

(4) Religious, moral, and political values; deliberate submission to the "new values," feigning enthusiasm; then moments of real frenzy; the way back.

(5) Images of and feelings about friends or fellows who are submitted to the same process, at the same time.

(6) Dreams.

The therapist complained he could not listen quietly to the patient's account because that account was too close to the therapist's own feelings. He felt that this is the reason why he had also thought of a play in which the tzurcan was playing the main role and was trying to demonstrate to them that they all resembled him. At the end he would say, "Do not hide it, confess you all love me." He said that perhaps the tzurcan on stage was himself. All this could have been to make the feelings more bearable by sharing them with an imaginary audience.

The therapist felt he was really "in Mr. B's shoes" and felt suddenly relieved. But later, when his repeated account was getting to this point, namely to the transformation into a torturer, the therapist confessed that he was feeling upset and secretly wanted him to stop short of telling this part of his story.

The patient declared that he certainly could not have resisted. He would have become a torturer, but he felt lucky because he had came to the Piteshti prison with the last series of prisoners.

In these transformational events, torturers re-educated and the re-educated tortured. Travel is a transfer from one state of mind to another. Hence, education is a travel/transfer; torture is an education/travel. Symptoms (consequences) of torture are diseases, and diseases are addressed by torture. This Romanian institution illustrates how violence can feed on itself, and rather than be depleted, will instead be amplified—perhaps across generations as well as through the life-history of the victims.

References

Cucliciu, Ion. (1994). *Presentations and Panel Discussions*. PSAMRA Workshops, 8–12 October 1994.

Eco, Umberto. (1986). *Travels in Hyper-reality: Essays*. Translated from the Italian by William Weaver. San Diego: Harcourt Brace Jovanovich.

Freud, Sigmund. (1933). *Neue Folge der Vorlesungen zur Einfürhung in die Psychoanalyse.* Leipzig and Vienna: Deuticke. Translated from the German by James Strachey as *The New Introductory Lectures on Psychoanalysis,* pp. 112–135.

Kohut, Heinz. (1977). *The Restoration of the Self.* Madison: International Universities Press.

Lifton, Robert Jay. (1961). *Thought Reform and The Psychology of Totalism: A Study of 'Brain Washing' in China,* New York: Norton Publishers.

Manea, Ion. (1994). *The Cincinnati Psychoanalytic Institute, The PSARMA Workshop,* 8–12 October 1994.

Peterfreund, Emanuel. (1971). *Information, Systems, and Psychoanalysis. Psychological Issues* 25/26, New York: International Universities Press.

Vygotsky, Lev Semenovich. (1962). *Thought and Language,* translated by E. Hanfman and G. Vaka. Cambridge: The M.I.T. Press.

Chapter XXVI

The Moral Cycle of Egotistic and Altruistic Violence: A Century of Bloodshed in Colombia

Mario Fandino

The Puzzle of Historic Violence in Colombia

The last 150 years of Colombian history reveal the tragedy of virtually permanent and widespread bloodshed, commonly referred to as *la violencia*. Sometimes gravitating around political or organized crime lines, and sometimes being just anarchistic, this violence surpasses in its recurrence and multifaceted nature the violence experienced in most if not all other national states of the modern era. This paper deals with such phenomenon in terms of patterns and concepts derived from several sources in social theory.

To give an exact definition of the object of analysis now is a rather elusive task; a simple empirical characterization of it, in terms of certain kinds of crimes or victims, or modes of action, runs counter the specific concern of our analysis which involves the transformation of social "behaviors" (observed isolated violence acts with no imputable macro-purposes) into "social agency" kinds of violence. For this reason the objects of analysis are constructed and specified along with the development of the argument, rather than given at the outset.

The puzzling aspect of Colombian violencia has been essentially the lack of any plausible explanation for the exceedingly high levels, varieties, and recurrence of violent deaths and violent crime in general, especially throughout the last 100 years. This phenomenon of violence includes political and non-political kinds, and within the latter, organized and non-organized types, in great excess of what could be considered "normal" parameters of the phenomenon from comparable countries in Latin America (Comision de Estudios sobre la Violencia, 1987; Sanchez and Penaranda, 1995; Camacho and others, 1997).

Our concern here is with the pattern of recurrence of such kinds violence, which shows, for instance, that Colombian guerrillas are the oldest in Latin America, and yet, even after the collapse of Soviet Socialism, continue to threaten the Colombian political establishment with more force than ever: they control vast areas of the nation's territory, and have "infiltrated" (i.e., made their permanent presence felt by intermittent symbolic or real violence acts) practically all regions of the nation, to the point of provoking several rounds of "peace talks" with the central government, directly and through intermediaries, abroad and within Colombia itself. Yet, el bandolerismo, referring to the flourishing of violent gangs in the rural areas and small towns without structural or macro-level purposes, in some periods of time has had extremely high visibility. Such phenomenon can be compared with the case of the Northeast Brazilian Cangaceirism and perhaps with others of that kind, but its origin is generally associated in Colombia with extreme instances of the traditional political conflict between the two major political parties, the Liberal and the Conservador, and also—and perhaps more importantly—with the anarchistic residual of such extreme forms of traditional political confrontation.

This rather commonsense view has clearly something important to do with the question of la violencia. Yet, the recurrence of the phenomenon, and especially its eventual divorce from within traditional politics, sealed with "El Frente Nacional," requires a much deeper and comprehensive explanation. El Frente Nacional was that unprecedented political agreement between the two traditional parties which arranged for them to share the exercise of government for sixteen years, taking turns for the presidency, and dividing all state bureaucracy positions equally.

The Colombian case of la violencia represents then, much more than spurts of regional political protest movements such as the case of Chiapas in Mexico. The "Sendero Luminoso" movement in Peru perhaps did come to represent at some point a threat to the central government, but the overall force of such movement was much weaker; and most importantly, Sendero does not follow a century or more of continuous armed insurrection and/or anarchistic violence, as is the case in Colombia. The same basic difference in relation to the Colombian violencia appears in the case of the Central American guerrillas, especially in El Salvador and Nicaragua, the two most prominent movements in that region of the world.

There are also in recent history several examples of long-lasting, large-scale violent social conflicts in other parts of the world besides Latin America, and many have involved guerrilla warfare, including Yugoslavia, Lebanon, Vietnam and many other Asian and African conflicts. Yet, in all of these, again, in spite of the clear-cut racial, religious, or class nature of the conflicts, or some mixture of them, they were never intertwined with a comparable volume of long-lasting periods of anarchistic violence. Thus, clearly, neither religious, ethnic, nationalistic, or class conflicts, by themselves or in combination, nor the autonomy of culture, widely recognized today (Alexander and Seidman 1990), can account for the puzzling pattern of historic bloodshed in Colombia. What is different in the latter? How do any such differences account for the extremely high levels, recurrence, and mixed pattern of la violencia?

A Durkheimian View of Social Violence: A Scientifically (In)correct Approach

Durkheim's law of social gravity (Collins, 1994) is not usually seen—or applied—in conjunction with the equally important "moral agency" role imputed by Durkheim to social groupings, as adaptive and constructive mechanisms of (socio)moral life. Thus, what is frequently taken from Durkheim is the notion that little social integration through shared social norms (not necessarily reflected in the legal systems) is associated with general non-integrative behavior such as anomic suicides. Similarly, weak ties of the individual to the group in terms of specific kinds and degrees of acceptance of norms are associated with egotistic suicide. Yet, the regenerative capacity of social group morality by solidarity effects from its internal contacts and from its ritualistic intermittent "effervescence" is much less known and applied. Such regenerative capacity seems crucial for understanding the dynamics of la violencia.

This is not the place to review Durkheim's law of gravity and laws of notion for moral life. For our purposes it suffices to recall that for many reasons, either endogenous to his historical trajectory model of social morality (such as division of labor) or exogenous to it (such as the siege and fall of biblical Jericho in the Durkheimian reference) (1951), social groups can lose their moral fabric and enter a state of aggravated anomie and egotism (leading in turn to mass suicides and other forms of non-integrative behavior.) The moral reconstruction of the group can take place, and will take place, given certain "functional require-ments" (not derived from any "functionalistic" theory of society, but from a structure of logical causes and consequences, pertinent to each case). The group thus provides inter-individual contacts (and its integrative multiplying effects), effervescence rituals (and their maintaining and/or generative morality), and its moral (re)construction tendencies, all de-rived from its social-gravity and moral motion forces. Yet, the group is also subject to ran-dom and unpredictable contextual factors, which may or may not permit the operation of the moral forces it possesses, and thus may (or not) block the final and more permanent re-construction and development of its moral life. If the larger context ends up blocking off moral (re)construction at a certain point in its trajectory, then the morals of the movements dissolve in the face of their "demonstrated" (by praxis) utopism back into an original ego-tism, from where, by moral mobilization and given adequate conditions, they re-take the path of moral re-construction. This is how the moral cycle of egotistic and altruistic violence can be perpetuated, as it is argued here for the Colombian case.

Not always explicit, then, there is in Durkheim a historical trajectory model of moral life which relates, in a causal sense, relative states of social anomie (lack of group moral density), (socio)moral gravity tendencies, group moral generating and maintenance mecha-nisms (ritual, mechanical, and contractual), altruistic and egotistic character of collective consciousness, and specific observable patterns of individual behavior, such as suicide or violent crime. "Social bandits" and Hobsbawm's "primitive rebels" (1965) can be seen as illustrative instances of a critical turning point in Durkheim's implicit model. It should be indicated here that the historical trajectory model of Durkheim in *The Division of Labor* (1933) relating mechanic and organic solidarity to epochal changes in the division of labor is not the one referred to here, even although some of the genial insights from that work are consistent and make explicit some of the elements of the moral life model here utilized, es-pecially the case of the multiplicative effect of individual contacts on group solidarity.

It is never an exaggeration to emphasize that "anomie," "egotism," and "altruism" here are social or group rather than individual categories, and that the observable forms of indi-vidual behavior are taken as individual-level consequences of the former. Similarly, for the lesser-versed reader in Durkheim's moral integration theory, it should be clear that the con-notation of the word "moral" in this context is quite specific and separate from other theo-retical or commonsense meaning of the term. A lack of understanding of the specificity of the term here would lead to gross misinterpretations of the overall argument.

Some important characteristics of such a model should be pointed out here:

a) The model as such is not meant to predict specific historical patterns, due to the un-availability of endogenous forms of inclusion of external and/or contextual factors, such as cultural patterns or global forces. The model is strictly a tool that contributes to understand-ing and predicting group patterns of moral behavior. Each case then has to be analyzed in conjunction with the presence of whatever exogenous factors, and taking into account the availability of logical functional requirements. No attempt is made here to specify the pecu-liar group traits and contextual location of the groups linked to la violencia, and which would make the analysis complete, even though these would be essential elements of a wider research agenda for la violencia.

b) From "a" above it follows that specific historical groups, like some peasant, craft and small-trade groups in Colombia, exhibit particular historical patterns of moral behavior, such as the—here argued—'circular" pattern of historical violence in that country. In Colombia, as we will show, egotistic and altruistic forms of violence end up exhibiting such a circular pattern. This happens as moral (re)construction trends within those specific groups (however limited or even primitive in their content), encounter, down the line, a "structural" blocking-off obstacle in the form of the power of the state. The power of the state counteracts and dissipates the moral reconstruction (revolutionary) trends, and thus sets the moral life of the (now) atomized aggregate back into the low end of the moral cycle. At that point, due to the location of the groups within the larger socio-economic and political establishment, and in conjunction with their peculiar habitus and cultural makeup, those groups, and more importantly their morally dismantled offspring, begin their new (socio)moral ascension. In other words, with the dissolution of the originally "revolutionary" (or "for itself") group (due to its long-run impotence in the face of the political and military power of the state), its moral fabric naturally disintegrates, followed by highly anomic and egotistic forms of violence, sometimes (and earlier here) referred to as "anarchistic violence." As the group slowly begins to recompose itself by its moral gravity force, a new moral cycle re-starts, which, in turn, may or may not encounter again the same or new contextual or structural blocking-off forces.

c) The marginal groups undergoing or undertaking again their moral aggregation, however, need not remain constant (and eventually do change), subject as they are to all kinds of internally differentiating contextual pressures, producing structural rearrangements and "moral contamination," especially when the larger blocking obstacles prove insurmountable. Group-dividing ethical dilemmas may surface, like the Catholic church clergy participation in the Sandinista revolutionary state bureaucracy, or the alleged coalition of leftist guerrillas with illegal drug trade ventures. In such scenarios, moral cycles may be redesigned or interrupted as their social base (the original moral groups) changes. The demographic social base from where la violencia results has seemingly being very consistent for more than a century, disturbed only by the inter-regional and rural-urban migrations in the country.

d) The social-construction nature of moral life in Durkheim makes any given form of social behavior and social relation ethically relative to its moral context. Ethical relativism is avoided only by placing the analyst himself (herself) in a given moral context. In relation to this, all classical social theories, including Marx, are in agreement. In this sense, the socio-moral evaluation of the Colombian guerrillas derived from Durkheim's model is not in principle more or less condemning than that of the state policies or the "bourgeois" opposite groups. Yet, the moral context of our day is a point of reference that certainly makes downright condemnable the egotistical and many instances of the altruistic violence practices there encountered. Our purpose here is not to articulate any such evaluation. A long-lasting peace in any genuinely social conflict, however, depends on the realization of the moral dynamics and moral context premises of moral evaluation. This essay ultimately aims at that kind of contribution.

e) The blocking-off obstacles to group moral ascension can be external or internal. For instance, for many Latin American minds, excluded from participation in a meaningful way in the economic and political life of their nations (or in solidarity with those unable to participate), socialism constituted a alternative for the moral (re)construction of the national social bodies. Here it is timely to recall the Durkheimian view of socialism where, in spite of its "economic" content at the substantive level, it is still a moral phenomenon (and then a social fact), as it intends to submit the economic sphere to the public/normative realm of society's norms and authority, in the hands of the state, as opposed to the liberal view of leaving the economic unregulated.

Now, for some time many believed that the industrial-financial capitalism of the first world was the basic (external) obstacle separating Latin American societies from the realization of their socialist development dreams. Yet, as it turned out, internal elements of the socialist project, particularly its bureaucratic and communal property inefficiencies, "demonstrated" by the fall of the Berlin wall and the whole collapse of the second world, proved to be more convincing objections and deterrents to the socialist way of economic and moral (re)construction. Internal rather than external inconsistencies of the Soviet socialist moral project prevailed in 1989.

Yet, external factors can account as well for the historical elimination of a moral group, as in the cited case of Jericho, where it was simply a prolonged military siege that provoked the fall of that ancient city, and which triggered massive suicides in the face of the physical impossibility of continuing the practice of moral life, as they defined it, on the part of its citizens (Durkheim 1951).

In the present essay we simply make an outline of the moral (re)construction model as can be applied to la violencia, but no attempt is made to evaluate possible or likely internal inconsistencies of the guerrillas' project(s), nor to identify and evaluate "moral contaminations," frequently alleged (especially related to drug trade involvement), that the model allows for. The overall question here in focus is a highly complex one, and we intend only to outline its analytical parameters.

f) In spite of the "deterministic" inputs of the model (factors known to operate in certain ways), and of the possibilities of logical prediction in conjunction with external factors and theoretical functional requirements, certainly (and because of those), there is a key place for human agency. Yet this aspect of the question is again out of our present scope.

Anti-system and Specialized Social Movements

The phenomenon of la violencia cannot be understood outside the framework of social movements, if we work with the hypothesis that such phenomena conforms in a significant measure to the Durkheimian model outlined above, relating—at the practical level and also at the collective consciousness level—bandolerismo, mafias, and guerrilla movements. Yet la violencia cannot be understood either within the framework of the new social movements, simply because la violencia in many of its historical moments is not a social movement by any definition of it, and also because the guerrillas do not operate on the basis of solving any one specific social problem, not even poverty and inequality. The analytical ingredient needed here is the concept of "anti-system movement" (Wallerstein 1975, 1984), which derives from the Marxian notion of revolutionary movement. Here, however, we do not imply either the class notion in Marx, or the world system one in Wallerstein.

The recent history of the guerrilla warfare in Colombia can be classified as an anti-system movement, in the sense that, rather than targeting a specialized problem area, it focuses on the global political and economic system. Of course the specific elements of the proposed changes rarely, if ever, are defined. Yet, the guerrilla movements up to the present have represented an unconditional and unpredictable break with the entire system of legitimate authority relations, whether political, economic, or religious.

It is important to indicate here that the anti-system nature of the movement in question conforms to the pre-political-to-political dynamics, identified in Latin American social movements literature, especially in the 1980s (Costella 1992). The pre-political face is characterized by a lack of a holistic view of the social problematic, much in the sense of the new specialized movements. The political face, on its part, presumes the development of a systemic or holistic view, and assumes that the solution of any given problem ultimately derives from a systemic change orchestrated at the level of the overall political system. The new social movements represent, in this sense, a regression of the social agency process to the "pre-political" level, not in the sense that new social movements avoid the political struggle to promote their views and ends, but in the sense of accepting, or at least resigning themselves to, the western style of electoral/multi-party democracies around the capitalist economic system, and operating within such a context.

This notion of the transition from the pre-political to the political character of social movements is quite consistent with the Durkheimian model, even though such an affinity was never identified in that literature, which virtually always rejected any Durkheimian theoretical inputs as "positivistic" and conservative. Actually, what separates Durkheim's model from the Marxist one is the "substantialism" of the latter as compared to the rationalism of the former (Johnson et al. 1984). One subscribes to a material dialectics behind the dynamics of social consciousness, whereas the other subscribes to ideal or representational dynamics. The Marxist model has to account for an elusive mechanical determination of social consciousness from economic conditions, however lagged, in an externally determined trajectory model of social ideologies. The Durkheimian approach postulates only the internal dynamics of (social) moral density for social groups and leaves opened the actual historical paths, as we saw.

Now, the anti-system character of the movement has two important consequences for our analysis. The first is that the opposition and counter-strategies to the anti-system movements tend to be much more forceful and radical, and not amenable to compromising, compared with the reaction to, and bargaining possibilities of, specialized social movements, including those with civil disobedience strategies such as the MST (landless movement) in Brazil. This is simply because the former threatens the entire order of the social fabric, whereas the latter represents a threat only to a fraction of it. The government, as the only legitimate monopolistic holder of violence means and its armed—and not armed—forces, reacts with its maximum force against anti-system—that is, anti-government—threats.

The second consequence is the very low predictability of the continuing growth of the Colombian guerrilla movement, in the face of a rather decadent status of systemic "insurrectional" ideologies in the present state of development of global capitalism. It is in this sense that the Colombian guerrillas case is particularly striking. After the downfall of Soviet Socialism, other remaining socialist regimes in the world are generally taken to be either in a collision course, or in a peaceful transformation into electoral multi-party democracies of the western style, however slowly, even the case of China. It seems all a matter of time. How then can not only the persistence but the continuing growth of the Colombian guerrillas, socialist/communist in principle, and non-electoral in struggle strategy, be explained?

The democratic ideal and widespread recognition of everyone's place as a citizen in the global civil society was undeniably set as an irreversible trend at the turn of the twentieth century. Thus, the most recent literature on, and practice of, social movements focuses rather on the "new" ones, characterized by specialized problem issues, such as gender, race, environmental, and sexual preference issues. Even social class movements, as in the work of Eric Wright, as it subscribes to electoral democracies, sees its fighting arena significantly specialized, as can be noted already in the title of a recent publication: "Class *Counts*" (1997) (emphasis mine).

Yet, independently of how definite this "end" of history trend might be, there remain in the world many instances where the critique of the political structure and process are approached by many in a holistic manner. This is because of the presence of either openly non-democratic regimes or of fundamental flaws in the party and electoral systems. This does not mean, of course, that in any given case systemic political change has to be or is going to be approached by violent means. But it is clear that the world is still very far from having extirpated violent attempts to systemic change.

Thus, anti-system movements, or "holistic approaches to moral (re)construction" as we should call them here, are being atomized by the impact of the "new social movements" of the first world, which regard the workings of their political systems as tolerable or necessary evils, at worst. From the point of view of Colombian social violence, the cyclical historical pattern of la violencia helps explain the questions raised here.

The Socio-structural Base for Colombian Historic Violence

From what was said previously, even a moral model of historical trajectory has to start from the economic, cultural, and demographic composition and context of the groups from whence the moral gravity forces emanate. What follows is only an outline of the argument, as it relates to some relevant elements of social history, and from where the internal dynamics and external context of the groups are seen as colliding systematically.

The social-structural bases for Colombian historical violence have to be traced back to the question of the distribution of the land as the main surviving input of the economy, along with the questions of the legitimate authority and power relations derived from, and structured along, the historical path of the country, and still, along with a deeply rooted cultural dualism derived from the very historical matrix of the formation of the country.

The contemporary stage of class conflict in Colombia exhibits a gradual dislocation of the social locus of the armed insurrection to the urban centers. It can be held as a working hypothesis that urban working sectors have been highly instrumental in mobilizing and leading agricultural populations to revolutionary ideologies and praxis. The actual participation of segments of the urban areas (large and small ones) at the base levels is probably impossible to be calculated, but their input should be substantial. So it can be argued that the urbanization process of the country has, in its historical path, carried along the class differences and conflicts set in place at the time of the birth of the Spanish colony of Nueva Granada. Yet, the geographical locus of the armed insurgence itself still is, and should remain, even for strategic reasons, predominantly rural. This dislocation of the social locus of the class conflict in the nation has to be taken into account as we apply the moral construction model to the highly dynamic history of this conflict.

In terms of an outline, we can summarize each of the four formative components of la violencia as follows:

a) The Land Distribution Question.

By the middle of the nineteenth century, and in many places much before, the distribution of the land had acquired in Colombia the well-known socio-ecological dual pattern most common on the continent. On the one hand, nuclear large landholders, localized in the more fertile flat lands, work their properties through the labor of selected privileged administrators and peons from nearby subsistence agriculture areas. On the other hand, there are the peripheral small-holders, localized in the less fertile and hilly areas, living off their subsistence cultivation of plots either of their own or rented or shared-cropped with the larger land holders, and eventually working as temporary labor in the bigger farms and estates.

Some important variations to such "functional dualism" (de Janvry, 1981) were introduced and developed especially in the late nineteenth century and through the twentieth century. Highly significant was the extensively studied colonization of the Antioquia region, not exclusively but predominantly by small entrepreneurial immigrants. Equally significant was the conquest of the hot valleys in the country by modern expansive and technical agriculture (most importantly the Cauca and Magdalena river valleys) requiring technical labor. These variations, coupled with the introduction of labor legislation after the 1930s, introduced some important modifications in the traditional agricultural labor and capital relations. Yet, the fundamentals of the here called socio-ecological dual scheme continues essentially the same to the present day.

b) Cultural Dualism.

Stemming from a variety of aboriginal and African ancestors, the large majority of the Colombian lower classes conform to what D. Ribeiro called "New Peoples" (from the Portuguese *povos novos*) (1971). That is, the Cundi-Boyacense, Cauca, and other aboriginal cultures notwithstanding, the majorities in question were neither transplants from Europe, nor die-hard bastions of the aboriginal cultures. They are new breeds of culture resulting from the elimination of aboriginal cultures and massive interbreeding mostly with the lower ranks of the conquering ones. Such a cultural makeup set any moral construction project in a more open road, free from ancestral nostalgias typical of the more genuine pre-Columbian surviving populations. Thus, easy assimilation of new ideologies and technical inputs render the Colombian lower classes, made up predominantly of povos novos, more prone to constituting an economic and moral "class for itself."

The Marxist concept of class for itself is certainly different from the construct of social moral in Durkheim. However, an important affinity between the two does exist which justifies its use here, at least to the extent that both refer to the moral construction within social groups. The former can be a specific case of the latter, as it involves the construction of moral life on the bases of the opposition to an "external" enemy. Within the social context in question, however, the conservative aboriginal cultures remaining in the country could in some cases be assimilated into the foreword-looking pattern of moral reconstruction, set by their mulatto brothers. The upper classes in the country, on their part, are constituted by a substantial Spanish hidalgo-linage segment, plus a large capitalist class coming from below, where the Antioqueno segment is prominent. Such upper classes have proven to be one of the most dynamic on the continent.

The above highly polarized class distinctions—dressed (and armed) with such cultural ingredients, where both law and money are deprived of their theoretical status as instruments and measures of individual moral statures, and which distinctions became, in the eyes of large fractions of the lower classes, mere instruments of oppression—constitute the scenario where la violencia flourished.

c) The Question of Power and Authority.

Here we borrow Weber's notions of power and authority to formulate this section of our model. Recall that power involves essentially the probabilistic ability of individual or collective actors to impose their will upon others, outside of any organizational or institutional framework, whereas authority refers to the probability of a command, from a leader or individual in a position of authority, being obeyed by the subordinated group, upon which the former exercises "legitimate domination." The passage from power to legitimate domination and authority presupposes an element of voluntary compliance which, in the case of low social integration (weak overall normative consensuality or collective consciousness), may prove to be the exception rather than the norm.

In the case in question, the class relations of power (relative abilities of the social *classes* to impose their will through the central state), exhibit historically an inverting tendency: they start with a weak central state which faced a weak lower-class power, both derived from a weakly integrated national society and economy at large. Such a central state grows in its legal-organizational power, but faces similarly growing lower class discontent and organizational power. This, in turn, represents growing legitimate domination instabilities and crises. As neither one of the two sides manages to win over the other, but the upper classes do manage to maintain the power (as opposed to the authority), and to dismantle the instructional oppositions in times of a legal authority crisis, the cyclical pattern of egotistic to altruistic and back to egotistic violence emerges. This kind of pattern is outlined in the following section.

An Outline of the Cyclical Trajectories of Egotistic and Altruistic Violence in Colombian History

Before outlining the historical record corresponding to our theoretical argument, it should be indicated that the pattern of "legitimate order crisis" derived from class/culture oppositions, here presented for the case of Colombia, is different from the Habermassian model of "legitimation crisis" (1975). Although the two phenomena are related, the Habermas model is an endogenous one, that is, one where the internal structure of legitimate authority enters into recurrent crisis due to its own way to deal with change. The class/culture based conflict model here postulated for la violencia says nothing about internal structure of legitimate authority, and relates only to pressures from below, systemically marginal and thus external in themselves to the internal structure of the broader legitimate authority. As a matter of fact, the Colombian traditional authority elites have proven to be very adaptable and enduring as legitimate authority sources. One remarkable instance of such adaptability, already relevant to our argument, is the previously mentioned *frente nacional* agreement between the two traditional parties. This agreement contributed to a possible record of the country for the region, in terms of political democracy, as Colombia exhibits only one five-year dictatorship period through its overall twentieth century history.

To facilitate the exposition, figure 1 presents the historical trajectories of both altruistic and egotistic violence for approximately the last 100 years. The rather inverse relationship between the two, in conjunction with the selected historical markers represented along the time dimension, is consistent with our moral cycle view of la violencia.

Before spelling out the contents of figure 1, it is necessary to indicate

a) The figure is to be taken only as a first step in a much more complex agenda for the empirical analysis of la violencia; it is intended mainly as a heuristic device, to help visual-

ize the relationships involved in our argument, rather than as an operationalized way of veri-
fication of the hypothesis;

b)   In order to approximate the empirical dimensions of the hypothetical paths of altruistic and egotistic violence in question, presumed levels of both kinds of violence are given.
Each point in each of the curves represents the weighted number of fatal instances imputable to "informal wars" and to "other human violent acts";

c)   The trajectories in the figure are meant only as outlines, and yet hypothetical ones,
representing only "educated guesses" of the actual levels; only the *direction* of the trends
and *positive and negative locations* of the levels of the phenomena in relation to their continental means (that is, whether the trends are upward or downward and whether the levels
are above or below the mean) in both altruistic and egotistic violence, are meant to represent
specific hypotheses derived from the literature and/or from the theoretical model; future
quantitative research will perhaps be able to establish the specific paths of the violent trajectories and the overall adequacy of this model;

d)   In order to allow for comparability between the two curves, the levels are thought
of in terms of standard deviation units from the continent's averages for each point in time.
Thus the total volume of violent deaths of each kind, for each "historical marker" (see figure
1), is taken as a reference point to measure the time-specific level of each kind of violence.
The interpretation of the figure follows.

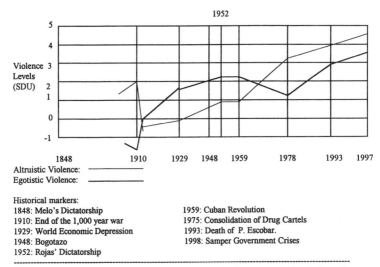

Figure 1: **Hypothetical Approximate Historical Trajectories of Altruistic and
           Egotistic Violence Levels in Colombia from 1910 through 1997. Measures
           Given in Hypothetical Standard Deviation units for Latin America.**

The altruistic-egotistic cycles in Colombia might be traced back even to the *Comuneros*
revolution in the late eighteenth century, if a certain continuity in the country's social history
is hypothesized. Yet, for our present purposes, we can take the One Thousand Year War of
the beginning of the nineteenth century as the first reference point. In a large measure, that
war represented the confrontation between large landholders and their mercenary militias on
the conservative party side, and the small farm and petty bourgeois class on the liberal one.

Of relevance here is the fact that after the end of the armed conflict, the militias from both parties were dismissed, leaving an enormous army of jobless peasants, versed in the "art" of violence. Marginalized from participation in the mainstream political and economic scenario, those groups fell into widespread violence, which, contrary to the practice in the war, had no higher social purpose, but resulted from either economic survival pressures or micro-interaction conflicts (Tellez 1987). This kind of violence corresponds to the egotistic category in Durkheim's model. Elements of anomic violence in the aftermath of the war were probably present, but their significance should be much less since, most likely, it was not primarily the lack or disappearance of social norms that triggered the violent acts, but rather the weaker ties of the ex-militias to the overall national collective consciousness. The war is here considered not a matter of conflict of norms but of social struggle and strategies. The norms continued to gravitate basically around religious values. The argument here is, then, that the most important component of the violence in question is an individualized or *personal purpose*, be it economic or affective, followed by a secondary component in terms of individual *internal distress* derived from the bankruptcy of the collective identity in the war.

The figure shows a peak of altruistic violence, and a corresponding valley for egotistical violence, at the end of the war. The latter is inferred simply from the theoretical inverse relationship between the two phenomena. That is, altruistic development in the group tends to cause a decrease in egotism. After the war, there can be clearly inferred drastic changes in direction of the two trajectories. Altruistic violence should fall somewhere below the continental mean and then begin a very slow recovery.

But recovery toward what? The answer to this question lies in a change in the organizational locus of altruistic violence, which should begin taking place somewhere in the first quarter of the twentieth century, from a liberal party affiliation to a far-left autonomous anti-system one, ending in the consolidation of Marxist communist and socialist ideologies and corresponding collective actors by the middle of the twentieth century. On the part of the egotistic violence trajectory, the expected low levels during the war (as most violence is absorbed by altruistically organized ends) begin to grow higher very rapidly, triggered by persistently poor, or perhaps worsening, economic and overall social conditions and symbolic capital. Colombian modern bandolerismo was born. The egotistic trajectory should exhibit some de-acceleration as altruistic forces begin to make significant gains. The latter can be seen for instance in the organization of FARC (Colombian Revolutionary Armed Forces) in the 1930s, the oldest leftist guerrilla group in the continent.

The 1940s and 1950s exhibit one of the most surprising transitions in Latin American modern history: from bandolerismo to Marxist guerrilla. However, this is not to say, or to agree with the view that, guerrillas are simply gangs of criminals camouflaged under ideological doctrine. Independently of what contours the process may have taken later, the transition in question is hypothesized here to have begun and be generally characterized as a genuine effort to moral (re)construction, consistent with Durkheim's law of moral gravity.

This is not just postulated on Durkheimian theoretical bases. Important empirical clues as to the historical adequacy of the model have been found. In the first place large groups of bandoleros under socially outstanding leaderships developed, including names such as Sangre Negra, Efrain Gonzales, Chispas, and many others, made famous in the country at large (Tellez 1987). They did live off their exercise of power upon, and extracted surplus from, the rural and small town communities. However, what is important about them is that their leadership did not gravitate only around egotistic criminal action, even though it might have started as just that. As it can be inferred from Tellez (1987), these leaders were also moral and charismatic figures *in their communities*, well beyond and ethically above their legally marginal and criminal pursuits. However, their leadership was exercised in a very primitive fashion, that is, without legal written codes, without formal-rational bureaucratic organization, and relying on grossly simplified and ethically immature procedures.

There is then here an ambivalent social position where, on the one hand the individual and his immediate followers represent the larger society's anti-values by any legal or moral standards, but yet on the other hand they remain loyal, instrumental, and authoritative (in the Weberian sense) in relation to their larger communities of social equals. These communities are marginal to the still larger legal system in terms of economic, social, and cultural capital, but *are not* outside the boundaries of the law, as their leaders are. Such ambivalence on the part of both the "social bandits" and their following, it should be noted, is not an exceptional and curious feature particular to Colombian social history. Rather, it is frequently observed among leaders of organized crime in many places, more noticeably today among drug-dealing mafias in Colombia, Brazil, Italy, and many other places. This kind of social relationship in the case of Brazil has been reported repeatedly in the mass media of that country in relation to Rio de Janeiro's *morro* social-ecological spaces, controlled by the mafias and where the police gains physical presence only exceptionally, by sheer brute force.

The problem here becomes, within the Durkheimian tradition, to find out the "functional requirements" for growing out of the purely egotistic character of the group into an altruistic one. For this essay, let us just say that the transition from bandolerismo to a more encompassing moral stance—including political ideology, struggle strategies, and eventually class-culture peace dialogues and from there to the prospect for structural healing and social amalgamation—is a most pressing and challenging question not only for the Colombian case, but for the Third World as a whole.

In the second place, specific instances of the change in question on the part of group leaders have been identified, especially the case of bandolero "Chispas" (Tellez 1987). However, the transition from bandolerismo to leftist guerrillas is not meant to imply some sudden "ideological conversions" as for the Catholic baptism of Jews. As Durkheimian facts, the epistemic correlates of the two phenomena, egotism and altruism, are group characteristics, of which individuals usually participate simultaneously, although in different degrees. So, "group levels" of these characteristics can be identified for each group as a whole. At the inception of the moral ascent of a group, possibly no one there makes any moves, or even speaks or feels in any concrete way the need for a socio-moral reconstruction, nor imagines any active participation of his (her) micro social unit in such an endeavor. At such point only some of the most elementary functional requirements for group moral construction begin to be met: more stable structuration of the groups through more stable contacts, development of leadership and charisma, group definition of "crime" and outer limits, among many others. Among the various empty spaces of the theory is not knowing when and why some groups do develop an altruistic and proselytistic view of their moral values, whereas others do not. The latter is the case of "organized crime" and mafias. The process is, in any event, established by the moral forces that may or may not succeed in the long run.

The transition in question from bandolerismo to guerrilla then involves the relative weight of egotism and altruism in relation to the illegal groups, which began to pass from a predominance of the former to a predominance of the latter during the 1940s and 1950s. Of course, it will not be until later, presumably in the decade of the '60s, that the two trajectories, for the country as a whole, and in the terms here utilized, cross over each other. The trajectories do not refer to absolute numbers of violent deaths of the two kinds, but to standard deviation units from their continental means. It should not be read between lines here that the guerrilla movement had as its only or primary source the bandolero gangs. As indicated earlier, the contextual conditions may dictate the direction and intensity of these movements, and yet, the transition from egotism to altruism is the result of much broader group moral makeup, where the bandolero and the guerrilla are only tip-of-the-iceberg type expressions.

The 1948 *Bogotazo* is the name given to massive riots in the streets of Bogota after the assassination of J. E. Gaitan, leader of the liberal left and candidate to the presidency of the nation. Following that event—an example of the moral transition expressed in anomic explosions triggered by the disappearance of a charismatic leader—the institutional order approaches critical levels which end up with the coup d'etait of General Gustavo Rojas Pinilla in 1952. During the dictatorship that followed, it makes sense to hypothesize a decrease, and perhaps a stabilization of, the violence trajectories, because of the peace talks and agreements, especially with guerrilla leader Guadalupe Salcedo (Fluharty 1957). In this particular instance, the decrease in altruistic violence does not mean an increase the egotistic kind, but rather it should carry along a decrease in its rate of growth or even an absolute decline. This is because the climate produced by the promises of the new regime.

After the Cuban revolution—and certainly in no small measure because of it—and also because of the failure of the dictatorship to bring about any structural solutions to the ongoing conflicts, altruistic violence experienced again intense and prolonged growth. Egotistic violence on its part, can be expected to exhibit a corresponding continuous decrease after that point. Bandolerismo had virtually disappeared, and the gains of altruistic groups probably absorbed increasing portions of the egotistic violent potential in the country. The very active role of the urban-based M19 movement constitutes a key development at the time, added to the apparently still growing forces of FARC (Colombian Revolutionary Armed Forces) and ELN (National Liberation Army).

These tendencies should have climaxed, according to the historical pattern of the country and of the continent, in another institutional order crisis of surely large proportions where, for a combination of internal and external forces, the establishment would have prevailed. From Argentina to Nicaragua, passing through Uruguay, Chile, Brazil, Peru, and El Salvador, to name only the most important cases, violent confrontations between left insurrection groups and the military, behind various institutional arrangements and processes, took place. Yet, by the time of the collapse of the Soviet Union, or shortly thereafter, all of them have achieved virtual control of the insurgent groups. Colombian guerrillas, however, in spite of significant government efforts to attract guerrilla personnel to regular civil life, grew even stronger. Why?

Outside of the altruistic violent forces at stake in the country, a new and quite unique development set Colombian violence paths in their exceptional historical configuration exhibited in the last quarter of the twentieth century, characterized by rapid and monotonic increases of both altruistic and egotistic violence. I am speaking of the consolidation of the drug cartels first in Medellin—tentatively marked around 1978, and then in Cali, after the death of Pablo Escobar, around 1994. This development sets in motion two parallel processes: one, the growing war against the cartels, fueled both nationally and internationally; and two, the renewed vigor of altruistic violence derived from likely participation of the guerrillas in the drug business at the levels of production, manufacturing, and conceivably commercialization.

The specific mechanisms through which the two phenomena could reinforce each other is still a very obscure matter. However, the upward direction of both kinds of violence paths, this time, is common knowledge. With the mounting efforts—including international ones—of the war against drugs, the death of P. Escobar, and the dismantling of the Medellin cartel, a deceleration of egotistic violence should have occurred. It should be indicated that in the face of the legal authority's failure to control such a scenario of violence, "paramilitary" mercenary armies have inundated the rural areas to protect agricultural businesses from "boleteo" (forced monetary contributions or "taxes" extracted by the guerrillas), genuinely or not. Thus, at the surface, a chaotic picture of hijackings, blackmailing, executions, and violent abuses of authority plague the nation, where ethical and unethical genuine informal war, altruistic violent strategies and counter-strategies confound with similar procedures from the egotistic side of the spectrum.

The overwhelming extent of the conflict today is widely documented by the mass media in Colombia and internationally. For our purposes it suffices to register than the report from DEA (*Washington Post* 1998) reveals that the guerrillas control more than 40% of the national territory, and that, at the rate of growth they have at the present time, very soon they will be in a position to defeat the national regular military forces.

References

Alexander, Jeffrey, and S. Seidman, editors. (1990). *Culture and Society*. New York: Cambridge University Press.

Camacho, Alvaro, A. Guzman, and others. (1997). *Nuevas Visiones Sobre la Violencia en Colombia*. Bogota: Fundacion Frerich Ebert de Colombia e Instituto de Estudios Politicos y. Relaciones Internales, Universidad Nacional de Colombia.

Comision de Estudios sobre la Violencia. (1987). *Colombia: Violencia y Democracia*. Bogota: Instituto de Estudios Politicos y Relaciones Internacionales, UNC, Colciencias.

Collins, Randall. (1994). *Four Sociological Traditions*. New York: Oxford University Press.

Costella, Maria. (1992). *A Igreja Catolica e o Movimento da Encrucilhada Natalino*. Porto Alegre: UFRGS.

de Janvry, Alain. (1981). *The Agrarian Question and Reformism in Latin America*. Baltimore: The Johns Hopkins University Press.

Durkheim, Emile. (1933). *The Division of Labor in Society*. New York: The Free Press.

———. (1951). *Suicide: A Study in Sociology*. Glencoe, Illinois: The Free Press.

Fluharty, Vernon L. (1957). *Dance of the Millions: Military Rule and Social Revolution in Colombia 1930–1956*. Pittsburgh: University of Pittsburgh Press.

Habermas, Jurgen. (1975). *Legitimation Crises*. Boston: Beacon Press.

Hobsbawm, Eric. (1965). *Primitive Rebels: Studies in Archaic Forms of Social Movement in the 19th and 20th Centuries*. New York: W.W. Norton.

Johnson, Terry, Christopher Dandeker, and Clive Ashworth. (1984). *The Structure of Social Theory: Dilemmas and Strategies*. London: Macmillan.

Ribeiro, Darcy. (1971). *The Americas and Civilization*. New York: Dutton.

Sanchez, Gonzalo, and Ricardo Penaranda (editors). (1994). *Pasado y Presente de la Violencia en Colombia*. Bogota: CEREC.

Tellez, Petro Claver. (1987). *Cronicas de la Vida Bandolera*. Bogota: Planeta.

Wallerstein, Immanuel. (1975). Class formation in the capitalist World Economy. *Politics and Society* 5.3: 367–375.

———. (1984). *The Politics of the World Economy*. Melbourne: Press Syndicate of the University of Cambridge.

Wright, Eric. (1997). *Class Counts. Comparative Studies in Class Analysis*. New York: Cambridge University Press.

Part Five

Loose Ends: Reflections and Epilogue

The case histories in previous sections each focus on a genre of violence within a circumscribed relationship or group. The narratives speak for themselves; they cannot be summarized in any meaningful way, nor do they lead to packaged conclusions. Yet, in many instances, those examples of violence shaped by culture are accompanied by antidotes within the cultural frame, and sometimes even prophylactic preventions. In still other cultures, we have become familiar with other approaches to curb and heal violence as it has waxed and waned throughout history. Drawing on these observations, this volume will end with two chapters, both by the editor.

A case history reflecting on the Saami people, an indigenous ethnic minority living in arctic Fennoscandia and northwestern Russia, defies placement in any of the four sections of this volume. In fact, it was composed to pull together features about the family, the interpersonal, the institutional, and larger systems from a single cultural group, interrogating those systems for indicies and relations of violence. This chapter serves other ends as well. First of all, the Saami are relatively tranquil as a society, and would not ordinarily be included in a treatise on violence. However, the seams in their social and environmental relationships do bear tinges of the violent, and they stand as victim vis-à-vis the linguistic and cultural assimilationist policies of the state and of global events such as Chernobyl. At the same time, the chapter explicitly raises serious questions as to the attributions of and definitions for violence within a particular culture.

The epilogue picks up on categories and definitions of violence, being in part a response to the promissory note of the introduction. The case histories present data and analyses about a finite number of cultures and genres of violence. Some of those genres are tested, as it were, on the Saami in the penultimate chapter, where one discovers some, but only some, common constellations of violence. In the epilogue, the case histories and a wider literature are summarized to inspect a greater variety of categories and theories of violence, in order to foreground the variety of cultural counters to violence. These preventative measures, neutralizing gestures, and social policies are likewise shaped culturally. Yet, even though solutions cannot be transplanted, they permit a gentler landing for a volume on the cultural shaping of violence.

Chapter XXVII

Reflections on the Saami at Loose Ends

Myrdene Anderson

One More Case History: The Saami of Lapland

The cultural setting where I am personally most comfortable happens to be largely tranquil, at least when the surface is viewed by outsiders or even from the inside. That setting would be among the Saami reindeer-breeders of Norwegian Lapland, where I've enjoyed many years of research and just plain visiting since 1972. Over the thirty-plus years, I've tallied more than seven in combined durations of fieldwork. For the most part, when there, I live among the reindeer-managing minority, but I also focus on sedentary Saami in other occupations, who are the plurality, and on Norwegians—who are often a local minority in this arctic region of Norway, as are the Saami reindeer-breeders themselves. [See Anderson (1978) for a comprehensive ethnography, based largely on Norwegian Lapland; and Anderson (1991) and Paine (1984) about Saami-Norwegian relations.]

The Saami do not exhibit any truly spectacularly violent habits. Indeed, were this arctic setting a strident one, with noticeable violence against persons and property, I may not have persevered in my research. This is an occasion, though, for me to foreground and reflect on some genres of violence and nonviolence in Saami culture, as documented historically and as unfolding ethnographically. In this case history, it's possible to tap into some history and unpack various institutions affording us insight into the interplay of child-rearing, ethnicity, identity, environment, bureaucracy, and concerned culture-bearers.

Childrearing: Starting at the Top, or the Bottom

Children are highly valued in Saami society, and they almost raise themselves while immersed in a permissive social environment. The physical environment exerts more limits than the social, at least traditionally. The social environment will include, beyond the nuclear family in a neolocal residence, other relatives, neighbors, and even tourists, plus, yes, an ethnographer or two. These combined environments teach the child about hot and cold, wet and dry, sharp and soft, deep and shallow—along with how to deal with the overwhelmingly positive feedback from significant humans. Are children "spoiled"? Perhaps. Children do play with knives, essential to daily life for adults; fortunately, at a very young age a baby will generally have neither the strength nor the motor control to hurt itself or others with a dull knife.

Boy babies earlier than girl babies become impatient with being swaddled and toted around by handy humans, and the virtual infants manage to walk independently at an early age. In some houses and tents, crawling is not an option. I was alert for any consequence of these infants skipping the crawling stage and noticed nothing alarming.

Once mobile, there is no stopping these children, born into a very mobile and even nomadic culture. Children wander at will outdoors, without going beyond some constantly enlarging familiar perimeter. Saami activities calling for skill are not the subject of didactics, but rather of individual initiative—of the child. The child may fail the first few tries in executing a task, but the effort will be socially rewarded regardless, even when the failure entails material loss to the family or group, or even injury to the child (Anderson 2000).

People find the mobility of toddlers exceedingly amusing, and the same is true about the activities of the elderly. Occasionally, every individual will have to push her own physical limits in a life-and-death situation, and seeing babies, older folks, and other creatures doing this of their own volition is reassuring, even inspiring. To be sure, if people move about, they are also transporting things, and at every scale the built environment moves, from furniture to houses. Even sparse forests come indoors to be tapped for energy.

However much children are indulged in Saami society, infanticide and abortion have always been known to occur. Infanticide often boils down to accident or extenuating circumstances extrinsic to the mother, such as blizzard conditions at the time of birth. Infanticide victims return as ghosts on occasion, voicing themselves on the tundra and in school dormitory bathrooms. These locations correspond to the places where infanticide might most likely have occurred. The noises made by these ghosts would be frightening, were people not able to recognize them as little souls asking to be baptized and named. That's what people do, verbally giving each ghost the names of both Adam and Eve, names not otherwise used in the community. Actual infanticide these days would be rare, while abortion, usually a medical procedure, is more commonplace without being frequent and carries minimal stigma. Basically, the Saami are pragmatists and accept matters as they happen. Suicide is still less frequent than abortion and infanticide; not well comprehended, the puzzle of suicide is more apt to foster stories, often about the model suicide being young, male, and disappointed in love. Being young and male are also features characterizing most accidental deaths. As discussed later in the epilogue to this volume, traditional infanticide in most cultures does not bear the signs of being violent at all, nor does abortion or suicide, and none of these practices appears so among the Saami. That is, these infrequent acts are neither aggressively motivated nor carried out with rage. Certain classes of accidental death, though, can arise through abuse of vehicles and/or alcohol, which practices constitute a fuzzier sort of violence.

Enter Habit and Consequence

Children are afforded the leeway to take risks, and usually do so with impunity. Accidents do happen, but more often to older children and adults, especially male adults, and particularly when either or both machines and alcohol are involved. Persons may scheme against each other but seldom fight. Physical altercations do not happen in the absence of alcohol, but since knives are worn on the person, these fights may escalate beyond scuffles. Of these recurring patterned tragedies—accidents and altercations—the latter category clearly classes as violent. The abuse of material culture or alcohol may also reasonably be asserted to be an index of violence if not violence itself. Alcohol will re-enter this narrative later, regarding a historical incident where the Norwegian providers of alcohol are as responsible for violence as the Saami imbibers.

What about the Saami treatment of animals, of their machines, of their built environment, of the natural environment? These are arenas where behavior can vary. Dogs are essential to reindeer management, and for the most part, they are a part of the family, sheltered and fed generously. However, dogs are not coddled pets; they are working partners and, as such, must be disciplined on occasion. Those occasions seldom coincide with a "teachable moment" but rather with a frustrating one. Reindeer livestock reside on the tundra, under variable surveillance. They can be driven harshly into corrals, will be earmarked, and eventually slaughtered, if nature or predators have not already counted coup. Herders are more apt to let out their frustrations with animals verbally, when the animal is out of kicking reach. Between the dog and the reindeer, the former is the handier target of both verbal and physical abuse. I can't say that I've ever seen an implement of punishment come into the equation, unless it already happened to be in the hand. In fact, most physical touching between individuals is incidental.

The Saami find a culture of "discipline and punish" utterly alien, unless they should translate some of their own subtle ways to communicate horizontally between peers and vertically, up and down between unequals. Hence, clever feats of revenge and provocation circulate in discourse to entertain and educate for a long time—such as stories about tricking the German occupiers during the Second World War, outwitting second-cousin reindeer-rustlers, pulling the plug to the freezer of someone out of favor, or fibbing to a curious journalist or ethnographer. Given all this handy raw material for narration—which not only entertains but contributes toward reputation of narrator and subject(s)—how could anyone promote a story about beating a dog!

Snowmobiles and other machine-driven vehicles entered the domestic scene in the 1960s. When machines break down there ensues no automatic natural process of healing, self-correction, or learning, unlike what happens when dealing with animals. Some individuals take extraordinary care and enjoyment with their machines, but others do not, especially if finances, or subsidies, permit their replacement. This leads the environment to become cluttered with spent artifacts of various sorts, including those designed for obsolescence without options for reuse or recycling.

Since these particular Saami have been, to an extent, nomadic, and their material culture largely organic, they have relied on the environment to tidy up after them (Anderson 1994). Contemporary trash and garbage and other "refused" items, large and small, now litter communities and the hinterland. Furthermore, outsiders, such as tourists, now massively contribute to this state of affairs. Besides an expanding road system, the tracks of wheeled terrain vehicles now crisscross the tundra, leading to serious degradation of landscape and pasturage, with both locals and outsiders being responsible. While only the subset of Saami reindeer breeders are responsible for the overgrazing on the remaining territory, another major category of environmental insult—dams for hydroelectric power plants—crowns the list of threats to Saami rangelands and Saami culture itself (Paine 1992), as discussed presently. Finally, the Saami also live downwind of the 1986 Chernobyl disaster and next door to the earlier Soviet atomic testing grounds in Siberia. Not unlike other indigenous ethnic minorities and other just plain minorities, the Saami have been on the receiving end of structural violence from colonizers and the wider world as well.

Transforming Historical Shame and Imposing Colonial Guilt

I am comfortable referring to irreversible damage to machines, built environment, material artifacts, and landscape as violence. But, as far as I can tell, my Saami friends would either disagree or not understand at all. To find an instance of violence they would agree on would take us back to 1852, when a small group of Saami—inspired by Laestadius, an activist part-Saami preacher in Sweden, and acting out against perceived colonial evils such as alcohol—terrorized an entire village, injuring both Saami and non-Saami, and killing two non-Saami: the sheriff and the trading-post manager. Saami arriving from a nearby smaller settlement were able to apprehend the score of perpetrators. There was no precedent for this tragedy, and no violent incidents to follow.

That event in 1852 is now called the Guovdageaidnu massacre. For generations hardly anyone mentioned it, neither the Saami nor the Norwegians. It was almost as though everyone agreed the massacre was so out of character for the Saami that in a spirit of fairness or due to shared embarrassment, it need not be recalled. To find out more, one had to seek out particular historical treatments of this unique happening. With the rise of ethnic identity about thirty years ago, this event was dusted off and reinterpreted—as a Saami revolution of sorts. It is now the topic of refreshed oral lore, written stories, performances, and films, as well as scholarship (Bjørklund 1992, Zorgdrager 1989/1997).

However, the contemporary indigenous interpretation of the violent encounter doesn't settle so much on the Saami perpetrators of the 1852 massacre, who can even be portrayed as culture heroes, but on the Norwegians and some Saami whose behavior—particularly centered on the place of alcohol in the colonizing mission—precipitated the conditions prior to the massacre. In the recently re-emerging narrative, the violence foregrounded is not that of the Saami perpetrators of the massacre, but that of the Norwegian colonizers in general, and to the particular Norwegians who sought justice afterwards, and to the dominant Norwegian culture which took possession of the bodies of the perpetrators thereafter, and which participated in the (partial) erasure of this discursive event.

The Norwegian authorities arranged for a trial, in a larger town, resulting in short-term incarcerations, life sentences, and five death sentences—of these all but two commuted to life imprisonment (one of the five died). In 1854, two men were guillotined (or hanged), their heads (and perhaps bodies) sent to the nearest (not very near) university for "scientific" study. They were, after all, criminals and their skulls might hold some clues for science; they were also considered to be from a different "race," so the skulls might somehow confirm the significance of that distinction! In an ironic twist, it now has been revealed that the preacher, Laestadius, was known to disinter bodies in order to obtain skulls to sell to museum procurers.

Whatever the rendition, I had always assumed that those two sets of osteological materials, whether skulls and/or skeletons, were "properly catalogued" in the university museum in Trondheim, laundered for science as it were. But 140 years later, in 1997, it took kin quite an effort to locate them—one skull in Oslo, one in Copenhagen—and these were only then properly reclaimed by relatives to be buried in the same county as the Guovdageaidnu event of 1852, in caskets that looked very much like traditional cradles in the online photographs.

Current Challenges

By the time that the two skulls from 1854 were recovered and buried by descendents, "fourth-world" (Graburn 1981) ethnicity had been surging for several decades among indigenous ethnic minorities around the world and in Lapland, where it was fueled by

Saami reactions to and occasional protests about incursions on pasturage by settlement, extractive industries (mostly forestry and mining), military, roads, tourism, and finally, hydroelectric power plants. The title of a book by ethnographer Robert Paine, *Dam a River, Damn a People?* (1992), sums up very well the serious consequences of unbridled hydroelectric development, focusing upon the largest and most recent project in northern Norway.

While some of the protests to encroachments have been passive resistance (most noteworthy, a hunger strike outside the national parliament), or were intended to be passive resistance (such as occupying the dam development site), other incidents have been violent, as were the developmental incursions themselves. Oddly enough, outside the political arena, one doesn't hear any stories about these protests, or about "the" eventual dam, or other dams. Nor do they recall Chernobyl, unless maybe when asked. Instead, on the ground, Saami, particularly the nomads, busily take advantage of whatever situation that's come to pass with or without their input, protest, or ratification. Again, their pragmatism both serves and undermines their short-term and longer-term interests, respectively, although there has always been a minority of politically engaged, and enraged, Saami. These will include very few persons involved in primary subsistence activities; instead, they are members of a diffuse bureaucracy, able to speak freely while enjoying salaries from some organization or governmental department.

Reflecting over the past thirty and 300 years, cultural violence gradually merges with structural violence and, in turn, subsumes direct violence. No reversals in levels or rates of violence can be expected. Perhaps cultural violence reverberates through the emerging family structure as well, affecting child-rearing practices. If so, the influence is subtle to my eye; yet the current problems of Saami children in school have more in common with those found far away than they do with the local situation of mere decades ago. Many Saami do voice concerns about school practices, lax child-rearing, family breakdowns, deteriorating subsistence economies, addictive media, and increasing autonomy of children when nature itself plays less of a role in educating them. The occupational sectors of the society used to be more distinct: the seasonally nomadic reindeer-breeders vis-á-vis the sedentary farmers, entrepreneurs, and civil servants. These sectors have their own parallel occupational organizations but their concerns increasingly overlap. Now villages have become towns, and most Saami live in towns and small cities. A few have relocated to their national capitals, where various subsidies and conveniences have become prominent in their lives.

Addressing issues of education, public affairs, environment, language, and culture generally, since 1989, is the Saami Assembly in Norway (also called the Saami Parliament), corresponding to those founded in Sweden (1993) and in Finland (1973) (but absent in the Kola peninsula of Russia). The Saami Assembly and its relationship to the Norwegian government align with Convention #169 of the International Labor Organization, specifically its requirement that fourth-world peoples—indigenous ethnic minorities—be guaranteed self-determination and the protection of their indigenous culture. Nowadays Saami concerns can theoretically be resolved through their own political institutions, locally and nationally within the nation-state. In fact, in 1974 the Nordic Saami Institute was established to facilitate regional communication about issues shared between Saami in Norway, Sweden, and Finland, and, in 1975, the Saami were represented when fourth-world peoples met for the first time as the World Council of Indigenous

Peoples in Port Alberni, British Columbia. Fifteen years later, the Saami, residing in the arctic of all four nation-states of the Pan North, adopted a flag which one sees more and more frequently—even (or especially, perhaps) when Saami descendents gather in North America, as they now regularly do. North American Saami have discovered their roots at the same time as many Saami in their Fennoscandian homelands.

Nowadays, ethnic identity is assumed to be a matter of voluntary self-ascription, although it may arise on the scene first as a non-voluntary construct of "othering" by outsiders, or through a collaborative co-construction. For several centuries, some Saami had been absorbed into their overarching dominant societies, with or without intermarriage, and with or without the violence of an assimilationist policy by their colonial states. The flow reverses today. When there is incentive plus inclination, a person or a family may declare itself Saami—the motivation may be economic subsidy or voting rights in the elections for the Saami Assembly; some even learn the language of their ancestors. The consequence, in many cases, is that siblings may be in different political and bureaucratic camps, whereas earlier, when the distinction was largely traditional and occupational, it would be, at most, distant cousins who would be holding competing or contradictory interests in policy promulgations. There was a tendency for Saami and outsiders to assume that the typical Saami would be a reindeer-breeder; this led to local resentment against the colorful nomads with their plentiful meat and adventures, not only on the tundra but with tourists and ethnographers (Anderson 1991). Today, some of these "authentic" Saami choose not even to register as Saami, and hence distance themselves from the political scene.

With greater autonomy, no longer is it so logical for Saami to point a finger exclusively at violations of the dominant society, but this fact does not mean that either new problems or old habits of attribution disappear. In daily life, both nomadic and sedentary Saami frequently question the good judgment of others, their responsibility, their accountability for actions and nonactions, but seldom come to solutions.

Bureaucracies, in a systems model, are by nature rigid, post-mature, overdetermined, and therefore every bit as pathological as they have rendered themselves necessary (Salthe 1993, Salthe and Anderson 1989). For Saami, the local, regional, national, and occupational bureaucracies which have proliferated in their lifetimes protect them, frustrate them, and perplex them, as already these bureaucracies have set deep and adventitious roots—a constraint entailing violence imposed through the boredom of the bureaucrats, the arbitrariness of their actions, and the frustration of the citizen-victims. This no doubt sounds familiar to people outside of the fourth world!

References

Anderson, Myrdene. (1978). *Saami Ethnoecology: Resource Management in Norwegian Lapland*. Ph.D. dissertation, Yale University. (University Microfilms, 1979.)

———. (1991). Reindeer and magic numbers: The making and maintenance of the Saami stereotype. In *Self and Society, Stereotype and Ethnicity*, edited by Myrdene Anderson and Karen Larson. Special issue, *Ethnos* 56.3–4: 200–209.

———. (1994). Trashing and hoarding in words, deeds, and memory: A sampler from the fourth world Saami. In *Refiguring Debris—Becoming Unbecoming, Unbecoming Becoming*, edited by Myrdene Anderson and Walter R. Adams. Special issue, *The American Journal of Semiotics* 11.1–2: 257–249.

———. (2000). Saami children and traditional knowledge. In *Ecological Knowledge in the North: Studies in Ethnobiology*, edited by Invar Svanberg and Håkan Tunon (*Studia Ethnobiologica,* 9), pp. 55–65. Uppsala: Swedish Biodiversity Centre.

Bjørklund, Ivar. (1992). The anatomy of a millenarian movement: Some organizational conditions for the Sami revolt in Guovdageaidnu in 1852. *Acta Borealia* 9.2: 37–46.

Graburn, Nelson H.H. (1981). 1, 2, 3, 4: Anthropology and the Fourth World. *Cultur/Culture* 1.1: 66–70.

Paine, Robert. (1984). Norwegians and Saami. In *Minorities and Mother Country Imagery*, edited by Gerald L. Gold. St. John's, Newfoundland, Canada: Institute of Social and Economic Research.

———. (1992). *Dam a River, Damn a People? Saami (Lapp) Livelihood and the Alta-Kautokeino Hydro-Electric Project and the Norwegian Parliament. IWGIIA Document* 45.

Salthe, Stanley N. (1993). *Development and Evolution: Complexity and Change in Biological Systems*. Cambridge: MIT Press.

Salthe, Stanley N., and Myrdene Anderson. (1989). Modeling self-organizing. In *Semiotics 1988*, edited by Terry J. Prewitt, John Deely, and Karen Haworth, pp. 14–23. Lanham and New York: University Press of America.

Zorgdrager, Nelllejet. (1989/1997). *De rettferdiges strid, Kautokeino 1852: Samisk motstand mot norsk kolonialism.* Translated from the Dutch (*De strijd der rechtvaardigen Kautokeino 1852; religieus verzet van Samen tegen intern Noors kolonialism*) by Trond Kirkeby Garstad. Nesbru: Vett & Viten. *Samiske Samlinger*, 18. Oslo.

Chapter XXVIII

Epilogue: Denaturing Cultural Violence

Myrdene Anderson

The Various Genres and Worlds of Violence

The introduction to this volume promised an expanded discussion of the concerns surrounding violence. Hence, this epilogue will broach and further probe a number of issues and genres of violence beyond those discussed in the previous chapters. Primary among the *issues* will always be the tangle of relations between "culture" and "biology"; most salient among the *genres* would be, at this moment in the West, "terrorism." The preceding case-histories stand on their own without cause for summary, but are tapped here for examples of successful culturally-shaped preventions of and responses to violence. The epilogue goes on to pull together still other approaches to arrest violence and to point us toward more positive futures, even though eradication of violence cannot be the task of this modest volume.

Violence at any level—whether a direct aggressive event, a structural domination process, or yet more endemic cultural patterns (indeed, if distinguishable, adapting Galtung 1990)—has been more regularly associated with putative "causes" or "explanations," than with "solutions." Whether pointing at "aggression," crystallizing especially at the direct, local, personal level, or at "power," at the cultural and structural level (which often subsumes the local), these constructions have led scholars deeper into linear, deterministic, and therefore simplistic narratives rather than toward a nuanced appreciation of the complexity characterizing cultural dynamics. Causality is a superstition, Warren McCulloch has claimed (1965), inspired no doubt by Wittgenstein. Far-from-equilibrium dynamics (Prigogine and Stengers 1984/1979) and anticipation theory (Rosen 1985) have since expanded on McCulloch to emphasize that in dynamical systems, prediction is illusory and control impossible. Like much else, violence resists simplification (cf. Cromer and Wagner-Pacifici 2001, Keane 1996, Scheper-Hughes and Bourgois 2004, Turpin and Kurtz 1997).

The organization for the genres of violence indexed in this volume move from examples close at hand, in the family; to other antisocial behavior in small- and large-scale societies; to more dedicated institutions of violence; and finally to extreme examples of escalating collective destabilization. Represented in each of the five parts of the volume are discussions of societies of the first-, third-, and fourth-worlds, with the penultimate part also including a study drawing on the second-world. These somewhat journalistic categories, the notion of "worlds," are crudely relative (societal scale and economic type) and provisionally heuristic (Graburn 1981). The "first world" includes Western (post-) industrial and especially "capitalistic" societies, the "second world" the secondary industrial and perhaps "socialist" powers, and the "third world" the balance of the nation-states rapidly folded into the global economy, although often more focused on survival than wealth. The third world has also been called, in succession and ethnocentrically: "undeveloped," "underdeveloped," "developing," and "lesser-developed" or, now, "LDCs," the acronymically laundered "lesser-developed countries"—all expressions being examples of violence in ordinary language. These three "worlds" came to be labeled; they did not name themselves, nor did their constituents, if we exclude the journalistic commentators from the first world.

Finally, and in important contrast, the "fourth world" consists not in nation-states but in indigenous ethnic minorities within the countries of the first, second, and third worlds. This world *did* name itself, when representatives of a number of indigenous ethnic minorities from around the globe gathered for the first time, in 1975 in Port Alberni, British Columbia, to compare their respective tribulations. The World Council of Indigenous Peoples has met many times in many places since 1975. A fourth-world people may be small in population and limited in resource base, but this does not translate into either homogenous or simple. Insofar as one may summarize their concerns, they pivot on cultural survival within a dominant national culture and a global hegemony, at least as much as on more mundane, corporeal survival—each a potential site of violence. Some fourth-world peoples are still buffered from deleterious global economies by their traditional subsistence activities, relying on a "nature" still more kind than the monoculture barreling toward them. These smaller groups often have distinctive languages as well as cultures, and even today the public probably associates anthropology with research in the so-called fourth world. Some fourth-world peoples, especially in North America, think of themselves as "first nations," and are recognized as such, somewhat ironically, just as the notion of "nation" itself has come up for deconstruction (e.g., Anderson 1983, Friedman 2002, Guéhenno 1995, Scott 1998).

Conceptual Accountability—Culture, Society, Behavior

As we perch on the emerging edge of the new millennium, the first two worlds seem to be becoming structurally indistinguishable, and at the same time increasingly distinct from the latter two worlds, which, while never merging, share many features and concerns. Sometimes the first two worlds have been called the "north" or the "have's," and the third world the "south" or the "have-not's." The fourth world, pertaining to peoples or "first nations" rather than nation-states, sometimes falls through the cracks.

As outlined here, the various worlds nurture and tolerate different genres of violence at both the direct and structural levels. To appreciate some of these variables, it will be useful to inspect more closely certain of the units of analysis common to social science, and how these interpret violence.

However seriously anthropology continues to interrogate the notion of "culture" (e.g., Bhabba 1994, Fox and King 2002, Henry 1963), the discipline still attaches to it meaning which is both broad and deep: broad, because culture is inclusive of all individual and collective social (and anti-social) practices; and deep, because culture underlies those institutions, materials, beliefs, and behavior, without determining them. Hence, culture self-organizes the spatial and temporal, the material and informatic, and can be recognized by its traces of spatial pattern and temporal continuity in empirical relations—the very society we find around us.

Culture is neither determined by biology, nor reducible to society or human behavior. Yet, culture powerfully shapes society and behavior, even as those activities feed back into ongoing culture; and culture certainly shapes the biological species while it has itself been enabled, not determined, by biology.

Consequently, it makes little sense to inquire: "What are the main forces—political, social, economic, psychological, linguistic, and cultural—that cause and sustain patterns of violence?" (Steger and Lind 1999: xiv–xv), because *culture* is "all of the above." Well, we would be advised to remove the "linguistic" from this "all of the above" litany, but not from the list itself, inasmuch as languaging operates alongside culture, not just within it, in most enterprises including the violent. Were we comfortable with pointing at "causes," we could likewise say, "all of the above," and more. But would such a list direct us onwards? It is difficult to build on the above sequence as it includes just a few institutions, two noncoordinate phenomena of the social and linguistic, the still more superordinate cultural, and also conditions such as the psychological.

Just to start with, to flesh out an inventory of institutions which may hold clues to and/or be sites of violence—beyond the political and economic often singled out as criterial—we should add law, science, education, religion, media, art, and, of course, the family. Each institution emerges from the cultural to the social, where it, other institutions, and cultural actors may mutually define each other. Each and all of these abstract institutions and concrete actors may be implicated in violence, and at either end of it—if indeed we should be thinking dichotomously.

One might ask why and how the four worlds seem to be coalescing in some respects, and moving apart in others. The short response acknowledges similarities arising through hegemonic cultural formations domesticating ever more of the planet, and to differences arising from the asymmetric flows from the sites of most intense commodification and media outwards (Gottdiener 2000, Gramsci 1995, Lasn 1999). The media mediate, naturally enough, and naturalize violence or neutralize it, turning it into entertainment and escape (Tuan 1998). Via the media, war is transformed to sport, and vice versa. While most institutions are bounded by culture, various media have the capacity to spread indiscriminately, especially since there are few barriers erected at the receiving ends— where a passive populace is seldom just saying "no."

Languaging itself is a partner in the crimes of violence—before, during, and after the acts and facts, and in many guises (Gay 1998, Halliday 1978, Lecercle 1990, Lemke 1995, O'Connor 1995). Metaphor will shortly be mentioned with respect to medicine; it is even more muscular with respect to war (Lakoff 1991) and ethnic cleansing (Ahmed 1995). English usage favors rather transparent militaristic metaphors for discussing medicine, sports, the stock market, and ordinary conversation, so it is amazing how our language manages to launder the real thing: war. Despite human intelligence collectors and the softening before a full-scale attack, there is always collateral damage. Further linguistic laundering is accomplished through acronyms, which thrive in bureaucracies where discourse becomes a string of increasingly opaque abbreviations, acronyms, and initialisms. How long will WMD survive—the acronym as well as the CBRM (chemical, biological, radiological, and/or nuclear) weapons of mass destruction sprinkled liberally around the globe? None other than United Nations Secretary-General and Nobel Peace Laureate Kofi Annan has referred to AIDS in Africa and around the globe as a weapon of mass destruction (2003). Indeed, the acronym WMD has already "mutated" in the title of one scientific article referring to certain genes as "weapons of mutational destruction" (KewalRamani and Coffin 2003), and the field of immunology has been labeled a "weapon of mass distraction" in another article (Chin 2003). Denaturing somber labels through paraphrase may divert our concentration, although not for long.

Cruelty, Not Quite a Deadly Sin

Some acts of violence are perpetrated by individuals who seemed, up to that point, ordinary; however, many perpetrators advertise their aptitude through danger signs and continue from one act to the next unimpeded. Many of the latter individuals may have been socially or environmentally at risk from a very early age, and/or may have exhibited their malaise through childhood acts of cruelty. One of the easiest signs to detect is alloanimal abuse (Arkow and Ascione 1999, Lockwood and Ascione 1998). One can go further and suggest that abuse for abuse's sake of other living things, such as of plants, and destructive behavior generally, even of inert "things," all signal a system overdue for feedback, but by that time the situation can have become very complex. Self-abuse indexes other pathological behaviors as well, as seen in phenomena from eating disorders and self-mutilation to neuroses.

There are many medical practices that are at odds with sympathetic logics and environmental sensibilities, however culturally ingrained the procedures may be. Circumcision comes to mind. Most of the critical discussion focuses on female circumcision, but closer at hand is the example of pervasive male circumcision in cultures without any religious or ritual reasons to practice it. Many other medical trends and procedures turn out to be misguided or even dangerous, and in any event divert resources from situations of more straightforward needs. In medicine and much of culture we have not internalized any responsible, and consensual, guidelines for triage. The medical profession in the West reveals its macho stance in the military metaphors it adopts, conquering cancer, for example (Hardin and Baden 1977). The pharmaceutical industry joins forces with advertising to brainwash consumers to think they can buy beauty and eternal life (Lasn 1999), illustrating other examples of violence in language. Doctors overlook their natural ability to deal with, even heal, whole persons, and, complying with patients, sometimes administer serial, lucrative "cures" for merely spurious symptoms. The pharmaceutical industry profits through its influence on all sides of the doctor-patient relationship.

While the global inventory of individual cultures and languages is steadily declining, human population increases. Our only substrate, the earth, continues to sustain a burgeoning human population, but barely (Hardin 1968, 1993, 1999), and this is not just a recent phenomenon. At the same time, many other species have been lost at a rate which would not be "natural" were humans not so dominant in the equation (Murray 2003). Regardless of societal scale, the human impact on the environment is massive, because each culture tends to expand, to extract, and to waste unsustainably. Of course, the per-capita footprint on the earth by the contemporary industrial and post-industrial first and second worlds in particular dwarfs each and all other and previous insults to our blue marble. Discussion of this matter tends toward self-flagellation-unto-bragging by well-meaning observers, who may go on to romanticize fourth-world peoples (Edgerton 1992, Knauft 1987). No one is innocent, sadly, but some cultural practices are more violent than others. Regardless of the society, since it is we humans who most damage the earth, overpopulation could be our most egregiously violent practice, even and especially when matched by affluence.

The greater the number of people, the greater the consumption and waste. The more affluent and immune to limits the society appears in the short term, the more it is afflicted by the seven deadly sins of lust, greed, gluttony, envy, anger, pride, and sloth; the first four are related through their consumption of objects and essences, and the final three are related through their consumption/erosion of self. These sins are luxuries; perhaps the poor can muster some envy and anger, but not to the degree of the affluent. Yi-Fu Tuan (1998: 118) remarks on the strange absence of cruelty in this litany of seven deadly sins (cf. Rosset 1993). Perhaps cruelty comes more cheaply. The infliction of pain may not be mortal but it is universal, and the types of pain many. With or without implicating each other in every instance, cruelty and violence share deep cultural roots. Indeed, a perception of the universality of bodily pain may lend violence a cloak of transparency affording a communication which transcends ordinary language—language only to be cracked through translation, and at the risk of doing violence to the original (Ruch 2002, Žižek 1989).

Everyday language reveals some of our assumptions about aggression and power. Nor has public discourse been passive in the face of changing cultural habits. For instance, our concern for other animals used to index "cruelty" as an issue, while now "abuse" can cover human as well as alloanimal maltreatment; indeed, these happen to be correlated behaviors. Cruelty remains an interesting term, though, as it only applies to action by a human being against the presumed most sensate of living things, while violence can be stretched at both ends, allowing for more categories of perpetrators and of their targets. While we credit other animals with a capacity for compassion, they cannot be cruel, and, as discussed with respect to infanticide, only in exceptional circumstances can they be violent. Built into the ontologies of these concepts is an assumption that cruel or violent transgressors are endowed with other and preferable behavioral pathways.

Also, the adjectival forms, "cruel" and "violent," focus more narrowly than the substantives, "cruelty" and "violence." The distinctions are more emphatic when considering who or what can be on the receiving end of cruelty and violence. If in our culture we cannot empathize with the victim, it will not classify as cruelty, whereas violent behavior need not claim only sentient victims, nor even be limited to living ones. Ratcheted up from the interpersonal to the cultural, cruelty readily morphs to torture and terror (cf. Baumeister 1999/1997, Daniel 1984). Thus, violent behavior can damage inert objects, and institutionalized violence can damage nature and culture alike, all hiding behind habit.

Resituating "Aggression" and Deflating "Power"

While there remains with respect to violence a strong current of biological determinism in the scientific culture if not in society itself (e.g., Blumstein 2000, Shipman 2001), social science remains largely skeptical if not also critical (e.g., Grossman 1995; Montagu 1968, 1976, 1978; Sampson et al. 1997; Stone and Kelner 2000; Wrangham 1999; Wrangham and Peterson 1996). Even some biological scientists join the social scientists and humanists in distancing aggression or violence from any biological origins (e.g., Lewontin et al. 1984, Ridley 1997). It resolves nothing to attribute "aggression," let alone "war," to genes or instincts or biology, especially when we observe such a variety among cultures in the styles of violence, and of its mediation, if it can be detected at all (Levinson 1989). Also among related primate species, violence is not a given in their repertoires of social interaction. If anything, alloprimates appear eager to resolve incidents when they do occur—even "kissing to make up" (Waal 2000, Harcourt and Waal 1992), and the bonobo's peaceability has aroused almost as much attention as its sexuality (Waal 1997).

So, at the direct and personal level of violence, if we dismiss any deterministic biological programming, we can proceed to scrutinize sociocultural conditioning, yet leaving room for the operation of uncommon but undeniable biochemical differences between individuals. Some biochemical differences may themselves stem from environmental toxins, such as lead, known to result in impaired attention span, impulsive aggressivity, or relentless violence without regard to outcomes and impervious to feedback. Aside from such unusual cases, humans respond to socialization and enculturation, becoming similar in behavior and belief to the patterns exhibited around them, whether these be deleterious or congenial, and go on to replicate those patterns, irrespective of societal scale (Scheper-Hughes 1987). These processes of socialization and enculturation actually begin *in utero*, not long after conception, and do not wait for kindergarten, let alone college. Current attention to honoring cultural, racial, religious, sexual orientation, and individual differential-ablement diversity intends well, but will not suffice to modify deeper structures of difference, and indifference, harboring potential for the violence learned much earlier. First in, last out, seems to be the pattern.

Nor is difference, or structures of the "other," a necessary precondition or predictor of "aggressive" violence. Hardly, when in many if not all societies, direct personal violence is intimate if not actually residing within the home (e.g., infanticide, domestic abuse, child molestation and neglect, and rape; cf. Ronai 1995; Holtzman, chapter VII) or within supposedly nurturing institutions such as schools (cf. McDonald, chapter II). All too easily, structural violence filters down to the local, and cultural responses via regulation may not be effective. Nor can one distinguish the structural from the direct in a way that illuminates the violence at large.

Alongside aggression, another common assumption about the cause or precipitator of violence revolves around power—a term more than a concept, a universal solvent, a formula much used and abused in the social sciences and the media. Most often power has been brought into the discussion of structural violence, but sometimes it figures in theories of direct violence as well. Looking at policing in the U.S., hardly a nurturing institution nowadays, Lutes and Sullivan (chapter XIII) assert that aggression is not violence pure and simple. Perpetrators, victims, and mediating structures such as police all tap into cultural norms, deploying and sidestepping legalities in playing their roles.

It is refreshing to read Hannah Arendt's essays, *On Violence* (1969), because she takes no prisoners in her deconstruction of a bevy of loose relatives to violence; besides power, she brings up authority, force, strength, and might. The latter notions tilt strongly toward direct behavioral violence rather than structural violence; they could even be sociocultural refinements of some imagined underlying biological determinants, such as the popular scapegoats of "aggression" and "dominance." Power, though, is both more general and more interesting as an ingredient in discourse about violence.

Arendt asserts that power and violence may overlap but essentially are in complementary distribution, at least in their pure forms (1969/1970/1999: 9–10). Power is tied to ends in dyadic interaction, and must be accepted as legitimate, as such needing no justification. In contrast, violence may be justifiable but will never be legitimate. Arendt understands violence as an instrumental means, often literally employing instruments to magnify human force. More importantly, violence appears where power is uncertain (cf. Hautzinger, chapter VI; Jimeno, chapter XI), meaning that impotence can breed violence—anticipating McLuhan's (1968) observation about vacuums, the absence of feedback. Violence never contributes to power, and in fact tends to destroy whatever power may inhere in the system. Instead, violence can breed further violence in positive feedback loops (Arendt 1969/1970/1999: 10). Arendt also addresses terror, which will enter this epilogue again at a later point.

Many formulations of power emphasize its hegemonic habits of subjugation, for when asymmetric relations are internalized, they become natural, indelible, opaque (Gramsci 1995, Wilden 1987), like culture itself. Given that culture exhibits patterns and continuities (Fox and King 2002), it's not surprising that culture—along with numerous other complex phenomena—falls into a class of anticipatory systems (Rosen 1985). It follows that violence itself, with its patterns and continuities, will likewise be constituted in anticipatory systems—virtually linking self-fulfilling prophecies with closed loops of entailment. Victims lock into self-destructive habits whenever horizons are blocked by the blinders of early enculturation and later addiction; if negative or positive feedback is interpreted as inconsistent or intermittent, addiction is further assured (Bateson 1977). The roles of media cannot be over-emphasized in this regard. Addressing our collective denial, research regularly revisits the contention that media violence contributes to violent behavior, controlling for the possible attraction of the predisposed perpetrators for violent programming (Grossman and DeGaetano 1999). Once more, TV violence not only engenders violent behavior, but does so in the long term as well as in the short term, looking at eight-year-olds over three years, and again 15 years later (Huesmann et al. 2003).

One condition fueling violence is fear (Berry 2001, Foucault 1995: 58; Suu Kyi 1991/1995), or, more pernicious, fear of fear itself. This was touched on in the introduction, as was the psychological phenomenon of intermittent reinforcement. These loops linking anticipatory self-fulfilling prophecy, fear, and intermittent reinforcement point toward an overdetermined system, and by and large overdetermined systems can be diagnosed as pathological (Salthe 1993, Salthe and Anderson 1989).

Another way of broaching such systems is to unpack the very notion of feedback in that intermittent reinforcement. Marshall McLuhan (1968) regarded "violence as a response born out of a 'lust for compensatory feedback'" (quoted in Ryan 2001: 3). Given such a framework, Gregory Bateson (1972) might consider schizophrenia as an index *as well as* a type of violence, when it emerges out of inconsistent or absent feedback in social relations, whether or not there be some underlying genetic preconditions. Basically, with legitimate power coursing through the system of relations, based on openness, provisionality, habit, and respect, there will not be violence—or not unless or until there is some cataclysmic revolution contesting such power (Arendt 1969/1970/1999: 11).

Other philosophers of power also dwell on it residing in systems of relations (Foucault 1980, Wilden 1987) which subjugate individuals and collectivities through regularities, habit, self-induced repression, and insecurity via inconsistency. This medley of conditions invites comparison with the features contributing to addiction and domestication that characterized concentration camps (Kotek and Rigoulot 2001, Todorov 1996), as well as media and consumer culture today (Lasn 1999, Lutz and White 2002, Roy 1999).

The Body and Other Natural Environments

Cultural violence encroaches on the individual body as well as the body politic, and these can be linked, sometimes through the natural environment. In the first and second worlds, so much incidental waste and intentional discard is produced at every level that some of it has been literally exported to the third world and onto the lands of fourth-world peoples. The first option, though, has always been to situate waste where no one will notice it or where no one who does notice can complain. Dumps in pristine areas occur from every historical period, and nowadays with nature in shorter supply, waste is often unloaded on the disadvantaged. The consequences offend both eye and public health. Addressing these concerns is the recent articulation of environmental ethics, which, if practiced with a sensitivity to all interests, may also be prophylactic (Barsh 1990, Homer-Dixon 1999, Meeker 1980, Nash 1989, Williams 2003). Pollution is violent and breeds violence, it seems appropriate to assert.

Many ordinary environmental practices of the past have returned to haunt us as well, for instance, lead-based paints (Markowitz and Rosner 2002). In affluent neighborhoods, inherited dangers in the built environment are noticed and eradicated, while the poor—faced with other exigencies—may remain oblivious or without recourse. Crimes of person and of property associate strongly with disadvantaged classes and abused environments: that is, the victims of inequality are re-victimized with impunity, and again if they land in penal institutions (Foucault 1995, Gilligan 1997, Gramsci 1995). Sometimes the connections between environment and behavior reveal themselves to be chemical and biochemical; usually there will be overlays of the sociocultural and linguistic. Problems that do not lap over to mar the horizons of the advantaged may resist recognition and treatment indefinitely. Investigations have documented deliberate obfuscation of public safety issues, such as those about lead in the U.S., implicating policy as well as advertising (Markowitz and Rosner 2002, NIOSH 1996). This has put certain populations at greater risk than others. While we decry the practice of restricting information and of bookburning ("libricide," usefully coined by Knuth [2003]), the public has very little assurance about the reliability or validity of what comes into their ears or before their eyes.

The typically more direct and singular "-cides" (infanticide, homicide, suicide), unlike the more structural and multiple "-cides" (genocide, ethnocide, linguacide), are not exclusive to the disadvantaged at all, but do leave deeper tracks there. One could argue that suicide's violence against self might cancel itself out, were the practice careful not to impose on significant others or on strangers who do not sympathize with the decision. Violence enters suicide when the latter act is motivated against the nonself, and when it obliges others to set the scene aright after the fact. Suicide enacted by self-described martyrs actually bent on homicide attains and surpasses the violent (Atran 2003). "Terror," "terrorism," and "terrorist" are terms that now take up the slack left by an exhausted "violence." Terrorism will return to the discussion yet again.

Richards' (2000) study of infanticide has been mentioned in the introduction. One could argue that infanticide carried out in the incidental manner most typical in traditional cultures might not constitute violence (Piers 1978). As described with respect to the Saami people of Lapland (Anderson, chapter XXVII), incidents of infanticide—however traditional—can almost be accidents, when inexperienced persons give birth unassisted or when birth occurs under severe weather conditions. In many other cultures, as well, infanticide entails no more than the mother exposing or abandoning the newborn marked by situational inconvenience, cultural attribute, or individual condition. While something like that occurs in our contemporary culture, too, the majority of Richards' cases clearly qualify as violent when carried out longer after birth, by individuals (of either sex, related or not) while in rage, or by individuals with some extended, premeditated outcome in mind. Consequently, this latter common category of infanticide is only distinguished from ordinary homicide—that is, murder—by the (arbitrary) young age of the victim. While infanticide is a human universal, "shaken-baby syndrome" is not; it joins other culture-bound syndromes such as multiple-personality disorder (now DID, dissociative identity disorder), pre-menstrual syndrome (PMS), and sudden infant-death syndrome (SIDS) in North America. Again, note the domesticating acronymic habits of language.

Some situations of violent infanticide might have parallels in alloanimal societies, where incoming males taking over a harem have been known to kill the younger offspring of females, and even to abuse those pregnant. The too-convenient sociobiological explanation rests on the assumption that the incoming males will sooner be able to propagate their own genes if they dispose of the progeny of recent males (Dawkins 1976/1989). This line of reasoning is too facile, and, in fact, has found no resonance in Richards' data on human infanticide in the U.S (2000)—nor could it inasmuch as human sexual behavior is not constrained by estrous.

Few public controversies in the U.S. wax with more heat than that surrounding abortion and abortion rights, the latter only assured nationwide in the U.S. since *Roe v. Wade* in 1973, though possibly to be revisited again. Abortion is another practice that appears to be a cultural universal, carried out in a variety of ways and for a variety of reasons. Contemporary medical abortion might well appear more violent than traditional abortions; there is premeditation in each case, and a complex of fear (not just of the procedure, but of the pregnancy condition too, and of any alternative outcomes), yet aggressive rage is absent, and the motivations are usually benign, taking into account short- and long-term quality of life for self and for others.

An interesting demographic study will link these cultural practices of infanticide and abortion to the sometimes overlapping domain of crime. Of course, crimes of all sorts are by broad definition apt to be violent, as are the punishments. Most U.S. Americans feel the weight of crime acutely, and are puzzled by statistics reporting its decline. Many tentative explanations—explaining the decline away—don't hold up to scrutiny, but there is an interesting contender. Donohue and Levitt (2000) suggest that the decreasing crime rate is real, and that it really can be explained. Specifically, their data indicates that, following 1973, *Roe v. Wade* made it possible for more women to avoid having unwanted babies, babies who would certainly discern their precarious situation as they grew up in socially unsupportive environments. Medical abortion, then, whether viewed as violent or not, might in some cases be culling lives that would be unfulfilled to the point of becoming self-destructive as well as violent against others.

A Fifth World? Displaced Persons and Peoples

The four worlds came into our vocabulary gradually over the past generation—first the three categories of countries and finally, circa 1974, the fourth world of indigenous ethnic minority peoples. Very tentatively, a few writers have ventured to extend this inventory to five, but inconsistently and without persevering. Given George A. Miller's familiar algorithm, "The magical number seven, plus-or-minus two" (1956), cognitively, we could handle going above four worlds, and for convenience more than conviction, I will do so here.

One can document kinds and degrees of violence in the other worlds, but, in addition, each of those worlds contributes to the fifth, which I will simply call displaced persons and peoples, who may continue to affiliate with some other world or worlds at the same time. The Nuer refugees studied in the U.S. Midwest by Holtzman (chapter VII) are people from the fourth world, immigrating from the third world to live in the first world, but as fifth-world refugees. Persons and populations are more difficult to describe when they and their ideas move about freely, willingly or otherwise. Furthermore, some cultural groups pre-date the jigsaw puzzle of nation-states, and are not displaced but have been rendered asunder by the cuts of history and/or their own peregrinations, such as Jews, Gypsies, Kurds, and even Saami.

The first world absorbs, at least temporarily, displaced groups coming from the third and second worlds. But the first and second worlds together have precipitated more displaced individual persons than the third and fourth worlds—despite or because of their sometimes relative affluence. These are the homeless, literally or figuratively extruded from their first-world or second-world family, community, job, society. A lesser number of homeless are just psychologically isolated, still living with their families, whom they cannot support or properly face. Some homeless claim they have chosen this way of life; others clearly did not. While structural violence is implicated in their displacement, direct violence may have also played a role. Once displaced, there follow more indignities and violence.

Displaced individuals in a third-world setting will not have the wealth of discard to harvest that is especially available along the alleys of the first world. In the fourth world, displaced individuals may be absorbed by their overarching first-, second-, or third-world country, because their own small-scale society may have no roles of last resort for them. There have been roles and stereotypes for the displaced in nation-states for some time; the problem is not novel, but its intensity is.

Some displaced individuals make radical relocations to another cultural setting, again, voluntarily or unvoluntarily; sometimes dramatic transnational moves involve whole families and much larger groupings (Warshall 2002). When this happens, emigration and immigration records may yield statistics, if translocations are legal; otherwise the extent of these global flows of population is as untabulated as those of the individual homeless. In the case of centrifugal exodus, whether voluntary or involuntary, violence is one element people would like to leave behind. In the case of centripetal flows, violence also plays a role in rendering the unknown so plausibly better than the intolerable familiar, that migrants give new settings the benefit of the doubt.

Throughout history and prehistory, where there have been migrations, there have been back-migrations, and these can sometimes be tallied. In 2000, 600,000 refugees voluntarily returned "home," of the perhaps 22 million displaced transnationally from 120 countries (UNHCR 2000). A less certain but equal number of persons has been displaced as groups within their nation-states, due to ethnic and religious strife, famine, natural disasters, and, ironically, development projects. In 2000, about 15 million refugees could not return home because of anticipated persecution or death. Sometimes persons and groups become expelled from host countries—77,000 in a recent year—to face violence in their home countries. "If one can speak to the moral heart of the world, those violently forced to flight may be the most accurate signal of planetary human cruelty . . ." (Warshall 2002: 40–42).

As has been the case with natural ecosystems, interference in these *natural cultural* systems can backfire. Any well-meant adjustment may have an infinity of unintended and deleterious consequences, accompanying or not accompanying the intended beneficial one. Some general conclusions can be gleaned from experience, some being hardly surprising. Armed conflict seems ludicrous as a solution to anything, and spews animosities and landmines without so much as a half-life. Food aid appears to benefit corporately-connected donors at one end, and intercepting vandals on the other, more than the actual population at risk. Humanitarian aid in general amplifies local and transnational dislocations, installing codependencies and intensifying inequities with irreversible consequences. Finally, the restructuring of "free trade" has added stress to the system, at all levels.

Terror and Other Unsustainable Violence

All violence is unsustainable, logically, even when virally ensconced in a culture. It is certainly unjustifiable. Earlier I suggested that violence is entropic, uncreative, closed, dark—erosive of self, society, culture, ecosystem. It should, really, just self-destruct. Instead, we foster it, and through the complicity of anticipation we assure its maintenance.

Insecurities breed fear, and fear can be an ingredient in violence, if not a major connective tissue (Berry 2001, Lischer 1999). Insecurities compromise futures, in this anticipatory system called culture. As suggested earlier, a contribution to compromised futures is found in inadequate and/or inconsistent feedback from the past, whether immediate and personal or extended and environmental. In numerous settings, from family to civil strife, various scholars have described McLuhan's "vacuum" seeking feedback (1968) more narrowly as "affect hunger" (Goldschmidt 2003) and "father hunger" (Herzog 2001).

If again I mention children, it is not because I seek "causes," but rather that children are sculpted in the crucible of culture plus a wider environment and then go on to become adult actors (Kadushin and Martin 1981, Korbin 2003). Children are not passive, blank slates, or dependent variables, but instead they play creative roles at every stage of their development. No matter how dismal their chances, some individual children will not just survive but thrive. However, there are no convincing clues as to what permits such good fortune, or how the more auspicious variables somehow sort themselves out. And then, there are unexplained cases of youngsters well-endowed in every way who fail, or whom we fail.

Innocent and not so innocent children participate in the escalation of violence close to the domestic sphere, and far from it as well, while becoming victims themselves (Moffatt 2003). Briefly, examples would be the massacres in public school settings in the U.S.—one already documentarized by Michael Moore as "Bowling for Columbine" (2002). Incidents of school massacres carried out by a child or children now occur from coast to coast and also outside the U.S., one major tragedy in Germany. On the streets, and sometimes in the schools, gangs are more commonplace, sometimes involving girls as well as boys. Another conjuncture for youth and violence points to child soldiers in the third world—or everywhere, if 18-year-olds are deemed children (Cohn and Goodwin-Gill 1997). There are connections between these, and primarily the connections would be weapons (Grossman 1995) and media (Grossman and DeGaetano 1999; NTVS 1996, 1997, 1998/2000). I will not externalize responsibility, except to note that we do have, individually and collectively, a say in the cultural institutions we have propagated, and evidently tolerate and thereby support (Kanner and Kasser 2003, Lasn 1999).

Ink as well as blood has been spilled on the general subject of violence and the special topic of terrorism, before and since the pivotal events of "9/11" or "911" (e.g., Bennis 2003, Denzin 2003, Glanz and Lipton 2003, Kushner 2002, U.S. Department of State 2002, and four volumes of Stout 2002). For some months after that date, commentators wavered between referring to "nine-eleven" and "nine-one-one," perhaps recalling that hundreds or thousands of victims were calling the "nine-one-one" emergency numbers as well as their loved ones from the World Trade Center.

A further tragic twist, beyond terrorism, is "suicide terrorism." This is troubling because for some onlookers it is incomprehensible. However, as Atran (2003) points out, not even suicide terrorism is a recent innovation; he traces its discontinuous record throughout history, including Western history.

Reviewing the installation of habits and institutions of violence before 9/11 lessens the surprise of this otherwise unprecedented set of events (see Gardner 2002). When societies tolerate and promulgate direct interpersonal strife involving different ages, sexes, and classes; and when societies export strife in the form of weapons, addictions, and inequalities: could these practices themselves approach or even constitute terrorism? To terrorize is to initiate an intransitive relation which will implode on itself. Contemporary international terrorism differs from that lamentable but more ordinary terrorism generated by the intra- and inter-cultural codes of violence exampled in the preceding chapters. Whether or not international terrorism can be tied to its own culture(s) of violence, it does contrast in ways which put those other codes into high relief. Quotidian violence exhibits some checks and balances, at least, theoretically. The targets might be able to step outside harm's way, even if it's a big order to suggest that one can step outside one's own culture, to decline to participate, to defy abusers, to keep one's head low, to flee from communities under siege.

Often the potential victims of quotidian violence know they are at risk. They live in unhealthy-unto-pathological families, neighborhoods, communities, or institutions, or they are marked individuals out of place and time, as women in the marines (cf. Moore, chapter XVI). Perpetrators of violence acting more randomly outside of these cultural environments are certainly deemed terrorists, and indeed they have the capacity to psychologically terrorize an entire population, even *without* acting. An individual running amok or a group of bandits on the loose concentrates social awareness in two directions—one direction toward the deviant body and its capture and control, and the other direction inward as the social group and its constituents realize a collective impotence. Such episodes of aberrant behavior rarely destabilize the host society, unless they are memorialized or recurrent, unless they are internalized.

Exactly that is happening in the U.S. There is a Department of War, transformed to a Department of Defense, but no Department of Peace, not even in the wings, unless HR 1673 proposing a Department of Peace should make it through the bureaucratic hoops

(Department of Peace 2003), or unless the fledgling Institute of Peace would qualify (Holden 2003). The U.S. is now staging costly Terror Drills, the first in Seattle in May 2003. Also freshly hatched is a U.S. Department of Homeland Security, and, in at least one university, a new academic department and major, similarly labeled, potentially naturalizes paranoia and gives degrees in it. When was the last time in history we encountered the term "homeland"—or the first time? The U.S. National Science Foundation solicits research grant proposals for the ACT program through NSF 03-569; ACT stands for Approaches to Combat Terrorism—note the choice of verb. The military are already engaged in literally and figuratively combating terrorism; some participants may have been recruited not centripetally on grounds of patriotism or centrifugally from unemployment, but as video game addicts. The U.S. Army recently spent $6 million to develop a video game to attract potential recruits; if expenditure be a measure, the game is probably above average sophistication, as ordinarily such a game costs but a fraction of that amount (Barron 2003).

Is this altogether just one more growth industry? It does seem so.

Recapitulating the Interlocking, Amplifying, and Inhibiting Institutions of Violence

While the subject of violence remains as dark as the habitual practices it concerns, violence does permit a level of unpacking. Throughout these chapters, authors have avoided attributing violence to straightforward, simple, linear causes, or addressing violence through correspondingly simple solutions. Indeed, in the cultural settings themselves, folk analyses of violence are typically complex, taking into account historical time and personality quirks. Not uncommonly, those at risk of violence find that the cultural setting affords first approximations of rationalization and defense, although not always prevention.

In the home environment which bleeds, figuratively and literally, into school and society, each child approaches fear of violence and violence itself from within a personal perspective colored by unique relations with kin, neighbors, and friends—all responsive to personality, age, gender, birth order, and past behavior of self and kin. Violence against the most helpless in a society, the children and other living things, frequently is moderated as well as inculcated by those very victims. McDonald (chapter II) mentions the various configurations of social and antisocial relations that buffer the victim in her urban U.S. school setting. McDonald, and Rogers (chapter IV), both document child survivors establishing a sort of apprenticeship within a peer group. Children's narratives acknowledge a missed childhood, while focused on the sources of danger over which they as actors hold no or minimal control. Rogers' Irish subjects benefit from more enlightened social services; bullying, at least on school grounds, was eradicated through a reconciliation program, and children were trained as peer mediators.

Insofar as all social systems operate through both feedback and feedforward loops, it's not surprising that expecting violence in a population can contribute toward its happening. In urban U.S. schoolyards, the expectation of violent behavior during recess has led some schools to do away with recess altogether. In a closer observation of actual recess interaction, Beresin (chapter III) noted that children only became unruly at the time of the closing bell. This liminal phase, between the playground and the classroom, precipitated mock violence which was temporary and easily controlled. She points out that ethologists have established that mammalian interactors in mock violence will stay together, and face-to-face, following a bout, as the tenor of behavior returns to normal. Serious violence fractures social relations, while mock violence is more of a pastime. One can imagine that interfering with mock fights, and separating the protagonists, could quite unintentionally reify their mis-alignments.

Interpretation, over-interpretation, and under-interpretation exacerbate social and anti-social roles in other cultural settings as well. Hautzinger (chapter VI) finds in her Brazilian setting that male and female participants and the outsiders in an altercation must be able to distinguish between ordinary conflict and violence. A culture endows ordinary conflict with transformative potential, as it is part of an open dynamical system which has always and will always be in flux. Violence tests the limits of that system, and in fact can destroy it. Hautzinger notes that male insecurity tips social relations toward more serious imbalances.

Hautzinger observed couples and others in close relationships in Brazil, finding that there were checks and balances within the culture itself. Fonseca (chapter X) and Jimeno (chapter XI), also carrying out research on relationships in Brazil and Colombia, respectively, find that a medley of emotional states work together to moderate violence. Recurring in all these chapters is the interplay among love, fear, respect, reciprocity, and reputation. Jimeno boils this down as love plus fear equaling respect. Women hold many of the strings in incidents of partner conflict.

Much the same has been documented by Winkler (chapter V) and Sault (chapter IX) in Mexico, and by Holtzman (chapter VII) among Nuer immigrants in the Midwest compared to their domestic structure in Africa. In addition to noting the nature of the interaction between primary protagonists, these authors also observe how kin and kin groups figure in preserving and in modifying social conventions. The practice of bride-stealing and rape documented by Winkler has tapered off when the Mexican community as a whole exerted control over practices and reputations. Sault points out that there is often a tendency to overlook the impact of women in regulating mock and serious violence. She particularly focuses on the power of the godmother. On the other hand, when an individual family or an entire group of persons migrates, kin and fictive kin relations often fail to consolidate in the new cultural setting. This is manifestly the case with respect to the Nuer immigrants studied by Holtzman. Social service agencies have had to cope with different kinds of violence, different cultural definitions and expectations surrounding violence, as well as different explanations for unfortunate incidents. Thus far there has been too little time to judge whether the Nuer and their new neighbors are moving toward a more positive rapprochement.

Repeatedly, faced with the complex antecedents and inputs of what one intuitively terms "violence," researchers mention moderating and meliorating factors such as trust, respect, and something as subtle as politeness (Cohen and Vandello, chapter XII; Brown and Levinson 1987). In the past 20 years, social scientists have returned to look more closely at emotions as expressed in behavior (Lakoff and Johnson 1980, 1999) and language (Wierzbicka 1999). Regarding both external behavior and internal emotion, universal patterns obtain—some ethnological and cross-cultural, and others more deeply ethological.

Looking at violence at close hold—in family, school, and neighborhood—individuals have been socialized to accept what's meted out, and in the process they learn all sides of the relationship, becoming in due time the abusing (or blind) parent, spouse, teacher, neighbor. This said, each cultural setting is replete with contradictions which can be mined by the individual, regardless of age or sex. At the same time, stepping back to let some common variables fall into place, Mackey (chapter VIII) pinpoints the pivotal role of fathers in child-rearing cross-culturally. Despite the variety of social systems, each functioning at some adequate level, Mackey can demonstrate patterns in murder levels tied to the absence of fathers. Exactly what all the fathers contribute to the less pathologic of families is unclear, but it will not reduce to either financial stability or "discipline." Perhaps here also the ephemeral factors of trust and respect figure in the crucible of forging social selves. One recalls also the recent research of Donahue and Levitt (2000), linking decreasing U.S. crime rates to the liberalization of abortion since *Roe v. Wade* in 1973.

Socialization affects not only the young in family and school, but adults as they enter all manner of institutions. Socialization in either instance can be soft or severe. In the case of policing in the U.S., as pointed out by Lutes and Sullivan (chapter XIII), officers must attend to the legal limits of their enforcing *of* the law. That is, force itself becomes a philosophical practice. The same dilemma obtains with respect to military training, which licenses killing while also training recruits how not to be killed, as documented by Ben-Ari (chapter XV) in Israel and Moore (chapter XVI) in the U.S. marines. Legitimate killing costs heavily, psychologically, both before, during, and following the act (Grossman 1995, MacNair 2002). Some analyses suggest that the individual has to be broken down through physical and mental violence, built back up as a soldier, dissolved into the group, and thereafter subjected to authority. The cruel rigors of military training may inculcate the ability in the recruit to "do" violence, while secondarily it serves as a pre-test, and pretext, of the recruit's ability to withstand torture. Recalling Bateson's (1936/1958) observation that persons learn role relations, not autonomous single roles, military training must simultaneously consist in lessons in torture. Along the same vein, intermittent reinforcement inclines the subject to fix the behavior (Bateson 1977).

When it comes to war, "necessary" and spurious violence can be placed in the same frame as positively valued behavior, such as bravery, and be thereby positively regarded. War occurs in only some larger-scale societies. Men in particular may recall with some degree of pleasure their bonding with mates in training and in battle, and, in smaller-scale societies, in inter-family feuds (as coming up in Smith, chapter XX). While provincial feuds are not oiled by specialized training, mercenaries usually do have prior training in conventional state-bound forces, illustrating a by-product of military training whether in peace or for war. Hacker (chapter XIV) adds that war, whether deemed justified or not, will be sporadic, while military institutions are enduring, and within their training programs and petty bureaucracies one will not find the likes of bravery. Indeed, bureaucracies promote other genres of violence. One is the random and motivated exercise of hierarchical privilege, and another is the foothold of bureaucracies among the resource priorities of a society. Still another factor in the naturalization of violence, throughout culture and cultures, is the obfuscation of open and provisional heterarchies through the expectation and acceptance of deterministic hierarchies.

Torture crops up in cultures throughout history and around the world today. It is not exclusively a concomitant of warfare or conventional military practices. Many pathologic domestic practices are tantamount to physical and mental torture. The taunting by a rapist or stalker cannot be called anything less than torture. In Winkler's narrative (chapter V), the persistence of her voice eventually brought about a resolution that removed one dangerously violent rapist from the streets. This should not be a luxury, and indeed it was not enough for Winkler. Before and since the arrest, trial, and sentencing of the perpetrator, Winkler has been in the public eye as an educator about the system which generates and protects rapists, batterers, and stalkers (Winkler 2002, cf. Buchwald et al. 1993, Matoesian 1993, Websdale 1998).

Naveh demonstrates how insidious a culture of torture can be, this in Romania (chapter XXV). While the art and craft of torture can be readily taught to the first wave of victims, who are inducted to become perpetrators, it has proven extremely difficult to treat the collective perpetrators-survivors as they seek curing in order to return to ordinary society. In Guatemala, a culture of impunity has legitimated torture, murder, and every imaginable inhumanity; Afflitto (chapter XXIII) is hard pressed to bring more than the witness of survivors against this violence. The bloodbaths in too many such societies in too many regions of the world are matched by the bloodless spiriting away of the disappeared. Perice (chapter XXIV) relates how oppressive it is to be watched in Haiti, and to have to watch others as well, just to calculate one's next move. Long-term armed conflicts whose tactics range from murder, to torture, to mobster-like guerilla operations, can mix with politics, as Fandino relates from Colombia (chapter XXVI). There, power can seem to slide into authority. Urban gangs sometimes behave like guerillas when they articulate demands, especially when they can maintain some continuity through time and across space. Trappey's (chapter XXII) Taiwanese case illustrates how rampant gangsterism can become before the citizenry recognizes the scope of the problem. Indeed, the phenomenon of gangsterism resonates with adult crime, urban schools, sports events, hooliganism, and the media—which can reward behaviors emerging in all these venues (e.g., BBC 2003, Bower 2000, Brownstein 1999, Vigil 2003).

In the contemporary third world, the first world has been experienced as occupier, colonizer, usurper of voice, and rapist of both humans and resources—at various times, literally and figuratively. Beyond the historical patterns and particularities, the third and fourth worlds now serve as the dumping ground *and* playground for the affluent other worlds. Among the Saami (Anderson, chapter XXVII) and throughout the Pacific islands (Teaiwa, chapter XVIII), in very different climes and terrains, tourism has been introduced, and welcomed by some. Tourism, even ecotourism, extracts money from some visitors, which in turn distracts some locals about the larger and larger dis-economies at work. While many parts of the world are now plugged firmly into a tourism economy, the Saami and Pacific islands share a more unique souvenir from the outside world: radioactive contamination from atomic bomb tests and nuclear accidents. Because the health and environmental consequences of this known radioactivity cannot be established for many years, and then only by indirect statistical inference, the victims themselves find the situation they're in rather hypothetical.

Around the globe many individuals choose to smoke a known carcinogen, yet populations such as those in radioactivity's path have no option but to continue their traditional lifeways, even if it means eating, drinking, and inhaling poisons. Complaints about these toxic conditions have to be addressed in many directions, from local authorities and their own state apparati, to global powers, yet the transgressions occurred decades in the past far beyond the pale of accountability. In monitoring ongoing environmental conditions, what's going on today may be flying under the radar. Few of us have the expertise to judge the alleged dangers from nuclear energy or genetically engineered crops, especially when scientists themselves cannot attest to "safe" levels of toxins when nonlinear hormesis effects may be the rule rather than the exception.

Here also a critical awareness has often been the only antidote to conditions that render some victims silent (see Elia, chapters XVII and XIX). While language serves violence, even in torture, as documented by Naveh (chapter XXV), language can also be enlisted in intentional protest as well as be unpacked as inadvertent documentation (cf. Lemke 1995). This is true in instances of brutalized children exploring their own logics to explain violence (Rogers, chapter III), in the case of the structures of myth and rhetoric serving the diverse populations of the Peruvian Andes (Dean, chapter XXI), and in any structures of pornography (Dworkin 1999/1988) and other crimes against person and property (Fox 1996).

Violence—precipitating stochastically or from individual, societal, cultural or even biological "habit"—can be anticipated and triggered by those very systemic patterns. Ironically, perhaps, public outrage against some violence can provoke reactionary and escalating violence, as in the case facing environmental movements (Helvarg 1994). A seldom acknowledged prefigurement to violence is fear, itself a form of violence. This situation sums up the art and craft of terrorism very well: one can instill terror without acting, or at most only intermittently reinforcing that substrate of terror.

However, if habit can sustain actual and perceived violence, habit can also undermine it, theoretically.

Positive Futures or at Least the Cultivation of Optimism

Although good fences make good neighbors, sometimes, fences themselves can also index bad neighbors, distrust, even fear—past, present, and future. Fences can fence in or fence out, or both, or neither. Words and language generally serve functions similar to fences at every level, joining and separating individuals and groups. Words, and silence, accompanied by other behavior, lead up to discord and also accompany its occasional dissolution. Discourse figures in the very registering of violence, in bringing it into the realm of comprehension. At another level, witnesses to violence communicate the passing incident or pathological condition through language. Many of the efforts to bring individual and collective antagonists together rely on the goodwill of language, and the bulk of the social philosophy of violence has to resort to that ordinary human faculty, human verbal language and its written congeners.

It appears that history is riddled with rhymes, unheeded ones. Humans do not have a good track record when it comes to learning from "mistakes." At the same time, in almost every age, scholars recite recurring litanies of woes. Besides regular complaints about the intolerable deportment of children, the erosion of the family, the faltering state of schooling, proliferating bureaucrats in general, politicians everywhere, and "armed conflict," or war—citizens everywhere voice their increasing concerns about violence, adrift from the outriggers of old. Religion enters the scenes of these crimes often as perpetrator, occasionally as mediator, seldom as solution (cf. Fox 1999, Girard 1977/1972, Kakar 1996, Mahmood 1996, Smith-Christopher 1998, Stern 2003), and ethnicity can endow protective identity as well as fuel inter-ethnic conflict (cf. Ahmed 1995, Appadurai 1998, Fox 2002). Sometimes reflecting on the alarms of the past trivializes those ills, comparing them with the enormity and proliferation of today's problems, which really are *deadly* serious. Yesterday's problems were overcome, or ignored, or diligently denied, only to revisit us with impunity, and with global brushstrokes (Hall 1991).

One might surmise that global pathologies call for global counter-measures. Yet global pathologies manifest themselves locally even as they are masked there—which is to say, here. Global pathologies include excesses of population, pollution, displacements, disparities, drug trafficking, other criminality, terror, disregard of human rights, and globalization itself—all merging with, without causing, local and intimate suffering (Barber 1996, Bauman 1998, Natrajan 2003). It makes no sense to defer to and wait for international or national or municipal bodies or heads of households to act or react when most problems are so immediate, and especially when some problems implicate those more inclusive bodies as perpetrators. As a most sobering example, the International Criminal Court has been endorsed by only 90 governments, and considers its mandate to deal with the overlapping categories of genocide, war crimes, and crimes against humanity—but only after the fact. Too late.

Institutions particularly charged with the shaping (both limiting and enabling) of future behavior in many societies may rely on negative feedback almost to the exclusion of positive feedback. This pattern may be manifest in the family and education as well as in any military, and with pets and livestock. Taking one more step, it is worth mentioning that we may not think in terms of the responsive behavior toward *and of* the natural environment or of material culture, whether it be collected or crafted, yet negative "feedback" to material culture does hasten its demise. Some cultural observers regard the care that extends the "life" of natural and artifactual material culture to foster habits applicable to the living world. The attention afforded houses, tools, toys, gardens, orchards, pets, and livestock may be extended to children and others—and/or vice-versa. Whether deemed generous, adequate, or deleterious, this care may correlate with other cultural relations, if only as habit.

Permissive child-rearing and traditional immersive learning, as practiced among the Saami and many smaller-scale societies, will not mesh smoothly when a larger entity imposes a social, commercial, or military establishment. Even where the family may be organized hierarchically in some societies, military recruits are strained to meld into a rigid military organization, as exemplified by the subjects of Ben-Ari and Moore (respectively, chapters XV and XVI). The soldier is shaped through disciplined violence to execute violent discipline upon an enemy. The connotations of noun and adjective contrast with what is perceived by the recruit as "violence" vis-à-vis what is perceived by the indoctrinated recruit and larger system as being unfortunately, but legitimately, "violent," although in a routine which merely controls, domesticates, or disciplines a situation. Seldom does one hear warfare summed up as mutual killing.

The particular mix of hierarchic and heterarchic organization in much contemporary violence does not reduce to any finite number of hypothetical variables, either, although the interplay of long-term civil strife and a population (especially of males) otherwise underoccupied suggests certain endemic flash points.

It's not surprising that violence in culture, in general and in the specific, has been addressed almost as often as it has been noticed, sometimes with satisfaction but seldom satisfactorily. Individuals and societies, operating inductively, deductively, and abductively, have amended the settings and conditions generating malaise (Sullivan and Kuo

1996), have amputated the diseased members of society, have voted for peace and quiet (Hunt 2002), justice and equity (Farmer 2003, McGovern 1964), forgiveness and reconciliation (Abu-Nimer 2001, Avruch and Vejarano 2001), and prevention of violence has focused on breaking pernicious habits and their positive feedback loops (Leatherman et al. 1999).

In the academy, research programs emerge to emphasize the potential positive, as the Living Beyond Conflict applied anthropology seminar at the University of Uppsala, Sweden (LBC 2001, 2002). More and more universities everywhere have peace studies available as a major or minor. Scholars have also looked afield for inspirations coming from other cultures and eras (Montagu 1978, Sponsel and Gregor 1994); "Respect for the rights of others is peace," Douglas Fry reports from the Zapotec (1992). Some observers defer to the violent actors themselves to generate their own solutions (e.g., Hoffman 2001). Others look to "human nature" itself, with its potential for creative health and healing (Kohn 1990, Ridley 1997). Finally, abstinence—the absence of violence—may result from a commission of a positive act or an omission, of abstinence (Nagler 2003).

Nothing can compare with establishing an actual community of peace, especially if it is self-sufficient, taking root in the eye of a violent storm. That describes the utopian settlement of Gaviotas in Colombia (Schorlemmer 2003). Even though in real dynamical systems, neither successful nor unsuccessful experiments can be replicated, learning about utopias can captivate the imagination.

Assuming, perhaps, that while meditating on a mantra one can do no harm, many persons like to dwell on their favorite texts—perhaps utopian, perhaps religious, perhaps mythical, and sometimes pragmatic. Arundhati Roy's *The God of Small Things* (1997) and *The Cost of Living* (1999) keep coming up in some circles. Academicians feel better feeding at the trough of tough love, seeking the latest words from a respected authority such as Johan Galthung in his most recent co-authored academic book, *Searching or Peace: The Road to Transcend* (Galtung, with Jacobsen and Brand-Jacobsen 2002/2000).

Still and all, generations of efforts of the pen and pulpit promoting nonviolence have not enjoyed even minimal rewards. No wonder that one politician, former U.S. president Jimmy Carter, wrote *Talking Peace* for young people (1995/1993), and another scholar, Johan Galtung, has addressed his latest book to very young children. Perhaps there, with younger generations, one can begin to make a difference that is, indeed, a difference. Galtung, whose thoughts on violence and its prevention have been brought up both above and in the introduction (chapter I), published his children's book in May 2003, in Norwegian (*En Flyveappelsin Forteller*), and it immediately had to be reprinted. If in glancing around, anyone notices an aerial edible fruit darting about, sharing wisdom about peace and justice, it will be Galtung's book in translation, a fable about a wise and adventurous orange. Whether oranges translate well into every language and culture won't matter; in Norway itself, oranges are imported, yet commonplace. Why not a flying apple? In the Middle East, a date? In the Pacific, a breadfruit? A piece of peace for everyone.

References

Abu-Nimer, Mohammed, editor. (2001). *Reconciliation, Justice, and Coexistence: Theory and Practice*. New York: Lexington Books.

Ahmed, Akbar S. (1995). "Ethnic cleansing": A metaphor for our time? *Ethnic and Racial Studies* 18.1: 1–25.

Anderson, Benedict. (1983). *Imagined Communities: Reflections on the Origin and Spread of Nationalism.* London: Verso.

Annan, Kofi. (2003). Press conference, 18 December 2003, reported same day by BBC.

Appadurai, Arjun. (1998). Dead certainty: Ethnic violence in the era of globalization. *Public Culture* 10.2: 225–247.

Arendt, Hannah. (1970/1969). *On Violence.* New York: Harcourt Brace Jovanovich. Excerpt pp. 35–60 republished in 1999 in *Violence and Its Alternatives: An Interdisciplinary Reader*, Manfred B. Steger and Nancy S. Lind, editors, pp. 3–11. New York: St. Martin's Press.

Arkow, Phil, and Frank R. Ascione, editors. (1999). Prevention and intervention. *In Child Abuse, Domestic Violence, and Animal Abuse: Linking the Circle of Compassion for Prevention and Intervention.* West Lafayette, Indiana: Purdue University Press.

Atran, Scott. (2003). Genesis of suicide terrorism. *Science* 299 (7 March 2003): 1534–1539.

Avruch, Kevin, and Beatriz Vejarano. (2001). Truth and reconciliation commissions: A review essay and annotated bibliography. *Social Justice: Anthropology, Peace, and Human Rights* 2.1–2: 47–108.

Barber, Benjamin R. (1996). *Jihad vs. McWorld.* New York: Ballantine.

Barron, Michelle. (2003). Playing at war: Militarism and media. Interview of Nina Huntemann, producer of "Game over: Gender, race, and violence in video games." www.mediaed.org/news/articles/militarism.

Barsh, Russel. (1990). Indigenous peoples, racism, and the environment. *Meanjin* 49.4: 723–731.

Bateson, Gregory. (1936/1958). *Naven; A Survey of the Problems Suggested by a Composite Picture of the Culture of a New Guinea Tribe Drawing from Three Points of View.* Stanford: Stanford University Press.

———. (1972). *Steps to an Ecology of Mind.* New York: Ballantine.

———. (1977). Some thoughts about intermittent reinforcement. Unpublished article manuscript. Bateson Archive, University of California, Santa Cruz.

Bauman, Zygmunt. (1998). *Globalisation: The Human Consequences.* Cambridge: Polity.

Baumeister, Roy F. (1999/1997). *Evil: Inside Human Violence and Cruelty.* New York: Henry Holt and Company.

BBC/British Broadcasting Corporation. (2003). Hooligans. Documentary on violence at sporting events, Sunday, 18 May 2003.

Bennis, Phyllis. (2003). *Before and After: U.S. Foreign Policy and the September 11th Crisis.* New York: Interlink Publishing Group.

Berry, Wendell. (2001). *In the Presence of Fear: Three Essays for an Unchanged World.* Orion Society. www.oriononline.org.

Bhabba, Homi. (1994). *The Location of Culture.* New York: Routledge.

Blumstein, Alfred. (2000). Violence: A new frontier for scientific research. Editorial. *Science* 289 (28 July 2000): 545.

Bower, Bruce. (2000). Inside violent worlds: Political conflict and terror look different up close and local. *Science News* 158 (5 August 2000): 88–90.

Brown, Penelope, and Stephen C. Levinson. (1987). *Some Universals in Language Usage.* Cambridge: Cambridge University Press.

Brownstein, Henry H. (1999). *The Social Reality of Violence and Violent Crime*. New York: Allyn and Bacon.

Buchwald, Emilie, Pamela Fletcher, and Martha Roth, editors. (1993). *Transforming a Rape Culture*. Minneapolis, Minnesota: Milkweed Editions.

Carter, Jimmy. (1995/1993). *Talking Peace: A Vision for the Next Generation*. Revised and updated. New York: Penguin Books.

Chin, Gilbert. (2003). Immunology: A weapon of mass distraction. *Nature Medicine* 9: 1269. Quoted in *Science* 302 (7 November 2003): 951.

Cohn, Ilene, and Guy S. Goodwin-Gill. (1997). *Child Soldiers: The Role of Children in Armed Conflict: A Study on Behalf of the Henry Dunant Institute, Geneva*. Oxford: Clarendon Press.

Cromer, Gerald, and Robin Wagner-Pacifici. (2001). Introduction to the special issue on narratives of violence. *Narratives of Violence*, edited by Gerald Cromer and Robin Wagner-Pacifici. *Qualitative Sociology* 24.2: 163–168.

Daniel, E. Valentine. (1984). *Fluid Signs: Being a Person the Tamil Way*. Berkeley: University of California Press.

Dawkins, Richard. (1989/1976). *The Selfish Gene*. Second edition. Oxford: Oxford University Press.

Denzin, Norman K., editor. (2003). *9/11 in American Culture*. Walnut Creek, California: AltaMira Press.

Department of Peace. (2003). www.dopcampaign.org.

Donohue, John J., III, and Steven D. Levitt. (2000). The impact of legalized abortion on crime. Stanford Law School, Public Law Working Paper No. 1; Stanford Law and Economics Olin Working Paper No. 204; University of California, Berkeley, Law and Economics Paper No. 200. *Quarterly Journal of Economics*.

Dworkin, Andrea. (1988). Pornography and grief. In *Letters from a War Zone*. New York: Dutton, pp. 19–24. Republished in 1999 in *Violence and Its Alternatives: An Interdisciplinary Reader*, edited by Manfred B. Steger and Nancy S. Lind, pp. 129–132. New York: St. Martin's Press.

Edgerton, Robert B. (1992). *Sick Societies: Challenging the Myth of Primitive Harmony*. New York: Free Press.

Farmer, Paul. (2003). *Pathologies of Power: Health, Human Rights, and the New War on the Poor*. Berkeley: University of California Press.

Foucault, Michel. (1980). *Power/Knowledge: Selected Interviews and Other Writings 1972–1977*, edited by Colin Gordon. Brighton: Harvester Press.

———. (1995). *Discipline and Punish: The Birth of the Prison*, translated from the French by Alan Sheridan (*Surveiller et punir*; London: Allen Lane, 1977). New York: Vintage Books.

Fox, K.V. (1996). Silent voices: A subversive reading of child sexual abuse. In *Composing Ethnography: Alternative Forms of Qualitative Writing*, edited by Arthur P. Bochner and Carolyn Ellis, pp. 330–356. Walnut Creek, California: AltaMira Press.

Fox, Jonathan. (1999). Do religious institutions support violence or the status quo? *Studies in Conflict and Terrorism* 22: 1919–139.

Fox, Jonathan. (2002). *Ethnoreligious Conflict in the Late 20th Century: A General Theory*. New York: Lexington Books.

Fox, Richard G., and Barbara J. King, editors. (2002). *Anthropology Beyond Culture.* Oxford and New York: Berg.

Friedman, Jonathan, editor. (2002). *Globalization, the State, and Violence.* Walnut Creek, California: AltaMira Press.

Fry, Douglas P. (1992). "Respect for the rights of others is peace": Learning aggression versus nonaggression among the Zapotec. *American Anthropologist* 94.3: 621–639.

Galtung, Johan. (1990). Cultural violence. *Journal of Peace Research* 27.3: 291–305.

———. (2002/2000). The state/national dialectic: Some tentative conclusions. In *Searching for Peace: The Road to Transcend,* edited by Johan Galtung, Carl G. Jacobsen, and Kai Frithjof Brand-Jacobsen, pp. 126–141. Second edition. London: Pluto Press.

Galtung, Johan. (2003). *En Flyveappelsin Forteller.* Illustrated by Andreas Galtung. Oslo: Kagge Forlag.

Galtung, Johan, Carl G. Jacobsen, and Kai Frithjof Brand-Jacobsen. (2002/2000). *Searching for Peace: The Road to Transcend.* Second edition. London: Pluto Press.

Gardner, Jean. (2002). The World Trade Center: Fuel cells instead of terrorists cells. 8 March 2002. www.metropolismag.com/html/wtc_gardner_03072002.html.

Gay, William C. (1998). Exposing and overcoming linguistic alienation and linguistic violence. *Philosophy and Social Criticism* 24.2–3: 137–156.

Gilligan, James. (1997). *Violence: Reflections on a National Epidemic.* New York: Vintage Books.

Girard, René. (1977). *Violence and the Sacred.* Translated from the French (*La violence et le sacré*; Paris: B. Grasset, 1972) by Patrick Gregory. Baltimore: Johns Hopkins University Press.

Glanz, James, and Eric Lipton. (2003). *City in the Sky: The Rise and Fall of the World Trade Center.* New York: Times Books/Henry Holt and Company.

Goldschmidt, Walter. (2003). Affect hunger and the evolution of human behavior. *Human Evolution*; special issue of *International Journal of Anthropology* for XV-ICAES, Florence, Italy, 2003: 97–112.

Gottdiener, Mark, editor. (2000). *New Forms of Consumption: Consumers, Culture, and Commodification.* Walnut Creek, California: AltaMira Press.

Graburn, Nelson H. H. (1981). 1, 2, 3, 4: Anthropology and the Fourth World. *Cultur/Culture* 1.1: 66–70.

Gramsci, Antonio. (1995). *Selections: English: 1995*; *Further Selections from the Prison Notebooks,* edited and translated from the Italian by Derek Boothman. Minneapolis: University of Minnesota Press.

Grossman, David. (1995). *On Killing: The Psychological Cost of Learning to Kill in War and Society.* New York: Little, Brown.

Grossman, David, and G. DeGaetano. (1999). *Stop Teaching Our Kids to Kill: A Call to Action Against TV, Movie, and Video Game Violence.* New York: Random House.

Guéhenno, Jean-Marie. (1995). *The End of the Nation-State.* Translated from the French by Victoria Elliott. Minneapolis: University of Minnesota Press.

Hall, Stuart. (1991) The local and the global: Globalizations and ethnicities. In *Culture, Globalisation, and the World System.,* edited by Anthony D. King, pp. 19–39. London: Macmillan.

Halliday, Michael A.K. (1978). *Language as Social Semiotic.* London: Edward Arnold.

Harcourt, Alexander H., and Frans B. M. de Waal, editors. (1992). *Coalitions and Alliances in Humans and Other Animals*. Oxford: Oxford University Press.

Hardin, Garrett. (1968). The tragedy of the commons. *Science* 162 (1968): 1243–1248.

———. (1993). *Living Within Limits: Ecology, Economics, and Population Taboos*. New York: Oxford University Press.

———. (1999). *The Ostrich Factor: Our Population Myopia*. New York: Oxford University Press.

Hardin, Garrett, and John Baden. (1977). *Managing the Commons*. San Francisco: W.H. Freeman.

Helvarg, David. (1994). *The War Against the Greens: The "Wise-Use" Movement, the New Right, and Anti-Environmental Violence*. San Francisco: Sierra Club Books.

Henry, Jules. (1963). *Culture Against Man*. New York: Vintage Books.

Herzog, James M. (2001). *Father Hunger: Explorations with Adults and Children*. Hillsdale, New Jersey: The Analytic Press.

Hoffman, Bruce. (2001). All you need is love: How the terrorists stopped terrorism. *Atlantic Monthly* (December 2001): 34–37.

Holden, Constance. (2003). Giving the Peace Institute a chance. *Science* 302 (14 November 2003): 1145.

Homer-Dixon, Thomas F. (1999). *Environment, Scarcity, and Violence*. Princeton: Princeton University Press.

Huesmann, L. Rowell, L. R. Moise, C. P. Podolski, and L. D. Eron. (2003). Longitudinal relations between childhood exposure to media violence and adult aggression and violence, 1977–1992. *Developmental Psychology* 39.2: 201–221.

Hunt, Scott A. (2002). *The Future of Peace: On the Front Lines With the World's Great Peacemakers*. San Francisco: HarperCollins.

Kadushin, Alfred, and Judith A. Martin. (1981). *Child Abuse: An Interactional Event*. New York: Columbia University Press.

Kakar, Sudhir. (1996). *The Colors of Violence: Cultural Identities, Religion, and Conflict*. Chicago: University of Chicago Press.

Kanner, Allen, and Tim Kasser, editors. (2003). *Psychology and Consumer Culture: The Struggle for a Good Life in a Materialistic Society*. Washington, D.C.: American Psychological Association.

Keane, John. (1996). *Reflections on Violence*. London and New York: Verso.

KewalRamani, Vineet N., and John M. Coffin. (2003). Weapons of mutational destruction. *Science* 301(15 August 2003): 923–925.

Knauft, Bruce M. (1987). Reconsidering violence in simple human societies. *Current Anthropology* 32: 457–500.

Knuth, Rebecca. (2003). *Libricide: The Regime-sponsored Destruction of Books and Libraries in the Twentieth Century*. New York: Praeger.

Kohn, Alfie. (1990). *The Brighter Side of Human Nature: Altruism and Empathy in Everyday Life*. New York: Basic Books.

Korbin, Jill E. (2003). Children, childhoods, and violence. *Annual Review of Anthropology* 32: 431–446.

Kotek, Joël, and Pierre Rigoulot. (2001). *Le Siècle des Camps*. Paris: J.C. Lattés.

Kushner, Harvey W. (2002). *Encyclopedia of Terrorism*. Thousand Oaks, California: Sage.

Lakoff, George. (1991). Metaphor and war: The metaphor system used to justify war in the Gulf. *Journal of Urban and Cultural Studies* 2.1: 59–72.

Lakoff, George, and Mark Johnson. (1980). *Metaphors We Live By.* Chicago: University of Chicago Press.

———. (1999). *Philosophy in the Flesh: The Embodied Mind and Its Challenge to Western Thought.* New York: Basic Books.

Lasn, Kalle. (1999). *Culture Jam: How to Reverse America's Suicidal Consumer Binge—and Why We Must.* New York: HarperCollins.

LBC. (2001, 2002). *LBC Newsletter.* The Living Beyond Conflict Seminar. Department of Cultural Anthropology and Ethnology, Uppsala University, Sweden. www.antro.uu.se/lbc.

Leatherman, Janie, William DeMars, Patrick D. Gaffney, and Raimo Vayrynen, editors. (1999). *Breaking Cycles of Violence: Conflict Prevention in Intrastate Crises.* West Hartford, Connecticut: Kumarian Press.

Lecercle, Jean-Jacques. (1990). *The Violence of Language.* London: Routledge.

Lemke, Jay L. (1995). *Textual Politics: Discourse and Social Dynamics.* Washington, D.C.: Taylor and Francis.

Levinson, David. (1989). *Family Violence in Cross-Cultural Perspective.* Newbury Park, California: Sage Publications.

Lewontin, Richard C., Steven Rose, and Leon J. Kamin. (1984). *Not in Our Genes: Biology, Ideology, and Human Nature.* New York: Pantheon Books.

Lischer, Rarah Kenyon. (1999). Causes of communal war: Fear and feasibility. *Studies in Conflict and Terrorism* 22: 331–355.

Lockwood, Randall, and Frank R. Ascione, editors. (1998). *Cruelty to Animals and Interpersonal Violence: Readings in Research and Application.* West Lafayette, Indiana: Purdue University Press.

Lutz, Catherine, and Geoffrey White. (2002). Emotions, war, and cable news. *Anthropology News* 43.2: 6–7.

MacNair, Rachel M. (2002). *Perpetration-induced Traumatic Stress: The Psychological Consequences of Killing.* New York: Praeger.

Mahmood, Cynthia Keppley. (1996). *Fighting for Faith and Nation: Dialogues with Sikh Militants.* Philadelphia: University of Pennsylvania Press.

Markowitz, Gerald, and David Rosner. (2002). *Deceit and Denial: The Deadly Politics of Industrial Pollution.* Berkeley: University of California Press. See also www.cincinnatichildrens.org/leadadvertising/.

Matoesian, Gregory M. (1993). *Reproducing Rape: Domination through Talk in the Courtroom.* Chicago: University of Chicago Press.

McCulloch, Warren S. (1945). A heterarchy of values determined by the topology of nervous nets. *Bulletin of Mathematical Biophysics* 7.2: 89–93.

McCulloch, Warren S. (1965). *Embodiments of Mind.* Cambridge: MIT Press.

McGovern, George Stanley. (1964). *War Against Want: America's Food for Peace Program.* New York: Walker.

McLuhan, Marshall. (1968). *War and Peace in the Global Village.* New York: Bantam Books.

Meeker, Joseph W. (1974). *The Comedy of Survival: Studies in Literary Ecology.* New York: Scribner.

————. (1980). *The Comedy of Survival: In Search of an Environmental Ethic.* Los Angeles: International College, Guild of Tutors Press.

Miller, George A. (1956). The magical number seven, plus or minus two: Some limits on our capacity for processing information. *The Psychological Review* 63.2: 81–97.

Moffatt, Gregory K. (2003). *Wounded Innocents and Fallen Angels: Child Abuse and Child Aggression.* Westport, Connecticut: Praeger.

Montagu, Ashley. (1968). *Man and Aggression.* New York: Oxford University Press.

Montagu, Ashley. (1976). *The Nature of Human Aggression.* New York: Oxford University Press.

Montagu, Ashley, editor. (1978). *Learning Nonaggression: The Experience of Non-literate Societies.* London: Oxford University Press.

Moore, Michael. (2002). "Bowling for Columbine." Film. Best documentary Oscar at Academy Awards, March 2002.

Murray, Martyn. (2003). Overkill and sustainable use. *Science* 299 (21 March 2003): 1851–1853.

Nagler, Michael N. (2003). The time for nonviolence has come. *Yes: A Journal of Positive Futures* (Summer 2003): 38–40.

Nash, Roderick. (1989). *The Rights of Nature: A History of Environmental Ethics.* Madison: University of Wisconsin Press.

Natrajan, Balmurli. (2003). Masking and veiling protests: culture and ideology in representing globalization. *Cultural Dynamics* 15.2: 213–235.

NIOSH/National Institute of Occupational Safety and Health. (1996). www.nurseadvocate.org/silent_epidemic.html.

NTVS (*National Television Violence Study*). Volume 1 (1996); Volume 2 (1997); Volume 3 (1998/2000). Thousand Oaks, California: Sage.

O'Connor, P. E. (1995). Discourse of violence. *Discourse and Society* 6.3: 309–318.

Piers, Maria W. (1978). *Infanticide: Past and Present.* New York: W.W. Norton and Company.

Prigogine, Ilya, and Isabelle Stengers. (1984/1979). *Order Out of Chaos.* Translated from the French. New York: Bantam Press.

Richards, Cara E. (2000). *The Loss of Innocents: Child Killers and Their Victims.* Wilmington, Delaware: Scholarly Resources, Inc.

Ridley, Matt. (1997). *The Origin of Virtue: Human Instincts and the Evolution of Cooperation.* New York: Viking Press.

Ronai, C. R. (1995). Multiple reflections of child sex abuse: An argument for a layered account. *Journal of Contemporary Ethnography* 23.4: 205–426.

Rosen, Robert. (1985). *Anticipatory Systems: Philosophical, Mathematical, and Methodological Foundations.* New York: Pergamon.

Rosset, Clement. (1993). *Joyful Cruelty: Toward a Philosophy of the Real.* New York: Oxford University Press.

Roy, Arundhati. (1997). *The God of Small Things.* New York: Random House.

————. (1999). *The Cost of Living.* New York: Modern Library.

Ruch, Alex. (2002). The rhetoric of incommensurability and the threat of violence. www.duke.edu/~jad2/ruch.htm.

Ryan, Paul. (2001). Threeing and peace. www.earthscore.org.

Salthe, Stanley N. (1993). *Development and Evolution: Complexity and Change in Biology.* Cambridge: MIT Press.

Salthe, Stanley N., and Myrdene Anderson. (1989). Modeling self-organization. In *Semiotics 1988*, edited by Terry J. Prewitt, John Deely, and Karen Haworth, pp. 14–23. New York: University Press of America.

Sampson, Robert J., Stephen W. Raudenbush, and Felton Earls. (1997). Neighborhoods and violent crime: A multilievel study of collective efficacy. *Science* 277 (15 August 1997): 918–924.

Scheper-Hughes, Nancy, editor. (1987). *Child Survival: Anthropological Perspectives on the Treatment and Maltreatment of Children.* Dordrecht: D. Reidel.

Scheper-Hughes, Nancy, and Philippe Bourgois. (2004). Introduction: Making sense of violence. In *Violence in War and Peace: An Anthology*, edited by Nancy Scheper-Hughes and Philippe Bourgois, pp. 1–31. Oxford: Blackwell Publishing.

Schorlemmer, Robert. (2003). Gaviotas founder Paolo Lugari, Colombia. www.friendsofgaviotas.org/2003retreat.htm.

Scott, James C. (1998). *Seeing Like a State: How Certain Schemes to Improve the Human Condition Have Failed.* New Haven: Yale University Press.

Shipman, Pat. (2001). On the nature of violence. *American Scientist* 89: 488–489.

Smith-Christopher, Daniel L., editor. (1998). *Subverting Hatred: The Challenge of Nonviolence in Religious Traditions.* Maryknoll, New York: Orbis Books.

Sponsel, Leslie E., and Thomas Gregor, editors. (1994). *The Anthropology of Peace and Nonviolence.* Boulder: L. Rienner.

Steger, Manfred B., and Nancy S. Lind. (1999). Introduction. In *Violence and Its Alternatives: An Interdisciplinary Reader*, edited by Manfred B. Steger and Nancy S. Lind, pp. viii–xxvi. New York: St. Martin's Press.

Stern, Jessica. (2003). *Terror in the Name of God: Why Religious Militants Kill.* New York: Ecco/HarperCollins Publishers.

Stone, Richard, and Katrina Kelner. (2000). Violence: No silver bullet. *Science* 289 (28 July 2000): 545.

Stout, Chris E., editor. (2002). *The Psychology of Terrorism.* 4 volumes. Westport, Connecticut: Praeger.

Sullivan, W. C., and F. E. Kuo. (1996). Do trees strengthen urban communities, reduce domestic violence? *Technology Bulletin* 4. Athens, Georgia: USDA Forest Service, Forestry Report R8-FR 56.

Suu Kyi, Aung San. (1995/1991). Freedom from fear. In *Freedom From Fear and Other Writings*, revised edition, translation by Michael Aris, pp. 180–185. London: Penguin. Republished in 1999 in *Violence and Its Alternatives: An Interdisciplinary Reader*, edited by Manfred B. Steger and Nancy S. Lind, pp. 313–316. New York: St. Martin's Press.

Todorov, Tzvetan. (1996). *Facing the Extreme: Moral Life in the Concentration Camps.* Translated from the French by Arthur Denner and Abigail Pollak. New York: Henry Holt.

Tuan, Yi-Fu. (1998). *Escapism.* Baltimore: Johns Hopkins University Press.

Turpin, Jennifer, and Lester R. Kurtz. (1997). Untangling the web of violence. In *The Web of Violence: From Interpersonal to Global*, edited by Jennifer Turpin and Lester R. Kurtz, pp. 207–232. Urbana: University of Illinois Press.

UNHRC (United Nations High Commissioner for Refugees). (2000). *The State of the World's Refugees*. New York: Oxford University Press.

U.S. Department of State. (2002). Patterns of global terrorism. May 2002, available at www.state.gov/s/ct/rls/pgtrpt/2001/.

Vigil, James Diego. (2003). Urban violence and street gangs. *Annual Review of Anthropology* 32: 225–242.

Waal, Frans B. M. de. (1997). *Bonobo: The Forgotten Ape*. Berkeley: University of California Press.

——. (2000). Primates—A natural heritage of conflict resolution. *Science* 289 (28 July 2000): 586–590.

Warshall, Peter. (2002). Human flow: Global migrations. *Whole Earth* (summer 2002): 39–43.

Websdale, Neil. (1998). *Rural Woman Battering and the Justice System: An Ethnography*. Thousand Oaks, California: Sage.

Wierzbicka, Anna. (1999). *Emotions across Languages and Cultures: Diversity and Universals*. Cambridge: Cambridge University Press.

Wilden, Anthony. (1987). *Man and Woman, War and Peace*. London: Routledge and Kegan Paul.

Williams, Michael. (2003). *Deforesting the Earth: From Prehistory to Global Crisis*. Chicago: University of Chicago Press.

Winkler, Cathy. (2002). *One Night: Realities of Rape*. Walnut Creek, California: AltaMira Press.

Wrangham, Richard W. (1999). The evolution of coalitionary aggression. *Yearbook of Physical Anthropology* 42: 1–30.

Wrangham, Richard W., and Dale Peterson. (1996). *Demonic Males: Apes and the Origins of Human Violence*. New York: Houghton Mifflin Company.

Žižek, Slavoj. (1989). *The Sublime Object of Ideology*. New York: Verso.

Contributors

Frank M. Afflitto teaches sociology at Lane College, one of the oldest historically Black colleges, in Jackson, Tennessee. He is the principal author of a forthcoming book on his research in Guatemala, entitled *The Quiet Revolutionaries*, about the struggles for, and perceptions of, justice for the family members of the disappeared and politically murdered. He has been actively involved in reconciliation efforts in Latin America and the Middle East, and is currently researching the gunfire deaths of Palestinian children.

Myrdene Anderson teaches anthropology, linguistics, and semiotics at Purdue University. She has engaged in ethnographic research in a variety of settings, ranging in the United States from community garden associations to the artificial life movement, but she is best known for her research among Saami reindeer-breeders in Norwegian Lapland. There, she has spent more than seven of the past thirty-two years among quite peaceful reindeer pastoralists. As an anthropologist, Anderson's concerns about violence emerge not because of but in spite of her good fortune in cultural research settings.

Eyal Ben-Ari is professor of anthropology at the Hebrew University of Jerusalem. He has carried out fieldwork on Japanese white-collar suburbs, Japanese kindergartens, the Japanese community in Singapore, and the current Japanese Self-Defense Forces. In Israel he has carried out research on various social and cultural aspects of the Israeli military. His recent books include *Body Projects in Japanese Childcare: Culture, Organization and Emotions in a Preschool* (London: Curzon, 1997) and *Mastering Soldiers: Conflict, Emotions, and the Enemy in an Israeli Military Unit* (Oxford: Berghahn Books, 1998).

Anna Richman Beresin teaches folklore, child psychology, adult psychology, and ethnographic methods to art students at The University of the Arts. She also is an adjunct to the Folklore Department at The University of Pennsylvania and serves as an educational advisor to local schools. Her research has centered around the study of children's peer culture, video-ethnographic methods, and play.

Dov Cohen, a social psychologist, teaches at the University of Illinois. His research interests include cultural variation between and within nations. Topics studied have included violence, honor, reciprocity, individualism, gender, memory, and the phenomenological experience of the self and social worlds.

Bartholomew Dean teaches anthropology at the University of Kansas, and serves as the anthropology coordinator for the Museum Studies Program there. At time of publication, he is once again in Peru, this time on a Fulbright Scholar grant awarded to support his work with the Amazonian Studies Program at the Peruvian National University, San Marcos (Lima). He serves on the editorial board of *Amazonia Peruana*, the flagship journal devoted to the scholarly study of the Peruvian Amazon, and has recently co-edited the volume *At the Risk of Being Heard: Identity, Indigenous Rights and Postcolonial States* (University of Michigan Press, 2003).

Nada Elia started writing about violence as a journalist covering the Lebanese war. Since then, her writing has covered a large number of manifestations of national, global, and domestic violence particularly as it affects women of color. She is equally interested in the subcultures that develop parallel to such violence, as well as in strategies to dismantle the political and economic structures of oppression. Her book, *Trances, Dances, and Vociferations: Agency and Resistance in Africana Women's Narratives*, examines alternative modes of expression among postcolonial and diasporan Africana women. She is currently completing a second manuscript, *Spell-Bound, Un-Bound: Conjuring as the Practice of Freedom*, which examines empowerment through the retention of alternative spiritual beliefs in the African diaspora.

Mario Fandino, born in Colombia, teaches and carries out research at the Federal University of Brazil (Porto Alegre). His research interests include crime and violence in Latin America from both policy-oriented and theoretical-historical standpoints, as well as in the areas of development and social theory as related to crime and violence.

Claudia Fonseca, born in the United States and trained in France, teaches anthropology at the Federal University of Rio Grande do Sul. She centers her research on kinship and gender relations in Brazilian working-class neighborhoods, with special emphasis on human rights issues and international adoption. Recent publications include *Caminhos da Adoção* (Editora Cortez, 2002) and *Família, Fofoca e Honra: Etnografia de Relações de Gênero e Violência em Grupos Populares* (Editora da UFRGS, 2000), as well as articles in journals such as *Law and Society Review, Law and Policy*, and *Men and Masculinities*.

Barton C. Hacker oversees the armed forces history collections at the Smithsonian's National Museum of American History, where he has curated major exhibits on submarines in the Cold War (2000) and on West Point in the making of America, 1802–1918 (2002). He has held a variety of academic, government, and corporate posts throughout the United States, most recently serving as Laboratory Historian at Lawrence Livermore National Laboratory. Hacker has published extensively on the history of twentieth-century military technology, the military history of women, and the comparative history of military institutions.

Sarah Hautzinger teaches anthropology, women's studies, and Latin American studies at Colorado College. She is completing the ethnography *Violence in the City of Women: Gender and Battering in Brazil* and plans further research on men's groups on anger management and violence prevention throughout Latin America. In the United States, she oversees student research in economic anthropology comparing two Colorado communities, Trinidad and Vail.

Jon D. Holtzman teaches anthropology at Western Michigan University and directs its international and global studies program. His research has centered on African populations in the United States and in Kenya, and is the author of *Nuer Journeys, Nuer Lives: Sudanese Refugees in Minnesota* (Allyn and Bacon, 2000), as well as a variety of articles in such journals as *American Anthropologist, American Ethnologist* and *Current Anthropology*.

Myriam Jimeno teaches at the Universidad Nacional de Colombia and is an associate re-sercher of the Centro de Estudios Sociales Universidad Nacional de Colombia. She has been Directora Instituto Colombiano de Antropología, and in 1995 she was awarded with a National Prize in social sciences in Colombia. Her interests center on social conflict and violence, ethnicity, state policy, and ethnic minorities. Some recent significant publications include *Crimen pasional: Contribución a una antropología de las emociones* (in press); "Violence and Social Life in Colombia," *Critique of Anthropology* (2001); and *Identidade e experiencias cotidianas de violencia* (G. De Cerqueira Zarur org.; Brasilia: Universidade de Brasilia, 2000).

Steven V. Lutes is principal analyst for the San Francisco Police Department, and for a number of years worked in Latin America and Southeast Asia and with American Indian tribes on projects concerning population studies, economic development, and local institution building. He is now involved in assisting the SFPD to respond to community concerns about possible racial profiling and addressing appropriate police accountability measures and institutional transparency. He focuses on the tension between traditional and community-policing models, the challenges of defining and applying "legitimate" force in a complex, multicultural society, and balancing the competing demands for civil order and personal freedom in a way that allows both to endure.

Wade C. Mackey has surveyed the father figure in twenty-three cultures in twenty countries. In general, he attempts to understand the father role as it relates to bio-cultural evolution. In particular, he has a special interest in the role of the father in affecting unwanted social behavior, e.g., violence on the part of his sons who have grown to adulthood and in affecting the mating patterns in his daughters who have grown to adulthood. In the second particular, he—with co-author Nancy S. Coney—is addressing the trajectory of the feminist paradox wherein, across generations, women's enhanced options are systematically followed by curtailed options.

Linda McDonald became trained in educational psychology after twenty years of classroom teaching, and now her work has further shifted from direct involvement with children in the classroom to that of child advocate through policy and systems change by implementation of programs for children. Her research examines the personal narratives and knowledge of urban and suburban children to discern the forces that shaped their development from their environments of home, school, and community. Currently McDonald is a research associate with RMC Research, Arlington, Virginia, working on literacy projects and providing technical assistance to state departments of education. She continues to provide technical assistance to high-need, low-performing school districts in Ohio and Pennsylvania. McDonald also serves on the steering committee of the Ohio Learning First Alliance.

Rhonda J. Moore is a cultural and medical anthropologist, with post-doctoral training in psychiatry and behavioral sciences (Stanford) and in epidemiology (University of Texas' M. D. Anderson Cancer Center). Her interests include cultural issues that impact the experience of pain, oncology care and communication, the impact of suffering in advanced stage cancers, neurogenetics and neuroimaging studies of pain, and social inequality in cancer care. She is senior editor (with D. Spiegel) of *Cancer, Culture, and Communica-*

tion (Kluwer), and author of *Pain in the U.S. Marine Corps: Impact on Cultural Belonging* (forthcoming 2004).

Gila Safran Naveh teaches Judaic studies, semiotics, and psychoanalytic literary criticism at the University of Cincinnati. She has carried out extensive studies on the psychology and politics of violence, while working with former prisoners who have been tortured and subjected to brutal acts of violence in Romania and in other earlier communist countries. She has spent five years with women survivors of the Holocaust and is now publishing *Unpacking the Heart with Words: Women's Experience in the Holocaust*, a work that brings to the foreground the unique acts of violence perpetrated against women during the Holocaust.

Glen Anthony Perice has carried out ethnographic research in Haiti, South Korea, and the United States. His interests include political violence and the poetics of rumor. He is also a published poet and essayist, and he writes on the boundaries of creative nonfictional modes of representation. He co-edited a collection of creative writing by social scientists titled *AZ*. He is currently working on a book about television and another one about the U.S. military. He has taught at several universities and colleges around the world including Hong Ik Univesity and Marylhurst University.

Cara Richards was trained at Cornell, where, among other sites, she also instructed Peace Corps volunteers. She has taught anthropology at Ithaca College and now is retired from Transylvania University. Richards has undertaken substantial ethnographic research among Onondaga Indians in New York State, Navajo Indians in Arizona, and mixed populations in highland Peru, where she also taught in Escuela de Servicio Social, Lima, Peru. Her most recent book is *The Loss of Innocents: Child Killers and Their Victims* (Scholarly Resources, Inc., 2000).

Linda Rogers teaches developmental psychology in the human development program at California State University, Monterey Bay. In her investigations on children and trauma, Rogers has worked in Australia, Northern Ireland, the Cleveland area, and now Monterey County. She utilizes semiotics as an analytic lens to help teachers and children understand and craft their communication patterns. She is the co-editor of the *International Journal of Applied Semiotics*.

Nicole Sault currently teaches anthropology in the graduate program at the University of Costa Rica. Since the 1970s, she has conducted research among the Zapotec of Mexico, studying women's roles in community organization, healing with incense, sweathouse ceremonies, and religious conversion. Her writing also addresses the cultural context of body image, breast implants, "surrogate" motherhood, and the interplay of social and biological conceptions of parenthood, which appear in her volume *Many Mirrors: Body Image and Social Relations* (Rutgers University Press, 1994). In addition to working with traditional farmers in Mexico, she has also done research among organic farmers in California and Costa Rica, developing an anthropological approach toward understanding sustainable agriculture.

Glenn Smith is completing a doctorate in ethnology at l'Ecole des Hautes Etudes en Sciences Sociales in Paris, following a Diplôme d'Etudes Approfondies (ethnologie) from the EHESS and a BA in anthropology from the University of California, Berkeley. Since 1985 he has done research on agricultural households and their ecological, economic, and social adaptations on the island of Madura in Indonesia. Since September 2001, he has been in Jakarta participating in the Franco-Indonesian cooperative project with the Indonesian Institute of Sciences to develop social science capacities for the study of conflict (www.communalconflict.com includes a comprehensive bibliography on conflict and violence). Smith has also done research in South Sumatra on spontaneous migrant communities in a context of rapid deforestation.

Michael Sullivan has been with the San Francisco Police Department for twenty-six years in many capacities, and for ten years he has been the SFPD's coordinator for the Americans with Disabilities Act (ADA); on duty twenty-one years ago, Sullivan became the victim of a violent crime and has been disabled ever since. He served on the Joseph P. Kennedy Institute's Advisory Committee in 2000 to assist with the development of training for the Washington, D.C., Police Department regarding interaction with persons with disabilities. Sullivan investigates and responds to inquiries from the Equal Employment Opportunity Commission, the U.S. Department of Justice, and the SF Mayor's Grievance Committee. Sullivan also serves in an advisory role to other city departments and has been honored as San Francisco's ADA Coordinator of the Year.

Katerina Teaiwa wrote her piece for this volume in 1996 as she was starting a master's program at the Center for Pacific Islands Studies at the University of Hawaii. She recently completed her doctorate in anthropology at the Australian National University, producing a multi-sited thesis in text and film (DVD) on connections between Kiribati, Fiji, Australia, and New Zealand as a result of phosphate mining on the island of Banaba. She now teaches gender, popular culture, globalization, consumption, dance, and the body in Oceania at the University of Hawaii, Manoa.

Charles Trappey received his doctorate in consumer behavior from Purdue University and joined the faculty of the National Chiao Tung University, Taiwan, in 1992. As a professor of management science, he teaches marketing and consumer behavior at the National Chiao Tung University, executive MBA classes at the National Tsing Hua University, and international MBA students at the National Cheng Chi University. His research interests include consumption behavior, trade area analysis, and business process modeling. Trappey is a specialist in the development of consumer and marketing information systems. He has successfully developed integrated contact center solutions for firms in Taiwan and China and is currently developing systems for the business process outsourcing market in India.

Joe Vandello, a social psychologist, teaches at the University of South Florida. His primary research has examined cultural influences on aggression between males and within romantic relationships. Other research interests include gender, regional culture within the United States, social influence, and prejudice.

Cathy Winkler is an independent scholar and anthropologist. Her book, *One Night: Realities of Rape* (AltaMira Press, 2002), employs experiential anthropology to undertake a study of violence. She continues writing and focuses on other styles to be expressed in forthcoming books, including *Crazied* and *Poisoned Professor*.

Index

Page of first mention is preceded by the chapter number in roman numerals.